The Housing Rehabilitation Handbook

THE HOUSING REHABILITATION HANDBOOK

John Benson

Peter Colomb

Barrie Evans

George Jones

The Architectural Press : London

First published in book form by The Architectural Press Ltd:
London 1980
ISBN: 0 85139 293 8

Printed in Great Britain
by W & J Mackay Limited, Chatham

Contents

Notes on Contributors

Barrie Evans is executive technical editor on the *Architects' Journal* and prepared the original *AJ* series on which the present book is based.

John Benson is an architect with his own practice whose work has over a decade been primarily private sector rehabilitation.

Peter Colomb has had experience of housing rehabilitation in the public sector and now has his own practice which works largely on conversion and rehabilitation.

George Jones is concerned with urban renewal and has been responsible for a wide range of rehabilitation projects in five London boroughs and for two housing associations.

David Pearson runs the Housing Acquisition and Rehabilitation Unit, a multi-disciplinary team specialising in rehabilitation and modernisation projects within the London Borough of Hammersmith and Fulham.

John Pryke is a structural engineer with long experience of surveying damaged properties, designing underpinning schemes and supervising their execution on site, which has led to a specialist knowledge of foundation engineering and the major structural alteration and preservation of old buildings.

Section one: Introduction

Introduction

The Housing Rehabilitation Handbook is intended to fill a gap in the information currently available to architects, for although many books have been published which deal with the conservation problems of historically outstanding buildings, very few touch on the more pragmatic subject of rehabilitating the mass of our existing housing.

This handbook will take the architect through the entire rehabilitation process, including both its constructional aspects and its organisation. This first introductory section of the book sets the rehabilitation scene and then describes the scope and form of the information which follows. The second section of the book, Repair and maintenance, is diagnostic in approach and aims to provide an understanding of how the buildings under discussion were constructed, how they have been changed in the interim and the causes of typical faults.

The third section of the Handbook, Case studies, takes us through a wide variety of recent rehabilitation jobs in a documentary way, showing the nature and organisation of the architect's work, the drawings and other documents used. This section is of especial interest in that the case studies concentrate on relatively neglected aspects of rehabilitation such as community-based rehabilitation, tenant liaison, housing rehabilitation for the disabled, rehabilitated homes for single people and sheltered housing.

Section 4 of the book, Improvements and conversions, follows a useful 'plan of work' pattern. Ranging from briefing to details, it covers organisation, design and the technicalities of improvements and conversions. The Housing Rehabilitation Handbook then concludes with Section 5: Administration which deals with the vitally important questions of grant availability and the running of projects.

1 A mixed heritage

1.01 '*I never intended to have republished this book which has become the most useless I ever wrote; the buildings it describes with so much delight being now either knocked down, or scraped and patched into smugness and smoothness more tragic than uttermost ruin.*'

1.02 The industrial boom just past is not unique as a period of large scale demolition of serviceable housing. Booms, times of self confidence about the future, are generally times for neglect if not destruction of the existing heritage. In the quotation above from the *Seven lamps of architecture*, Ruskin laments the loss between the first and second editions, 1849 to 1880.

1.03 The housing we have inherited is a product of shifts of fashion and technology, built during booms and slumps. There are good materials and construction and bad. Occasional shortages of materials led to ad hoc measures. New developments were, as now, tried out by being built. A feature that on one building is sound may be found on another from 10 years earlier as a poorly understood, badly built prototype. And as the drawing illustrates, **1**, the builder understood the construction process well enough to offer clients considerable choice behind a uniform facade.

1.04 An architect rehabilitating houses can be confronted with an enormous variety of built forms of variable quality. The handbook can distill experience, exemplify an approach, offer advice and point out rules of thumb. But the architect must expect the unexpected, be prepared for surprises. It is one of the difficulties and fascinations of rehabilitating houses.

The challenge ahead . . . . .

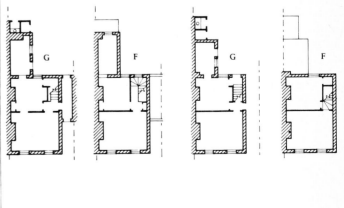
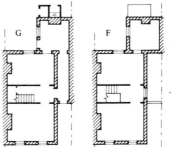

1 *A variety of plans behind a uniform facade, presumably negotiated between builder and client. Just which walls are structural, which way the joists run and other details can vary from house to house.*

2

2 Government policy

2.01 Most rehabilitation, whether public or private, goes on within a context of government policy. Though there have been grants available since the Housing Act 1949, it was not until the 1969 Act that the tide began to turn against redevelopment on a large scale, **2**. While grants are needed to make many jobs possible at all, it is the development of designated areas that has given the policy of promoting rehabilitation some coherence.

Designated areas

2.02 *General improvement areas* (GIAs) were intended to get the government's promotion off to a good start. LAs were asked to designate areas where rehabilitation has a good chance of success. Inevitably this advice plus uncertainty over the new process led LAs to play safe and most areas of acute housing need were left out.

2.03 *Housing action areas* (HAAs) were brought in to fill this gap. Considerable effort has been put into organising a sound base to work from in these areas which are recognised as areas of multiple, not merely housing stress. Many HAAs have been declared though the architects involved report little evidence of their being involved in a team approach to multiple stress. Schemes for HAAs are currently similar to those in GIAs except that the housing stock is generally in poorer condition and there are extra problems due to complicated tenure such as multiple occupation and absentee landlords. The HAAs are supposed to run for no more than five years. They can then be made GIAs as necessary.

2.04 *Priority neighbourhoods* (PNs) were devised at the same time as GIAs to be designated adjacent to them. They are effectively declarations of intent, commitments to future rehabilitation as it can be afforded. Designation is expected to limit if not prevent uncertainty about the neighbourhood's future. There is no grant available and to date very few have been designated. PNs appear to have been an afterthought and government has produced no very positive statement about their role or value.

3 Politics

3.01 This handbook is not a political treatise but the architect needs to be aware of the political context in which he is working. The use of designated areas is after all intended to lead to various socio-political ends, such as keeping communities together. The actions and intentions of LAs are specially important. For example, initial surveys or declarations of intent may have made occupiers suspicious of their motives and thus defensive. Some people may prefer no rehabilitation, or redevelopment. A policy of keeping communities together may be defeated by people preferring removal to prolonged decanting and when the job is over property values and rents may force the poorest to move on. All of course may go smoothly. But rehabilitation cannot be assumed to be simply working on specific houses for their current occupiers/owners.

3.02 The growth of rehabilitation, working on existing buildings often with known occupiers, plus changing attitudes, has led to more user involvement in rehabilitation than is common for new housing, both confrontation and co-operation, **3**. Some of the case studies in the handbook, eg ASSIST in Glasgow, illustrate recent developments.

2 *A major inhibitor of a shift toward rehabilitation was the difficulty very many government officials had in accepting that people preferred the rehabilitation of such areas to redevelopment.*

4

5

4 Scope of the handbook

4.01 The handbook is a guide for architects through all phases of housing rehabilitation, covering from the mid to late Georgian period to 1914. It is generally limited to housing that is grant aidable, specified by its rateable value (see Section 5: Administration, Information sheet 1, 'Grants'). Check though with local authorities for future revisions. This is the mass of simpler housing though it inevitably covers some listed buildings (all are listed before 1840).

4.02 Rehabilitation requires a different way of working to designing new houses. It is different both in the construction and work organisation. The time on site and knowledge of it must be much greater, spent in understanding how the houses were put together, diagnosing their faults and supervising the work on site. Site work cannot be expected generally to be as smooth as with the carte blanche of a new site.

4.03 Many checks and procedures can be systematised to allow more time for design. However, design is often on a small scale and highly constrained by the existing building. And on a one-off job the architect may well be competing with the local builder who will agree rudimentary changes in an evening over the kitchen table and produce a set of drawings for £25.

4.04 Though the scale of design may be limited this does not make it trivial. Changing houses to modern standards while preserving their essential character requires considerable sensitivity. Fortunately over the last few years there has been a softening of attitudes by LAs, and there is much less insistence for example in public housing on moving a wall 200 mm to force a Parker Morris shape into an old building. There is more respect for the proportions of rooms, preserving cornice lines and not renewing with antipathetic modern detailing. These are coming to be referred to as natural conversions. (On minimum ceiling heights planning officers remain dogmatic) **4, 5**.

4.05 Using the handbook the architect should be able to pursue a chosen strategy matched to the obsolescence of the housing. This obsolescence may be physical, financial, of tenure, functional (either for the occupant or community), or a mix of these. It may require for example a strategy of gradually renewing houses, repairing some, improving or converting others in sympathy with the occupants rather than only to achieve a chosen mix of housing stock for future use. But it must be accepted too that sentimental attachment to preserving houses cannot outweigh a mix of bad materials, bad design, bad construction and bad maintenance. As the outraged Ian Nairn puts it rather more bluntly, 'What was born in ugliness will die in it. Put that in your compassionate craw and choke on it.'

5 Form of the handbook

5.01 The handbook comprises five sections:
- Introduction;
- Repair and maintenance;
- Case studies;
- Improvement and conversion;
- Administration.

3 *Shelter Neighbourhood Action Project, 1969-1972, in the Granby district of Liverpool. Even with Shelter's assistance and expertise, there were long delays as rehabilitation required unaccustomed co-operation between corporation departments and decisions on matters not anticipated or delegated.*
4 *Before and* **5** *after rehabilitation; appreciating the quality beneath the decay leads to the transformation.*

Enquiry Department.

HOLLOW WALL CONSTRUCTION.

To the Editor of THE BUILDERS' JOURNAL.

SIR,—Can you give sketches showing the method of construction on each of the following section lines. I would also be pleased to

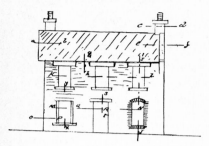

have any information about hollow wall construction.—Yours,   McK.

The accompanying sections will be found suitable for a small detached villa in an exposed situation; for less substantial property a 4½in. inner wall might be considered sufficient for the ground story, although this is not advised. It is usual to build these hollow walls with a 4½in. skin outside, as there is thus less substance to absorb moisture;

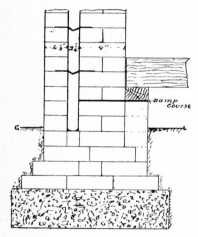

FIG. 1.—SECTION AT J.

and when wet it dries quicker; also the thicker portion being inside to carry the constructive timber, necessarily shortens the span and economises material. The hollow space between the two walls should not exceed 3in., and is more frequently 2¼in. The two portions are kept entirely separate between the ground line and the upper ceiling except at the reveals of door and window openings; these are formed, and the space closed, as shown in Figs. 3 and 7,

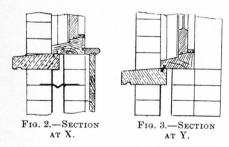

FIG. 2.—SECTION   FIG. 3.—SECTION
AT X.   AT Y.

by King closers, all the hidden portion of these latter bricks should be covered with tar or melted asphalte before laying to prevent the transmission of moisture to the inner wall. Starting about four courses from the ground, and at every third course thereafter, rows of

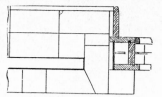

FIG. 4.—SECTION AT M AND R.

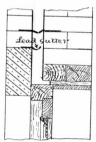

FIG. 5.—SECTION AT H.

wrought or cast galvanised iron ties, spaced about 3ft. apart, should be built in the brickwork, as shown in the sketches, to tie the work together; they should not be placed vertically over each other, but hit and miss fashion. These ties are made of various shapes, but those having a good dip in the middle are best. There are also purpose made

FIG. 6.—SECTION AT S.

bricks in the market, but in cases of unequal settlement these are very liable to break. It is not advisable to take the hollow below the ground line, as water will accumulate therein, but where this must be done to protect a basement the inner wall should be covered with asphalte up to the damp course, the

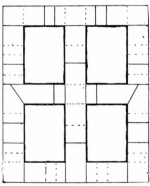

FIG. 8.—SECTION AT G.

top of the hollow should be closed at or near the ceiling line, and immediately above, a damp course must be inserted, as shown in Fig. 8. Over all doors and window heads a strip of lead should be built in the outer wall, and turned up to form a gutter as shown in Fig. 4; this should be long enough

to overhang each end about 2in. During the building of the wall, pieces of board laid on the ties will prevent morter, &c., falling into the space. Fig. 1 is a vertical section at the foot of the wall; Fig. 2, a vertical section through ground floor window. The stone sill must not quite bridge the space; both sills are grooved, and a strip of lead, bent and bedded in cement, prevents the ingress of water. Fig. 3, a similar section of first floor;

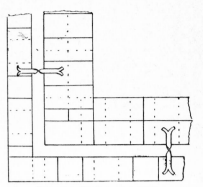

FIG. 9.—SECTION AT O P.

Figs. 4 and 5, horizontal sections through the reveals (dotted lines show courses above and below); Fig. 6, vertical section through head of doorway, showing stone lintel and lead gutter; Fig. 7, a horizontal section through the chimney breasts, the left half on the ground floor, the right half on the first floor; Fig. 8, a section through the eaves, showing top of the hollow wall; Fig. 9, section of

FIG. 10.—SECTION AT C D.

corner of wall at ground floor; Fig. 10, section of chimney above roof. Sections at gable and parapet are not necessary, as these will be built in the ordinary manner, but with the damp course taken all round at the same level.

IT has been virtually decided to provide the Royal Courts of Justice with lifts at an early date for the accommodation of those having business at the offices and chambers situated on the upper floors of the building. It is understood that about four lifts will be erected for this purpose, of which two will be situated in the east block, and one each in the western and main blocks.

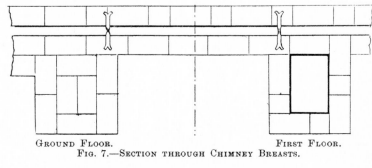

GROUND FLOOR.   FIRST FLOOR.
FIG. 7.—SECTION THROUGH CHIMNEY BREASTS.

Repair and maintenance

5.02 Though the architect will be thinking about design changes too at an early stage, repair and maintenance is a separate section as it requires a particular approach. The emphasis is on diagnosis, understanding how the building was constructed, how it has been changed in the interim and the causes of faults. Then follows advice on treatment.

Case studies

5.03 The handbook cannot hope to be exhaustive in its coverage of nearly 200 years of housing. The case studies document rehabilitation projects from start to finish, illustrating recent developments in organisation and the distribution of effort noted earlier (**4.02-4.04**). They put the detail of the rest of the handbook in context and show particular problems being solved, with costs, specifications and documentation.

5.04 It would of course be helpful to deal with these aspects exhaustively but the housing is too varied. So the studies concentrate on aspects of housing rehabilitation that have been relatively neglected. Some aspects are socio-political, the community-based approach of ASSIST and tenant liaison. Others cover so-called 'special purpose' housing, which is gradually being integrated into a more diversified view of housing requirements. The 'not-so-special purposes' covered are the disabled, single people and sheltered housing.

Improvements and conversions

5.05 Continuing from the design ideas and overview of rehabilitation in the case studies, this section will deal with particular aspects such as subdivision of buildings, fire-proofing, structures and services. There will be a selection of details; they cannot be 'standard details' but are for commonly met situations.

Administration

5.06 Checklists of work methods and procedures for obtaining grants and permission, detailed advice on building regulations, etc. are all given in the final section of this *Handbook*, Section Five: Administration.

6 Information on existing buildings

Pattern books

6.01 The information on existing buildings is unfortunately quite limited in the detail appropriate for rehabilitation. There are few pattern books available covering the simple dwellings dealt with in this handbook. And such was the builder's knowledge of the construction process and architects' intentions that the architect did not need to specify too closely by drawing. Then from the 1850s journals began to be published which took the place of the pattern books without fully duplicating their function. In *The Building News*, *The Builder* and *The Builders Journal* and *Architectural Record*, among others, there were published many model schemes of simple housing for 'improving the condition of the working classes'. But they were less specific than the pattern books had been and it is difficult to find out if they were built, and if so with what modifications.

6.02 This approach is also to be found in many pamphlets of the time, a large selection of which is in the RIBA Library. Both the journals and the pamphlets contain some useful specific information, **6**, but it is extremely laborious to unearth and generally for too high quality work.

Drawings collections

6.03 Drawings collections are held by the RIBA, the Victorian Society, the Society for the Protection of Ancient Buildings, other historic buildings societies and some LAs. But almost universally they are of outstanding buildings worthy of listing and conservation, not the common buildings of variable architectural merit in need of rehabilitation. Ordnance Survey drawings have plan shapes which over a period chart the date of construction and of major addition. Local authorities have some drawings but at least up to the late 1880s they will have been little more than block plans with drainage layouts. It may well be too that LAs have not insisted on depositing and retaining those records.

Construction books

6.04 These can be very useful if old enough editions can be found. Illustrations and text are often edited out as they become irrelevant to new building. Public libraries may have something in store.

Personal knowledge

6.05 Generally the most informed sources are the local building inspectors and surveyors who have had knowledge passed on to them or gradually relearned the nature of construction, how buildings relate to available materials and to local conditions of climate and ground. Other informed people will include a few local architects and builders, conservation/amenity societies and other enthusiasts. It will probably be necessary to find any local craftsmen by word of mouth too. They will usually be outside the rehabilitation price bracket but may be needed for attention to stonework, ironwork and thatch.

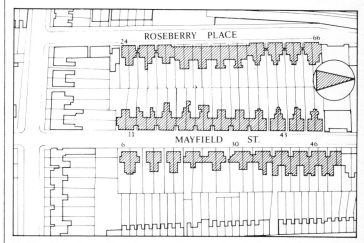

7 *Checking through such maps of successive Ordnance Surveys dates major additions and demolitions.*

7 Addresses

7.01 *Ordnance Survey*, usually accessible locally, contactable at: Romsey Road, Maybush, Southampton, SO9 4DH.

7.02 *Society for the Protection of Ancient Buildings*. This and the Victorian Society are mainly concerned with outstanding buildings. 55 Great Ormond Street, London WC1.

7.03 *The Victorian Society* 29 Exhibition Road, London SW7.

7.04 *CoSIRA* (Council for small industries in rural areas) mostly potters, jewellers and similar but a few constructional craftsmen. The CoSIRA guide is classified by county, available from: Advisory Services Division, 35 Camp Road, Wimbledon Common, London, SW19 4UP.

7.05 *Natural stone directory*, contains lists of quarries still producing, agents and trade, craft consultative and other bodies, from: Stone Industries, Ealing Publications Ltd, 70 Chiswick High Road, London W4.

8 Acknowledgements

8.01 A large number of people have contributed to the form and content of the handbook. Authors of specific articles will be acknowledged as the articles appear. The principal consultants for planning the handbook are architects JOHN BENSON, PETER COLOMB and GEORGE JONES.

Section two: Repair and Maintenance

Technical study 1
The approach to rehabilitation

Repair and maintenance will not be sharply separated from improvement and conversion during construction. But they embody a distinct approach in understanding the state of the building to date. It is important not only to recognise the construction but to distinguish where possible between the original and later amendments and to diagnose faults. Advice then follows on treatments. Much of the coverage of dampness in this section has been produced by H. J. ELDRIDGE, a consultant on construction formerly with BRE. Drawings for the two houses were compiled by PETER COLOMB.

1 Presentation

1.01 Repair and maintenance is focused on recognising and diagnosing faults. This section is not a potted course on building construction. The technical studies in this section are organised around a few main drawings; in the case of roofs for example there are three roof types used to exemplify the cause of most common faults. These drawings are accompanied by an illustrated text which breaks the main drawings into parts, dealing with each fault in turn, diagnosing and suggesting treatments.

Checklist

1.02 The subheadings through this section then constitute a checklist of items for examining buildings. This is not the only sequence possible. Architects may prefer to start inside or out, working up or down the building. The important point is to have a systematic sequence for covering the whole building which where necessary relates inside to outside. This is most necessary in diagnosing dampness and mapping the routes of pipes.

2 Aims

2.01 Repairs and maintenance are needed to relieve the accumulated rot of ages, the physical obsolescence of the fabric. Maintenance has usually been poor for many years, **1**, and it will now be necessary to deal with an accumulation of faults and to make the building sound enough to last for the specified life with minimum continuing maintenance. This may be from 15 to 40 or more years though the award of grants is based on encouraging a 30 year minimum. Significantly, the largest timber treatment and damp proofing company has extended its guarantee (ie insurance liability) period from 20 to 30 years. Others can be expected to follow suit.

Local conditions and character

2.02 Using the term 'faults' is in some ways a harsh judgment on houses that may be 100 years old. Though nowadays fixing timber in 9 inch brickwork would not be recommended, the houses are still standing. The choice was adequate considering the then current knowledge and the local exposure conditions. This latter should be borne in mind when recommending repairs. While current building construction books recommend hopefully fail-safe details for any exposure condition, less stringent measures may be adequate for many climatic situations and much more in keeping with the local vernacular. For example lead flashings and soakers are now recommended at chimney to roof junctions, **2**, but often a mortar fillet capped with slate or tile would be physically adequate and aesthetically more sympathetic, **3**.

1 *The product of years of neglect: fascia and gutter missing, flashing loose, gap at ridge/hip junction, missing pointing to flank wall and far chimney, slate missing from stack, flashing over slates liable to rain and snow penetration, no hip iron at hip end.*

3 New materials for old?

3.01 There will inevitably be compromises between desire to conserve and limited finances. Visually this is most evident as houses get reroofed with modern materials. And there are some good reasons for this. A slate roof for example is expensive to renew; interlocking tiles are a cheaper but heavier covering appropriate to the low pitch of slate. Though LAs generally are sensitive enough to replace slates, the owner occupier or landlord is usually less so. A package, replacing slate with tile, is commonly sold door-to-door, **4**.

3.02 The architect can of course urge the more expensive course but may help more materially by arranging to purchase materials from demolition or the salvaging of materials during repair. These usually become the property of the contractor and special clauses need writing into the prelims to secure them for future use. For example NBS clauses 1154-1156.

1154 *Materials arising* from the work are to become the property of the contractor except where otherwise provided. Remove from site as work proceeds.

1155 *Materials arising:* the following are to remain the property of the employer. Carefully lift or take down and store on site where directed. Protect until removed by employer or end of contract. (List materials and conditions.)

1156 *Materials arising:* where specified to be re-used, carefully lift or take down, clean as necessary and adequately protect from damage. Overhaul, adapt and repair as specified in other sections.

4 Dampness

4.01 Dampness is the single most important factor in the durability and maintenance of buildings. Materials deteriorate and conditions are favourable for fungal and insect attack. These notes indicate a general approach; particular advice will be given with each fault.

4.02 It is essential not only to make the building adequately dry but remedy any faults resulting from damp in the past. Attention should be given to parts that have been renovated previously because of dampness to ascertain whether the remedial work was effective and will remain so for the specified life or whether it was a stop gap measure masking the evidence without dealing with the cause.

Examination

4.03 All possible causes should be checked; dampness may arise from a variety of sources, eg rising and penetrating damp, leaking plumbing and humid air. 'Live' dampness ie currently wet areas, should be outlined on the surface so that if there is a chance to revisit any change can be noted.

Moisture meters

4.04 Care is needed in interpreting moisture meter readings. The common types measure the resistance between two metal spikes. Usually these spikes will penetrate only 1 or 2 mm into plaster or timber so that only a surface reading is taken. And the resistance reading will also be high if there is a high salt concentration in the material whether it is damp or not.

Other moisture indicators

4.05 Timber is the most useful material to examine since it is more sensitive than others and its deterioration is easy to see. Moulds are a sure indication of dampness; relative humidity must have been persistently above 70 per cent, generally due to 'live' dampness, often condensation. Efflorescence occurs if the building is damp or has been so; brush it off and note if it reappears. (This could take days or weeks.) Efflorescence suggests considerable damp in the structure since it appears when water which has passed through the structure, dissolving salts in the process, then dried out on the inner surfaces of walls and ceilings.

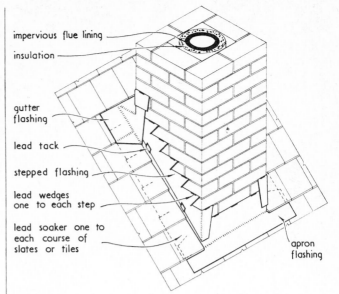

impervious flue lining
insulation
gutter flashing
lead tack
stepped flashing
lead wedges one to each step
lead soaker one to each course of slates or tiles
apron flashing

2 *'Ideal' detail, intended as fail-safe for any exposure.*

3 *Traditional detail, serviceable in its local setting if kept in good repair.*

4 *An individual choice. Later re-roofing of neighbouring houses may well be to a different gauge so the half round tiles on the slope must be kept. Asbestos slates are more sympathetic and similarly priced.*

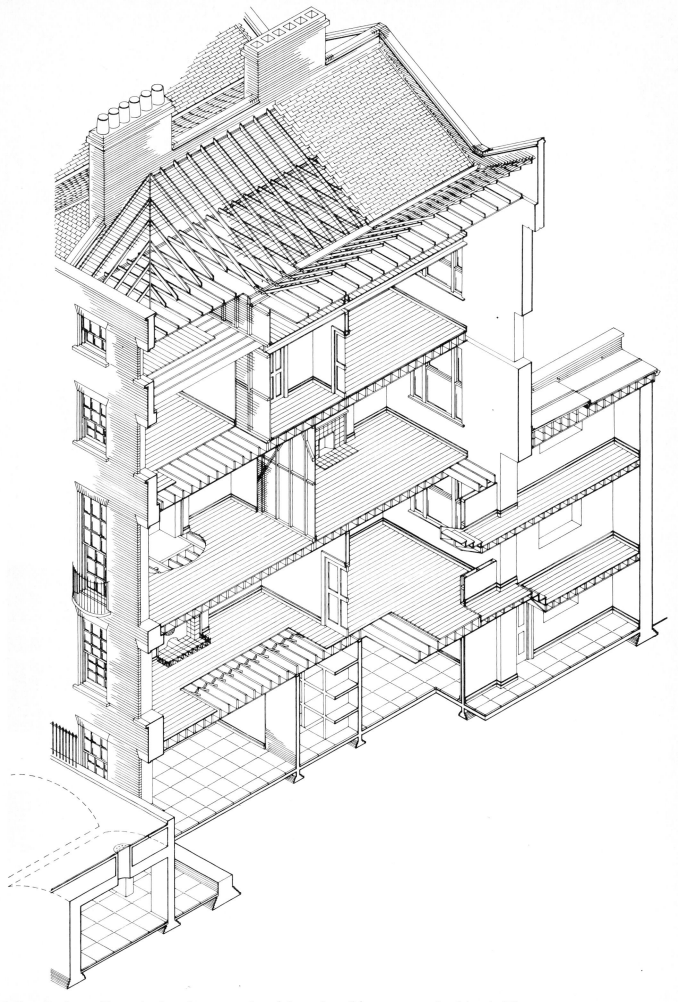

5 *Georgian house, illustrating how then current knowledge and traditions were translated into buildings.*

5 Two houses

5.01 The two sectional, annotated drawings of houses, one Georgian, **5**, one Victorian, **6**, illustrate the original approach to building to be found in houses for rehabilitation. They cannot stand for every feature of every house type but exemplify common approaches to detailing and the use of materials, the scale of components and the then current knowledge of how buildings function with respect to climate, structural strength and durability.

Climate and durability

5.02 Dampness both from penetration and condensation (mitigated by draughts) was much more accepted than it is now. (The northern textile towns were sited for the damp atmosphere.) It was not until 1879 that dpcs and site concrete were required in London, later elsewhere, and from 1900 onward when the building of cavities became common.

5.03 As the drawings show, **5, 6**, timber was frequently used but the main danger was thought to be fire rather than damp. Ventilation to subfloors is limited, to pitched roofs is through any gaps and to flat roofs is non existent. Timber is commonly found in solid external walls: bressummers, wallplates and the ends of joists and purlins. Carrying the party wall through the roof covering was also a fire precaution, discontinued in late Victorian times because it proved so troublesome. Party walls, along with parapets and chimneys, are most exposed on buildings and not easily accessible for maintenance.

Structural strength

5.04 Sizing of elements was largely a matter of tradition rather than understood principle until well into the last century. Though Georgian Building Acts prescribed wall thickness they seem to have been empirically based; buttressing was not prescribed. The use of structural timber partitions, based often on much less substantial foundations than external walls, may have led to sagging in roofs and floors. Sole plates and other partition members would have to be cut to make new openings and it may not have been easy to restore structural continuity. Sagging is also due to undersizing of timbers through cost cutting or where tradition had no ready answer for unconventional loading. Triangulation was known to be advantageous but the nature of forces was not necessarily understood. So nailing of joints and spiking to wallplates was often inadequate; the M roof for example, **5**, tends to push over a flank wall.

Quality: Georgian v Victorian

5.05 Though Georgian construction is often said to be inferior to Victorian this may not be apparent. By now the worst of each have been demolished and the atypically sound survive. There are unsound Georgian details such as the M roof, **5**, described by *The Builder* of 1844 as 'that notorious abomination'. Founded on structural timber partitions which sag, the central gutter beam loses its fall and pulls rafters from the wallplates. But if Victorian building is sounder in principle there are still often cases of expediency mixed with tradition to get quick results in the wake of the industrial revolution.

Local character

5.06 The properties of materials and the bases of their use are considerably uniform beneath the variety of appearance— Glasgow tenement, highland croft, Nash terrace, Welsh cottage, Gothic revival villa, Newcastle back-to-back. Slate for example is found through much of the UK built in the nineteenth century spread first by canals then by railways. And from around the middle of the last century uniformity increased, though much more so in urban areas than rural where traditional uses of materials and forms often survived. Frequently, the most significant local variation was in the quality of workmanship.

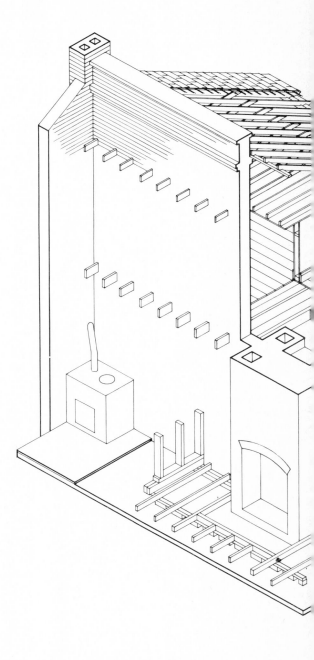

6 *Mid-Victorian house, in many ways more akin to Georgian than to modern houses in the approach to using materials.*

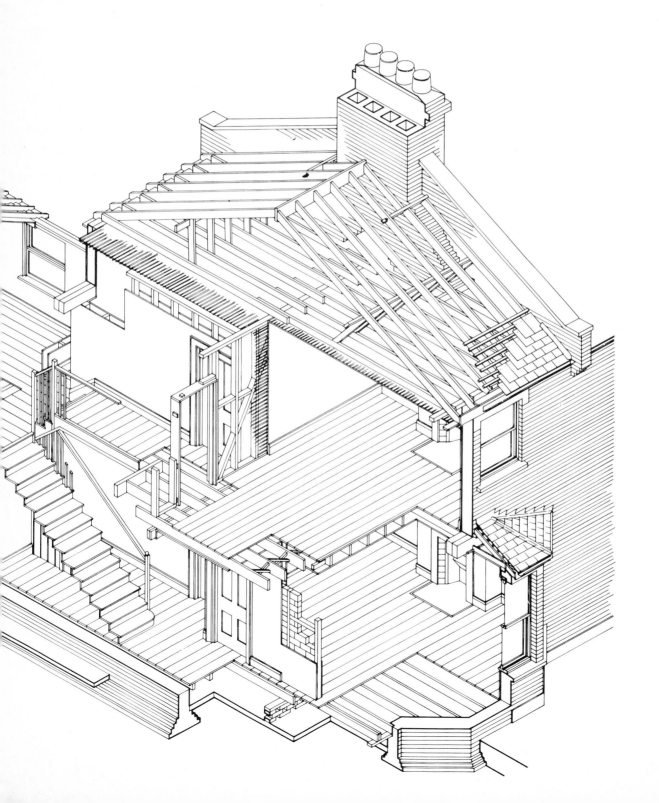

Technical study 2
Pitched roofs

Roofs are often the most elaborately constructed parts of houses and are prone to many defects, especially where exposed—at edges, chimneys, parapets and party walls. Roofs need close inspection. There is no effective substitute for getting onto and into the roof. Trap doors may have to be made. There are three key drawings: a M-roof (A), a mansard roof (B) and a single pitched roof (C). These show common defects. It is necessary to look at all three, since defects, though common, are often only illustrated on one. The text and other illustrations diagnose causes of defects and propose action.

1 Chimneys

Sources of defects

1.01 Chimneys are likely to be defective. They are exposed to the weather and atmospheric pollution and are attacked from within by combustion products and condensation. Where chimneys are inadequately ventilated they tend to stay damp (especially on external walls) and this reduces insulating quality, further promoting condensation. Hygroscopic salts from combustion will also retain moisture. Dampness makes chimneys vulnerable to frost.

Due to sulphate attack from both inside and outside of the chimney, the mortar may be decayed right through rather than just on the outer face. The masonry may be cracked through because of the heat stress of normal use and perhaps chimney fires. Though these defects may be considerable, in many cases atmospheric pollution is reduced and chimneys are no longer used for combustion. The chimneys can be repaired to suit these less rigorous demands.

Pots and flaunchings loose and broken

1.02 Flues are always in use for ventilation (except where fireplaces are bricked up) so pots should not be sealed if no longer used for combustion. They can be sheltered from rain simply with a half round tile set side on to the prevailing wind, **C**. If flaunchings (haunchings) are cracked or loose, pots probably need rebedding. Flaunching can be chipped off and renewed with concrete of small aggregate. A mix much stronger than existing masonry or flaunching will respond differently to wetting and drying, heating and cooling and tend to detach itself as a solid piece of concrete, **1**.

Flues unprotected

1.03 Condensation promoted by inadequate ventilation plus defective flue linings may lead to black staining on chimney breasts. This is greasy to touch. Stacks are normally lined with clay sections or parged (an internal render about 1 cement: 3 lime: 10 sand) but this may have been missed out or, more likely, be crumbling. The stack may be only half brick thick (stone is usually more substantial). These factors increase the likelihood that sulphate attack, heat and frost will have cracked through masonry as well as mortar.

1.04 Even unused flues may need sweeping. Capping pots, **C**, slows decay of linings. Re-lining is not generally necessary unless the flue is in use. The cheapest measure is to thread a flexible stainless steel flue liner down from the top of the stack. The end flange at the top retains the liner and the pot can sometimes be replaced. However, for gas fires and central heating a cowl is often required, or at least insisted on by installers, **C**. This is usually out of keeping with the pots and may be avoided (commonly for gas central heating) by using a balanced flue, ie venting at an outside wall. Check Gas Board regulations. Do not use liners with solid fuel appliances.

1 *Pot missing from ridge stack in foreground. Replacement flaunching already breaking off.*

1.05 If the stack is being taken down for rebuilding, parging or concrete sections can be set in over that part. For the enthusiast, re-parging can be done by drawing a damp sacking plug up each flue on a rope. The sacking contains a former (eg a piece of wood) the same shape as the flue. Parging is put on top of the sacking and runs off the plug into cracks and gaps as it is drawn up.

Cracked masonry

1.06 The effects mentioned above, rather than settlement, commonly cause cracking. Settlement cracks will continue through the roofspace and will probably also be visible through decorations to lower floors. In many cases settlement will have ceased (for wall movement see Technical study 4 Structural stability). A further load may be from a tv aerial, **C**. Generally, deep raking and repointing is adequate. Arrises of masonry will have weathered round, exposing the softer inside of bricks. Flush point the masonry in 1 cement: 1 lime: 6 sand (lime to BS 890: 1972). When further rebuilding is needed there is a temptation to demolish the stack altogether, but this tends to break up the rhythm of rooflines. If repairs are sound rendering should be unnecessary; but patch cracked render. (See later information sheets on damp.)

Chimney lean

1.07 If (unusually) the chimney is straight in itself the lean is due to settlement (see Technical study 4 Structural stability). Commonly, the stack is curved to where wind and sunshine produce the greatest drying effect. Salts in the mortar to the opposite side have more time to crystallise and expand, so swelling the mortar and pushing over the stack, **B**. If atmospheric salt content is now reduced and the lean is not markedly eccentric, ie the middle third of the top is above the base, it could be left raking and repointing or where convenient tied back (ie restrained, not straightened). Lean indicates that the mortar has deteriorated through, so rebuilding will often be needed.

2 *Slate listing stepped down side of chimney and set across face. Slates should be to every course.*
A *An M roof showing tile details and faults common to pitched roofs. Numbers after notes refer to paragraphs in text.*

Listings loose or broken
1.08 Listings are projecting drips of brick, stone, slate or tile, which stop rainwater running down the chimney onto the chimney/roof joint below, **A**. They may be stepped on a roof slope, **2**. Their function and exposure often make them wet, prone to sulphate and frost attack. They may be split and broken themselves and their bedding mortar is often decayed leaving them loose. Either refix/renew or remove slates/tiles, checking the weather tightness of the newly exposed junction below (see paras **4.06-4.09**).

2 Parapets and projecting party walls
Sources of defects
2.01 Parapets and party walls which project through the roof covering **A, B, C** are, like chimneys, relatively highly exposed. In solid wall construction there is hardly ever a dpc right through the masonry, and combating serious penetration is difficult. Penetration should be distinguished from leaks in the junction with the roof covering (see paras **4.06-4.09**) or the covering itself (see para **3.01**), though they may well occur together. For parapets and rooms in the roof, penetration through masonry will show on walls, whereas failures in roof covering will predominantly stain ceilings. If the roof space is open, the stain trails of specific leaks will be clearly distinct from diffuse penetration through the masonry. In this latter case, penetration through masonry is less serious because water can evaporate in the open roof space. One reservation is that wallplates, **A**, edge rafters, trimmers and other timbers **B, C** may be set against the masonry and should be checked for decay. (See information sheets on damp and timber decay at the end of this section).
2.02 Evidence of penetration is often difficult to distinguish

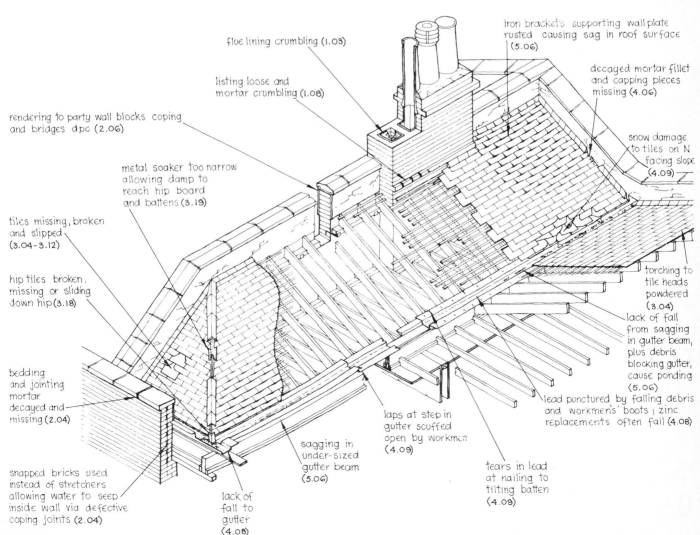

flue lining crumbling (1.03)

iron brackets supporting wall plate rusted causing sag in roof surface (5.06)

listing loose and mortar crumbling (1.08)

decayed mortar fillet and capping pieces missing (4.06)

rendering to party wall blocks coping and bridges dpc (2.06)

snow damage to tiles on N facing slope (4.09)

metal soaker too narrow allowing damp to reach hip board and battens (3.19)

tiles missing, broken and slipped (3.04-3.12)

torching to tile heads powdered (3.04)

hip tiles broken, missing or sliding down hip (3.18)

lack of fall from sagging in gutter beam, plus debris blocking gutter, cause ponding (5.06)

bedding and jointing mortar decayed and missing (2.04)

lead punctured by falling debris and workmen's boots; zinc replacements often fail (4.08)

laps at step in gutter scuffed open by workmen (4.09)

snapped bricks used instead of stretchers allowing water to seep inside wall via defective coping joints (2.04)

sagging in under-sized gutter beam (5.06)

lack of fall to gutter (4.08)

tears in lead at nailing to tilting batten (4.09)

A

from condensation. Ventilation was often not thought of so that penetration and condensation are likely to coincide. In the exposed position of roofs, usually with 225 mm brickwork, condensation is very likely in winter. There may be some opportunities for ventilating, and limiting rain penetration obviously helps in keeping down the supply of moisture and keeping down U-values. Ventilation and heating of the space in use help but are hardly in the architect's control. Roof insulation is one positive step. Where insulation is between ceiling joists, pipes and tanks should be lagged. If roof coverings are being renewed, a felt incorporating glass fibre (or other insulator) could be used. Ventilation to the roofspace must be maintained. (See heating study in Improvements and conversions section). Roof insulation is the only sort grant aided.

Reducing penetration

2.03 Where penetration is not serious, reducing it rather than keeping water out altogether can be effective through generally upgrading the construction. Checking local buildings may be a useful guide to what is effective.

2.04 Because old stocks or badly burned bricks are irregular, they produce an uneven finish when used as stretchers. They are therefore often found snapped, making a one-brick wall effectively two half-brick skins. Water may leak into the 'cavity' through defective coping joints, **A**. Inspect mortaring to coping bed and joint; check there are throatings. If stones are pervious, put a dpc below. For brick on edge coping, **B**, repair mortar and tile creasing. Rake out and repoint defective mortar, finishing flush with the brickwork. (Weatherstruck pointing will further deteriorate masonry arrises). Hack off cracked and spalling render/stucco to a firm base and patch. Check listing (uncommon) as for chimneys (see para **1.08**), **3**. Refix/renew any loose slates, bedding them in mortar, **4**, and laying to courses, running any dpc from below the coping over their top edge. (For render see later information sheets on damp.)

Keeping the water out

2.05 One option for party walls is simply to take them down and roof over. Where the ridge runs parallel to the front, **B, C**, better quality construction has the edge rafters set higher than others to tilt the roof covering away from the abutment. Unless these rafters are reset there will be a slight hump in the roof, most noticeable for close fitting slates, **4, 5**. This is accentuated by the different weathering of additional slates/tiles and the difficulty of nailing them in where they have no nibs. Tiles are easier and nibbed ones can sometimes be substituted. Slates can be fixed with lead tacks as shown, **C**. (Occasionally copper, they are variously called tacks, ears, tingles, latchets, bale tacks.)

2.06 The alternative to removal is to make the party wall or parapet impervious. The use of slate, **4**, or render, **A**, are attempts to do this. Render may have been added later, especially to late Victorian houses which used badly burned bricks. These were burned too fast, leaving a soft centre and brittle shell, often blown off by frost action. In this case render will be to the underside of the coping. It may have blocked the coping's throating and buried the end of any dpc, **A**. Bear in mind that render is intended to be impervious rather than to undergo cycles of wetting and drying as masonry does. So cracks will admit moisture that cannot then freely evaporate. Render needs careful maintenance, so that in the long term (over 30 years) it may be more expensive than installing a dpc through the masonry. If parapets are to be rendered (the back often already is) this is both a constructional and aesthetic choice requiring planning approval, **6**.

2.07 The simplest treatment, requiring renewal every few years, is to paint the masonry with clear silicone water repellant once the joints are raked out but before repointing. (For render and silicone treatments see the information sheets on

3

4

5

3 *Stepped stone listing set in party wall.*
4 *Slated party wall projecting through roof.*
5 *Roof after removal of party wall as illustrated in* **4**.
6 *Rendered parapet face, an aesthetic as well as a constructional choice.*

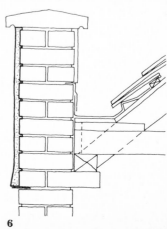

6

dampness at the end of this section.) Cheapness relies on managing without scaffolding.

3 Slope coverings

Sources of defects

3.01 Defects in roof coverings—slates/tiles, felt, boarding, battens—may lead to defects in the roof structure (see para **5.01**) such as decay and shifting of the roof. These in turn may cause further loosening of slates/tiles and other covering defects. Where the roof is misshapen, diagnosis must relate the two sets of defects: of structure and of covering. There will also sometimes be whole building movements as a result of settlement, **7** (see also Technical study 4 Structural stability). **3.02** Wind (and snow) are likely to lift slates/tiles, wear their fixing holes and loosen fixings. The water will lead to rust in fixing nails rusting and of oak pegs rotting, and permeate to timber below, promoting decay. In industrial areas, rainwater is (or at least has been) acidic, accelerating decay of slates/tiles and fixings. Over the last 200 years timbers have become more regular, slate/tile manufacture more standardised and thus roofs more even. Unevenness in older roofs is not necessarily a product of the greater decay.

3.03 Natural and asbestos slate roofs may be painted over with an impervious coating to give a complete seal. However, leaks (which often occur after only two or three years) are difficult to trace. Though the amount of water penetrating may not be greater than to other roofs, the coating inhibits evaporation, promoting timber decay.

7 *Displacement of tiles due to settlement of part of terrace. Gaps can be made up with single or slip (half) slates/tiles.* **B** *A mansard roof; common faults and pantile details. Numbers after notes refer to paragraphs in text.*

7

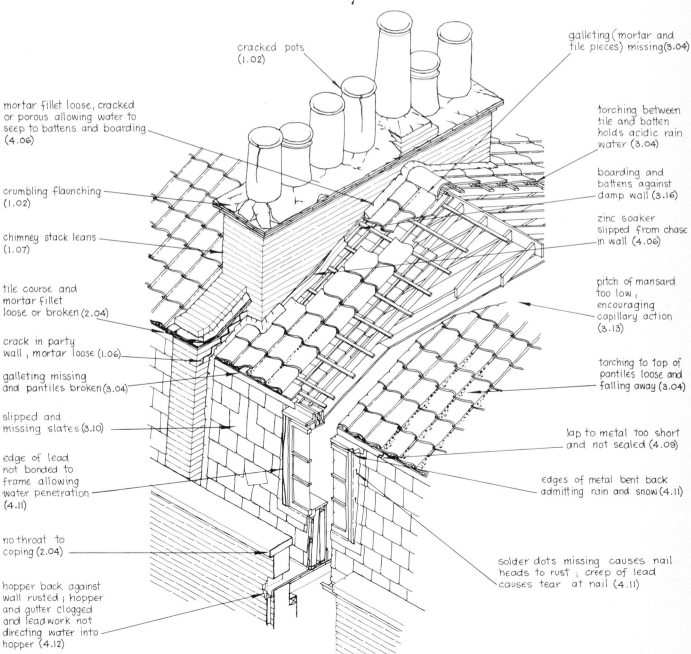

cracked pots (1.02)

mortar fillet loose, cracked or porous allowing water to seep to battens and boarding (4.06)

crumbling flaunching (1.02)

chimney stack leans (1.07)

tile course and mortar fillet loose or broken (2.04)

crack in party wall, mortar loose (1.06)

galleting missing and pantiles broken (3.04)

slipped and missing slates (3.10)

edge of lead not bonded to frame allowing water penetration (4.11)

no throat to coping (2.04)

hopper back against wall rusted; hopper and gutter clogged and leadwork not directing water into hopper (4.12)

galleting (mortar and tile pieces) missing (3.04)

torching between tile and batten holds acidic rain water (3.04)

boarding and battens against damp wall (3.16)

zinc soaker slipped from chase in wall (4.06)

pitch of mansard too low, encouraging capillary action (3.13)

torching to top of pantiles loose and falling away (3.04)

lap to metal too short and not sealed (4.09)

edges of metal bent back admitting rain and snow (4.11)

solder dots missing causes nail heads to rust; creep of lead causes tear at nail (4.11)

B

Irregular slates/tiles and torching

3.04 Tiles and pantiles, common before 1800, were hand made with no nibs. This made them irregular; plain tiles are cambered both along and across. They are vulnerable to windblown rain and snow penetration. These wind effects are inhibited by torching: filling between tiles with a lime mortar, sometimes containing hair or other reinforcement (eg reeds or cow dung). Tiles are torched between batten and tile from underneath, **A**. Pantiles are often also torched on top, **B**. The torching limits penetration but holds acidic rainwater against fixings and battens, causing rust and timber decay. (The fixings may be oak pegs hooked over battens.) Pantiles are also galetted at ridge and eaves, **B**, ie where the curved tile meets a straight edge. Galetting is a mortar filling with segments of masonry set into it—in this case pieces of tile.

3.05 It is difficult to match the original idiosyncratic shapes, especially of pantiles, and the appearance of weathering effects. If some are broken or split, one roof plane could be covered with new or secondhand tiles and the sound ones used to patch other roof planes. If replacement of natural slates with new is too expensive, asbestos slates are more sympathetic than tiles. Check load on structure if the covering is changed; (see BS 648 Schedules of weights of building materials).

Capillary attraction

3.06 Capillary attraction is most likely between pantiles and between slates. (Pantiles, because of their short lap and the chance that torching may have filled the gap, **B**. Slates, because they are close fitting with no camber; the gap between is likely to fill with dust, and so on.) Water may rise to rust nails or decay fixing pegs and wet timber. En route, acidic rainwater may promote frost damage and cause flaking in the overlap. Flaking is common for slates and must be checked for, though care is needed in lifting them. Slates may be nailed at the centre rather than the head, or cheek nailed—a nail at intervals at the side as well as head nailing. Centre nailing, **8**, is common in areas of high exposure; lifting the edge hard may snap the slate in the middle. Cheek nailing was sometimes used during cheaper construction where only one head nail was used. To keep the slates in line, with their edges parallel to the verges, they were nailed at the side at intervals either in a nick in the edge or a special hole. Either way, the nailing is vulnerable to water penetration from the gap between the slates above.

Breaking and splitting of slates/tiles

3.07 Frost and chemical attack, perhaps promoted by capillary action, are likely in time to lead to breaking and splitting. Attack either from above or below may lead to lamination. Obviously this is most likely in split materials, ie slates and stone slates, especially where they are thin such as on bays, **9**. But this should not be confused with worked edges common to stone slates and earlier, thicker slates. These are exceptional in looking considerably deteriorated yet maintaining adequate weather lightness. Compare other local examples, **10**.

3.08 Unless splitting and breaking of slates/tiles are associated with some specific cause such as the impact of workmen's boots and ladders, being too thin or highly exposed at eaves or verge then the quality of material is suspect. Nail heads may not be flush with the slate surface leading to wear and splitting in the slate above.

3.09 With more than 5 to 10 per cent defective slates/tiles, recovering will usually be necessary. The choice depends both on the client's priorities (renew now or in a few years' time) and on the defects. A few broken slates may be bad ones in the set or be in vulnerable or badly detailed positions. Patching could then be worthwhile. But if flaking or nibs breaking off are general, or slates/tiles are slipped indicating general decay of fixings, recovering is probably necessary.

8

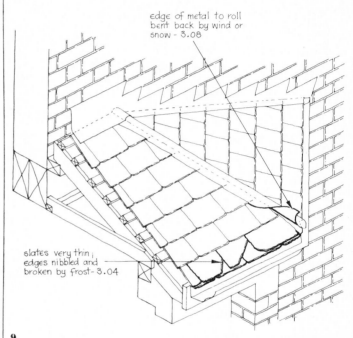

9

8 Slates centre nailed on a coastal site to inhibit uplift by wind. Slates missing due to rusting of nails.
9 Bay to Victorian house. As well as the defects noted, there is a lack of ventilation and the gutter is fixed to the fascia preventing painting.
10 Crude looking but effective stone slates to a laced valley. The curve is made without cutting or shaped elements.

10

Slipped and missing slates/tiles

3.10 Damp promotes decay in fixings. Nails rust especially if ferrous (not galvanised) and oak pegs decay. The action of wind, rain and snow moves slates/tiles, wearing the fixing holes to the edge. Frequently slates/tiles slip but are held by friction for a long time, maybe years, before falling to the ground. Replacement is necessary (see lead tacks, para **2.05**). Patching is often inadequate for a 30-year life and a few slates/tiles may need inspecting to check the general degree of decay.

3.11 Often an extra unevenness to the roof, slipped and missing tiles, and for slate several lead tacks, indicate that removal and relaying are required. Taking down, sorting and storing are an extra cost over destructive stripping. Five to ten per cent (see para **3.09**) of evident defects is enough to prompt relaying, but 50 per cent recovery for re-use is a good average. Nails should be non-ferrous for battens, zinc for tiles and aluminium for slates. For heavy stone slates, oak pegs can be replaced by brass screws or dowelling. Lichens and moss collect on asbestos tiles and they suffer some lamination from frost attack. When laid on the diagonal they tend to hang out of line at verges, further exposing them, **11**. Replace as necessary. The profusion of organic growth makes any new tile very evident by contrast.

3.12 Late Victorian/Edwardian tiles were often of poor quality. Decay is often considerable, even though the environment is not necessarily harsh.

Inadequate pitch

3.13 This is not a common fault. Slates can be set to a lower pitch than tiles; the larger the slate, the lower the pitch. Local custom is the best guide to effective pitch (ideal pitches are given in CP 142, see para **6.01**). There are however a few situations where inadequate pitch may be found, leading to seepage and promoting capillary attraction. Check roofs of bays and dormers, sprockets and valleys. A stone slate/tile valley can be thought of as a strip of roof to shallower pitch than the surrounding surface. Before preformed tiles, valleys were swept or laced (ie flat stones slates/tiles were built up, also cut in the case of sweeping) and laid to make a curved valley between planes. These require specialist skill to repair.

3.14 Where inadequate pitch promotes seepage or capillary action, the simplest step is to realign/renew slates/tiles. To be more thorough, battens can be replaced by pre-treated ones and any felt checked. Where they are sympathetic, larger sized slates/tiles can be used, to a larger lap. In many Victorian and Edwardian roofs (and sometimes over boarding) there is no felt. Add felt ensuring adequate ventilation for evaporation. Roofs such as bays, dormers and the shallow pitches of mansards can be made impervious by a metal covering (see Technical study 3 Flat roofs). Or, since inadequate pitch is usually a problem of minor slopes such as bays and dormers rather than principal slopes, firring or remaking to a steeper pitch can be cost effective.

Decayed battening and boarding

3.15 Many defects mentioned so far allow ingress of damp. Battening, **A**, **C** and where used, boarding **B**, are thus liable to decay. Inspect from below where possible; otherwise a few slates/tiles can be lifted. This may seem elaborate but is worthwhile to ensure a continued life. Too often decay is found only when the job is nearly complete. Unless considerably advanced, it is unlikely to be very noticeable in misalignment of slates/tiles. Signs to look for are ridging of rafters on slate/tile surface, sagging roof lines and patching on hip flashings and mitred hips.

3.16 Boarding, serving a similar function to roofing felt, is common in more expensive work but may also be found in cheapened form. Counter battens may be missing, **12a**, or feather edged boarding is used where tiles have nibs, **12b**. Either way, water seeping through the slates/tiles cannot run down the boards into the gutter and so soaks into the timber. Though water itself does not cause decay, insects and spores are common enough in the air to attack wherever conditions are appropriate (as with mould on food). Replacement should be with pre-treated timber and surrounding masonry sprayed to kill spores. (See information sheets on damp and timber decay at the end of this section).

3.17 Decayed timber, feather edged boards, boards and battens, should be removed. To make edge details simple, keep the roof surface at the same level. Use felt and battens for feather edged boarding and either thicken the battens or add firring to rafters where counterbattens were missing.

Loose and missing hip and ridge cappings

3.18 These are exposed, so that bedding mortar tends to

11 *Asbestos slates gradually working out of line at verge, so more prone to wind uplift. Dust collects on surface texture and at laps allowing growth of mosses.*

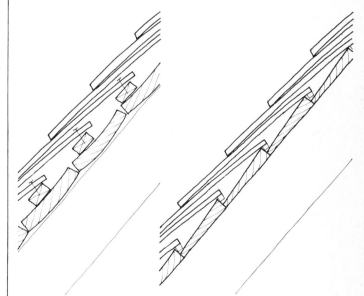

12a *No counter battens running down roof so boards not held flat. Seeping water trapped between boards and behind battens, promoting timber decay.*

12b *A cheap compromise for boarding and battening, feather edged boarding absorbs seeping water in its top edges.*

crumble, and wind may lift off the cappings leading to rot in hip and ridge timbers and rafter ends. Shaped tiles are usual, more often loose or missing than cracked or broken. If there is no hip iron, the hip tiles plus their bedding mortar may slip down the hip en masse. A gap at the hip/ridge junction will be evident, though this could just be missing mortar. Where there is a lead roll as on the bay, **9**, the edges of the lead tend to blow up in the wind. These can be bent back or bedded with bitumen. On ridges of more expensive construction, the edges of lead rolls are held down with lead tacks. These are not signs of repair. On cheaper work hips may be mitred or a mitred capping added (usually slate) bedded on bitumen.

3.19 Mitred hips tend to splay open, **13**, and need at least rebedding and two nails per slate/tile. Single nailing is common where slates/tiles at hips are only half width instead of slate/tile-and-a-half. A lead roll or hip tiles with a hip iron are more reliable than a mitre. Check that soakers have been installed under the hip tiles/slates and are in good repair.

4 Roof edges
Sources of defects
4.01 Edges are mostly exposed, and slates and tiles also often act as drips, making them specially vulnerable to cracking and splitting by frost action. Poor maintenance, mainly of bedding mortar and painted timber, and poor detailing are common.

4.02 Where metal flashings are used, avoid galvanic action of dissimilar metals, such as copper overflow pipes through zinc or lead flashings. Metals not close together in table I should not come into contact. Copper (number 9) should thus be kept away from most other common building metals. Where metals are in contact, the lowest numbered one will corrode. Copper can be adjacent to lead; lead is usually copper nailed.

Table I Electrochemical series

1 Magnesium and its alloys
2 Zinc, galvanised wrought iron or steel
3 Aluminium and its alloys
4 Mild steel, wrought iron, cast iron
5 Chrome irons
6 Lead, tin and lead-tin solders
7 Low copper brasses
8 Nickel and its alloys
9 Copper, high copper brasses
10 Stainless steel

13 *Mitred hip to bay opened because of single nailing and inadequate bedding.*

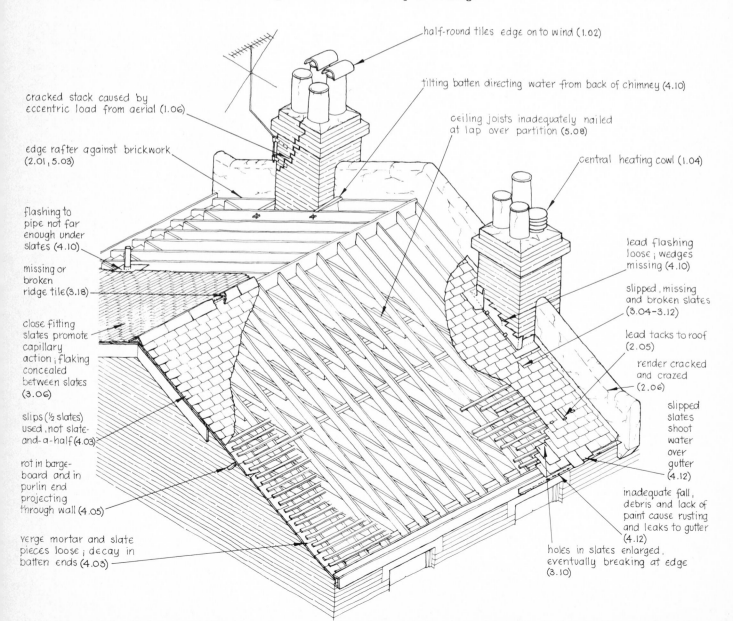

half-round tiles edge on to wind (1.02)

tilting batten directing water from back of chimney (4.10)

ceiling joists inadequately nailed at lap over partition (5.08)

central heating cowl (1.04)

cracked stack caused by eccentric load from aerial (1.06)

edge rafter against brickwork (2.01, 5.03)

flashing to pipe not far enough under slates (4.10)

missing or broken ridge tile (3.18)

close fitting slates promote capillary action; flaking concealed between slates (3.06)

slips (½ slates) used, not slate-and-a-half (4.03)

rot in barge-board and in purlin end projecting through wall (4.05)

verge mortar and slate pieces loose; decay in batten ends (4.03)

lead flashing loose; wedges missing (4.10)

slipped, missing and broken slates (3.04-3.12)

lead tacks to roof (2.05)

render cracked and crazed (2.06)

slipped slates shoot water over gutter (4.12)

inadequate fall, debris and lack of paint cause rusting and leaks to gutter (4.12)

holes in slates enlarged, eventually breaking at edge (3.10)

C *Victorian slated, end of terrace roof showing slate details and common verge defects. Numbers after notes refer to paragraphs in text.*

Defective tilting at verges

4.03 The roof covering is often tilted away from the verge to get rainwater to run down the roof, rather than spill over onto the gable. Tilting is achieved by setting pieces of slate/tile on top of the wall and running the battens over them, **C**. The only protection the batten ends have from damp is the mortar filling which, being exposed, is liable to decay. The mortar helps to support and adhere slates/tiles to the roof, so that rot in battens will be considerably advanced before there are surface defects. The first signs are usually loosening of fixings. The surface may also be irregular if the tilt is too steep or if slips (half slates/tiles) have been used rather than slate/tile-and-a-half at the verge. Gaps will be seen under the bottom edges, **C**. If the surface is irregular, slates/tiles should be lifted to inspect battens, fixings, and fixing holes, and slips replaced with slate/tiles-and-a-half. The slate/tile pieces under the batten ends can then also be checked. They are usually butt jointed and joints may coincide with joints in the slate/tiles above promoting seepage. Reset as necessary.

Verge tilting absent

4.04 This is very common. Edge slates/tiles are more vulnerable to frost action without the tilt directing away rainwater. Where the covering is flush with the gable, as on many cheaper Victorian houses, the water run off promotes decay of mortar and stains the gable. Run off is not usually serious enough to require tilting. But this is easier than making an overhang, which may not be in keeping with local buildings.

Rot in barge boards and fascias

4.05 If tilting is defective or absent and there has been a lack of regular painting, decay is likely in barge boards and fascias. Painting to the back is very rarely done when barge boards are set against the masonry, either initially or after the supporting purlins projecting through the masonry have gone rotten and been cut off flush with the gable. Replacements could better be set on spacers to allow some ventilation behind and to keep the boards away from the damp brickwork. This setting against the brickwork and the consequent maintenance problems are common to fascias to bays and extensions. Barge boards of treated timber and fascias should be given two coats of primer before fixing.

Loose/cracked mortar fillet to abutments

4.06 Depending on the locale and quality of work, the abutment of roof covering with parapet/party wall/chimney may be a plain mortar fillet or be capped with slate/tile, **A, B**. As it is not rebated into the masonry, it is vulnerable to some moisture bypass through the masonry. The fillet allows some evaporation, so decayed mortar should not be painted over with bitumen. Capping new mortar fillets with slate/tile provides worthwhile added protection. In Victorian buildings, there may be no soakers under the fillet, or it may be loose, **B**. Check and install as necessary.

4.07 Because of their shape, the edges of pantiles are relatively exposed, so mortar at abutments on more expensive work may mask an oversailing course of brick or tile. (Oversailing course: projecting masonry corbel or listing that shelters the edge of the pantile.)

Defects in soft metal: gutters, valleys and flashings

4.08 Soft metal, commonly lead and zinc (whiter), perish with age and chemical attack. Lead may last up to a century in adequate condition, zinc rarely half that time. Metal gets split by falling debris and workmen's boots which allow water to soak into the timber or masonry with little chance of evaporation. Decay in timber should be checked for. This is most likely where falls are small, where debris inhibits flow and in the case of the M roof, where sagging removes falls, leading to ponding, **A**.

4.09 On slopes (abutments and valleys) lead tends to creep down the slope. It expands on heating and tends not to move back up the slope on cooling, due to its high density. This strains and opens welts and reduces laps. Generally, this is not very serious. Welts can be resealed and laps will not be greatly reduced. If they are, take up and lay lead again. Metal to gutters and valleys is restrained from creeping by nailing to tilting battens, **A**. Tears at nails are not exposed and generally metal remains secure, though on M-roofs snow may melt on one face, slide into the gutter and up under the opposite edge, loosening metal and slates/tiles, **A**. Stepped flashings are held by wedges which may need replacing. On slopes, if lead is thick and not markedly slipped it can be restrained by nailing, covering the head with a solder spot. Check that metal is well secured and laps and welts are watertight to gutter outlets through parapets, **B**. Clear out debris from gutter and outlet. It is useful to think of gutters as flat roofs (see Technical study 3 Flat roofs).

Defective dressing to slates/tiles

4.10 Where metal is dressed over pantiles (and on later additions interlocking tiles and asbestos sheets) there is little to stop the metal from sliding down the roof unless the flashing is one continuous piece, **14**. The securing of soakers should be checked, **C**. The backs of chimneys (the face nearest the ridge) are vulnerable to penetration by rainwater run off and a tilting batten will help steer water away from them, **C**. Rooflights should be dressed round as for chimneys, **C, 15**.

14

15

14 Flashing to addition (with interlocking tiles) unrestrained by tacks, so slides down slope.

15 Rooflight to much repaired pantile roof. Flashing crudely done here but it is difficult to produce a neat finish by dressing over such an irregular surface. Torching to top of pantiles loose. Varied replacements: old at left, different profile interlocking tile at centre, new pantile at right.

The main difficulties with rooflights and trap doors through the roof covering are when the flashings are loose and the flashed upstand is too low to stop any build-up of water, which runs down the roof, from flowing over the upstand into the roofspace.

Loose metal dressing to dormers

4.11 Metal is often nailed or screwed to the cheeks of dormers. The nail/screw heads should be covered with a lead spot, but this may be missing and the heavy metal may be dragging on the nails causing tears, **B**. The edges of the metal are infrequently set into grooves and tend to blow back, letting wind-blown rain and snow onto the timber below which has probably never been painted, **B**. If the metal is not perished, check for decay in the timber, then bend it back. It may be worth holding the edge down with a cover strip, especially if it is exposed to wind.

Defective eaves, gutter and downpipe

4.12 Check for decay in bedding mortar to under tiles/slates, **C**, that the slates/tiles direct rainwater into the gutter and that any roofing felt and boarding leads seepage into the gutter too. Fascias may rot on the back if held against the brickwork. Cast iron, flat backed gutters, **C**, will very likely be unpainted to the back and, if flush against a fascia, the back may have rotted away. Gutters and gutter brackets should be set on spacers (bobbins) to keep them off the fascia. The same applies to the hopper head and downpipes. Leaks are generally obvious from stains. If in doubt, having removed debris from gutter and hopper head, pour water into the gutter. This also checks whether falls are adequate; often not the case. Holes should be cut in timber soffits or other openings left, allowing ventilation to roof spaces, not forgetting bays, **9** (say 30-40 mm diameter at each rafter spacing).

4.13 The detail, **16a**, is especially difficult to ventilate and timber is often decaying. Where decay is not extensive enough to require replacing the roof, several smaller changes can help. When replacing any decayed timbers with pretreated ones, one simple measure is to add a tilting batten to lift the slates/tiles off the gutter, **16b**. Do not set the slates/tiles so high that water run off overshoots the gutter. A lead dpm over the corbelling and up the fascia would limit direct penetration. More involved to install, a lead dpm capping to the brickwork would inhibit rising damp.

5 Roof structure

Access

5.01 The need to lift slates/tiles to inspect the timber from above has already been mentioned. For a 30-year life, the architect needs to be confident that no timbers are rotting so he should also inspect the underside thoroughly. Often this requires making a trap door. In rooms in the roof, ceilings need opening directly below covering and edge defects and where there are stains. This may seem drastic, but patching with plasterboard or plaster on expanded metal is not expensive as part of general works. Rooms in the roof are especially bad for timber decay because evaporation is limited and conditions favour condensation. Access is, of course, provided from above if the roof covering is removed. Once the roof is open, the dirt of many years will be evident. Vacuuming it out makes the roofspace more pleasant to work in.

Sources of defects

5.02 Most failures mentioned in this technical study lead to moisture penetration. Rot is likely where moisture cannot evaporate freely. As well as rooms in the roof, rot is common in timbers in or set against masonry, **A**, where there is torching, between roof boards, **B**, and where counter battens are missing or boarding is feather edged, **12**, **13**. Moisture may also come from condensation, leaking pipes and tanks and

from open gutters. Open gutters lined with lead are common in earlier Georgian houses with pitched roofs behind parapets. The gutter runs from front to back, **17**. Repair and cover this (or re-route water where possible). The other main sources of defects are inadequate or rusted nailing, overloaded timbers and the builder's limited knowledge of forces in structures, particularly on end of terrace houses which lack buttressing.

Decayed timbers

5.03 Replacement should be with pre-treated timber. Remaining timbers and brickwork in the roof should be treated. (See information sheets on damp and timber decay at the end of the section.) If boarding is rotten, it is cheaper not to replace it but to use thicker counter battens to keep battening at the original level, adding roofing felt. Where a few of the common members (rafters and joists) are decayed at the ends, the ends can be cut off and new timber bolted on, or the remainder supported on hangers (see Technical study 4 Structural stability). However, other members such as purlins and wallplates should generally be replaced completely. To keep rafter, purlin and joist ends out of contact with damp masonry, galvanised metal joist hangers can often be used.

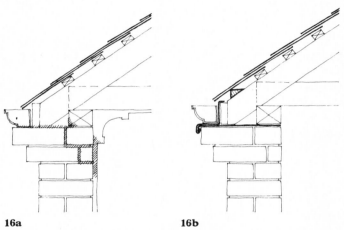

16a   **16b**

16a *Leaks from gutter and wind-blown rain below penetrate to ceiling and roof timbers. There is no eaves ventilation. Inspection is awkward: a mirror may help.* **16b** *Lead over fascia and beneath gutter will inhibit direct penetration. A tilting batten allows ventilation where there is no boarding or felt. If the roof structure is propped to remove the wallplate, the whole wall could be capped with lead to limit damp rising to the timber. This would require removal of the plaster cornice. Welt the two sheets of lead together to inhibit capillary action.*

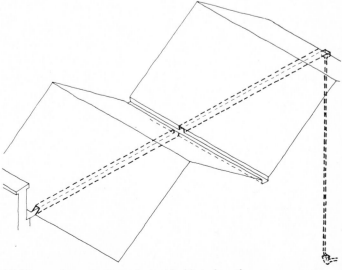

17 *Route of gutter through double hipped roof.*

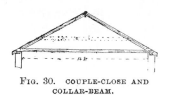

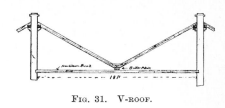

FIG. 28. LEAN-TO ROOF.   FIG. 29. COUPLE-ROOF.   FIG. 30. COUPLE-CLOSE AND COLLAR-BEAM.   FIG. 31. V-ROOF.

18 *From a journal of 1897,* advice on the size of spans at which tieing was needed. From left to right: *7ft, 11ft, 14ft, 18ft.*

Decay of wallplate support

5.04 Corbelling and wallplate brackets, **A**, are both under stress and damp and thus are especially likely to be defective. Surrounding masonry may also be decayed, requiring considerable rebuilding. If so, installing joist hangers may be more economical. (See Technical study 4 Structural stability.)

Overloaded timbers

5.05 Undersizing through cost cutting, extra load from changed roof covering, unusual patterns of loading falling outside the builder's experience, and shifts in the roof redistributing loads are the most frequent causes of overloading. Timbers can be doubled up, cutting a new one to match the existing, placing them side by side and bolting them together at 500 mm intervals. Extra bearers, struts and purlins can be added to redistribute loads on purlins, hips and other principal timbers.

5.06 Overloading is commonest for purlins and gutter beams. In cheap pitched roofs, purlins run between party walls without intermediate support. The gutter beam in M-roofs is prone to sag, **A**, and often needs strengthening. Doubling up timbers is effective. In M-roofs, however, there is often no purlin and it is simplest to install one half way down the slope, strutted off the party wall. This is best done when the roof covering is being changed (ie when elastic deformation is least). The roof can be eased back with props before bolting on extra timber, but this easing can only be slight as all elements of the roof will gradually have adjusted to the deformed roof shape. Re-lay the gutter to avoid ponding.

Deformation of the roof

5.07 Rotten timber ends destroy the structural integrity. The other main cause of deformation is movement in the supporting fabric. Walls settle and bow (see Technical study 4 Structural stability), timber partitions settle and deform, **A** (see Technical study 1 Approach) and redistribute roof loads. Strengthen any obvious weakness by doubling timbers or inserting extra purlins.

5.08 Roof tying may be inadequate. As ties are often the ceiling joists, they may have been sized to limit ceiling deflection rather than primarily to accommodate tying loads. The support of spiking to wallplates was often considered adequate, **18**, and where joists are lap jointed over partitions this is often with only a single nail. Hip rafters may not be tied at the feet because their wallplate is parallel to the joists. Galvanised metal straps can be nailed to the wallplate and to the adjacent three or four joists at 500 mm intervals to tie in the hip slope, **19**. Hipped corners can be restrained from spreading by laying a bearer across the corner and nailing it to the joists. The wallplates of both sides of the corner can then be tied back with straps, **19**.

6 Further information

6.01 CP3 *Code of basic data for the design of buildings* chapter V 'Loading' Part 1: 'Dead and imposed loads'. (Gr4). 1967. Part 2: 'Wind loads' (Gr10). 1972. Chapter IX 'Durability'. (Gr6).

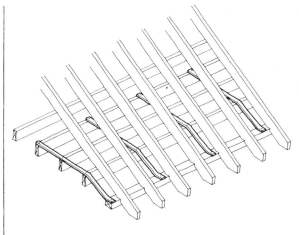

19 *Tying in of hip slope using metal ties to joists.*

CP 112 *The structural use of timber* Part 2. 1971. (Gr8).
CP 131 *Chimneys and flues for domestic appliances burning solid fuel* 1974. (Gr7).
CP 142 *Slating and tiling* Part 2. 1971. (Gr7).
CP 142 *Sheet, roof and wall covering:*
Part 5 'Zinc' (Gr5). 1960.
Part 11 'Lead' (Gr7). 1970.
Part 12 'Copper' (Gr6). 1970.
Part 15 'Aluminium' (Gr7). 1973.
CP 153 *Windows and rooflights* Part 2. 'Durability and maintenance'. (Gr5). 1970.
CP 308 *Drainage of roofs and paved areas.* (Gr8). 1974.
CP 326 *The protection of structures against lightning* (Gr7). 1965.
CP 337 *Flues for gas appliances* (Gr7). 1963.

6.02 Cecil C. Handisyde *Everyday Details*, The Architectural Press Ltd: London 1976.
21 Parapets in masonry construction, p. 99.
22 Pitched roofs: eaves, p. 105.

Technical study 3
Flat roofs

Flat roofs are common on additions and bays. The low pitches of mansards may also be dealt with as flat roofs. Unlike pitched roofs, the coverings are designed to be impervious to water. Flat roofs can be found with no fall at all and are often badly drained. They are generally poorly insulated and lack ventilation, leading to timber decay.

There are two key diagrams, A and B, showing several faults common to flat roofs. Both diagrams should be checked whatever the roof covering being worked on.

1 Metal roof coverings

Sources of defects

1.01 Roof coverings were usually made of lead till late in the last century when cheaper, lighter zinc became available. Earlier lead roofs have often been re-covered in zinc. Both metals react with atmospheric pollutants to form protective surface layers (primarily carbonate). The layer is much more effective on lead—which may last 100 years or more—than on zinc, where some chemical attack is not effectively inhibited. Zinc should last 40 years unless this attack (primarily by sulphur acids) is especially harsh; rate of decay depends on the local concentration of pollutants. Zinc also deteriorates by galvanic action when in contact with copper (eg overflow pipes). Very occasionally, there is reaction between lead and copper nails at rolls and drips, but by then the lead is usually decayed itself. Eventually, both metals become brittle and are blackened by chemical attack and grime.

1.02 The coverings are designed to be impervious to moisture. Joints are often sealed by lapping, A, B, so moisture penetration by capillary action leading to timber decay should always be checked for. Care is needed not to split coverings, especially where they are more brittle with age. Zinc is less malleable than lead. As the metals are soft, they are vulnerable to perforation from workmen's boots, falling debris, and general wear and tear where roofs are used for sitting out. This attrition may also open joints and poorly made repairs, and wear at any unevenness in the roof covering, causing splitting, especially if it has become too brittle to yield to impact. Even small perforations are likely to leak because of rainwater ponding. Falls are often small or non-existent, and in time roof structures may sag from the weight of covering and general structural decay ($2 \cdot 5$ mm lead weighs $29 \cdot 3$ kg/m^2, 14 gauge zinc weighs $5 \cdot 4$ kg/m^2).

1.03 Both metals expand considerably on heating, so joints and edge details must take up this movement. As well as this elastic deformation, lead tends to deform plasticly, creeping on slopes. It expands on heating and due to its weight tends not to contract back up again. Movement allied with irregularity in the roof structure (for lead or zinc), will distort sheets and pull at joints and edge details. So timber may be open to water by direct penetration or capillary action. Again, metal must be bent back carefully to avoid splitting. Underfelt between metal and deck eases free movement of metal. It may be missing.

1.04 Lead is restrained at rolls and copper nailed at the heads of sheets. Creep is evident as scallop shaped folds, shown exaggerated in **1**. The folds are permanent, liable to cracking and impact damage. Creeping lead tends to push open any clips at laps in sheets, tear at copper fixing nails (there may be too few) and to overhang eaves gutters, promoting rainwater overshoot. In pulling away from abutments, **B**, and rolls, **1**, the lap will be reduced. Check for timber decay.

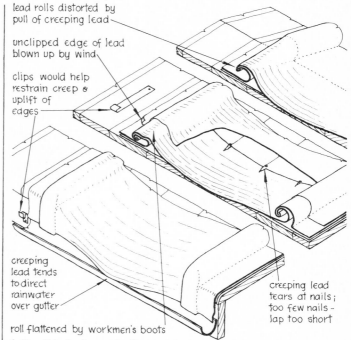

lead rolls distorted by pull of creeping lead

unclipped edge of lead blown up by wind

clips would help restrain creep & uplift of edges

creeping lead tends to direct rainwater over gutter

roll flattened by workmen's boots

creeping lead tears at nails; too few nails - lap too short

1 Possible faults on lead covered, flatter slope of mansard.

Creep is only likely to be serious where there is a pronounced slope: commonly the flatter planes of mansards. Where creep is minor, extra nailing, adding clips at overlaps and abutments, and carefully re-clenching lead round rolls is sufficient. If it is more marked a new covering needed; sheets will be too distorted to be re-laid. Unless creep is localised or life required very long, new lead will not be cost effective and zinc should be substituted.

Inadequate laps on slopes

1.05 The following laps are recommended for lead:
for 15° pitch 300 mm
for 20° pitch 225 mm
for 25° pitch 175 mm
for 30° pitch 150 mm
Though the slope angles coincide with those of lower pitched roofs, the detailing of metal is mostly as for roofs laid to a fall of say 1:80. The main difference is the use of laps; roofs to a fall should not have laps between drips, **A, B**.

1.06 The lap may be less than the figures given above but still effective. Undo any clips and lift the overlap. Water penetration by capillary rise will stain timber near the top edge of the underlap. A new longer overlap sheet can be fitted to prevent eventual timber decay (strip off covering and boarding if decay has started). If wind-blown rain and snow have opened laps there may be direct penetration or a reduced capillary path. Check for timber decay (see later information sheets), closing laps and fastening edges with copper clips, **1**.

1.07 The welted lap is generally sound in zinc coverings, **2**. One or two sample laps should be opened to check for timber decay from water ingress or condensation. Take care not to crack the zinc when bending it back or tear it at the clips.

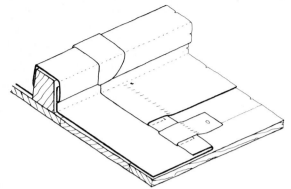

2 *Welting of zinc on a slope.*

Inadequate laps at abutments

1.08 Leaks from abutments tend to spread across ceilings; penetration through masonry is more evident in wall plasters. Because coverings must have freedom to expand and contract, they are formed into an upstand at abutments but should not be wedged into the masonry, **A**. If they are wedged, release them and fit a flashing. There may be cracking where the metal has been bent too sharply into the junction between wall and roof, **B**. If damage is localised in lead, it can be patched (see para **1.20**). Otherwise replace the lead or zinc sheets. The overlap of upstand and flashing may blow open on lead, **B**,

and should be clipped back at about one metre intervals. Zinc is stiffer than lead and clipping is not usually needed. The zinc flashing edge can be made into a welted or beaded drip, **3**. Check that the flashing is firmly wedged and the bedding mortar sound. At external angles an extra piece (gusset) should be welted, or for leaded, welded in, **B**.

1.09 In good work, upstands and flashings will be around 150 mm for lead and 100 mm for zinc with a 50 mm overlap. Check underneath for stains of penetration before increasing undersized details. Flashings may be too shallow where parapet walls are so low that there is no appropriate mortar joint for bedding the flashing, **A**. There may be a loss of lap at drips where the drip steps up by 50 mm and the mortar coursing holding the flashing steps up by say 75 mm, so reducing the lap to 25 mm, **A**.

Leaking rolls

1.10 Rolls on slopes must follow the fall of the roof. Where hollow lead rolls have been made they will be sound unless obviously distorted, **1**. Distortions can often be straightened but the lead may be split. If the roof is otherwise sound it can be patched (see para **1.20**).

1.11 Commonly lead and zinc sheets are jointed over wood rolls. To allow movement in lead sheet, it should underlap and be nailed at one roll and overlap at the next one across the fall, **B**. The lead should be clenched round the wooden roll. If the roll has sharp arrises or is not bossed smoothly at its lower end, cracks may develop in the lead. These are not repairable unless very localised, when patching is possible. Such splits signify poor workmanship and hence the likelihood of other defects. Replace the sheet and smooth the rolls. In extreme conditions, mainly where there is creep, lead may

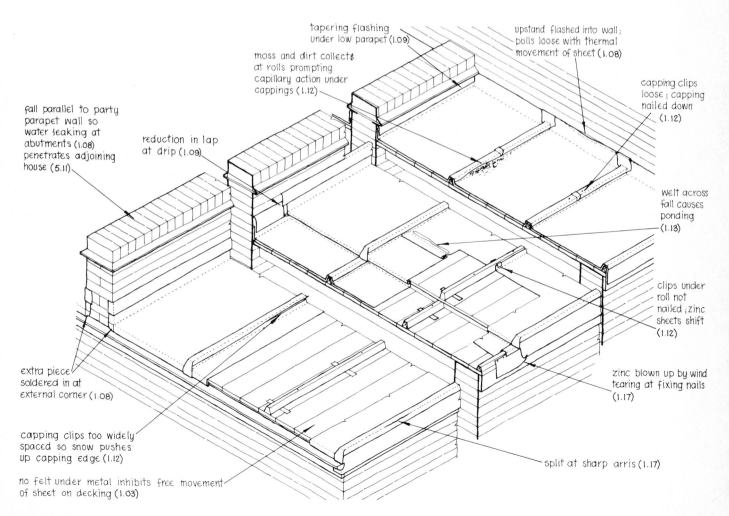

A *Common flat roof faults on a zinc roof. Numbers to notes refer to paragraphs.*

have pulled partly away from rolls, tearing at nailing and opening overlaps. Rain and snow may penetrate directly or the gap may clog with dirt, promoting capillary action. Bend back overlaps to check for timber decay. Generally, cleaning, some nailing and re-clenching is adequate. If tears and distortions are marked, eg on mansards, then re-covering will be needed.

1.12 Zinc rolls have sharper arrises without causing splitting. Movement is accommodated by clipping the sheet edges. The clips may not be held by nails through the wood roll and so shift, letting the sheet loose, **A**. Holding down clips for cappings should be at about one metre intervals. Longer spacings may allow snow to force them up, as they are held only by friction at their lower ends, **A**. Where holding down clips for cappings work loose, clips and cappings may have been nailed through, allowing rain penetration. Renew as necessary. Cappings may clog with moss and dirt, promoting capillary action.

Leaking drips

1.13 The interval between drips on flat roofs is about 2 m (the length of sheet used). There should thus be no welts across the fall. Because of the shallow (around 1:80) or non-existent fall and sag in roofs, ponding of water may build up behind any welt, ensuring penetration through even small perforations, **A**.

1.14 The drip should be at least 50 mm. Check weather-tightness of beaded or welted joints in zinc at tops of drips, **3b, A**. The underlap to lead drips should be rebated and copper nailed, **4**. Lack of rebate leaves a double thickness and ponding as for a welt, **B**. Clean and press down any turned up edges of sheets. (Construction books often show an anti-capillary groove, **4**. This is rarely found). Where drips are splayed, ie inclined rather than vertical, capillary action might seem more likely. Fortunately splayed drips give little trouble as they are used for higher drips, say 75 mm, on more expensive work.

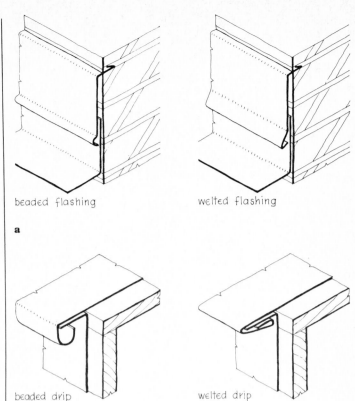

beaded flashing   welted flashing

a

beaded drip   welted drip

b

3 *Beaded (round) and welted (folded) details for **a** flashings and **b** drips.*

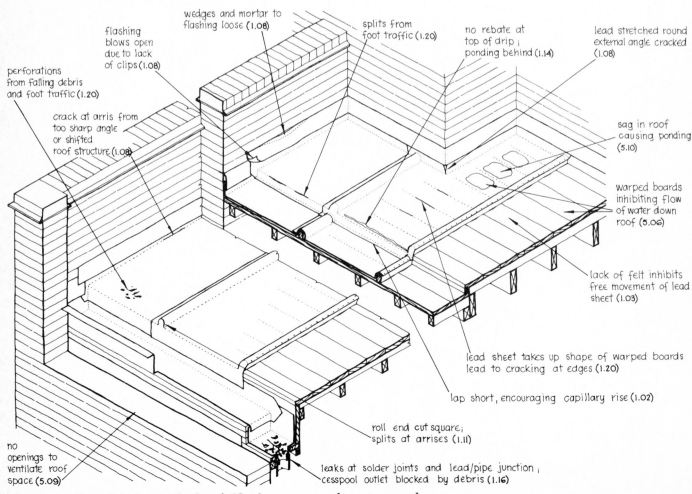

perforations from falling debris and foot traffic (1.20)

flashing blows open due to lack of clips (1.08)

wedges and mortar to flashing loose (1.08)

splits from foot traffic (1.20)

no rebate at top of drip; ponding behind (1.14)

lead stretched round external angle cracked (1.08)

crack at arris from too sharp angle or shifted roof structure (1.08)

sag in roof causing ponding (5.10)

warped boards inhibiting flow of water down roof (5.06)

lack of felt inhibits free movement of lead sheet (1.03)

lead sheet takes up shape of warped boards lead to cracking at edges (1.20)

lap short, encouraging capillary rise (1.02)

no openings to ventilate roof space (5.09)

roll end cut square; splits at arrises (1.11)

leaks at solder joints and lead/pipe junction; cesspool outlet blocked by debris (1.16)

B *Common flat roof faults on a lead roof. Numbers to notes refer to paragraphs.*

Leaking gutters

1.15 Gutters are in effect narrow flat roofs, with drips, **B**. Being the lowest area on the roofs, they are liable to fill up with debris, causing ponding which tests the watertightness of the drips and ensures penetration through any perforations. Where the gutters are adjacent to slated or tiled roofs perforation is more likely, caused by slipped slates/tiles or foot traffic (see Technical study 2 Pitched roofs, para **4.06**).

1.16 Where a cesspool is made in the roof, **B**, it should be folded from a continuous sheet or, for lead, welded. Cesspools often need unblocking, **B**. Leaks from perforations and poor joints are very difficult to pinpoint, and stains on walls and ceilings below give only a rough location. The junction of cesspool with downpipe should be checked. The pipe may have shifted because of loose fixing; the amount of metal dressed inside may be short and distorted by the impact of falling and waterborne debris. The pipe and metal can be realigned to make the junction sound, but the difficulty of finding leaks in the cesspool may necessitate its replacement. A more reliable detail is to route water through the parapet wall to a hopper (see Technical study 2 Pitched roofs, diagrams **A** and **B**).

Defective verges

1.17 A verge roll, **A**, has similar properties to other rolls. However, commonly there is no roll and the metal simply turns over the fascia with no gutter. It is simplest to fit a gutter, clipping the metal if it has been distorted by wind, **A**. Check fascia for decay.

Defective eaves

1.18 The possibility of creep leaving coverings projecting at eaves has been mentioned in para **1.04**. If the metal has been turned down too sharply there will be cracking at the arris, **A**. Lead can be patched locally, otherwise sheets need replacing. The metal may have been turned up at the edge by wind or by snow in the gutter. It can be turned down and held back either by a clip to the gutter, **1**, or by a clip nailed to the fascia, as at verges, **A**. In some cases there may be no gutter. Fit one after checking for decay in fascia.

1.19 The eaves, where the two slopes of a mansard intersect, may have an edge roll and continuous tack, but a simple overlap is more common. This is an exposed edge which can be blown up by wind, allowing rain penetration. The edge can be clipped back as at verges. Check that the arris is not sharply defined and so split. If it is, and there are no other defects, an extra layer of metal could be slotted under the existing metal, say 100 mm up the slope, and nailed. The two bottom edges can be welted together, **5**.

Perforations

1.20 Zinc is too thin (14 gauge is 0·8 mm) to renovate generally by soldering. If there are few blemishes, the zinc and lead can be cleaned with hydrochloric acid and soldered (solder to BS 219, Soft solder). For effective patching to lead, new pieces should be burned (welded) on. The presence of soldering or welding, or even painting over with bitumen should warn that there are probably small leaks to the repairs and other leaks undetected. If the source of perforation is obvious, eg falling slates/tiles, further patching may be justified. Generally, patching indicates that recovering is needed. Where perforations and splits occur over the edges of warped boards, usually on lead (see para **5.06**) the boarding itself needs replacing, **B**.

2 Concrete roofs

Sources of defects

2.01 Concrete roofs are uncommon except as roofs to bays, hidden behind low masonry parapet walls. They consist of around 225 mm of concrete, intended to be impervious: few

4 Drip in lead roof.
Underlap set into rebate and copper nailed. Anti-capillary groove is a 'textbook' detail, rarely found.
5 Junction of planes on mansard roof. New underlap protects against future leakage at weakened arris and acts as continuous holding down clip for edge.

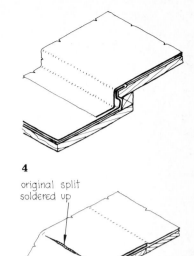

4

5

still are. Drainage is usually poor.

Treatment

2.02 Where concrete is cracked (reinforcement is probably nominal) a replacement flat or pitched roof will be needed. If structurally sound, it can be covered with an impervious layer. Choice of layer depends to some extent on the builder's skills and any extra cost of employing a specialist subcontractor. There may be no fall and usually poor drainage, so felt is vulnerable to any seepage at laps from rainwater ponding. Zinc is better because the covering can often be from a single sheet. If a roll is needed, zinc is only advisable if there is adequate drainage. Asphalt is a safe bet, but several such roofs would be needed to offset the expense of getting a specialist subcontractor on site.

2.03 Note the likely routes by which water will dry out from the concrete into the building, and ventilate where possible. Check any adjacent timber for decay.

3 Asphalt roof coverings

Sources of defects

3.01 Asphalt is formed into a durable impervious layer. Well made, it will last up to 60 years. Asphalt expands markedly on heating and so must be free to move on the deck. If there is no underfelt, asphalt may catch on irregularities (such as the edge of warped boards) and ripple. This makes it vulnerable to cracking, which is accelerated by foot traffic and falling debris.

3.02 Asphalt can tolerate some plastic deformation during movement but shear forces may crack it through. Shear may occur at abutments when the roof structure shifts or at sharp arrises. Sharp arrises are rare on purpose-made roofs; asphalt dates from late in the last century. But asphalt may have replaced metal and be layed over the sharp edges of drips and gutters.

3.03 Asphalt crazes soon after laying but this is only, a harmless surface effect. It is tolerant of ponding. However, in time it becomes brittle and resistant to movement, resulting in cracking through. This will occur sooner at any point where the asphalt is laid thinner than the rest. If new asphalt is laid, a top dressing of stone chips will reflect heat, reducing thermal movement.

3.04 The impression of some contractors is that the quality of asphalt has deteriorated recently; it is more prone to shrinkage. Keying at abutments is especially important.

Leaking upstands

3.05 The detail **6** shows several points to consider when making an upstand. If originally neglected, they may have caused failure. If the flashing has come loose (but gaps mortared over?) or was not bedded deep enough into the mortar joint, damp may have bypassed it, promoting decay in the timber decking and condensation both in the roof space and in the room below. This is particularly important where the masonry is exposed, eg a parapet. Also, a fillet is needed in the asphalt, backed by expanded metal, at the angle. A too small fillet is likely to develop a slot-shaped crack; decayed timbers may give a definite step.

3.06 If asphalt is defective, bonding on new sections can work for limited repairs (see para **3.11**). But, since most roofs are small, recovering is often worthwhile. However, several roofs will be needed to justify the expense of a specialist subcontractor. Otherwise the asphalt could be covered with felt.

Cracks

3.07 Cracks at concave angles such as abutments have been mentioned. But convex angles, eg at the tops of drips and side of gutters, may also have sharp arrises. The asphalt needs removing and the arrises rounding. Where there are drips and gutters, the repairs may be extensive and it may be cheaper to take up the asphalt, decking and firring and fit new firring so that the surface is to one constant fall (see para **5.10**).

Taper at verge and eaves

3.08 Metal nailed to the decking and turned over the edge should direct water into the gutter. Fit a gutter if none exist to inhibit wall staining and fascia decay. Asphalt may be tapered down onto this metal, **7**. Being thinner than the rest of the roof, it becomes brittle sooner. It may also have been kicked and broken at the edge by workmen climbing onto the roof. Asphalt can be softened and a thicker edge made (see para **3.11**).

Leaks at pipes through roofs

3.09 Pipes through the roof should have a metal collar flashing because the asphalt tends to shrink away from the pipe, leaving a gap for water penetration, **8**.

Surface defects

3.10 Cracks have been mentioned. There may be ripples because movement of the covering has been restrained, **9**. If patching is attempted, enough asphalt needs removing to provide access for repairing the felt or smoothing the decking. Bubbles occasionally occur from water vapour below the covering, indicating the absence of a vapour barrier. This could be patched though it does not deal with the cause and the decking may be decayed too (see para **5.05**) requiring replacement. Generally, old asphalt should be removed and new bonded on, especially if bubbling is at abutments. There may also be inadequate repairs. Commonly, cracks are filled with bitumen or covered with hessian bonded to the roof with bitumen. But these repairs last only a few years.

3.11 Bonding on new asphalt is a skilled job. Asphalt should not be cut but melted off. Hot asphalt is put over the defective area, melting the asphalt directly below. This is then scraped off. The process is repeated until the old asphalt is removed. Edges of holes are left tapered to allow smooth bonding of new to existing.

4 Built-up felt coverings

Sources of defects

4.01 Built-up felt is the cheapest, least durable (15-20 years) and often the least expertly laid roof covering. Felt is not inherently bad, but on small domestic roofs it is the only covering that many local builders feel able to lay. Costs may be cut by laying one or two layers. Felt belongs to a different

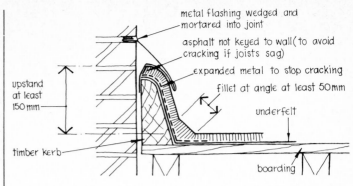

metal flashing wedged and mortared into joint
asphalt not keyed to wall (to avoid cracking if joists sag)
expanded metal to stop cracking
fillet at angle at least 50mm
underfelt
upstand at least 150mm
timber kerb
boarding

6

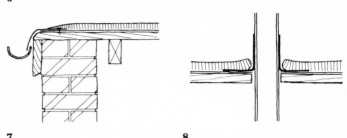

7   **8**

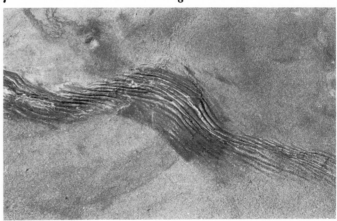

9

6 *Recommended detail for making an asphalt upstand.*
7 *Asphalt layer tapered down at the eaves, leading to early embrittlement.*
8 *Flashing to pipe through asphalt covering.*
9 *Ripples caused by localised irregularity in the roof check for defective underfelt inhibiting movement of the asphalt covering.*

age to metals and asphalt, relying on 'glueing' sheets together (with bitumen) to form an impervious layer.

4.02 Laid on roofs that may sag and have restricted or no fall, the lapped joints are vulnerable to ponding. Water vapour, either trapped during construction or due to condensation, causes bubbling and in time cracks. Felt is not very resistant to impact from boots and falling debris, especially where bubbled. Such impacts also lead to cracks where felt is dressed over or into sharp arrises, eg at drips, gutters and roof edges. Felt does not expand very much on heating compared with the other coverings, and the bottom layer should be nailed to the deck with the other layers bonded on top with bitumen. If nailing or bonding is inadequate, wind suction may lift the covering, perhaps leaving bubbles.

Repair or replacement

4.03 Some details—ill bonded laps and defective flashings at abutments—can be repaired. Isolated cracks and perforations can be masked by bonding on a piece of felt on top, which may last a few years. On small domestic roofs, recovering is advisable if there are only a few evident defects.

Leaks at abutments
4.04 Lift flashing and check for specific leaks and for diffuse staining from capillary action. The latter occurs with inadequate lap. The flashing may be loose from the abutment, or the metal perished and cracked. Renew/refix with wedges and fill the mortar joint. The angle may be too sharp at the abutment, or the roof structure may have shifted, causing cracking of the felt.

Leaks at laps
4.05 Laps may be badly bonded, scuffed open by boots or pulled open by movement in the roof. Laps across falls are also vulnerable to seepage from ponding and capillary action.

Other surface defects
4.06 Bubbles may form. They cannot be removed and are likely sites for premature embrittlement and cracking. Felt, like lead, tends to take up the shape of the deck, so cracking over warped boards. This, and cracking at bubbles, is made worse by impact. Generally, re-covering is needed.

5 Roof structure

Sources of defects
5.01 The roof structure—masonry supporting timber joists and decking—is subject to much the same decay as pitched roofs. Brickwork is solid, one brick thick (or, on some single-storey additions, even half brick, which will require thickening). So water bypasses flashings or leaks through gaps to the timber below and there is direct penetration through walls. This damp environment for timber is aggravated by the lack of vapour barrier below many coverings and by condensation. Flat roofs are usually poorly insulated and unventilated, except fortuitously through gaps, making condensation likely. (See later information sheets on damp treatments.)
5.02 Many problems of insulation, ventilation, penetration through coverings and thermal movement are particular to flat roofs. One treatment is simply to make the roof pitched, covering with slates/tiles.

Damp penetration via brickwork
5.03 Damp penetration occurs as for parapets to pitched roofs (see Technical study 2 Pitched roofs, para **2.01**. See also information sheets on damp treatments later in this section.)

Timber decay
5.04 Decay is quite likely, promoted by water seepage and condensation. This is less likely on metal roofs where laps, welts, rolls, and so on allow some fortuitous ventilation. On new asphalt roofs it is worth installing a proprietary ventilator for roofs of 10 m² or more which helps relieve vapour pressure, so limiting bubbling. It is necessary to open the ceiling to check the joists, even if the covering is removed allowing inspection of decking (and timber rolls) from above. (The lath and plaster can be patched with plasterboard or plaster on expanded metal fixed with galvanised nails.)
5.05 Remove all timber where there is decay. If joist ends are rotten they can be sawn off and the remaining ends extended with timber or steel (see Technical study 4 Structural stability).

Distorted boarding
5.06 Apart from decay, boarding may need removing if it is warped and laid in the wrong direction, causing ridging and cracking in felt and lead, **B**. Ridging can also be marked if board end joints are not staggered. Warping in the boards of not more than 1 to 2 mm is tolerable if it has not affected the covering and the boards do not run across the slope. Boards should have been laid downwards or diagonally on the slope so that the slight channels formed by warping in boards direct rainwater to the eaves.
5.07 Decay in boards or rusted nailing may lead to joists

shifting. Check that joists are strutted and fix new strutting as required.

Inadequate insulation
5.08 No comment has been made about re-boarding so far because of the need for insulation in most flat roofs. If the covering is not to be removed, insulation could only be from below. Insulation can be added at ceiling level as long as the space above is well ventilated. If the covering is removed, insulation can be added over a vapour barrier. The insulation must be firm enough to support the covering and sustain foot traffic, for example wood wool slabs. If the decking is to be replaced, the insulation boards can be laid as the decking over a vapour barrier, saving labour and materials. Wood rolls and the base layer of felt must be nailed through to the joists. Use of insulation board may require adjustment of the level of edge details.

Inadequate fall and ventilation
5.09 Fall and ventilation are linked because firring to give a fall (set at right angles to joists) allows air to circulate freely within the roof. Firring on top of joists makes spaces between joists into separate compartments.
5.10 If there is no fall, fir up the joists. If covering and decking are removed, also take out drips and internal gutters where convenient. Smooth away sharp arrises. Ventilate by letting air in at the eaves, eg **10**, and setting firring down the fall whichever way the joists run. If they also run in the direction of slope, gaps of say 50 mm at one metre intervals can be cut in the firring to allow air movement across the roof. Strutting is especially necessary. Recommended falls are 1:120 for lead, 1:80 for asphalt and felt, and 1:60 for zinc. If local authorities insist on (t & g) boarding, this can be laid diagonally or on battens across the firring for lead and felt. Battens allow boarding to be laid down the fall.

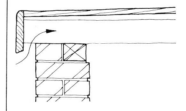

10 *One possibility for providing eaves ventilation. New timber built out beyond wall or pieces lap jointed to existing.*

6 Further information

6.01 CP3 Code of basic data for the design of buildings Chapter V Loading. Part 1: 1967 Dead and imposed loads Gr(4). Part 2: 1972 Wind loads (Gr10) Chapter IX Durability CP112 Structural use of timber. Part 2: 1971 (Gr8)
CP143 Sheet roof and wall coverings. Part 5: 1964 Zinc (Gr5) Part 11: 1970 Lead (Gr7)
CP144 Roof coverings Part 3: 1970 Built-up bitumen felt Part 4: 1970 Mastic asphalt

GLC *D & M Bulletin No 116* (2nd series) June 1978. Aluminium roof cladding: a failure due to fixing method.

6.02 Cecil C. Handisyde *Everyday Details*, The Architectural Press Ltd: London 1976.

18 Flat roofs: falls, p. 80.
19 Flat roofs: timber joist construction, p. 85.
20 Flat roofs: verges of timber joist roofs, p. 89.
21 Parapets in masonry construction, p. 99.

Technical study 4
Structural stability

Many problems of instability occur in the first ten to fifteen years of a building's life. Current structural movement should be attributable to specific, usually recent causes. This study sets out sources of defects and describes analysis of cracks and inspection of foundations. Finally appropriate remedial work is outlined. It is based on information compiled by **JOHN PRYKE** of J. F. S. Pryke & Partners. Structural stability is obviously vital. Architects should call on more expert help when in doubt in analysing a structural problem.

1 Sources of defects

Signs of instability

1.01 Overall, houses are very much stronger than structurally essential, so can tolerate considerable changes in load distribution without noticeable defect. When movement does occur the prevalence of timber and the elasticity of lime mortars often accommodate it without marked cracking. Eventually cracking, deflection and distortion can occur but even these may still be tolerable. Many openings in walls are out of square and cracks have been mortared leaving buildings acceptably stable. So architects should not over-react to apparent signs of failure. Often one source of defect is acceptable. Serious problems arise when defects occur in combination or when there is clear evidence of continuing movement.

Materials used

1.02 As earlier drawings of whole houses showed (Technical study 1 Approach, figures 5 and 6) many houses comprise a timber structure inside masonry walls. Steel, either in flitched beams, **1**, or lintels to openings such as windows and fireplaces, is hardly found before the turn of the century. In houses near iron or steel works, local availability and familiarity with the material may have led to earlier use.

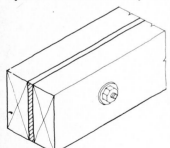

1 *Flitched beam. Steel provides compressive strength, timber inhibits buckling. Flitched beams may be found over large openings such as bays and shop windows.*

Materials decay

1.03 Timber joists and purlins provide tying to walls though this is not always very significant. It is not just walls parallel to the run of joists that bow. The ends of the timbers may be decayed reducing what tying effect there is. Boarded floors, timber partitions and triangulated roof structures provide some stiffness and buttressing to walls. Decay of timbers including loss of bearing and rusting of nails will diminish this support.

1.04 Masonry softens in time and could be more prone to crush under abnormal loads, for example at small bearing areas at the ends of lintels. The masonry cracks and flakes. But this is rare. Brick is not usually loaded in excess of one-twentieth of its crushing strength. Where jointing is irregular such as in rubble walls loose core material may shift in time leading to cracking or some limited collapse of the wall itself.

1.05 Masonry walls may crush or distort where timber included in them decays. There is a loss both of crushing strength and structural continuity. Wallplates at intermediate levels and lintels are obvious examples. In some Georgian buildings 'bonding timbers' were set in the wall behind the outer half brick facing skin. (These also levelled up the irregular coursing of cheap handmade bricks, including broken ones being used.) Size of bonding timber varies with house size. For the smaller Georgian houses encountered in rehabilitation, a convenient timber such as a floor joist might have been used. Considerable difficulties can arise when buried timbers are affected by 'wet' or worse 'dry' rot.

Dissimilar materials: shrinkage and movement

1.06 Shrinkage of materials is rare after the first few years but may continue in a minor way. Shrinkage or swelling will occur with changing weather and is often affected by a change in heating régime—for example if central heating is installed. Dissimilar materials shrink and swell, and move under load differentially. So there may be minor cracks, for example at the junctions of timber stud and masonry walls. Masking such movement cracks is one function of architraves and cornices. Larger movements occur due to long-term creep of stressed timber. This is often very noticeable on roofs, which develop sags between ridge and eaves or party walls when rafters are undersized. It also explains much of the relatively large distortion that develops in the timber framing of older buildings referred to at the beginning of **1.02**.

Tying of roofs

1.07 Tying of roofs has been mentioned (Technical study 2 Pitched roofs, para **5.07**). Ridged roofs tend to spread, pushing out walls at the eaves. M-roofs tend to push over end of terrace gables.

Bulging and bowing

1.08 Bowing of freestanding walls such as parapets may occur, brought about by the chemical effects inducing lean in chimneys (Technical study 2, Pitched roofs, para **1.07**). Bowing and bulging may also occur in time due to inadequate buttressing; tying fails (**1.03**), cross walls are sometimes inadequately bonded to facades, or walls are built too long or thin. Walls may have a half-brick thick skin of facing bricks hardly bonded to the rest of the wall (headers are often snapped before construction) so that the wall is effectively two skins and thus structurally more slender than its overall thickness suggests. New chemical bonding methods offer an economical solution. Bowing is often associated with some foundation failure.

Differential loading

1.09 Though houses are structurally stronger than necessary overall, there may be a pattern of differential loading along the foundation. Commonly, narrow brick piers between windows may apply concentrated loads. Generally only when the ground support of old foundations changes is this differential pattern of loading likely to lead to differential settlement.

1.10 The exceptions to this are generally bays and rear additions, partial basements (basements under part of ground floor) and internal timber partitions which have been settling differentially since they were built. Generally, deeper foundations are consolidated less by building loads. So chances of

Table 1 Soil identification

Soil type	Field identification	Field assessment of structure and strength	Possible foundation difficulties
Gravels	Retained on number 7 BS sieve and up to 76·2 mm	Loose—easily removed by shovel	Loss of fine particles in water-bearing ground
	Some dry strength indicates presence of clay	50 mm stakes can be driven well in	
Sands	Pass number 7 and retained on number 200 BS sieve	Compact—requires pick for excavation. Stakes will penetrate only a little way	Frost heave, especially on fine sands
	Clean sands break down completely when dry. Individual particles visible to the naked eye and gritty to fingers		Excavation below water table causes runs and local collapse, especially in fine sands
Silts	Pass number 200 BS sieve. Particles not normally distinguishable with naked eye	Soft—easily moulded with the fingers	More susceptible to frost than fine sand. It can be very difficult to obtain a good bottom in waterlogged coarse silt. Silt is perhaps the most difficult soil of all for the foundation engineer.
	Slightly gritty; moist lumps can be moulded with the fingers but not rolled into threads	Firm—can be moulded with strong finger pressure	
	Shaking a small moist lump in the hand brings water to the surface		
	Silts dry rapidly; fairly easily powdered		
Clays	Smooth, plastic to the touch. Sticky when moist. Hold together when dry. Wet lumps immersed in water soften without disintegrating	Very soft—exudes between fingers when squeezed	Shrinkage and swelling caused by vegetation
		Soft—easily moulded with the fingers	Long-term settlement by consolidation
	Soft clays either uniform or show horizontal laminations	Firm—can be moulded with strong finger pressure	Sulphate-bearing clays may attack concrete and corrode pipes
			Poor drainage
	Harder clays frequently fissured, the fissures opening slightly when the overburden is removed or a vertical surface is revealed by a trial pit	Stiff—cannot be moulded with fingers	Movement down slopes; most soft clays lose strength when disturbed
		Hard—brittle or tough	
Peat	Fibrous, black or brown	Soft—very compressible and spongy	Very low bearing capacity; large settlement caused by high compressibility
	Often smelly	Firm—compact	
	Very compressible and water retentive		Shrinkage and swelling—foundations should be on firm strata below
Chalk	White—readily identified	Plastic—shattered, damp and slightly compressible or crumbly	Frost heave
		Solid—needing a pick for removal	Floor slabs on chalk fill particularly vulnerable during construction in cold weather
			Swallow holes
Fill	Miscellaneous material, eg rubble, mineral, waste, decaying wood		To be avoided unless carefully compacted in thin layers and well consolidated
			May ignite or contain injurious chemicals

Crown copyright reproduced from BRE digest 64 by permission of the director of BRE.

producing appropriate-sized foundations at the appropriate depth to match the settlement due to consolidation of the main structure are not very high. Often additions and bays, and partitions almost always, are built on shallower, smaller foundations than the main structure so tend to sink relative to it. Additions and bays are often attached only by occasional bonding bricks or metal (maybe rusted) cramps.

Undermining of foundations

1.11 Undermining of foundations, the removal of ground support, may be due to major ground movements such as mining subsidence or swallow holes. Swallow holes are fissures in chalk and limestone which can 'swallow' up substantial amounts of soil. These potential hazards will usually be well known locally. Table 1 lists the characteristics of soils and the possible foundation difficulties which may lead to undermining of foundations. There are two common problems. Groundwater movement undermines silts and peats at coasts and rivers. Clays swell and shrink with moisture content, affected by rainfall and drought, leaking drains and the demands of plant roots.

Building on slopes

1.12 Buildings on slopes will normally be stable by now but there may be changes in groundwater which could affect clays and gravels as mentioned in table 1 so that the building not only settles but slips down slopes. Change of water content may affect built up ground, **2**, and retaining walls may eventually fail, **3**.

Man-made defects

1.13 Loss of soil support may be due to recent ground works; improvements in drains and other entrenching may be dug too close to existing buildings and/or loosely backfilled. Soil slips towards these.

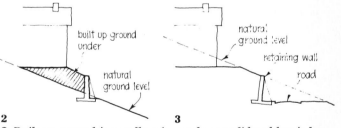

2 *Built up ground is usually adequately consolidated but is less so than uncut soils and so more vulnerable to groundwater movements.*
3 *Failure of retaining walls buttressing soil slopes may allow soil and building to slip. The wall might be to a railway cutting say 50 m away.*

Cycles of movement

1.14 Movements may occur in cycles, natural and man-made. Patterns of occupancy may change, varying the loading (not usually significant) and heating/cooling régimes. Weather changes will bring about expansion and contraction of materials and changes in soil moisture content. These cycles may result in cracks which fluctuate in size with the cycles or which get a little worse at each cycle.

2 Crack analysis

Crack direction

2.01 Cracks in old buildings are not as clear cut as in new buildings because traditionally used lime mortars are often much weaker. Cracks in the following figures are shown pronounced to illustrate shape and direction of movement. They are shown for brick walls with cracks along lines of greatest stress, modified by following the mortar joints. Cracks in dressed and rubble stone walls will be the result of similar strains but modified by large scale or irregular coursing.

Crack shape

2.02 Whole wall shifts opening either horizontal or vertical mortar joints are extremely rare, except for some shrinkage cracks. The normal pattern is for cracks to *taper* because movement is by *rotation*; cracks spring from the centre rotation, **4**.

Crack movement

2.03 Usually talking to occupants, noting likely causes of cracks and inspecting them will be enough to indicate whether movement is recent. Breaks in wallpaper or paint, sharp edges to cracks, clean interiors and discontinuities in any damp staining, all indicate recent movement.

2.04 A more thorough though longwinded approach is to use telltales. This could take months or even years if there is an annual cycle of movement. Two methods are illustrated, **5, 6, 7**. The use of glass telltales is not illustrated because of the difficulty of keeping them in place and of avoiding breakage on site. Measurements must be kept at regular intervals to check whether the movement is slowing, regular or accelerating.

Shrinkage cracks

2.05 Shrinkage cracks, if found, will usually be at the junction of timber and masonry, **8**, **9**. Generally shrinkage cracks will not exceed 2 mm and those above 3 mm are probably due to differential settlement. Shrinkage cracks tend to be of equal width along their length. Where there are shrinkage cracks between masonry and timber walls, these will probably not be continuous down the building.

2.06 There may be a vertical crack along a chimney or behind the fire back due to heat shrinkage, **10**. This is most likely where the chimney is on an external wall, subject to atmospheric cooling.

Deflection cracks

2.07 Internal timber-framed partitions may crack away from the rigid external walls or more rigid partitions that continue from floor to floor through the building. Cracks may be due to shrinkage, foundation problems or deflection. Cracking is explained not so much by the form of cracks as by the nature of structural support. Shrinkage is not very common and very unlikely to be continuous from floor to floor up the building. If there is settlement, and timber partitions are often poorly founded, cracks will run right from the lowest floor up the building. (In practice they could peter out toward the top as nailing and other restraints plus reduced dead loads support the partition without cracking.)

2.08 Deflection itself is unlikely to be marked in simply supported floors though deflection cracks may occur at ceiling edges and across the ceiling at the lowest point of sag. However, sometimes joists are undersized or bearing has been lost due to timber decay. (Lift the floorboard adjacent to the external wall to check for these.) Cracks tend to occur where partitions are inadequately supported, ie support is not continuous from floor to floor, **11**.

2.09 The other type of deflection is in simply supported members over openings. These could be bressumers (two or more timbers, probably nailed or bolted together) or flitched beams, **1**. Check for timber decay removing plaster as necessary. The crack pattern is clear. Masonry above the lintels will drop in roughly triangular formation leaving an arching of the structure above. Diagonal cracks spring from the ends of lintels to the centre, **12**.

Foundation settlement

2.10 Foundation failures are generally associated with a change in ground support for the foundation. Houses that have survived up to 200 years are not going to suddenly overload a foundation unless there is a substantial change in loading pattern. Overloading is anyway extremely rare in the UK except on fens and saltings. Heavier buildings, those over three storeys, are more prone to overload clay soils and are

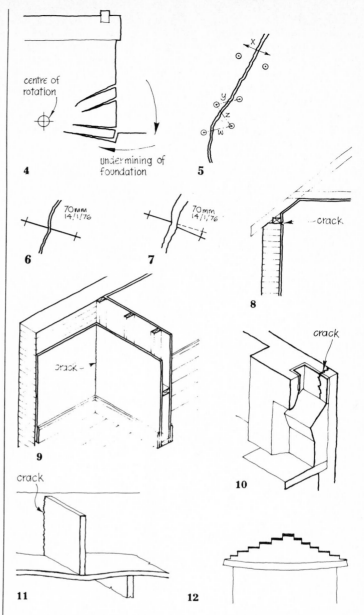

4 *Undermined end of terrace settles. Cracks are tapered and segments between cracks settle relative to a centre of rotation.*

5 *Using a proprietary gauge and metal studs glued to wall, measure change in crack width 'x'. Reading accuracy 0·02 mm (influenced by temperature); 'w', 'y' and 'z' interpreted to give width and shear. Extreme accuracy gives reliable results quickly but expensive to monitor.*

6 *Line drawn and noted.*

7 *Later readings monitor changed width and shear. Accurate to about 0·3 mm on flat.*

8 *Shrinkage and differential movement due to changes of temperature and humidity.*

9 *As 8 plus deflections due to timber creep and changed loading.*

10 *Heat shrinkage crack.*

11 *Partitions offset, supported on deflecting floors, pull away from more rigid walls.*

12 *Sag in lintel and brick, arch left over opening.*

therefore likely to fail where there are defects such as recent excavation nearby. Humped basement floors, often found in heavy 3 or 4-storey 18th and 19th-century brick buildings on clay soils, are typically due to long-term settlement as a result of overloading. Where there is a loss of foundation support the existing differential loading along the foundation may lead to differential settlement. Where settlement and distortion occur these may redistribute loading within the building so that other walls or perhaps non-loadbearing partitions are distorted and/or settle. The majority of house foundation failures arise where shallow foundations are constructed in clay soils. The most severe defects develop where large changes in foundation depth occur (such as where bays or extensions on shallow foundations typically less than 1 m deep in clay soils adjoin parts of a house built on basement walls) and there are vigorous trees nearby. All sizes of buildings are equally vulnerable to movements caused by clay shrinkage and swelling.

2.11 A sagging building tends to develop small cracks, **13**, whereas with hogging the same curvature, fewer (often only one) large cracks develop, **14**. Direction of taper indicates the type of movement. Where an area of soil beneath foundations is soft (or becomes so from water movement) softness is more tolerable at the centre, causing sagging. The foundations under walls at either end tend to buttress the movement. Where softness is at the end(s) there is no buttressing effect and settlement (hogging) is more marked.

2.12 When walls or piers sink differentially there are usually distinctive crack patterns. Differential settlement is always associated with sections of brickwork rotating relative to the remainder of the structure, and thus with tapering cracks. The crack patterns may be simple as in the case of a corner sinking, **4**, or more complex, as in the case of walls with a high proportion of window openings, **15**, **16**. These cracks taper from window corners vertically in pairs. It is thus possible to identify directions of movement; identify for 'blocks'—areas of masonry between cracks—and the direction of rotation and sinking required to form the tapered cracks. Thus the direction of foundation movement can be identified, **17a, b**.

Variable depth foundations

2.13 The likelihood of cracking where bays or extensions join the main structure, **18**, has been mentioned **1.09**. Consolidation of bay/addition is not matched to that of the main structure. Settlement may also vary long after construction when moving groundwater affects foundations differently at different depths. This could also apply to semi basements, **19**.

13 *A sagging building tends to develop several cracks tapering open toward the foundation.*

14 *The same curvature as* **13** *but hogging; there are likely to be fewer, larger cracks—often a single one tapering open toward the roof. See* **16**. *Such cracks are rare in walls without openings.*

15 *Pattern of tapering cracks around windows if centre wall settles.*

16 *Pattern of tapering cracks if end walls settle. Cracks are in similar locations to* **15** *but taper in the opposite direction.*

17a, b *Settlement of end of terrace. Window aprons tend to rotate as blocks. The foundation settles differentially with differential load from structure.*

17c *Settlement may be due to groundwater movement to right of windows. These are idealised patterns. Extensions should have better foundations than the building being extended, for example, design for the same bearing pressure but at greater depth.*

18 *Extension founded in shallower soil so more prone to consolidation, hence settlement, than the main structure.*

19 *Drying of soil to left due to transpiration of tree causes a relatively large (25 mm) crack. To the right, the extra consolidation of shallower foundations causes a much smaller (3 mm) crack. This example is based on a measured case.*

20 *Inspection pits should be as small as convenient and not undermine the foundation. Digging should be co-ordinated with inspection so that the foundation is not left exposed. 600 mm is usually wide enough; extra space can be made by digging away from the building.*

21 *Qualities of structurally adequate foundations. Poor foundation concrete sometimes diverts attention from the real cause of foundation failure.*

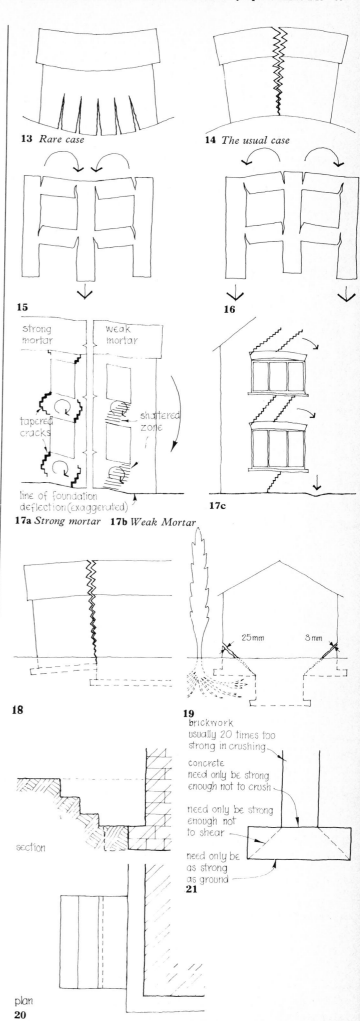

13 *Rare case*

14 *The usual case*

15

16

strong mortar weak mortar

tapered cracks shattered zone

line of foundation deflection (exaggerated)

17a *Strong mortar* **17b** *Weak Mortar*

17c

18

19

brickwork usually 20 times too strong in crushing

concrete need only be strong enough not to crush

need only be strong enough not to shear

need only be as strong as ground

25mm 3mm

21

section

plan

20

3 Foundation inspection

Sources of information

3.01 On the few occasions when original drawings are available, even these should be doubted. Foundations are the least likely parts of buildings to be built as drawn. So inspection pits should be dug to check depth and quality of foundations. Pits usually provide adequate diagnostic information but remaining uncertainties may require specialist soil tests for bearing capacity or for checking such major faults as swallow holes and mining subsidence.

3.02 Large scale Ordnance Survey maps provide information on marshes, streams and other features. Geological maps of most of Great Britain are available. A current list can be obtained from The Director, Institute of Geological Sciences, Exhibition Road, South Kensington, London SW7. Old maps in local archives may be even more informative.

Digging inspection pits

3.03 Digging pits should disturb foundations as little as possible. A failed foundation should not be exposed over its length but at the point(s) of greatest settlement. Where a corner sinks, eg **4**, the pit should be dug at the corner and not below the centre of rotation from which cracks spring.

3.04 Inspection pits should be narrow trenches (up to 600 mm wide), **20**. Any increase in working space should be dug away from the foundation. Digging should stop short of the bottom of the foundation, not undermine it. The last few shovelfuls are only removed when the architect is on site to inspect it. Hardly ever is remedial action immediate so backfilling should be done after inspection. A fairly dry concrete should be rammed under the foundation and spread round the footing. Soil should be compacted back.

Foundation quality

3.05 Foundation materials are hardly ever too weak in themselves, however poor their appearance. Even brick with earth in the joints, **21**, shows how relatively small the stresses usually are. There may of course be some failure from differential loading but this is likely to be due to soil weakness rather than foundation material failure.

Foundation depth

3.06 Foundations spread their load quite locally, **22**, so inspection of soil does not need to be widespread. Foundations should be deep enough to reach good soil. Soil may be natural, filling (look for brick and timber particles and other debris), loam or topsoil. In practice all will normally be consolidated though larger pieces of debris may take a very long time to decay. But if the soil is not natural it may be less supportive and more vulnerable to being leached away by moving water. Consolidation will have been greater than for natural soils. Remedial work will take foundations down to solid ground below such soil.

Soil quality

3.07 Table 1 indicates the field assessment that can be made of soils. Cohesionless soils—sands, gravels and silts—are vulnerable to having fines leached out by moving groundwater. Local pumping operations and other processes that pass water under the building, not merely wet the soil, are liable to do this. Moving water as well as foundation pressure may help move buildings that are on slopes if retaining walls fail, especially on fill, **2**. Clays are vulnerable to wetting and drying; they swell and shrink. As plant roots develop they drain clays more quickly so causing shrinkage; this may become very serious in times of drought. Alternatively (or simultaneously) clay may be wetted by leaking drains. Failure can be accelerated if initial foundation movement has ruptured drains.

3.08 If inspection of soils by sight and touch does not yield reliable information a sample can be handed to an expert with a colour photograph of where it was extracted. Or for clay a

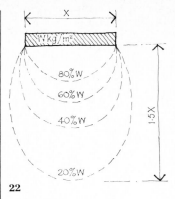

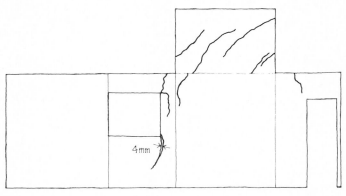

22 *Bulb of pressure distribution showing the confined area over which pressure dissipates.*
23 *One very useful method of recording crack patterns in three dimensions. The width of cracks of 1 mm or more and their directions of taper are noted. The diagram is an 'unfolded' set of linked elevations plus ceiling viewed from below.*

shear test can be done. (A vane of crossed blades is inserted into the soil and the torque needed to rotate it, ie to shear the soil, is read off a gauge.) Taking samples for laboratory analysis is a skilled job; samples must be undisturbed.

4 Treatments

Preliminaries

4.01 It is difficult to know how much more responsibility for safety has devolved on the architect with the new Health and Safety at Work Act. On humanitarian grounds alone the architect should think carefully about the safety and comfort of working that will be involved. It may be that some cheap method cannot be used because access to the workplace is too restricted.

4.02 Architects should also check what effect proposed works will have on neighbouring buildings. A survey is needed of:
● conditions of adjoining and neighbouring buildings with a record made of defects. Cracks do not photograph well so a crack diagram is a useful aid.
● extent of vaults, tunnels and other underground structures
● location of services
● nature, quality and legal definition of walls abutting the site. Regulations on party walls are not uniform nationally (see section 5 of the handbook, Administration). It is important to serve the appropriate party structure notice for work on party walls, or formalise agreement to any works in writing.

Approach

4.03 Since this section deals with repair and maintenance, discussion of propping etc does not extend to making openings and other design changes. But it is important to think how treatments for instability may be integrated with design of improvements and conversions. It may be, for example, that if a timber internal wall settles and more substantial or deeper foundations are needed, this is the moment to relocate walls and rooms in the centre of the house. There will be incidental damage and repairs needed to dpcs, roofs, drains, gutters and so on.

Materials decay

4.04 If ends of timbers are decayed, they can be cut off and the remainder supported or extended (see **4.16**). If masonry is crushed by concentrated loads, spread it or accommodate it by replacing crushed masonry with stone or concrete padstones. If timbers in masonry are decayed they can be replaced in concrete. Some needling and propping may be needed to temporarily support the masonry above (see **4.17**).

Dissimilar materials: shrinkage and movement

4.05 This is unlikely to be serious and can be left or masked by decoration. Paradoxically, rehabilitation may bring on shrinkage cracking by changing occupancy and/or changing the heating. Gradual shrinkage may go on for three or four years. Warn the occupant.

Deflection cracks

4.06 Unless timber bearing is decaying deflection cracks should not get worse. A design solution may be effective (**4.03**) or they can be masked as for other minor movement.

Bulging and bowing

4.07 Bowing freestanding walls like parapets can be tied back using steel cramps, **24a**, bedded in the brickwork and screwed into the rafters. This will require some flashing where it penetrates the roof covering. Sagging and hogging of buildings, **13, 14**, may also distort parapets. These movements will weaken or reduce mortar so rebuilding may be needed rather than tying.

4.08 Bowing walls should be tied back. Bowing is often associated with foundation failure so any cracks should be analysed. Tying back restrains masonry, it does not restore its original shape. Nor does it prevent further movement if there is active foundation failure. Only in timber partitions or roofs could props or blocks and tackles be contemplated for restoring shape. But since other elements will have shifted in sympathy simply tying is generally advisable even here. Tie in poorly bonded facades at crosswalls, **24b, c**. Where walls are parallel to joists tying can be achieved as shown, **25a, b, c**. Where they are at right angles, methods used to extend joists (see **4.16**) can provide additional restraint where joists' current bearing does not achieve this. **26** shows how little of a house may be tied in. Recent developments in epoxy resin bonding provide new, economical solutions.

Over-consolidation

4.09 Bays and additions are often partly detached from the main structure. If movement is not recent simply bonding in masonry may be adequate (**4.08**). Sometimes additions are poorly founded and jacking up (a specialist job) and underpinning (see **4.18**) will be needed, **27**. Alternatively they could be demolished. (Many faults are found in additions and they are sometimes awkward spaces to use well so the sum of their disadvantages may make demolition worthwhile.)

4.10 Bays that are unstable may also be jacked and underpinned. Those made of stone segments are built rather like a child builds with wooden bricks. They may collapse in a heap so the first step is shoring (**4.20**).

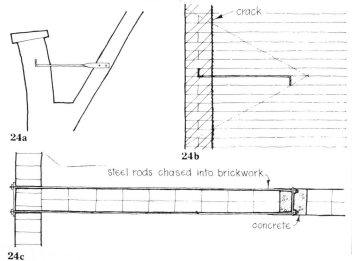

24a

24b

steel rods chased into brickwork

concrete

24c

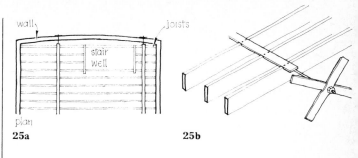

plan

25a   **25b**

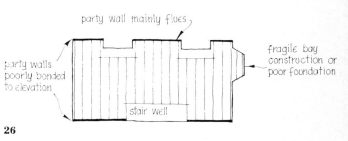

party wall mainly flues

party walls poorly bonded to elevation

fragile bay construction or poor foundation

stair well

26

27

24a *Steel flats (say 50 mm × 6 mm at 2 m intervals) tying back a leaning parapet. Flats must be primed after bending. Cutting out brickwork to set in flat will require resetting masonry giving a firm anchorage. If mortar is seriously decayed, rebuild instead.* **b** *section of flank wall (left) poorly bonded to crosswall (right). Steel flat (say 70 mm × 9 mm section at 1 m vertical intervals) bent and primed. Modify interval to make workplace accessible where necessary. Dotted lines indicate direction of failure cracks in cross wall if its mortar is decayed. A more robust but elaborate method is shown in* **c**. *Primed, threaded steel rods (say 12 mm diameter) are bolted to a flat on the outside and to a plate set in concrete cast into the brickwork to form a sound anchorage. Tie rods should run in a chase. Repeat at 2 m to 3 m vertical intervals, say at least one per storey height, length not less than spacing.*

25 *Tying in a wall parallel to joists.* **a** *steel flats, 5 m long or more where possible are notched into the joists—though not at their mid points. Ties have to be offset round openings. Screw new steel flats to joists to anchor wall to floor which acts as stiff diaphragm transferring load to side walls when boards and ceiling are in position.* **b** *flats (say 75 mm × 6 mm section) with a 20 mm diameter × 600 mm long rod welded on for 100 mm. Tie notched and screwed into joist. Rod threaded and primed steel flats bolted to the outside. (Decorative plates and shaped flats are hardly ever obtainable now.)*

26 *Little of some house perimeters is buttressed. Joists tie a limited length and elevations may be poorly bonded to crosswalls.*

27 *Jacking up a house with spanner operated jacks at about 600 mm centres. Where consolidation has about ceased, the house can be jacked up and the gap plugged with concrete or masonry. Jacking up corners, maybe 100 mm or more, should be costed as an alternative to rebuilding. (There is no written guarantee for jacking, unlike underpinning.) When 'combined' with underpinning, jacking is very cost effective and the underpinning will still be guaranteed.*

28 *Foundations tend to settle before the rest of the building, often failing along the dpc line. Inhibit subsequent collapse of wall by hammering in hardwood wedges. This saves shoring. Check whether wedges need hammering further in at about two-week intervals.*

29a *Joist end cut off (after propping) and supported on galvanised hanger set into hole with dryish mix of 3 sand: 1 cement.* **b** *where several ends are cut off, a steel angle (say 80 mm × 60 mm × 6 mm) can be bolted to the wall (at say 500 mm centres). Joists are screwed on from below. This requires predrilling of fixing and screw holes so can be useful for contractors with their own workshop. Put expanded metal over lower arm of angle before plastering.*

30a *Where more than the bearing of the joist needs cutting off, a trimmer can be set between sound joist. New pieces of pretreated timber are set into the (now dry) wall and nailed to the trimmer. For one or two joists cut off, doubling up of adjacent joists supporting the trimmer may not be needed for support but help reduce deflection. If existing timber is not in best condition, joist hangers should be used rather than simple nailed butt joints.* **b** *for isolated members, a lap joint coach bolted can be used with a lap of say 500 mm.*

31a *Screwing up props in sequence can generally raise a ceiling where necessary. If further force is needed a jacking strut (say 100 mm × 100 mm) can be used, impelled by a car jack set between props in turn. It should be nailed to the top spreader so that if it loosens it is suspended in place.* **b** *Where a joist is propped the joist end in the wall may be free to lift several cm. Pack the end with 3 sand: 1 cement mix or otherwise wedge.*

32 *Underpinning by site contractor. Get careful workmen and use expert aid in supervision for the first few times. If there are very concentrated loads, eg a narrow pier between windows in a high building, this will*

need needling and propping expertly. **a** *pits should be dug down to good soil (usually this is not more than double the depth of foundation). Dig pits in sequence about 1 m wide, all the number 1 pits as the first round of underpinning. Do not start the second round till 48 hours after the pinning up of the first round pits. All number 1 pits should be dug and inspected as an investigatory exercise. If good ground varies in depth work from deepest pit towards shallowest to avoid risk of undermining completed work.* **b** *excavate leaving the bottom firm and fill a nominal 1:8 mix or BS 5328 Prescribed Mix grade C10P, preferably with SRPC mix of rapid hardening cement to within 75 mm of the underside of the foundation. (No reinforcement or special shear keys between pits of successive rounds are needed.) After setting a mix of 1 rapid hardening cement: 3 fine sand should be rammed in the 75 mm gap (pinning up). A dryish mix is used; one that holds together in a ball when squeezed in the hand. Keep a record of work actually done.*

33 *Specialist contractors usually form a supporting beam before excavation of more widely spaced holes or forming supporting piles and pilecaps. Here patent 'stools' are set in the wall then the remainder removed. Reinforcement is threaded in and a beam cast in situ. Without stools, the contractor would use needles as temporary support and cast the beam below.*

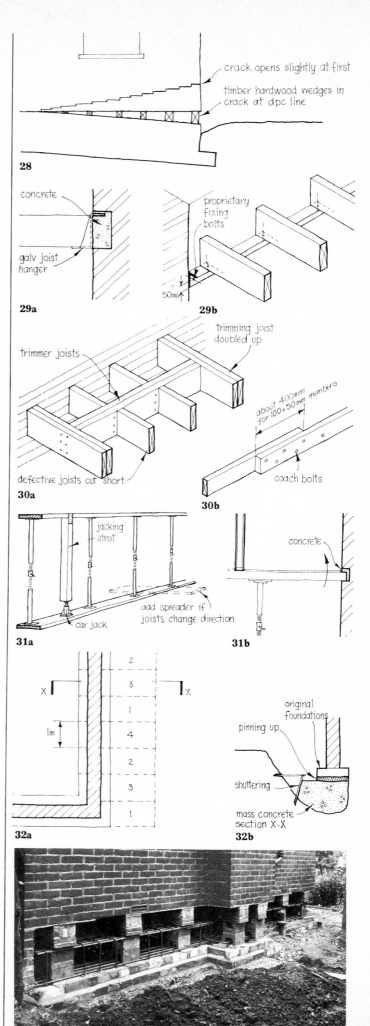

crack opens slightly at first

timber hardwood wedges in crack at dpc line

28

concrete

galv joist hanger

29a

proprietary fixing bolts

50mm

29b

trimming joist doubled up

trimmer joists

defective joists cut short

30a

about 400mm for 100×50mm members

coach bolts

30b

jacking strut

car jack

add spreader if joists change direction

31a

concrete

31b

2
3
1
4
2
3
1

X   X

1m

32a

original foundations

pinning up

shuttering

mass concrete section X-X

32b

33

4.11 Recent and/or continuing differential foundation movement is either due to seriously decaying foundations such as timber piles, which is very rare in the UK, or due to an external cause which must be identified, for example, nearby excavations, or changes in subsoil water levels and moisture content. If foundation materials have decayed they can be replaced where necessary and the existing foundation underpinned with a concrete beam.

Undermining of foundations

4.12 If trees affect clays badly, felling or lopping the top (it will die eventually) will lead to clay swelling. Movement can be controlled by judicious pruning to control the rate of transpiration. This requires continuing attention. If the tree root system existed beneath the foundations *when the house was built*, heave due to swelling can be a serious problem although there would probably be a long history of foundation trouble if that were the case. If trees are younger than the house, then there is unlikely to be trouble when a tree is lopped or felled unless the root growth has already caused distortion and cracking. Removal of the tree would tend to restore levels, but if cracks have been filled in or stitched then uplifting pressure may cause new cracking.

4.13 Major ground problems like mining subsidence and swallow holes will need expert treatment. Passage of water should be stopped or diverted at source.

4.14 If the end of the terrace is subsiding the foundation usually settles before the rest of the wall. If this can be caught in time the crack can be plugged with hardwood timber wedges, saving shoring, **28**.

4.15 Once causes of failure have been arrested the foundations can be underpinned by taking the foundations down to good ground. The exception is slipping on a slope, where the building must be braced at ground level. This needs an expert.

Decayed joists

4.16 The most convenient method of repair is to cut off decayed ends and support them on galvanised joist hangers, **29a**. Where many are to be cut, a steel angle could be bolted to the wall and screwed to the joists, **29b**. Where more is to be cut off the joists, the gap can be trimmed round, **30a**, or a lap joint made secured with coach bolts, **30b**.

Needling and propping

4.17 The main principles for temporary support (including shoring **4.20**) are:
● to consider the total pattern of loading in the building, supports and foundations. For example, the feet of inclined struts need both vertical *and horizontal* support
● to take supports down to firm ground
● to arrange supports so that they do not obstruct remedial works.
Screw props are commonly adequate on domestic work though a car jack may come in useful for extra leverage, **31a**, **b**. Where the sole plate of the propping is resting on a timber floor check that there is adequate support below.

4.18 Where substantial loads have to be borne, prop and needle sizes need checking by calculation so beware the contractor not using an engineer.

Underpinning

4.19 Local underpinning is suitable for most problems, underpinning the whole building is an unnecessary expense. The procedure shown in **32a**, **b**, can be carried out by the contractor. The depth of underpinning must always be determined by inspection and testing on site and should never be decided until the cause of failure is known. For most domestic work experience indicates that underpinning to a depth between 1·5 m and 3 m can be expected. The minimum safe depth in shrinkable clay soils is 2·4 m provided that all excavations are checked to ensure that dried clay or roots do not penetrate

deeper than this. **33** shows a proprietary method. The principle involved is first to form a continuous beam and then to take the foundations down to solid, undisturbed ground on piers.

Shoring

4.20 Much over-rated, often a form of visual reassurance. Flying shores (horizontal) between buildings may be needed if there is selective demolition in a terrace. Raking (inclined) shores are in fact supporting almost vertical loads so wedging of cracks or temporary jacking may be effective. Shores should be calculated so use someone with expertise. When they are installed they must bear against the wall at each floor level, **34**. They are especially important for fragile structures such as two-storey bays with stone mullions or cast iron columns.

5 Additional information

5.01 AJ Failures in building construction series:
1 The cracked corner 9.10.74 p865
3 The cut priced extension 20.11.74 p1221
4 The detached garage 18/25.12.74 p1445
5 The unstable retaining wall 1.1.75 p45.
BS Code of Practice 2004:1974 Foundations (Gr 11).
BRE digests:
63 Soils and foundations: 1
64 Soils and foundations: 2
67 Soils and foundations: 3

5.02 See Section 4, Technical study 11, 'Structures' for integrating repairs with conversions.

34 *Bays, where they are stone or concrete segments or have cast iron columns, are fragile and need solid shoring applied at each floor level.*

Technical study 5
External walls

This section covers walling in stone and brick, including openings. Damp treatments such as render (plus stucco), vertical tiling and painting masonry are included in the later section on dampness. The main problems are gradual decay to masonry and a lack of continuing maintenance to woodwork.

1 Masonry

Sources of defects

1.01 Analysing apparent defects may reveal little significant damage, only surface irregularity. For example, cracks and bowed walls are often the result of settlement, by now minimal or ceased, or of wartime damage. Try to establish what wartime damage occurred. Without major structural defects (see Technical study 4 Structural stability) there are not likely to be failures due to loading. The main problems will be due to the action of water (perhaps bearing damaging chemicals).

1.02 *Bricks* Old stone and brick are often irregular without being defective, **1**. Bricks may be cracked through due to structural movement or heat shrinkage in chimneys (see Technical study 4 Structural stability para **2.01**) or their face blown off by frost action, exposing the softer interior, **2**. This interior is (relatively) highly absorbent and promotes water penetration through the wall. Sound bricks harbour dirt which may be removed with a stiff (not wire) brush and water. Check if the bricks and the budget will stand it.

1.03 *Stones* Stone in rehabilitation is usually rubble, often squared, **3**, though ashlar (finely dressed stone) may be used as quoins and around openings. Rubble fails rarely, perhaps from frost damage or chemical attack. Failure is more common in the often softer, more workable stones of ashlar, **4, 5**. Water

1 *Brick, more irregular than is common now but adequately weatherproof. Regularity provided by tuck pointing; flush pointing colour matched to the brick then ribs of putty mortar applied.*

2 *Frost has blown off faces, leaving relatively porous interior exposed.*

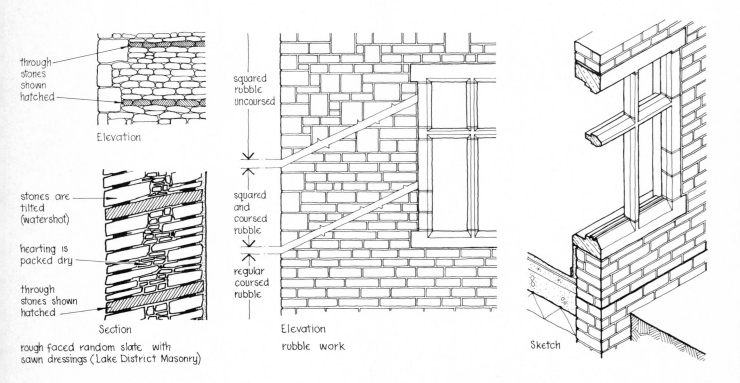

through
stones
shown
hatched

Elevation

stones are
tilted
(watershot)

hearting is
packed dry

through
stones shown
hatched

Section

rough faced random slate with
sawn dressings (Lake District Masonry)

squared
rubble
uncoursed

squared
and
coursed
rubble

regular
coursed
rubble

Elevation
rubble work

Sketch

3 *Rubble walls, showing bonding types and construction through wall. Through stones tie the wall together. The hearting laid dry here is similar in performance to no-fines concrete.*

4 *Calcium sulphate solution from limestone is crystallising in the sandstone causing decay.*

5 *Damaging salts contained in sand of pointing or bedding mortar leads to decay, first seen around joints.*

6 *Defective stone cut out for piecing in new stone.*

is the main agent of stone decay, so unless there is some obvious recent source such as a leaking pipe, deterioration may have been proceeding steadily since construction. Whether this is seen as a defect requiring repair depends on its rate (a matter of local knowledge) and the life expected of the property.

1.04 If cleaning is desirable and within the budget, ideally it should be done before remedial work is chosen because cleaning may show up defects. For example, on better quality work, ashlar is jointed with metal cramps. Sometimes stone will have spalled off as rusting cramps expand; but if this is only imminent, dirt may clog cracks and mask stains from rusting. For a full discussion of stone cleaning, fault diagnosis and repair see AJ Stone handbook (CI/SfB Ye) especially the section on Maintenance: Technical study 1 Cleaning and surface treatments (AJ 2.7.75 p39) and Technical study 2 Diagnosis and repair methods (AJ 16.7.75 p141).

1.05 *Projecting courses* Cornices, projecting string courses and other projecting features are vulnerable because liable to be soaked by water running down the wall, accelerating masonry decay. They are often capped with metal (usually lead or zinc) which may have perished, cracked at arrises or come loose from its chasing into mortar joints, requiring replacement or patching. Remedial work should ensure that water is thrown clear of the wall surface. If there is no capping and no marked damage relative to the rest of the masonry by now, it is not worthwhile fitting one.

1.06 *Mortar* Original mortars of sand and lime may have become soft and friable, requiring repointing. Often walls have already been repointed using a Portland cement and sand mix, which is too strong. It does not adhere well to the masonry and rainwater reaching it tends to move to the adjacent, more porous arrises, promoting frost damage. (Occasionally, the reverse is true and mortar is much more porous than bricks so water is drawn into the wall via the mortar joints). Ideally, there should be about even porosity over the whole wall surface, though only very marked differences usually lead to defects.

1.07 Mortars for stone are often stronger than for brick, matching the less pervious quality of stone. Though there is generally much more mortar bonding rubble together than in a brick wall (but not for ashlar), the core may be laid dry giving a resistance to moisture penetration akin to no-fines concrete, **3.**

1.08 *Cavities* Few brick dwellings built before the first world war, and probably a minority of inter-war ones, have cavities. (The London model by-laws 1939 had no requirement for cavity walls.) Cavities were not immediately standardised at 50 mm; they can be found at 20 mm, with cavity bridging by many adjacent mortar joints. Where wall ties were installed, they may have corroded. This is not generally a problem for rehabilitation but will become so in future, aggravated by any foundation settlement. Over areas of walls, the skins of brick may begin to bow apart.

1.09 Apart from these planned cavities, there may be fortuitous ones. In Georgian buildings, bricks of varying sizes can be found. Walls constructed of a skin of facing bricks backed by cheaper bricks of a different depth were usually only bonded where inner and outer skin course levels coincided. Then, and later, the bonding of skins was often done inadequately. Irregularity of brick length meant headers could give an irregular surface, so sometimes they were snapped. Also broken bricks were used. As with corroding ties, there may be local bulging as skins separate—though this is unlikely to happen after so long unless mortar is seriously weakened or there is more general structural instability, providing new stresses.

1.10 *Bond timber and wallplates* Bond timbers are long timbers built into walls which provide structural continuity and compressive strength (being part of the wall) and level up irregular brickwork. The latter was an advantage to the bricklayer laying the inner skin of cheaper, more irregular bricks. After several courses, the top course would not be level and bedding on a timber provided a new, level surface to start with the next course. Bond timbers and wallplates are little loaded in bending (unlike lintels) so they tend to decay considerably before compressive forces crush them. Plaster spalls and the outer skin may bulge. There is no way of knowing where bond timbers are.

1.11 *Tie bars* Tie bars restraining bulging walls may be seriously rusted. Generally, they cannot be repaired effectively and must be replaced (see Technical study 4 Structural stability para **4.09**).

Remedial work to ashlar

1.12 The references given in para **1.04** cover repairs to ashlar. Stonemasonry is expensive by rehabilitation standards; illustrations **6-10** indicate some of the repairs that can be made. Cleaning is also expensive, whether by water, blasting, abrasion or chemical cleaning. The principle of washing is to abrade as little as possible with a fine water spray and stiff (not wire) brush. For openings and quoins on a group of houses, the cost of a specialist contractor may not be prohibitive; and clients may have resigned themselves to meeting the cost of cleaning. Rusting cramps require the expense of removal and replacement of cramp and stone. For possibilities of replacing carved stone with plastic mouldings see AJ 16.6.76 p1199, CI/SfB Ye (W5). Mouldings should have metal cappings and flashings as for stone to give consistent appearance, to provide drips and evenness of discoloration from water run-off.

1.13 Plastic repair (replacing defective ashlar with mortar mixes) is often the only on-site procedure which can be afforded. Note whether 'stone' is in fact natural stone, cast or rendered brickwork (eg mullions of bays). Ideally plastic repair of stone requires a skilled craftsman, and it is worth getting an estimate. Plastic stone tends to look drab and dead compared with natural stone, but the junction with existing stone is often less obtrusive than replacement with new. The mix can be coloured, though this may weaken it. Colour changes with drying out, so test experimental samples, recording mix composition. Crushed stone is not generally a good aggregate.

1.14 Plastic stone is suitable for cavities and losses between 25 mm and 75 mm deep. Decayed stone should be cut back to a firm base, preferably regular in shape and parallel to coursing. A key is formed by undercutting round small areas, dovetail-like, so that inner dimensions are larger than the face. For larger areas use copper wire (say 3 mm diameter) or other non-ferrous reinforcement. For cornices and heavy projections heavier reinforcement will be needed. After cutting out, wash out to clean and reduce suction then fill in one or two coats (the outer 25-50 mm thick) with no feather edges. Tamp around reinforcement. Leave finish slightly rougher than surrounding stone. To fill across a joint, make the joint and point later; do not score the plastic mix. Plastic mixes (and pointing) should be weaker than the stone—1 cement: 1 lime: 6 sand for the soft stones usually found, 1:1:4 for tougher stones, 1:1:2 for tougher stones in exposed places such as parapets, copings and chimneys. With an interested builder, rubber moulds could be made of existing damaged features such as pilasters, for casting replacements.

Replacing and pointing bricks and stones

1.15 Where a few bricks or stones are defective from localised causes, they can be cut out and replaced. Mortar mix depends on required porosity (see para **1.05**). For brick, a stronger mix is 1 cement: 1 lime: 6 sand, medium say 1:2:9, or weak around 1:3:12. For stone see para **1.13**. Where there is ashlar, it is unlikely that loose stones can be reset as tight as new ones, so very deep raking and ramming in the mortar may be more

7a   **7b**

7a *Decayed stone head cut flat and* **b** *new carved piece glued on.*
8 *Moulding with decayed surface cut back to a firm stone.*
9 *Grp replacement for stone; cheaper and lighter than stone and can be made very 'realistic'.*
10 *Cleaned stonework. Poor repairs, surface defects and decayed arrises also revealed.*

8

9

10

11 *Blind window makes wall thinner than rest and may allow localised rain penetration.*

12 *Inner leaf of cavity gable wall stopped off inside roof. Strut to purlin and edge rafter rests on stopped off inner leaf.*

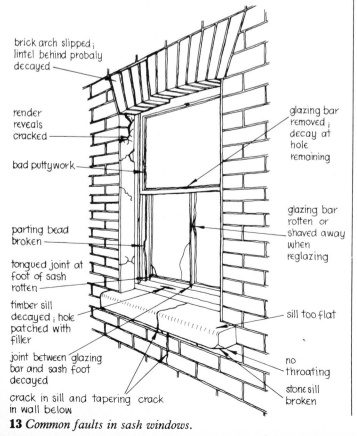

brick arch slipped; lintel behind probaly decayed

render reveals cracked

bad puttywork

parting bead broken

tongued joint at foot of sash rotten

timber sill decayed; hole patched with filler

joint between glazing bar and sash foot decayed

crack in sill and tapering crack in wall below

glazing bar removed; decay at hole remaining

glazing bar rotten or shaved away when reglazing

sill too flat

no throating

stone sill broken

13 *Common faults in sash windows.*

effective. For brick, rake out 20 mm; for stone rubble, at least this much to get back to a firm surface. Point up to at least as far as the original mortar to avoid newly exposing any arrises to frost action. For brick, there may be no satisfactory form of pointing. Weatherstruck or recessed pointing often looks better, but exposes arrises. Flush pointing protects the bricks but tends to destroy the line. A derivative of tuck pointing, **1**, might be tried, making an edge within the mortar joint to provide a line of shadow.

Dampness

1.16 Damp treatments are dealt with in the information sheets published after this technical study. Whole walls may require treatment to make them impervious, due to faces blowing off bricks, other general deterioration of brickwork or expectation of higher standards then when the houses were built. Walls may be too thin in places, resulting in both penetration and condensation. Local thinning may be found as blind windows, **11**, where wall thickness diminishes up a building several storeys high, or where the inner leaf of a gable wall is stopped off inside the roof, **12**. Single storey rear extensions built after the main house may have one or more wall of thin rubble or half brick thickness.

Bonding of brick skins

1.17 Where there is no designed cavity but masonry skins are relatively independent in brick or stone, the wall can be filled by pressure grouting, requiring a specialist contractor. The ad hoc method of gravity grouting (pouring washing water then a grout of cement in water) is not generally recommended because of the difficulty of washing out enough dirt to ensure adhesion, and avoiding grout missing much of the wall. (In stone this also removes the 'no-fines' character of the hearting of some walls). The alternative, safe though laborious, is to cut out and install headers in brick or through stones in stone walls.

Cavities

1.18 Where wall ties are rusted leading to bulging, there is no very cheap measure. Cutting out and setting in new ties is simple and effective, but laborious and therefore expensive. Rebuilding the outer skin is usually more costly. Recently a cavity fill foam, Tyfoam, has received an Agrément certificate (No 75/344). Effective as other foam insulants, it also stabilises the wall by adhering to both faces of the cavity. It is certified effective as a replacement for wall ties in excess of 25 years.

Bond timbers and wall plates

1.19 If bond timber decay has lead to crushing and bulging in adjacent brickwork, it can be jacked back into level using screw props and needles (steel flats or timbers)—see Technical study 4 Structural stability para **4.18**. Once propped, the timber can be cut out and a precast beam set in or a concrete beam cast in situ with nominal reinforcement (in general, there is negligible bending stress). A decayed wallplate can be freed by propping the joists and breaking out any nails or cutting through them. The plate is better replaced in concrete, as for bond timbers, unless the ingress of moisture and the form of decay (fungal or insect) can be eliminated. (See the following information sheets on damp treatments).

2 Openings

Sources of defects

2.01 *Doors and windows* The most obvious defects will be deteriorated paintwork and timber decay. Few doors and windows will have been thoroughly maintained continuously through their life and patching with plastic wood, putty or hard-setting filler is common. Push a knife or screwdriver into the timber to check if it is sound. Decay is commonest in subsills, bases of jambs and mullions, lower rails of opening lights and glazing bars. Decayed timber is easy to push a knife into along the grain. Filling could have removed all sign of obviously decayed timber (especially if done immediately prior to sale) but timber is likely to be soft around the filling. Check that beading or mortar fillets seal the abutment of joinery and masonry. Canopies over bays and doors can generally be treated as pitched roofs (see Technical study 2) or flat roofs (see Technical study 3).

2.02 Doors often have no weatherboard and are at the same level as the street outside. Both these factors allow water under the door to decay the adjacent floorboards.

2.03 Diagram **13** shows a variety of faults found in sash windows. The crack in the sill may adjoin one in the wall below, with tapers open two or three mm wide, below the sill, **13, 14**. Where the sill is brick on edge or tiles, these may be crumbling. The details of reveals, arch and glazing, **13**, may be repeated in the door. Where reveals are not rendered there may be gaps in the window-to-wall joint, **15**.

2.04 *Lintels* Externally, stone lintels may decay due to weathering or, unusually, may crack due to imposed loading and self weight. Brick is usually formed in an arch which may settle as part of structural movement and/or due to mortar failure, **13, 16**, or rusting of an iron hoop supporting the soldier bricks.

2.05 Internally, lintels are usually of timber and somewhat different to bond timbers. They are easy to find, **17**, and are loaded in bending, so if they decay there is a gradual sag and spalling of plaster. Hack off some plaster under the lintel next to the window frame (the nearest point to the outside which is accessible) to check for timber decay when there is no sag or cracked plaster. Where there is a metal (lead or zinc) cavity tray it may have failed, or the cavity may have become clogged, producing localised damp patches above the window which require cutting open and taking out.

Window and door repair

2.06 Piecing in timber, eg sills and glazing bars, is usually more economical than replacement. Check that all decayed timber is cut out and small gaps filled, and that new timber pieced in is pre-treated. Prime before filling, puttying and pointing. Repair render to reveal. Seal round window or door-to-wall joint and junction of sill and timber subsill with mastic. Replace window and door ironmongery as necessary, checking working of locks and catches and condition of hinges Where floor and outside ground are level, lower outside level say 100 mm, adjust drainage accordingly and fit weatherboard to the door.

2.07 Renew sash cords as necessary. Where glass or the whole sash is replaced, there will usually be an increase in weight. New, heavier weights are often too large for the frame and tend to jam, so retain the old weights. Thread washers or lead pipe into the cords before tying on the old weights. This will slightly reduce the range of movement of the sash.

Stone sills and lintels

2.08 Fine cracks in stone sills are common and at 1 or 2 mm wide are not usually associated with serious structural instability. Cracks in stone sills and lintels may require opening out to, say, 5 mm so that filling can be rammed well down inside (say 25 mm); do not feather-edge the repair. Mixes and methods as for paras **1.13** and **1.14**. Replacing seriously cracked sills and lintels may be possible from demolition, precast or casting in situ (see para **2.10**). A clear, waterproof paint can be used to inhibit damp penetration (see later information sheets on damp). Capping sills with metal (zinc or lead) requires very careful detailing at corners and setting in at edges, and is often out of keeping with surrounding openings. A rasp could be used to file a throating to a sill without one.

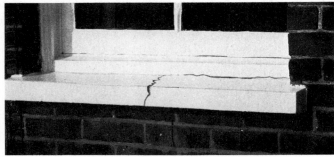

14a

14b

14a, b *Cracking due to minor settlement of brick piers either side of window relative to window apron.* **15** *Mortar fillet at window-to-wall joint fallen away.*

15

16

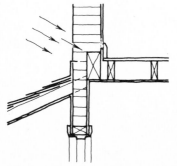

16 *Brick arch over window collapsing from defective mortar and some minor structural movement.* **17** *Where there are single-storey back additions, half the wall may be stopped off by a lintel. This is easily checked by measurement. The lintel is vulnerable to decay.*

Brick and tile sills and lintels

2.09 Patch brick and tile sills or replace them, **18**. Shaped bricks can usually be found to match, though if not exact, the whole sill will need replacing. Waterproof with clear paint as for stone (see para **2.08**). Brick arches over openings should be reset, replacing any rusting iron hoop supporting the soldier bricks with galvanised iron.

Timber lintels

2.10 Replace decayed timber with concrete. If the stone outer lintel has failed, both can be cast as one, **19**. Screw props and needles will be needed to support the opening and reinforcement calculated. Usually the timber depth of 150 mm or 225 mm in brick will be a convenient beam depth. In houses of several storeys, especially of stone, lintels may be much bigger, eg 250 mm × 200 mm. Instead of in situ casting, a pre-stressed concrete lintel could be set in. (A rsj, first clad in concrete as damp protection then set in, is not usually cost effective unless the rsj is second hand.)

Wall thickness

2.11 Where thin walls allow damp penetration or promote condensation, the simplest step is to paint the masonry with clear water repellant, inhibiting penetration and reducing U-value. (See later information sheets on damp.) There may still be a need to increase insulation, especially where walls are half-brick thick. Externally, an extra half-brick leaf could be added or insulation followed by vertical slating/tiling or boarding. Inside, a dry lining could be used (see Technical study 6 Interiors). The interior treatment generally gives greater problems in dealing with openings, wall edges and existing fixtures and fittings. But it gives better thermal response to intermittent heating.

3 Further information

3.01 Cecil C. Handisyde *Everyday Details*, The Architectural Press Ltd: London 1976

7 Masonry walls: jambs with timber window frames, p. 29
10 Cavity wall lintels, p. 47
11 Window sills, p. 52
12 External doors: position of frame, p. 58

13 External doors: thresholds, p. 60
3.02 CP 121: Part 1: 1973 Walling part 1: Brick and block masonry (Gr 10)
CP 121. 2.01: 1951 Masonry walls ashlared with natural stone or cast stone (Gr 7)
CP 121. 202: 1951 Masonry rubble walls (Gr 8)
CP 151. Part 1: 1957 Wooden doors (Gr 7)
CP 153: Part 2: 1970 Windows and rooflights: durability and maintenance (Gr 5)
CP 231: 1966 Painting of buildings (Gr 9)

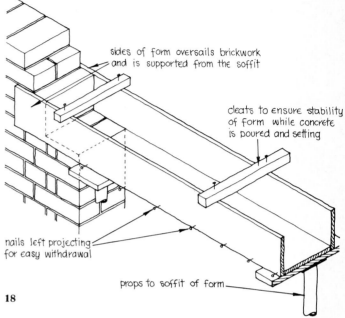

sides of form oversails brickwork and is supported from the soffit

cleats to ensure stability of form while concrete is poured and setting

nails left projecting for easy withdrawal

props to soffit of form

18

18 *Casting a lintel. Window is removed and props in window space support soffit of shutter (say 0·5 m intervals). Needling say three courses above the shutter provides space for getting in concrete and tamping it round reinforcement.*
19 *Examples of gauged brick arches over windows. Gauged bricks are usually rubbed or sawn to fit closely with a fine putty mortar (lime putty) joints. Repair is a skilled job.*

Technical study 6 Interiors

So far this book has concentrated on weather-tightness of the shell. Though interiors are affected by weather, the emphasis is more on wear and tear of materials. Often these have a shorter life than materials used outside and will need renewing. Many of the items noted, especially services, are part of improvements and conversions (Section 4).
When buildings are listed, the essentials may not be clearly specified so an inspector will have to specify precisely.

1 Cost and standards

1.01 Several features of interiors will not match building regulations, or Parker Morris Standards, where they apply. (As money for rehabilitation has dried up, local authorities have insisted far less on Parker Morris standards.) While updating to meet these will not generally be necessary during repair and maintenance, there could be considerable cost in meeting them if improvements and conversions are carried out. For example, basements may need digging out, attic ceilings raising and walls bringing in to provide required headroom, **1**; vent stacks and associated piping may need relocating inside, and re-positioned stairways may require a new staircase to a lower slope (taking up greater plan area). These costs should be borne in mind when deciding whether further work is needed beyond repair and maintenance.

1 *Long, low room (below regulation 2·3 m) cheaply treated by replastering. More elaborate changes could require raising ceiling to regulation height.*

2 Joinery

Doors
2.01 *Renew or remake ?*
Where joints are loose, panels split or doors ill-fitting, it may be cheaper to get a joiner to remedy the faults, rather than replace doors. If doors are not replaced throughout the house, appearance may be discordant (unless secondhand replacements are used). And though new doors are relatively cheap even when made to non-standard sizes, fitting them to frames distorted by settlement can be laborious.

2.02 *Fitting and filling*
Small losses can be filled and larger ones pieced in, eg where locks and hinges have been moved. (Filling splits in door panels is usually ineffective.) Timber may have been added to or cut from tops and bottoms of doors to fit them to frames. Check that added pieces are firm and will be inconspicuous when decorated (or replace) and that there is adequate clearance all round including over any proposed floor finish. Damaged architraves are usually better filled, modelling filler to mouldings, as replacements rarely match.

1

2.03 *Ironmongery*
Ironmongery may be of poor quality or worn out. Check that locks, catches and hinges are firmly fixed and work smoothly. Hinges may need repositioning if repairs with new screws in the past have broken up the timber of the door or frame behind hinges.

Windows
2.04 Probe for decay and check faults such as loose parting beads, broken catches and sash cords. (See Technical study 5 External walls, figure **13**.) Release lights screwed or painted up. Repair or replace architraves, which may be in worse condition than for doors, having been damaged by fixing curtain rails and pelmets. Repair, replace or remove curtain rails and pelmets.

Shutters
2.05 Take care when opening unused shutters; they may be screwed shut with screw heads painted over. Check timber of shutter and shutter box for decay. Check framing, panels and ironmongery as for doors. Shutters are worth putting in working order. If well fitted they provide good insulation against heat loss, **2**.

2 Shutters are often repairable and useful for thermal insulation.

Skirtings
2.06 Repair skirtings as for architraves. If damp treatments are needed, skirtings and grounds may be decayed. Deep, moulded skirtings cannot usually be matched exactly so it may be worth renewing one room and using the sound skirtings removed to repair another.
2.07 In some cases skirtings are of plaster. Their decoration is different to timber and they are flush with wall plaster; mouldings are cut in rather than protruding. Patch plaster.

Stairs
2.08 *Movement*
Stairs may shift with settlement of buildings or because joints have worked loose. They could be tied with steel straps or screwed and wedged. First, it may be worth trying to straighten the staircase with screw props.

2.09 *Rigidity*
Timber stairs may decay in strings against damp walls and where stairs meet solid floors. Under stairs is one of the commoner sites of insect attack. Cut out and piece in if possible, or replace the staircase.
2.10 If treads are loose they may be tightened with wedges screwed and glued between treads and risers. (This will require breaking open any plastered soffit.) Worn nosings can be cut out and replacements pieced in though this is expensive, **3**.

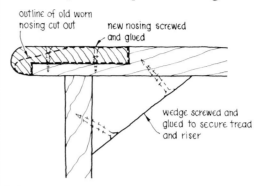

3 Renovating existing stairs. Wedge glued and screwed between tread and riser for stiffening. Worn nosing cut out and replaced.

Balusters may need replacing or screwing and glueing. Handrails on the open side of stairs may bend due to loose balusters and newel posts and/or being of too small section. Stiffen by securing newel posts with dowel pegs or screws, and screwing and glueing balusters. A post of the same section as the newel set at the midpoint of the handrail, provides extra support.
2.11 Handrails fixed to walls may be loose, needing refixing. Where plaster and masonry is soft and plugs are difficult to secure, drill out a hole twice the diameter and a little longer than the plug. Wet to wash out and reduce suction. Fill completely with hard stopping then press/hammer in a plug and scrape off the excess stopping forced out. Allow to set.

2.12 *Standards*
Stairs may be excessive pitch by modern standards, perhaps more than 50°, narrow and with low headroom. They are often too expensive to replace but this may be worthwhile for narrow attic stairs where space allows, **4**.

4 Attic stair, narrow and steep with a confined entrance doorway at the bottom; difficult for the infirm to negotiate or for furniture moving. Improving access, though expensive, would make the space more generally usable.

Paint

2.13 In general do not burn off paint as a good surface for decoration is unlikely to be achieved; knots and old filling are likely to be found. Sand well before painting, fill losses, sand and prime before general undercoating. Where paint is many layered, chips may be thick, **5**. Smooth out by sanding or fill.

3 Walls and floors

Partitions

3.01 *Crack patterns*
Examine cracks in plaster, distinguish the roughly equal width cracks which sometimes occur at changes of construction, such as stud to masonry, from the usually diagonal, tapering ones of structural movement. Partitions are often on nominal foundations, even if carrying the load of floors and the gutters of double-pitched and M-roofs. Any effects of settlement may be increased to give a marked sag if openings have been made which cut the timber framing of the partitions. The bottom of such framing is often built above floor level and there may be diagonal struts, **6**. (For crack analysis see Technical study 4 Structural stability.)

3.02 *Masonry*
Once any cracks in masonry have been filled it will need little other attention. Brick on edge partitions are generally adequately stable. Clinker blocks found in some inter-war buildings tend to crumble when cut, eg when making openings or chasing. If cutting is likely they are better replaced (they are not usually structural).

3.03 *Studs*
Stud partitions may be hollow or filled, eg with brick on edge or even solid plaster. Where partitions abut damp walls or ceilings, decay may occur—where partitions are filled this can be very advanced before deformation is noticed, even in structural partitions. Strip off plaster in damp regions and probe for decay, especially where noggings tie partitions into external walls, **7**, and in porches where lath and plaster may be used externally.

External and party walls

3.04 *Thin walls*
(For crack patterns and treatments see Technical study 4 Structural stability.) Party walls and occasionally flank walls are only half-brick thick. They may need strengthening with an external skin, or an internal skin could be built through the house either side of the chimney, **8**. Where not strengthened, insulation by dry lining (**3.17**) will be needed to half brick external walls. (Or an external finish incorporating insulation could be used. For tiling, slating and weatherboarding see Information sheet 5 Separate layers.)

3.05 *Timber*
Where plaster is stripped off check bond timbers, wall plates, lintels, studs and noggings for decay. In external walls it is safer to replace decayed timbers with reinforced concrete but while this is often practical for lintels, it is not for common sizes of wall plates and bond timbers (eg 100 mm × 50 mm). So use pressure impregnated timber. Do not replace these with brick or tile as these materials remove structural continuity. Where decayed timber is cut out, lap old to new by say 500 mm, or more if timbers are deeper than 100 mm.

Fireplaces

3.06 Blocking up a fireplace is not generally necessary, and with our uncertain energy future it is becoming easier to persuade clients not to bother. However, open fires are very inefficient thermally and hearths take up valuable space in small rooms. An alternative use is for fireplaces to accommodate unit heaters, perhaps with back boilers.

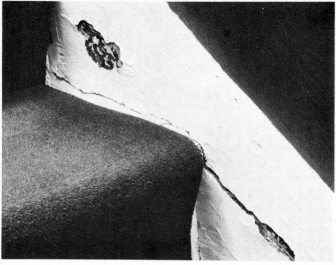

5 *Chips in accumulated layers of paint may be too deep to sand smoothly, requiring filling.*

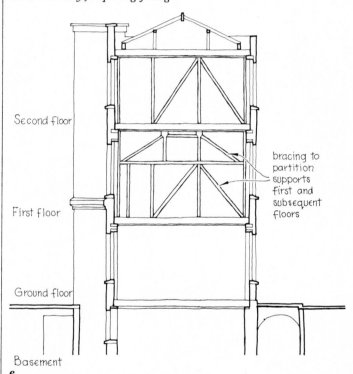

Second floor

First floor

Ground floor

Basement

bracing to partition supports first and subsequent floors

6

6 *Framing more elaborate than in most houses. To create an open ground floor the first floor partition is braced, supporting the first floor itself and floors above. Any new opening would require a diagonal member to be cut. In other houses horizontals and verticals might be cut. If openings are necessary, strip off all plaster to reveal framing. Analyse distribution of forces and redistribute using extra timbers.*

7 *Stud partition abutting external wall, bonded at about 1·5 m centres by noggings (check for decay). Gap between wall and stud due to bulge in external wall.*

7

8 *Half brick wall rendered outside and strengthened with a leaf of blockwork inside on either side of the chimney breast, from foundation to attic.*

9 *Rusted iron bar that supported flat brick arch over fireplace.*

10 *Stone beams providing support both for hearth (now removed) and chimney-breast. Beams pass through wall supporting stacks back-to-back in adjacent houses.*

3.07 If the fireplace is to be retained, reset brick arches as necessary, replacing rusted iron supports, **9**, with galvanised. If the fireplace is filled, ventilate near ceiling or floor (eg in skirting) to inhibit condensation in the flue. Condensation will promote masonry decay and moisture drying out to the inside of the room may bring with it tarry black deposits from the flue. If for some reason the hearth is removed, dismantle cautiously. It may be supported in a variety of ways, eg on the fireplace brickwork, on timber framing, on stone beams, **10**.
3.08 Smoke doors sometimes found on interwar chimney breasts can generally be blocked up.

Panelling
3.09 Generally found in more expensive conservation work rather than rehabilitation. Occasionally matchboarding will be found up to dado height in basements and may conceal damp. Strip some off to check for damp and for matchboarding decay.

Floors
3.10 *Decay*
Take up floorboards adjacent to external walls and check for decay in joists. Occasionally, apparently solid floors are based on timber; there will be more 'give' than is usual for concrete. This detail may be found in entrances, **11**. The timber is usually poorly ventilated and decaying. Renew in timber and ventilate, or cast a slab. See Information sheet 6, Condensation, and Information sheet 7, Timber decay.

3.11 *General defects*
Floors may be uneven, sagging, creaking and/or springy. Remedying these to make floors as good as new can be very expensive. If floors are very uneven it is probably due in part to decay in joist ends which will be remedied. If floors slope in one direction firring to near level can be successful. But the effects of settlement may produce floors distorted in three dimensions so that any firring would have to be individually cut for each joist. Altering floor level may also give problems at doorways where floors meet.

3.12 Sagging may be due to undersizing of joists or notching for services. Undersizing could be remedied by adding extra joists, though this would require taking up all floorboards. New joists should be 10 mm less deep than existing ones to clear the plaster key projecting between laths. Alternatively, timbers say 100 mm × 25 mm could be screwed to joists to support them and provide a level edge for boarding, **12**.
3.13 Notched joists, **13**, could be strengthened, eg by a steel bar, **14**. Creaking may be reduced by full nailing of infrequently nailed boards, though where floors are springy nails may pull out, so screws are required. Excessive springiness may be due to joist decay undersizing, notching and/or lack of strutting. Adding strutting is a fairly straightforward process. A row of solid strutting (dwangs) requires only one or two boards to be lifted. Joist-sized members shallow enough to clear plaster keys in lath and plaster ceilings are nailed through joists, offset, **15**. Remember to wedge between edge joists and walls.

Plaster
3.14 *Lath and plaster*
(For crack patterns see para **3.01**.) Ceilings and stud partitions generally have lath and plaster surfaces. Solid walls are often plastered direct but may have laths on battens nailed to wall-plates, bond timbers, lintels, and so on. If battens to walls or any laths are decayed the plaster surface will be springy when pressed. It will require stripping off and renewal. Generally, laths may be decayed, detached from wall timbers, too close together so plaster lacks a key or be fixed against broad elements, eg large beams, so that there is no space behind for a plaster key. It is fairly easy to tell poor plaster from the hollow sound when tapped. Disturbing plaster by chasing or pulling off wallpaper may well cause large losses. Quality may vary

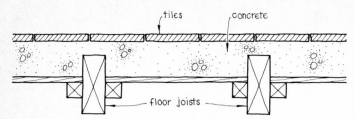

11 *Timber joists supporting concrete and tiles may be found in entrances. Timber is very prone to decay.*

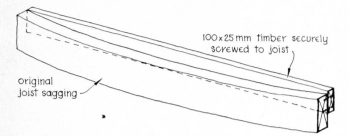

12 *100 × 25 mm timbers solidly screwed to sagging floor joists provide some strengthening and give a level surface for boarding.*

13 *Notched joists. Notching does not usually require remedial action; but see* **14**.
Threading through timbers is best done at the centre, the neutral axis.

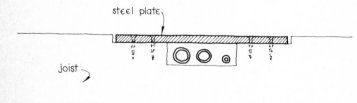

14 *A possible strengthening of a notched joist. Steel bar in compression. This remedial measure secures joists; they remain sagging.*

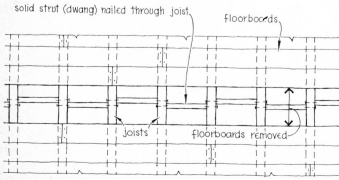

15 *Solid strutting (dwangs) nailed through joists to reduce springiness in floors.*

considerably over a single wall so do not replaster completely after limited soundings, **16**. Generally two-coat work is adequate but three coats will be needed over very uneven walls.

16 *New and old (wallpapered) plaster. No very obvious reason for location of unsound plaster on this dry party wall; unsoundness located by tapping wall. Thorough checking in this way saves wholesale replastering.*

3.15 *Repairs*

Crazing may be sealed with emulsion or liquid stopping painted on. Repair with plaster that expands slightly on setting (class B, CP211:1971—see **5.01**). Small cracks should be cut back to a firm edge, undercut slightly to 3 or 4 mm wide. Wet to wash out and reduce suction. Fill with skim coat, or two coats if crack is full depth. If the surface is powdery or pitted it can be rubbed down and skim coated. Wet thoroughly and use a wet plaster mix to avoid suction leading to peeling or bubbling, **17**. For larger areas where laths are removed, galvanised nail on expanded metal and plaster over or nail on plasterboard and skim. If walls are uneven and mortar soft, render could be used with expanded metal if necessary, then skimmed. Render would help bind the surface.

17 *Bubbling of skim coat. Skim not bonded to old plaster due to suction.*

3.16 *Mouldings*

Mouldings such as plaster cornices and roses are relatively heavy; roses especially may be loose. Fix with brass screws with brass washers (to increase bearing area) into ceiling timber. Extra timber may have to be added from above. Countersink for screw heads and washers, then fill over. Replacement mouldings are available though patching is often preferable for cost and appearance. New mouldings which exactly follow the line of existing ones might not be made. And while new detail will be sharp the old is usually softened (or obscured) by many layers of paint. It is often possible to remove many layers of distemper by brushing it with water using a stiff bristle brush or a wire brush (very gently) so revealing the fine detail.

Dry lining
3.17 *Selection*

Dry lining might be done to improve thermal performance

and/or as part of a damp-proofing treatment. The first decision is whether some other treatment would be preferable. If lining is used, ventilated behind, solely to provide a surface for decoration immediately after injecting walls or external damp-proof treatment, then an internal render with additive would be cheaper. (See Information sheet 8 Basements and solid floors.)

3.18 If a combined thermal and damp-proofing treatment is required, an extra masonry skin, or weatherboarding/slating/tiling on counterbattens with insulation between would be an alternative (see Information sheet 5 Separate layers). Following trades and occupants could then chase and fix to the wall at will. The cost advantages depend on what damp-proof treatment is combined with dry lining.

3.19 If a thermal treatment alone is needed, dry lining is generally cost effective. Sandwich boards are usually most effective in cost and construction, made of plasterboard, vapour check and rigid foam (perhaps paper covered). Granular as well as rigid foams are practicable where battens are used rather than the simpler fixing with plaster dabs. Granular foam does not adhere well to plaster. Corrugated pitch impregnated fibre sheets also provide some insulation, having air pockets behind. Nailed, say to bathroom walls, leaving gaps for appliances, plastered sheeting reduces condensation.

3.20 *Dab and dot fixing*
On fairly dry walls, 50 mm thick dabs of plaster can be laid on at say 300 mm horizontal centres and 600 mm vertical centres. Keep dabs at least 25 mm from board edges so that when boards are pressed on, plaster is not squeezed into joints. Put a batten at the bottom of boards to provide a clearance between floor and board while dabs are setting. An alternative with some boards is to fix by shot firing, **18**.

3.21 Dabs are good on true walls but where they are uneven it is difficult to get accurate alignment of boards. Dots of bitumen impregnated fibre, say 75 mm × 75 mm, on plaster set on walls before boards are fixed can be used to aid alignment, **19**. The plaster is of varying thickness to take up unevenness in the wall so that board pressed against dots will be level across the wall. Dabs are still used for adhesion. A board is pressed against the dabs until it comes up against the dots. Considerable practice is needed to set dots accurately.

3.22 *Boards on battens*
More expensive than dots but simpler to construct, boards can be nailed to pressure impregnated battens nailed to the wall. Nailing into walls tends to scrape off galvanising, so non-ferrous nails are preferable for fixing battens. Battens aid greatly in aligning boards on uneven walls. Batten spacing can be say 400 mm horizontally and 600 mm vertically to suit 2400 mm × 1200 mm sheets.

4 Services

Approach
4.01 Many services will be found near the end of their life, physically and/or functionally. Sometimes these are mixed with defunct services such as conduits, gas pipes to mantles and tubing for bell pulls. Many existing services will not last a further 30 years so there will be limited remedial work plus recording of what exists in case anything can be salvaged. Where services and appliances are kept, servicing should be done. When services are renewed it may be worth relocating gas and electricity meters and service heads. Design of new services is covered in section 4 Improvements and conversions. Servicing gas and electricity supplies as far as meters and water to stop cocks will be carried out by statutory undertakers. They or other qualified operators should be commissioned for any servicing of the remainder of systems.

18 *Dry lining using nails plus washers, shot fired direct into the wall.*

20 *Lead rising main with characteristic bulbous wiped joint meets drain cock, stop cock and copper piping.*

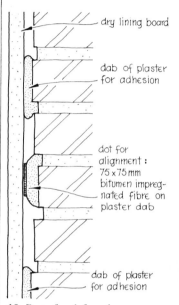

dry lining board

dab of plaster for adhesion

dot for alignment: 75 x 75 mm bitumen impregnated fibre on plaster dab

dab of plaster for adhesion

19 *Dots fixed first for alignment on uneven walls, then dabs used for adhesion.*

21 *New plasterwork to attic with inspection panel left for cold tank and pipes.*

Water
4.02 *Stop cock*
Find the stop cock and associated drain cock and check that they work. The stop cock may be immediately inside the house where the rising main enters or, for older houses, out in the street. If, as sometimes happens, the stop cock cannot be found in the street, a new one should be fitted immediately inside the dwelling. Occasionally a rising main may be found serving two houses in series, so that one stop cock controls both. This arrangement is generally not worth changing as long as the second house in line is fitted with a stop tap. But there may be logistical problems during rehabilitation work when a contractor wants to turn off water in the first house.

4.03 *Piping*
Note the material of pipes. The rising main to the stop cock will probably be of lead, **20**. Lead beyond this is worth replacing. If plumbing is copper, it is usually durable enough to retain, though some or all of the layout may need changing. Trace piping through the house, where possible checking piping, taps, valves and drain cocks for leaks. Make inspection panels at tanks and fittings as necessary so that U-bends, pipe-to-tap junctions, ball valves and so on are accessible, **21**. Fix extra clips to pipes where support is poor. Pipes and cisterns in uninhabited spaces such as roofs, basements and under ground floors should be lagged with water resistant materials.

Check outlets from fittings are clear, cleaning U-bends as necessary.

4.04 In hard water areas pipes may be furred. If so, a hot pipe will sound markedly duller than an adjacent cold pipe when tapped. Where there is a water tank the flow rate will be less than expected for the existing head, but this is difficult to judge. If in doubt cut out a small section of pipe. A proprietary solvent can be put in the water tank to percolate round the system and dissolve the deposit. But where there is no water tank there is no simple means to introduce solvent. Either replace piping or install a tank.

4.05 *Tanks*
Check for leaks in any tank, in ball valves and balls. Tanks are relatively cheap so it is worth replacing galvanised tanks with any sign of rust. Where convenient, a cold tank outside (usually on an addition roof), should be replaced with an internal one. New hatches will usually be needed or existing ones will need to be enlarged to get a tank in, though plastic ones may be bent to get through small openings and existing ones left in the roof. Boarding laid over ceiling joists provides ease of access to the tank for maintenance.

4.06 Lag tanks. Lagging is obvious for hot tanks, but is worth doing to cold ones to guard against severe winters and the colder conditions produced by putting insulation between ceiling joists in the roof space. Check overflow pipes are clear. Lag overflows. A sectional hot and cold tank is more compact than separate ones.

4.07 *Bath/wc/basin/sink*
Generally replace vitreous clay or enamelled ware if chipped, cracked, rusted or irretrievably stained. Check the condition of plaster round baths, basins and sinks (including any communal sinks on staircases). Check for timber decay in floors at fittings and cupboards below sinks and basins and around wcs and baths (remove side panel). Sometimes beneath wcs there is a lead tray with a lead tube outlet through the wall. This outlet is often blocked and the lead may be perished, leading to decay of timber below. Repair decayed timber, remove lead and fit to modern standards. Check watertightness of joints to wc outlet trap. (Cleaning with bleach removes most stains but often the vitreous or enamel surface is no longer intact.)

4.08 *WC cistern*
Frequently cast iron cisterns are rusted and a source of noise annoyance, especially in multi-occupied dwellings. These are cured by replacement. If cisterns are kept check that brackets are securely fixed to walls, ball valves are watertight and balls are not punctured. To limit sound transmission, put rubber pads between brackets and cistern, and avoid fixing directly to wall where possible (or if necessary, put rubber washers on fixing screws). Occasionally the cistern will be a lead-lined tank outside the lavatory, perhaps in a cupboard in an abutting room.

Back boilers
4.09 Gas or open fires may have back boilers for heating water. These are prone to spring leaks at, very roughly, 15 to 20-year intervals, though some last much longer. They are laborious to dig out for maintenance. If kept, warn clients of the possibility of failure.

Gas
4.10 Check for any gas leaks. Check that visible pipes are not corroded and that taps work. Do not assume that an existing supply is suitable for central heating. Existing pipes are often of too small bore, so new supply pipes will be needed. Service supply pipes and appliances may be retained. (In fact a simple check of heater efficiency can be done by the architect. Read off rating (usually on maker's plate), run appliance on full for a few minutes and take meter readings before and after running. Metered consumption divided by time taken should match the

rating.) However, the problem is not usually that the appliance is inefficient of its type but that the type is inappropriate for the expected use.

Electricity
4.11 Service wiring, eg for earthing, polarity and appliances if they are to be retained. Wiring lasts 30 to 40 years efficiently. Aged circuits are recognisable by round pins, rubber sheath wiring and a shortage of outlets, **22**. Open up sockets and switches, especially on damp walls, to check cable type and rust. Usually rewiring will be needed to provide adequate outlets. It is tempting to leave lighting circuits but not usually worthwhile, since the disruption of installation is much more tolerable during general rehabilitation than later.

22 *Wiring physically and functionally obsolescent. Even if physically sound, there are usually too few outlets for modern usage.*

4.12 If there is an immersion heater, check that it and its thermostat work (install one if not included). The thermostat can be checked by switching off everything, setting the thermostat low then letting water heat up. When the meter stops, turn the thermostat up and check that it starts again. Feel the water as a crude temperature measurement. It is important to have control rather than a precise temperature scale.

Central heating
4.13 Occasionally, old central heating systems with cast iron radiators will be found. Though these are relatively inefficient it would generally take many years to pay off the cost of removal and new installation out of the fuel costs saved. Part of these savings will inevitably be taken up in fuel use for increased comfort. Replacement may be disruptive visually where special cages have been made for radiators, eg fretworked timber.

4.14 For any system, check that controls are adequate. There should be at least a two-period timer for intermittent heating and a thermostat. Single thermostats are fairly poor controllers for whole houses, especially if the system is not adequately balanced to give temperature differences in different spaces. A better form of control is to use a thermostatic valve on each radiator (costing £2 to £3 more than conventional ones). These rely on the boiler thermostat to cut the system in and out.

4.15 Where hot water and heating are combined in one system, independent running of hot water is required outside the heating season and control of priority is useful within it. Apart from a control unit, a diverter valve for switching between heating and hot water circuits would be the minimum required. Some systems will not be readily modified while for others change may be impossible, eg for a radiant heater with back boiler. Check with a heating engineer.

5 Further information

5.01 CP211:1971 Internal plastering (Gr7).

Technical study 7 Drainage

Often drainage systems are in an adequate state of repair, apart from routine maintenance such as painting, cleaning out gutters, hoppers and gratings, and removing any blockages. Below ground there is only a limited range of repairs worth carrying out before it is preferable to renew pipe runs, ensuring continued life.
Where improvements and conversions are to be carried out, the system will often need completely reorganising about ground level.

1 Development

1.01 Drainage systems went through rapid development in the latter half of the nineteenth century. Systems were installed in new and existing buildings with varied understanding of principles, materials, devices and workmanship. After the use of cesspools, ash pits and earth closets, soil waste was directed to a public sewer. Sometimes a flushing tank was used, in effect a cistern for the whole system, installed in the roof or at ground level. Flushing tanks were primarily filled with rainwater but were topped up if necessary from the rising main. The stormwater usually ran to a soakaway, though some boroughs collected it in a public reservoir.

1.02 Gradually experience grew of the potential defects of drainage, **1**. By around 1890, drainage systems were fairly standardised, like the two-pipe systems built until recently. Vestiges of old drainage systems may be found, (some perhaps still in use) such as flushing tanks, cesspools, inlets to manholes from outside wcs, curved pipe runs, **2**, and vent pipes to various appliances, **3**.

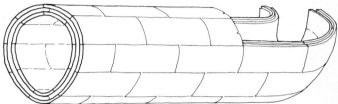

2 *Taken from a catalogue of 1853, these patent drainage bricks were an early alternative to fireclay and stoneware. Bends were quite sharp.*

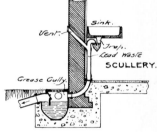

3 *Sink with vented outlet and grease trap, as recommended by the 'Builder's Journal' and 'Architectural Record', 1897.*

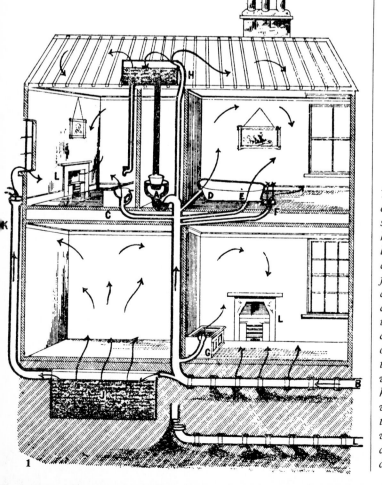

1 *Illustration from a book of 1878 by T. Pridgin Teale entitled 'Dangers to health; a pictorial guide to domestic sanitary defects'. Key: A Water-closet in the centre of the house. B House drain under floor of a room. C Waste-pipe of lavatory—untrapped and passing into soil-pipe of WC, thus allowing a direct channel for sewer gas to be drawn by the fires LL into the house. D Overflow pipe of bath untrapped and passing into soil-pipe. E Waste-pipe of bath untrapped and passing into soil-pipe. F Save-all tray below taps untrapped and passing into soil-pipe. G Kitchen sink untrapped and passing into soil-pipe. H Water-closet cistern with over-flow into soil-pipe of WC thus ventilating the drain into the roof, polluting the air of the house, and polluting the water in the cistern, which also forms the water supply of the house for drinking and washing. J Rainwater tank under floor, with overflow into drain. K Fall-pipe conducting foul air from tank fouled by drain gas, and delivering it just below a window. L Drain under house with uncemented joints leaking; also a defective junction of vertical soil-pipe with horizontal drain; the drain laid without proper fall.*

2 Preliminaries

Permissions
2.01 Check with the local authority and/or deeds as to whose responsibility the drainage system is. Adjoining houses may share systems. If any alteration is proposed, the local authority must be informed (under the Public Health Act 1936). If connection is to be made under the road to the main sewer, the highways department should be informed and generally a specialist contractor will be required.

Records
2.02 Records of drain runs are better than for many other facets of buildings, following the Local Government Act 1858. This was made locally as by-laws soon after. For example, in Carlisle in 1860 by-laws required that every person intending to erect a new building should provide:

> 'ground plans, plans of elevations and sections of every floor of such intended new building, drawn to a scale of not less than one inch to every eight feet, showing the position, form, and dimensions of the several parts of such building, and of the water-closet, privy, cesspool, ash-pit, well, and all other appurtenances; and such plans and sections shall be accompanied by a description of the materials of which the building is proposed to be constructed, of the intended mode of drainage, and means of water supply.'

2.03 Set against this, however, are the possibilities that records have not been retained and that construction underground (as with foundations) is the least likely aspect of a building to be built as drawn.

Finding drain runs
2.04 Records are important because drain runs are often difficult to find. They frequently run under buildings and may have no manholes, or manholes have been covered with paving, soil, and so on. Exploratory excavation is possible, or simply abandoning drains where testing shows leaks. Of for the appropriately sensitive, divining works well.
2.05 Where several drain runs are close together, just which manholes are connected may be obscure. Adding a dye and watching it emerge elsewhere indicates connections.

3 Defects

Appliance wastes
3.01 Check that joints on outlet pipes from appliances do not leak, that traps are clear and water seals deep enough. There may be a smell in properties vacated for some time, due to evaporation of the seal. In some cases wastes will be of drawn lead, which is still generally serviceable. A thimble is needed to make connection of lead to stoneware, **4**.

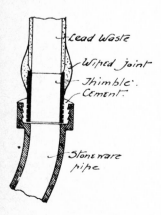

4 *Connection of lead waste to stoneware pipe for sink shown in 3, using brass or gunmetal thimble.*

Hoppers, gutters and downpipes
3.02 Hoppers, gutters and downpipes will generally be of cast iron or lead. Leadware is generally little affected by being flush against masonry. If leadware has perished in small areas, a patch could be soldered in. Cast iron, however, should be fixed by brackets on bobbins (spacers) to keep them from damp walls and allow painting. This is often done for downpipes but less so for hoppers and gutters. Fit bobbins as necessary. Put a wire netted cowl at the top of the vent stack.
3.03 Leaks and overflowing encouraged by blockage can often be seen from staining. Clear out gutters and hoppers and run water through to check downpipes, **5**. Leaks in leadware can usually be repaired by soldering. Cast iron, once rusted, generally needs replacing. Downpipe joints should be lead filled but putty is often found, promoting rust. Lead or cast iron downpipes which disappear into the ground as though to a soakaway may in fact be blocked with earth. Rainwater fills these pipes, leaking from joints and overflowing hoppers.

5 *Rainwater pipes out of sight and out of mind. This plant flourishes. Hoppers often contain bits of slates/tiles and mortar fillets plus other debris from repairs higher up the building.*

3.04 Gutters are often flush against fascias, so they not only rust themselves but prevent painting of fascias. Check for decay. Set gutters on spacers as necessary. Gutters frequently have inadequate or no falls though they may collect from several adjoining houses. So reset to falls as necessary and/or install larger gutters. Gutters may be overshot by rainwater run off if slates/tiles at eaves have slipped or if sagging in roofs channels rainwater run-off to one length of gutter. Fix slates/tiles and reset gutters as necessary. Existing gutters may be over 100 mm; ensure replacements are big enough.

Gulleys
3.05 Take out gratings and clean them. Pour water down any smelling gulleys to establish seal and check that it is at least 25 mm. Some old gulleys have very shallow seals, and are thus likely to smell often. Try rocking the gulley (gently) to check that it is securely jointed to inlet and outlet pipes. Also check if surrounding ground is especially wet (from leaks not overflows). Gulley designs are generally similar overall, though several variants may be found, eg **6**. If gulleys abut house walls, check that wall is rendered to same height as kerbs on other gulley edges.

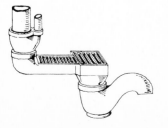

6 *Variation on the back inlet gulley designed to allow dispersal to the atmosphere of any odour bypassing the water seal.*

Manholes

3.06 Manholes were often advocated as good practice, **7**. However, frequently the inspection chamber was not included, rather the pipes join up under the house and a pipe runs under the house roughly in line with the hall. Usually there is an interceptor rather than direct connection to the sewer. There should be a cap on the bypass of the interceptor manhole outlet; a chain should be attached to this so that if the trap gets blocked the cap can be pulled out without grovelling in a manhole full of sludge, **8**.

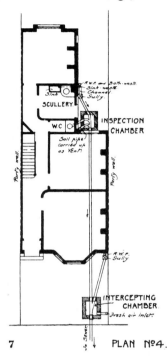

7 Good practice as advocated by the Builders' Journal and Architectural Record, 1897.
8 Interceptor trap to match 7. Bypass of water seal at outlet is capped but there should be a chain attached with its other end held at the manhole rim.

9 Manhole put in after house was built, probably interwar. Two inlets to right, to outside toilets, are no longer in use.
10 Manhole covers commonly corrode from below. Wire brushing and priming will be adequate.

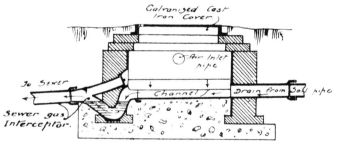

3.07 Check junctions of inlet and outlet pipes and mortar from inside as necessary. Some inlets may no longer be in use, eg from outside wcs, **9**. Wire brush underside of cover and prime as necessary, **10**. (Replace if seriously corroded or if lifting eyes are useless.) Grease round edge of cover to form seal (this also makes sure the cover comes up easily for maintenance or checks).

Pipe runs

3.08 Pipe runs, like manholes, often diverge from recommended practice. By 1900 by-laws required that:

'no drain shall be constructed so as to pass under any building except in any case where any other mode of construction may be impracticable, and in that case such drain shall be so laid in the ground that there shall be a distance equal to the full diameter thereof between the top of such ground under such building. Such drain shall also be laid on a solid foundation in a direct line for the whole distance beneath such building, and be completely imbedded in, and covered with good and solid concrete, at least six inches thick all round.'

In practice, the runs may not be straight and are often found resting on bare earth and there may be 'Y' junctions without manholes.

3.09 Check for blockages by rodding. If blockages will not budge—perhaps the run is disrupted by settlement or tree roots—rod from both sides of blockage, measure rods, and so establish location of blockage. Dig down to pipe and repair.

3.10 Trace pipe runs as far as possible. Where there are no inspection manholes, and the pipe run lies exposed on bare earth beneath a suspended floor, plug the interceptor manhole inlet, check water seals and carry out a smoke test. If there are any inspection manholes, water test runs between manholes and then branches to appliances. Where a drainage system has been out of use for some time the joints may have dried, and so leak. Fill pipes with water and allow to stand for half an hour before topping up and testing for leaks by noting any loss of head. Leaks can be located precisely in straight runs, by floating an inflatable plug down the pipe, inflating it at intervals and noting where any loss of head occurs. However, if a run leaks, all joints are suspect.

3.11 Specialist contractors will pressure grout pipe runs to seal them if their inspection satisfies them that treatment can be successful. Otherwise if there are leaks, replace the pipe run. Pipe runs under floors may be difficult to work on as boards will be taken up but joists will obstruct the workspace. Long cast iron pipes are easier to install than short clay ones. Leaks sometimes occur, where pipes pass through walls and are grouted in, due to settlement. Leave 50 mm round new pipes as they pass through walls. It may be possible to route pipes round rather than under houses, but there is the extra expense of longer runs and the costs of concreting near foundations to backfill trenches, **11**.

Cesspools

3.12 Cesspools are storage vessels, usually brick waterproofed inside and out with render. Current regulations require there to be no soakaway, though they may be found to existing tanks. Empty cesspool and check vent pipe is clear and cesspool is watertight. Render may be crumbling, so repair render or tank inside with asphalt. If cesspools are waterproofed outside there is no danger of asphalt being dislodged by water pressure, so loading floors and walls will not be needed. If decay is serious it may be cheaper to replace cesspools with septic tanks. These are much smaller ($2 \cdot 7$ m³ minimum compared with 18 m³ for cesspools) and require less frequent emptying.

Septic tanks

3.13 Like cesspools, septic tanks are likely to be found in rural areas but are of more recent origin so less in need of repair. Septic tanks process effluent by bacterial action, not merely storing it. The water resulting passes to a soakaway. Repair as for cesspools. For new septic tanks it may be cheaper to install a prefabricated plastic tank, **12**; this will require a soakaway, **13**. It may be necessary to negotiate with local inspectors about manholes since the usual requirement is for one supported on brick which is problematic to arrange around a plastic tank. Where possible site tanks down wind of houses, and downhill to reduce excavation costs. Size and length of runoff vary with porosity of subsoil and local habit. The local health department will usually provide approved details for septic tanks in their area.

3.14 If tanks are new or cleaned, or if the crust is partly destroyed by the use of detergents, microbial action can be (re)generated by 'priming' the tank with a dead (festering) rabbit, or similar sized animal.

4 Further information

4.01 CP 301: 1971 Building drainage (Gr 8)
CP 302 200: 1949 Cesspools (Gr 4)
CP 304: 1968 Sanitary pipework above ground (Gr 6)
CP 308: 1974 Drainage of roofs and paved areas (Gr 8)

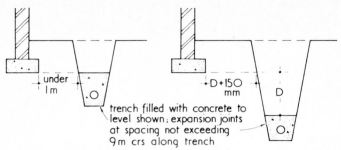

11 *Building regulation N14 for drains adjacent to foundations requiring concreting where runs are rerouted past ends of terrace.*

12 *GRP septic tank. Set on 150 mm concrete base, backfill up to connecting pipes and fill with water at the same time, connect up inlet and outlet and backfill to neck adding integral manhole frame and cover.*

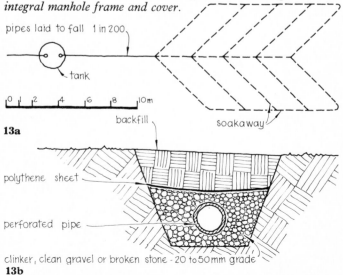

13a *Typical plan and* **b** *detailed section for a soakaway. Note relative area of soakaway compared with tank. Actual size required will vary with local tradition and soil porosity.*

Technical study 8 External works

External works, those particular to individual dwellings, are generally more decayed than the dwellings themselves. Since external works do not in general materially affect weathertightness they tend to have been relatively neglected in any past remedial expenditure. So the cost required to make external works as good as new can be substantial. The standard required, and thus what actually is spent, varies very much from client to client.

Details for entrance steps, figures 12 and 13, were provided by JOHN BENSON.

1 Ironwork

Existing ironwork

1.01 Ironwork will be found as railings, balustrades, balcony supports, fanlights, grilles, plant boxes, etc, **1**. Bars and plates will be used, sometimes wrought into curves but cast iron will generally be found for more elaborate decoration. Cast iron largely took over from wrought for this purpose in the early 1700s due to its relative cheapness.

Nature of decay

1.02 An even layer of rust might easily be dealt with but rusting generally occurs irregularly, with pitting and flaking of the surface disrupting line and detail, **2**. Once rusting has started rust should ideally be entirely removed before repainting. Paintwork deteriorates much faster over rusted than rust-free ironwork.

1.03 Rusting is often more advanced where ironwork is fixed to masonry, whether grouted in or fixed with molten lead, **3**. One effect is that the expansion of iron due to rusting may split the masonry, a more damaging effect in stone than brick, **4**.

Approach

1.04 Generally, the amount of ironwork on houses for rehabilitation is small. So, though individual items of remedial work may be relatively costly, total expenditure may not be great. The choice is between remedial work little and often, and more thorough, longer lasting treatments. For example the common approach of wire brushing evident rust and then painting does not effectively remove rust. The paint is disrupted from below in a few years. More thorough treatments which remove flaking and clear rust from pits provide in effect a new start, giving longer paint life.

1.05 Tests reported in CP 2008 (see **6.01**) showed that a four coat paint system (eg two primers, one undercoat, one top coat) lasted on average 10·6 years if the metal was first blast cleaned, or 9·6 years if instead it was pickled in acid. But after exposure on site and wire brushing the same paint system lasted on average only 2·3 years. (Flame cleaning using an oxyacetylene torch leads to a paint life of around five to six years.) These tests were for new metal, removing mill scale and rust. To match this order of difference on old ironwork, the factory processes would have to scour rust from pits and remove flaking.

1.06 Ironwork should be fixed into masonry with lead. On or near the horizontal, melted lead should be run into the hole round the end to be fixed, **3**. Where lead cannot be poured, lead sheet can be wrapped round the end of the iron and further lead hammered into the surrounding gap to fix it tightly into the masonry.

1.07 Where ironwork is severely rusted it is worth costing repairs and replacements as alternatives to prolonging life for only a few years by painting, or removing ironwork altogether.

Simple section bars can be replaced with steel bars, flats and tubing. Wrought iron curves can be copied. Castings can be made in iron or aluminium of simple shapes, such as the railing heads in **2**. For example, a broken off railing head might be reproduced in aluminium, fixed by threading the head and railing end, and the joint sealed with lead for less than £10.

Cleaning

Cleaning on or off site

1.08 The type of cleaning determines the life of the paint system used. Off site cleaning methods are generally much more effective and workmanship also tends to be better. Removing ironwork may be simple; fixings may well be loose. But in some cases, eg where each railing is sealed into masonry with lead, removal would generally be too expensive.

1 *Though the quantity of ironwork is small, it may be an important visual linking element along a terrace.*

2 *Prolonged rusting has caused pitting and flaking, disrupting surface and line.*

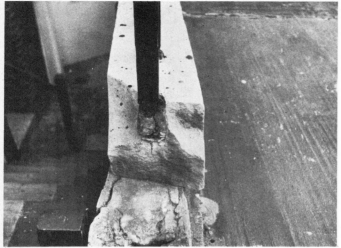

3 *Lead, lightened by stone dust, around railing end formerly securing it in socket in stonework.*

4 *Stonework disrupted by rusting. Cracked kerb has been rendered over and this in turn is cracked and flaking.*

Hand cleaning

1.09 Mechanical methods include rubbing with emery cloth and wire brushes, chipping, and grinding with power tools. These methods are only really effective for light rusting on simple shapes. Work is monotonous and tends to be skimped on site. Flaking and pitting is often left, just painted over, **2**, leading to early breakdown of the paint system. Even on metal not flaked or pitted, the finish is often rough, requiring particular primers—see table I. Hand cleaning can be done on or off site.

Flame cleaning

1.10 An oxyacetylene torch plus wire brushing will remove rust and scale. It can often be used on site with care though is restricted to ironwork 5 mm or more thick as thinner sections may collapse in the heat. It is more expensive and thorough than hand cleaning alone and is worth contemplating when there is say 20 per cent rust by area. Flame cleaning will, incidentally, remove old paint though it is not economic solely for doing this. It should not be used on bitumen or tar paint. It is advisable to wear respirators: they are required if paint contains lead and there is no simple way of knowing if it does.

Blast cleaning

1.11 Shot or grit blasting is generally the most effective method of cleaning though it may be very difficult to carry out on site. Priming should take place within four hours of cleaning. Since blasting makes a lot of dust even with vacuum collection, work, on site at least, will have to be organised in phases of blasting then priming. Use a quick drying primer.

On site chemical cleaning

1.12 Phosphoric acid washes and acids generally, pickling jellies and pastes and other proprietary chemical treatments are available. These can be combined with hand cleaning. They are generally much less effective than off site chemical cleaning. Ironwork requires careful washing down and drying between cleaning and priming. Avoid run off of chemicals onto other materials, including masonry, during cleaning and washing down. Priming should follow as soon as possible after cleaning.

Off site chemical cleaning

1.13 Pickling and phosphating involving immersion in hot acid and thorough drying are essentially factory processes. Forming a surface film of metal phosphates (to BS 3189—see **6.01**) improves rust resistance under paint, especially if treated subsequently in a chromate bath. Priming should follow as soon as possible after cleaning.

Bitumen and tar coatings

1.14 Bitumen or coal tar pitch paint may have been used on ironwork (they may also be found on cast iron rainwater goods). They are not very good coatings to start using since they rely on surface completeness for protection; they do not inhibit rust chemically. (Their inertness may be valuable in chemically, very harsh atmospheres.) However, they are very difficult to clean off, so rub down any rusting and apply two more coats. Or, if another finish is required, use an aluminium primer as well before painting.

Painting

Replacements

1.15 Replacements are often better cleaned and primed in the factory since factory cleaning—by blasting or pickling—is a much better preparation for painting new metal too than the wire brushing common on site. Rusting of unprimed metal delivered to site is sometimes not seen as bad since it helps loosen any mill scale, but subsequent wire brushing leaves significant rust and scale (see **1.05**). When ironwork is primed off site, provision should be made on site for cleaning and touching up any priming chipped by delivery or site handling.

Priming

1.16 On site, remove any grease with a solvent eg white spirit. Make sure the metal is dry before painting; apply paint to warm metal after flame treatment to avoid condensation. Brush the first coat of primer into all irregularities or clean and touch up any imperfections in factory priming. Apply other priming coats, undercoats and top coats with a brush, roller or airless spray. Check with paint manufacturers that primers applied on or off site are compatible with later coats. Where other metals are coated as well, eg aluminium, copper, lead, check with manufacturers that paint systems for ironwork do not promote corrosion in these other metals. Coal tar/epoxy paints and some zinc-rich paints can be used without primers.

Table I Primers for ironwork	
Form of cleaning	**Primer**
Hand	*Red lead Metallic lead
Flame	*Red lead Metallic lead
Blast	Etch primers Prefabrication (eg zinc-rich) primers Inhibitive primers† (often quick drying brands are required)
On site chemical cleaning	Zinc chromate and other inhibitive primers† (often quick drying brands are required)
Off site chemical cleaning	Zinc chromate and other inhibitive primers† (often quick drying brands required)

* Generally, 'tolerant' inhibitive primers. These are tolerant of the surface texture left by cleaning.
† Inhibitive primers: primers which contain pigments that chemically inhibit corrosion such as red lead, metallic lead, zinc chromate, zinc dust, zinc phosphate. Note that red oxide is not an inhibitive pigment.

Harsh atmospheres
1.17 Undercoats and top coats of ordinary gloss paint can be used after priming though special purpose paints are preferable in chemically harsh atmospheres, eg polluted air or near the sea. For examples apply undercoats and top coats of micaceous iron oxide paint or two coats of bitumen or tar paint. Unfortunately bitumen and tar paints form impervious layers which inhibit drying of primers, so primers should ideally be left for a month to harden before being painted over. A top coat, of bituminous aluminium paint, inhibits chalking and crazing due to sunlight. These paints are not, chemically, rust inhibitors, so that thick layers are especially advantageous. Paints forming thick layers are called high build paints

Balconies
1.18 Balconies, like other ironwork, tend to rust more markedly where they meet masonry, **5**. Restoring support by replacing brackets is an expensive and difficult job. Alternatively, a balcony supported in part from below could have extra, matching columns added. Or rsjs could be used to support a cantilevered balcony (the same could apply to a cantilevered bay). The size of joist will need calculation, resulting in joists of, for example, 150×75 mm I sections at $1 \cdot 5$ m centres. These would run in the depth of the floor from a party wall through the external wall projecting as cantilevers to support the balcony, **6**.

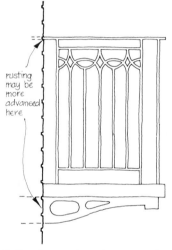

rusting may be more advanced here

5 *Rusting tends to be more advanced at fixings to masonry. This can be very expensive to repair for balconies.*

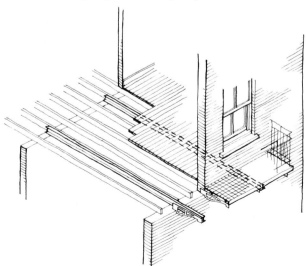

6 *Rsjs threaded through floor from internal wall to support balcony with rusting brackets; relatively cheap but inelegant. Obviously this method relies on appropriate direction of joists, adequate joist depth and convenient height of balcony relative to floor.*

Cracked masonry
1.19 Where rusting at fixings has disrupted brickwork, the brickwork is usually easily replaced. In stonework where ironwork is not rebedded, disruption is likely to continue so seal cracks with mastic. Where rebedding is done, plastic repairs can be made to stonework—see Technical study 5, External walls.

2 Boundaries and shared areas
Legal definition
2.01 Legal problems are dealt with in section 5 of the handbook, Administration. It is worth treading carefully as establishing who owns an area or boundary, and thus who pays for repair and maintenance, can be contentious. Hopefully tenancy or other agreements cover shared areas such as yards and ginnels, and title deeds define boundaries. (Entries on the land register are not legally definitive in themselves unless the Land Registrar has made a precise definition, though they will usually be accepted by the parties involved.)
2.02 Boundaries are complicated by their having no precise definition in common law. Where ownership is not clear neighbours are each generally taken to own the half nearest their land. In case of dispute several 'presumptions' apply, for example that a fence faces outward, **7**, but even these can be challenged in court. Inner London and Bristol have special legislation on party fence walls. (Other areas too have variations on common law.) To carry out work on the wall written agreement should be obtained from the adjoining owner. The alternative is to serve a party structure notice on him at least a month before work begins. This will involve the costs of appointing surveyors and, probably, delays.

Masonry
2.03 Having established legal responsibility (who pays the bill) the boundary structures will often be found in poor repair. Masonry walls are frequently in need of repointing, **8**. Large, often multi-occupied, dwellings may have long, tall boundary walls very expensive to repoint. Walls are often structurally slender with nominal or no foundations. Buttressing may be needed to restrain further leaning or bowing. Copings often need renewing. Masonry arches over gates may have slipped, requiring resetting.
2.04 In very dry weather walls on shrinkable clays are especially likely to be unstable. Tieing with buttresses could lead to further instability when rains eventually swell clay, lifting wall and buttresses. A temporary expedient, requiring occasional inspection, is to jam any cracks with hardwood wedges, loosening them as the clay swells.

Damp penetration
2.05 There is sometimes localised damp penetration into

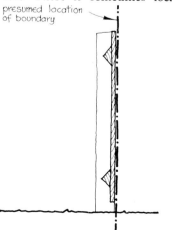

presumed location of boundary

7 *Example of legal 'presumption' for a fence is that the fence faces outwards; the fence including supporting posts are the responsibility of the owner to the left of the boundary.*

8 *Frequently such areas are reorganised by local authorities or housing associations. The existing structures are often shabby without being in danger of collapse.*

dwellings with solid walls where they abut boundary walls or outbuildings. This occurs at the top of the abutting wall due to spray from falling rain, and sometimes soaked copings, **9.** Several measures could be tried, singly or in combination: replace or cap brick on edge coping with a weathered one, use a sharper angled coping, separate the walls, **10a,** incline the coping, **10b,** flash the wall, **10c,** add a horizontal dpc.

Trees

2.06 Instability and differential settlement are often promoted by water movement caused by tree roots. Felling trees may drastically affect the water flow. Clays previously dried by trees' transpiration may swell. Soon roots will rot away causing some settlement. Heavy pruning is preferable. There is a legal 'presumption' that the roots of neighbours' trees can be cut as can overhanging branches. However, this does not seem to have been tested in court. (Re)move saplings from near walls before their roots get established.

Fences

2.07 Timber deteriorates very little due to the effects of water, though differential wetting and drying may lead to splitting. Rather, dampness encourages fungal growth which is the cause of all marked rot even though spores and fungal strands are not usually visible. To stem rot or before painting use a fungicide. Fences (and gates) often touch the ground, and may be decayed. Lower the ground level and/or shorten fence or gate. Where necessary cut out decayed timber (see Information sheet 7, Timber decay) and piece in new timber.

2.08 Fence posts merely loose can be tightened by ramming earth or packing in concrete. However, looseness in timber is often due in part to decay. New or replaced posts should be treated with preservative and can be hammered into ground or set in concrete, or supported on concrete stubs above ground.

Gates

2.09 As for fences, treat timber or replace as required. Tighten framing and bracing of gates by nailing or screwing as necessary. Check that hinges, catches, locks, bolts and other ironmongery are working. Hinge and catch supports in masonry are often loose, needing resetting. However, slightly loose ones could be tightened by hammering lead into the gaps round the fixings. Clean and paint ironmongery as necessary.

3 Paving

Unevenness

3.01 Much paving will be uneven but note if there is marked localised and/or recent movement (indicated by clean cracks and edges exposed by differential movement). Marked movement may be caused by drain collapse and water effects on soil due to tree roots, leaking drains or water movement behind retaining walls. Additional water will cause swelling of shrinkable clays but there may be settlement if silts, sands or gravels are gradually washed away.

Levelling

3.02 Causes of recent and localised movement should be established before any levelling is done. Details for bedding paving vary with ground condition and personal preference, ranging from hardcore, concrete and mortar dabs to sand on compacted earth. Generally, earth will have been sufficiently compacted by existing paving to use 50 mm of rolled sand directly on the earth. Joints can be filled with sand, stabilised by mixing it with grass seed. Despite laying paving to falls, local settlement may develop in time so joints and bedding that allow water to drain through are especially useful. Bedding on sand is generally adequate for paviors as well as slabs.

Drainage

3.03 Adjust levels so that paving drains to a trap or soakaway,

eg flower bed. Take special care to keep water away from dwelling walls and external stairs. If direction of falls is not evident pour water over paving and down any rwp draining onto it. Try external taps too; water tends to stand against adjacent walls.

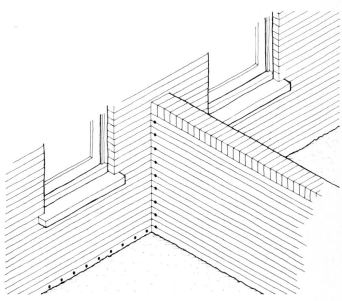

9 *Damp penetration is common through solid walls where they abut boundary walls. The spots on the walls indicate where dpc injection may have been carried out. But this does not usually protect the top of the wall from spray, leaking copings and coping joints.*

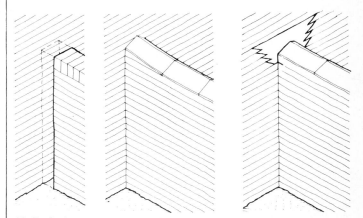

10 *Reducing water penetration through solid wall abutting boundary wall;* **a** *separating the two walls;* **b** *adding an inclined coping;* **c** *more obtrusive; flashing the wall.*

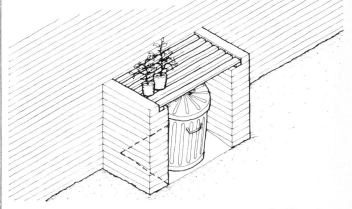

11 *Bin store with slatted top and inclined base to facilitate cleaning by rainwater and occupants.*

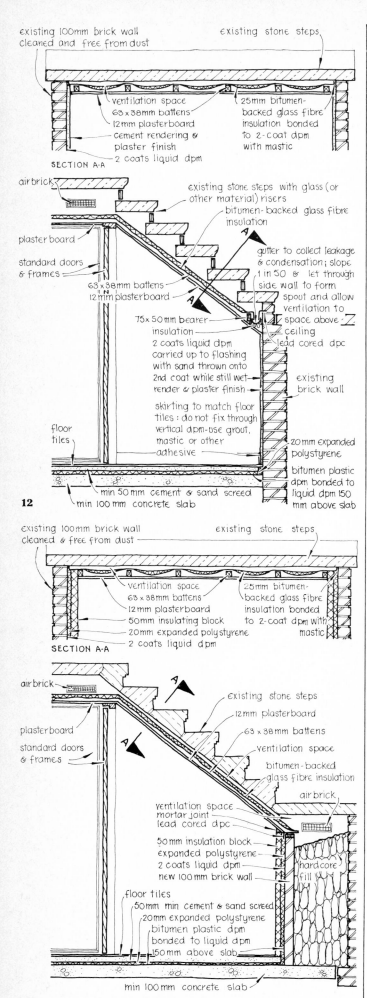

SECTION A-A

existing 100mm brick wall cleaned and free from dust
existing stone steps

ventilation space
63 x 38mm battens
12mm plasterboard
cement rendering & plaster finish
2 coats liquid dpm

25mm bitumen- backed glass fibre insulation bonded to 2-coat dpm with mastic

air brick

plaster board

standard doors & frames

existing stone steps with glass (or other material) risers
bitumen- backed glass fibre insulation

gutter to collect leakage & condensation; slope 1 in 50 & let through side wall to form spout and allow ventilation to space above

63 x 38mm battens
12mm plasterboard

75 x 50mm bearer
insulation
2 coats liquid dpm carried up to flashing with sand thrown onto 2nd coat while still wet render & plaster finish

ceiling
lead cored dpc

existing brick wall

skirting to match floor tiles : do not fix through vertical dpm-use grout, mastic or other adhesive

floor tiles

20mm expanded polystyrene
bitumen plastic dpm bonded to liquid dpm 150 mm above slab

min 50mm cement & sand screed
min 100mm concrete slab

12

existing 100mm brick wall cleaned & free from dust
existing stone steps

ventilation space
63 x 38mm battens
12mm plasterboard
50mm insulating block
20mm expanded polystyrene
2 coats liquid dpm

25mm bitumen- backed glass fibre insulation bonded to 2-coat dpm with mastic

SECTION A-A

air brick

plaster board

standard doors & frames

existing stone steps
12mm plasterboard
63 x 38mm battens
ventilation space
bitumen- backed glass fibre insulation

air brick

ventilation space
mortar joint
lead cored dpc
50mm insulation block expanded polystyrene
2 coats liquid dpm
new 100mm brick wall

hardcore fill

floor tiles
50mm min cement & sand screed
20mm expanded polystyrene
bitumen plastic dpm bonded to liquid dpm 150mm above slab

min 100mm concrete slab

13

4 Outbuildings

4.01 Work done will vary very much with client's priorities and expected use. Generally, check roof drainage, ironmongery and weathertightness of roofing, walls and openings. Rising damp in walls and floors is almost certain and usually tolerated. Check that exposed pipes to taps are lagged, and wiring to outlets plus fittings are sound. If outbuildings are to be demolished, check that support is not lost to abutting walls. Outside toilets can usually be kept in working order at little cost. Where outbuildings which abut a dwelling are demolished, the dwelling wall may need weatherproofing, eg with clear waterproofer or render. See Information sheet 3, Penetrating damp.

4.02 Where refuse has to be kept at the front of houses, bin stores may be useful to contain spillage and shield bins from wind, view and/or vandalism. Stores may also be required to support a metal frame for plastic sacks where a local authority uses these in preference to bins. Stores could simply be a leaf of screening wall or more elaborate, **11**.

5 Stairs

Timber stairs

5.01 Timber stairs are usually found as rear access to first floor flats. They may be subject to fungal and occasionally insect attack—see Information sheet 7, Timber decay. Rot is especially likely where stairs meet the ground and at joints. If stairs are replaced, incline treads to promote water runoffs and so inhibit frosting.

Stone stairs

5.02 Worn treads are not usually worth replacing but where treads are split replace them with concrete or secondhand stone. Risers, whether of concrete, stone or glass, are often poorly sealed to treads so water leaks through. Stairs may be found open, resting directly on the earth, over a store or a habitable space.

Dealing with leakage

5.03 Sealing with mortar is fairly effective at first but tends to deteriorate after a few years even when carefully done. Several proprietary compounds are available but none are of proven long term effectiveness. Asphalting is generally completely weathertight but is often visually discordant. Alternatively to sealing, leakage can be allowed and drained off. The details **12, 13** are suggestions that have been tried in practice. They preserve the appearance of the steps by leaving them relatively untouched while sealing the space below. Some local authority inspectors may question the sealing of liquid dpm to fabric dpm, and indeed the principle of draining off leakage rather than sealing steps. However, there seems to be no proven detail for sealing steps, except for asphalt.

6 Further information

6.01 CP 2008:1966 *Protection of iron and steel structures from corrosion* (Gr9).
BS 3189:1973 *Phosphate treatment of iron and steel* (Gr6).
BRE Digest 70 *Painting: iron and steel*.
BRE Digest 71 *Painting in buildings 2—Non ferrous metals and coatings*.
AJ Legal handbook (*Second edition*) E. Freeth and P. Davey (eds). The Architectural Press Ltd: London 1978

12 *Sample detail for collecting leakage through steps rather than sealing to stop leakage, allowing the space beneath to be used for storage.*
13 *As for 12 with another variant of stairs. Blockwork lining to allow chasing and fixing by workmen and occupants. This is likely to be needed where storage is part of habitable room.*

Information sheet 1 Dampness in buildings

A building may be damp from penetrating and rising damp, condensation and defects such as leaks. These may occur alone or in combination, promoting decay of materials and making the building unhealthy to live in. This section notes sources and signs of damp.
Others cover diagnosis and treatment of rising and penetrating damp, condensation, and insect and fungal attack in timber. Where the budget is limited, explain to the client the degree of reliability of any treatment.

1 Sources of dampness

Rising damp
1.01 Damp usually rises no more than one metre up walls. There is a characteristic 'tide-mark' at a level where the rate of rise matches rate of evaporation, **1**. Masonry becomes more prone to rising damp with time.

Penetrating damp
1.02 Penetration depends on exposure and materials. Porous materials such as masonry may be too thin or decayed to inhibit penetration, **2**. Impervious or near-impervious materials such as lead or render may be cracked or otherwise perforated. Any moisture passing has difficulty evaporating and is likely to penetrate to the interior. Damp staining is likely to be localised from perforations.

Condensation
1.03 Generally condensation is much more diffuse than rising damp, **3**. The internal conditions of damp air and materials, and poor heating and ventilation associated with condensation are also conducive to mould growth. Relative humidity needs to be persistently above 70 per cent for mould to flourish. Mould may result from other dampness.

Leaks
1.04 External leaks in pipes, **4**, roofs, etc, will generally produce localised stains inside. Try to inspect during wet weather. Drain leaks provide water for underfloor condensation. Faulty plumbing, especially lead piping to baths, basins, toilets and sinks leads to wet surrounding timber.

2 Interaction

2.01 Inevitably some or all of these four sources of dampness will coincide. This is especially likely for condensation. There must be a supply of moisture (though this could be provided by occupants; three people produce about 10 litres per week). And dampness in masonry reduces its insulation value, making condensation more likely (except in hot weather). Apart from appearance, **1-4**, ways of distinguishing various sources are detailed in individual sheets.

Live dampness
2.02 Is damp 'live', ie is damaging moisture still entering? Absence of occupants will reduce moisture input but may also reduce ventilation. Remedial work may have been done recently, either thoroughly or to mask the evidence. Efflorescence brushed off should not recur within two weeks without live damp though it may recur gradually if walls are drying out. Mark round damp patches with an indelible pencil and look for changes over as long a period as is available. Hygroscopic salts may have been drawn up the walls over a long

period. These absorb water from the atmosphere, increasing wall moisture content.

3 Moisture measurement

3.01 Moisture meter readings can be unreliable because high readings are given where there are soluble salts in the wall. Also the metal prongs usually take only a surface reading, penetrating 2 or 3 mm.

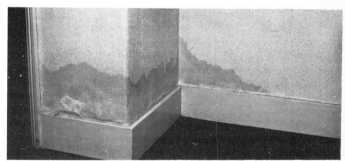

1 *Tidemark of rising damp.*

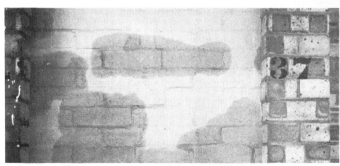

2 *Patches of penetrating damp.*

3 *Diffuse condensation stains covered in mould.*

4 *Common problem of leaks in cast iron rainwater goods.*

Information sheet 2
Damp-proof courses

It is often very difficult to separate rising damp from other sources. Some experimentation with treatments may be useful to establish the extent if any of rising damp. For example replacing plaster and improving heating and ventilation may be adequate. But this takes time and clients often want rapid results. So treatments used tend to be relatively fail-safe, and expensive. Where the budget is limited, explain to the client the degree of reliability of any affordable treatment.

1 Damp-proof courses

Movement of moisture

1.01 Considerable moisture over a long period is generally required for damp to rise say 1 metre up internal or external walls, **1**. Where evaporation is restricted on one side, eg by render or slating, the rise will be increased. Continuing dampness reinforces itself in two ways. Hygroscopic salts are drawn up the wall which, at their appropriate relative humidity, draw moisture from the atmosphere. And as walls age they become more prone to capillary rise; largely it is thought by moisture movement leaching lime from mortar, 'improving' the capillary paths.

Dpc in walls

1.02 The 1875 Public Health Act made dpcs mandatory though in practice their installation was not universal at once. Dpcs may be bitumen-based, slate, lead or engineering brick. These are likely to have failed where there is cracking from structural movement. Where a dpc is sound it may be bridged by pointing, screeds to floors, external render, either as a plinth **2** or to the whole wall, or by high external ground, **3**. Mortar in dpcs of engineering brick may have become soft and porous. Lead may be corroded by Portland cement mortar.

Rising damp in floors

1.03 Usually basements, kitchens and sculleries have solid floors of concrete, stone flags or quarry tiles. There is unlikely to be a dpm. Damp may be evident from efflorescence. If not, lay a piece of roofing felt on the floor which, will become wet on the underside in a few days if there is no dpm. Some rising damp may be tolerable to some clients if evaporation matches rise of damp so that air humidity is acceptable. If the floor is to be covered then coverings and any adhesives must be resistant to, or at least tolerant of, moisture. A continuous damp proof layer is required linked to dpcs, protecting thresholds and sealed to pipes passing through it (see Information sheet 8 Basements).

Copings

1.04 Water falling on parapets, projecting party walls, etc may penetrate copings. The usual source of leakage is not the coping stones themselves but decay of the mortar bedding. If a well bedded coping allows water penetration then any common dpc material can be used. Bonding at laps is recommended in bitumen-based dpcs. Beware though of attributing damp ceilings to faulty copings. Water may be blown onto the sides of walls bypassing the coping. Either insert a dpc at roof level (requiring rebuilding) or more simply, give the masonry a treatment inhibiting penetrating damp (see Information sheet 3).

1

2

3

1 *For solid walls, rising damp may also affect external walls. Here, rising damp evaporating beneath the windows is depositing salts which stain and disrupt the stone surface.*
2 *A small mortar plinth, just enough to bridge a dpc fixed around floor level. Plinths may be 10 mm or more of render up to around 5 m up the wall.*
3 *Concrete area level with dpc and in some places above. Render covering dpc has already been hacked off.*

2 Treatments

Bridging of dpcs

2.01 Bridging by internal screeds is part of damp proof floor treatments (see Information sheet 8 Basements). Externally, render, plinths and pointing should be cut away. If the ground is too high, a channel can be dug adjacent to the wall down to 150 mm below the dpc and filled with very coarse aggregate or large stones, **4** (beware vandalism). Facing the cut slope with concrete would tend to hold water and dirt. Make sure that adjacent ground does not drain into the channel. Lowering the ground is more elaborate but requires less maintenance. Where this is done downpipes and gulleys may need protecting, **5**. Decayed mortar around engineering bricks is inaccessible so generally a new dpc will be needed. Deep raking and repointing could be tried if there are months to experiment.

Choice of dpc

2.02 Insertion of dpcs may be appropriate for repairs, eg to slate broken by structural movement. But for whole houses, chemical and electro-osmotic treatments are generally priced to undercut insertion and are in most cases a lot quicker and less messy. There may also be lower prices for treating several adjacent units.

2.03 Several manufacturers and installers have agrément certificates; a useful assurance. And often, 'guarantees' are given for 20 to 30 years. In fact these are insurance against costs of any future remedial work, though how far this extends in terms of disruption is not clear. If a guarantee is important, eg to a client or building society, then look for a company that seems likely to be around in twenty years time to pay up in the event of failure. Specifying a treatment that the general contractor can carry out avoids the unreliability of guarantees from small specialist contractors.

2.04 Also check where the dpc will be fitted. Some installations look dangerously high, near floor level. They will protect the wall itself but may not prevent wetting of joists and any plate.

Inserting a dpc

2.05 Insertion provides a positive barrier to rising damp.
A horizontal slot is cut in a convenient mortar joint using a mechanical saw preferably with attached dust extraction, **6**. Handsaws may be needed in awkward corners. The dpc material is inserted in 1 m lengths, lapping say 100 mm and pointing up with quick setting mortar. Any of the usual dpc materials can be used except slate. Saws do not generally cut a wide enough slot for slate and laborious chipping out is needed. Even so any slight settlement from making the slot should be easily accommodated.

2.06 Working on internal walls is difficult with occupants in residence. A party structure notice or other writen agreement should be obtained for working on party walls. Insertion is not of course an appropriate technique for stone walls of random coursing.

Chemical treatments

2.07 On few occasions is the general contractor able and willing to buy chemicals and carry out chemical damp-proofing himself. Chemical damp-proof treatments are based on impregnation of the wall at the appropriate level with solutions of waterproofers such as resins, latex and siliconates, either singly or in combination. The dpc becomes operative when the solvent dries out. A line of holes is drilled into the wall and solution forced in under pressure, **7**, or allowed to flow from suitable reservoirs, **8**, or in one case inserted as ice sticks. It is worth leaving holes open for as long as possible to encourage drying out.

2.08 Chemical treatments do not all form an impervious layer. Many inhibit capillary rise (by changing the way water behaves in the pores of masonry). Penetration of chemicals to form an impervious layer is especially difficult in damp walls

4

5

6

4 *Ground cut out to 150 mm below dpc and stones placed in the gap. Light gravel topping to ground here is acceptable but more gravel would tend to fill between stones, collect dirt and rebridge the dpc.*
5 *An afterthought. Ad hoc detailing of drainage following lowering of path.*
6 *Saw for cutting chase to insert dpc. Sawing combined with dust extraction.*

with pores partly full of water. So pressure methods are preferred since impregnation is likely to be more complete. However, choices about effectiveness are generally the province of the specialist installer.

Electro-osmosis

2.09 Electro-osmotic treatments also require holes drilled, less frequently than chemical treatments, plus a chase cut between holes. A continuous soft copper strip is set into the chase and looped into holes. The strip is then usually connected to rod(s) in the ground; sometimes there is an applied potential of a few millivolts instead. The holes and chase are mortared over. The evidence of treatment may be a small junction box connecting strip to rod, **9**, or a voltmeter monitoring the applied potential. This can often be put adjacent to other electricity meters.

2.10 Electro-osmosis has been the subject of controversy because some people, especially BRE, find explanations of how it works unconvincing. The effect might be 'explained away' by changes in plastering, heating and ventilating. However a guarantee is generally provided and BRE have found no definite failures among thousands of installations.

Condenser tubes

2.11 One method claimed to be especially effective for rubble-filled and other irregular masonry walls is the installation of perforated brass tubes inclined to the outside. Water is claimed to condense in these in winter and their piercing the wall provides drying in summer. A specialist contractor will judge how many are needed to adequately inhibit damp.

Vertical damp proofing

2.12 Paints, special renders and other membranes are not generally recommended. They mask rather than cure the problem in walls and generally lack durability. They offer no protection to floors.

Plastering

2.13 Whichever method is used, it is likely that plasterwork in the lowest part of the wall has become impregnated with salts which tend to keep the wall wet. So plasterwork should be removed to at least 300 mm above the line of dampness. Installers giving a guarantee may specify the amount of replastering. Once dpcs are installed, walls dry out depositing much of their salts in the plaster. So leave plaster as long as possible before replacement.

Decoration

2.14 Rehabilitation may be done in a few weeks. Drying out very wet walls takes a much longer time. So it is advisable to use a porous paint or may require a foil-backed impervious paper if wallpapering is done immediately. If very wet, a dpm should be put behind the skirting, itself given two coats of primer.

3 Further information

3.01 BRE Digest 27, *Rising damp in walls.*
BRE Digest 77, *Damp-proof courses.*
CP 102: 1973, *Protection of buildings against water from the ground* (Gr 7) (Deals only with conventional materials, not chemical or electro osmotic treatments.)

7

8

9

7 *Internal damp-proofing by pressure impregnation.*
8 *A gravity method of introducing chemicals.*
9 *Small junction box connecting copper strip to rod in ground.*

Information sheet 3 Penetrating damp

Damp penetration through walls above ground may have been in progress for many years, perhaps since construction. Materials deteriorate and standards have changed.

This section covers the recognition of penetrating damp and outlines the range of treatments. Section 4 deals with directly applied treatments and their maintenance—waterproof paints, renders, stucco and textured finishes. Section 5 deals with separate surfaces—slating, tiling weatherboarding and extra masonry skins.

1 Penetrating damp

Penetration or rising damp?

1.01 Penetration is usually fairly easy to distinguish from rising damp by observation and deduction. Rising damp generally leaves a tide mark on internal decorations and rarely rises above sill level. There can be few conditions of exposure that would produce this effect. Also penetration is associated with particular direction(s) of windborne rain whereas rising damp may occur in any wall, internal or external. Efflorescence is generally a sign of penetration. Water passing through wall picks up salts which crystallise on the inside.

Penetration or condensation?

1.02 Penetrating dampness increases wall U-values, introduces moisture to the inside atmosphere and its evaporation causes some cooling. So it is likely that penetrating damp and condensation will occur together. Condensation tends to occur at colder points in rooms such as corners which may well be most exposed. And often in summer the only evidence is some residual staining of decorations.

1.03 Condensation is likely on the inside of any wall whereas penetration is associated with rain from specific direction(s). Knowledge of local microclimate can be obtained from local people and checking the orientation of neighbouring damp proofing—render, slating, tiling, weatherboarding. (For general climate see BRE digest 127, *Index of exposure to driving rain*.) Condensation is also more likely to be associated with mould than is penetrating damp (though the two may be combined). Mould and condensation require high relative humidities (mould 70 per cent) whereas penetrating damp may evaporate in a well ventilated room with much lower resultant humidity.

2 Treatments

Surfaces for treatment

2.01 The condition of external wall surfaces is a major determinant of treatment. Directly applied treatments (Information sheet 4) require a sound wall which will remain stable over the life of the treatment. There may have been chemical attack which is especially damaging to dressed stone and frost action may have blown the faces off masonry, **1**. But old masonry is often more irregular than modern without being defective, **2**.

2.02 If walls are in poor condition a separate surface (Information sheet 5) could be needed, supported on battens.

Where walls will not support battens or are too irregular it is usually possible though laborious to fix counterbattens as an alternative to adding an extra masonry skin. When counterbattens are used there is a chance to add insulation between them eg foam slabs or mineral wool batts. Check U-values. The decision to install insulation should be part of an overall strategy of environmental control.

Choice of treatments

2.03 Directly applied treatments are cheaper than separate layers, with waterproof painting the cheapest and shortest lived. It requires renewal every few years and there is the 'hidden cost' of making good the wall before painting. Painting reduces porosity but this may not be enough in severely exposed conditions. Renders are prone to failure due to lack of key and reaction with chemicals in walls, requiring care in specification and supervision. Dashed finishes may be more durable, and break up the flow of water down walls.

2.04 Choice of separated layers depends partly on the intricacy of the shape to be treated, its size and the available skills of the contractors staff. Non-rectangular areas, arrises and openings may be easier for render on expanded metal to accommodate but (asbestos) slating, tiling and pvc or timber weatherboarding require very much less maintenance. Timber weatherboarding is a commitment to frequent repainting. Appearance is often the deciding factor, though it is desirable even with pressure impregnation to keep timber battens from any possible source of damp.

1 *Faces blown off bricks exposing soft, friable interior.*

2 *Old irregular bricks. Shallow cracks from manufacture.*

Information sheet 4 Surface treatments

Surface treatments for penetrating damp included are colourless water repellants, coloured paints, textured coatings, render and stucco, wet dash (roughcast, harling) and dry dash. This section works through treatments in order of cost and of state of decay of the wall. Reducing porosity or making surfaces impervious increase the chance of interstitial condensation. Section 5 covers separate layers: slating/tiling and weatherboarding.

1 Colourless water repellants

Selection

1.01 Clear repellants require masonry in good condition, **1**. Though application is cheap, there is often the added cost of making good anything wider than a haircrack, perhaps repointing walls. Repellants should last 10 years on moderately exposed walling, though projecting features and exposed areas such as sills and parapets need a new application after five. Treatment will encourage any water entering the wall through cracks or from other sources (such as rising damp) to evaporate inside the building. Be sure wall movement causing racking has ceased. Do not use repellants internally, eg on stone windows as this leads to spalling.

The repellant

1.02 Clear water repellants, usually silicone based to BS 3826, reduce porosity but do not seal masonry. There is still some absorption and evaporation of water. The duck's-back effect of rain droplets running down the wall lasts for only a short while after application. Repellants generally have a minimum shelf life of six months.

1.03 There are three classes of silicone-based repellant:

Class A Silicone formulations for clay brickwork, hydraulic cement-based materials and cast stone masonry of a predominantly siliceous nature. (Siliceous—silica containing, such as quartz, including igneous rocks, eg granite, and sandstones.)

Class B Silicone formulations for natural and cast stone masonry of a predominantly calcareous nature and calcium silicate brickwork. (Calcareous—carbonates, such as calcium and magnesium, including limestones.)

Class C Aqueous siliconate solution for natural and cast stone masonry of a predominantly calcareous nature.

If in doubt use Class B.

Application

1.04 Brush or spray on repellant to manufacturer's instructions. It can be applied to one wall (orientation) only. It should normally be continuous from the roof line downward. At door or window-to-wall joints, apply repellant to walls (and windows if stone) before sealing joints with mastic. Follow manufacturer's instructions on acceptable dryness of walls to allow application.

2 Coloured paints

Selection

2.01 It is usually cheaper to use clear repellants so that coloured paints are usually chosen for aesthetic reasons. There may be an added benefit in that some cementitious paints seal cracks better than clear repellants. Painting masonry masks some patching but tends to show up anything that casts a

1 *Walls may be very uneven yet easily treated as long as surfaces are sound. Cracks must be filled.*

2 *Texture of masonry changed by painting. Wiring and conduits more pronounced.*

shadow, whether masonry arrises, conduits or wiring, **2**. The texture of masonry is considerably changed. Durability varies with type and manufacture; somewhere between three and ten years. See manufacturer's instructions (or BRE Digest 56:2 —see para **6.01**).

Repairs

2.02 Rub down flaking, bubbling and cracking paint, repainting to manufacturer's instructions. Two or three old layers will generally support repainting but further layers may eventually result in loss of adhesion. However, limewash should be scrubbed down before renewal. Often this has not been done and a crust has built up. If this is not flaking, any cracks can be filled with hardstopping (proprietary water plus powder mixes) and recoated.

3 Textured coatings

Selection

3.01 Textured coatings (not rough cast and pebble dash) are generally sprayed on by specialist contractors on walls in fairly good condition; they mask more patching than does coloured paint. Textured finishes break up the flow of water downwalls more than smooth ones, so pattern staining at poor details, eg ends of sills, is less marked.

3.02 A BRE report in 1972 on textured coatings stated that 'comparative tests indicate that cost-in-use over 50 years at a

3a

 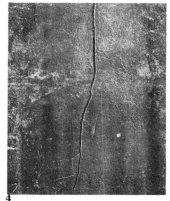

3b 4

3a *Textured coating stained and with fine cracks six months after installation. (Cracks touched up for printing).* **3b** *Coating follows moulding. It is especially*

exposed on top of parapet and cornice.
4 *Crack due to structural movement. There is usually some loss of adhesion; render sounds hollow when tapped.*

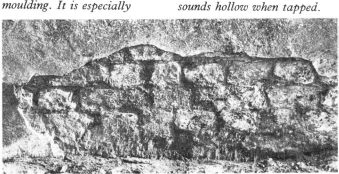

5 *Adhesion failure promoted by frost action. Crack direction is random.*

6 *Advanced sulphate attack on render. Cracks following mortar joints.*

redecorating interval of 10 years would not be lower than for much cheaper emulsion paint recoated every four to five years (at normal costs for labour and materials)'. In some cases a 15-year guarantee is given but the report noted that 'the guarantee, increased by some operators to 15 years, may be accepted as a valuable feature but its benefits depend on the quality of workmanship and the integrity of contractors. It may cover only limited forms of failure of the coating, not consequent defects in the base surface or structure.'

3.03 Things may have changed for better or worse since 1972. Usually a longer lasting and tried treatment such as render or roughcast would be safer. Clearly a lot depends on the contractor. The coatings tend to be thin, taking up any stains from walls and fairly dense, so liable to crack with structural movement and shrinkage, **3**. Coatings not applied continuously tend to dry patchy.

4 Render and stucco

Selection

4.01 Where clear waterproof paints cannot be applied to masonry deterioration, or more permanent treatment is required, the usual alternative is render due to its cost, durability and its blending with the locale. Sometimes there is the smooth finish of stucco nearby. Render may have become part of the local vernacular through its use on parapets, projecting party walls and other exposed walling and features. Though render has a deserved reputation for failure due to poor workmanship and poor (or non-existent) specification, there are few situations where successful rendering in some form is impossible.

Stucco

4.02 The dividing line between stucco and other renders is a hazy one. Generally, stucco is taken to be render with no portland cement (so generally early last century or before) applied over cheap brickwork in imitation of dressed stone.

Defects in existing treatments

4.03 *Paint on stucco*
Stucco imitating stone was generally left unpainted to match colour and can still be found so. However, changes of fashion and difficulties of keeping stucco clean in dirty industrial atmospheres have lead to frequent repainting, building up a crust of 2 mm or more. So there may be marked flaking and cracking which on inspection is found to be only in the paint layer.

4.04 *Cracking and spalling*
The render itself may be defective due to structural movement, **4**. Spalling plus lack of adhesion may be due to poor workmanship, frost action and/or sulphate attack. Often too strong a mix has been used, resulting in shrinkage cracks (random in direction) and loss of adhesion to porous or friable walls. Any loosening or cracking is made worse by frost action blowing off the render, **5**. Cracking from sulphate attack is likely to be more evidently patterned. Where sulphate concentrations are high such as in chimneys and/or where portland cement: sand mortar has been used for bedding or repointing, sulphates tend to crystallise, expanding and so blowing off render. Cracks are random at first but later tend to follow mortar joints, **6**.

Repairs

4.05 *Stucco paint and small cracks in render*
To make up gaps from paint flaking and small cracks, cut away loose material to firm edge and rub down wet. Wash out dirt. Fill with hard stopping (not oil-based or gypsum plaster fillers). Paint with an alkali resistent primer and undercoat when filler is dry, then undercoat the whole wall. If flaking is general, **7**, the whole wall will need wire brushing and rubbing

down wet before priming and painting. Cleaning off flaking paint very often pulls off some stucco, requiring making good.

4.06 *Defective areas of render*
Cut away loose render to a firm edge, undercutting it a little. Cut away for about 100 mm around any movement crack. Fill cracks in masonry behind. Wash out the gap. If structural movement has not definitely ceased, or the masonry surface is friable or oily from old oil mastic then nail on expanded metal with non-ferrous nails. Fill in several coats, depending on thickness; the outer one should not be more than 10 to 15 mm. Use 1 cement: 1 lime: 6 sand. For painting, use an alkali-resistent primer and undercoat before general undercoating. If it is not to be painted, trial mixes could be used to colour match the finish. Colour can be modified by choice of sand and cement, and the use of pigments. Wait until completely dry to judge colour. Colour matching is very difficult, **8**.

4.07 Proprietary methods are available for sealing up slightly cracked mortar. One method involves placing a nylon mesh over the render and painting with bitumen paint. Chemically compatible paints can then be added. This sort of treatment seals render so water must not be admitted from any other source.

New and renewed render
4.08 *Chemical attack*
Renewing render to chimneys as in **6**, and indeed applying it to any masonry likely to contain high concentrations of salts is risky. One factor that can be usefully controlled is the movement of water which promotes crystallisation. For example, capping unused chimneys with a half-round tile and putting a dpc above the render would help greatly. However, the common practice of rendering projecting party walls over the top is asking for trouble and a coping with dpc would be safer, **9a**, **b**.

4.09 Where there are known or likely to be considerable salts in masonry, render is better separated from the masonry using metal lathing or expanded metal on metal battens fixed with non-ferrous nails or, if the wall is friable, with expansion bolts or bolts grouted in. Using timber battens, even pressure impregnated, as part of this damp proofing treatment is usually an unnecessary risk.

4.10 *Adhesion*
Where masonry surfaces are friable, **10**, or where removing old render pulls off the surface, rendering may not adhere directly to the wall. Use metal, including battens where necessary—see **4.09**.

4.11 Where adhesion is poor because masonry is too smooth and not porous enough, or if porosity is variable across the wall, a first spatterdash coat can be used. This should be about 1 cement: 3 sand thrown on; throwing is essential for adhesion. This should be about 5 mm thick, not levelled to fill out irregularities.

4.12 *Ventilation*
If walls are wet, rendering leads to drying out to the inside. The use of battens or, more economically, nailing on corrugated bituminised felt as a base for render allows air movement between the render and the wall, so allowing some drying outwards. This also lessens the movement of salts to the inside and reduces the chance of interstitial condensation.

4.13 *Mixes*
BS 5262 'External rendered finishes' goes into great detail on wall condition and exposure for rendering. However, recommended mixes are often similar and the following recommendations allow simple specification. This simplicity helps keep the price down (generally the more you write the higher the price) and makes it more likely that builders will follow specification rather than using their usual mix if these differ.

7

8

7 *Paint badly flaking but stucco appears sound below.*
8 *New render around a new opening. Sands, cements and mix may be of different colour to original (which has been coloured by weathering).*

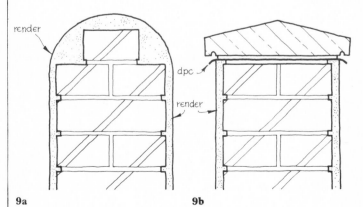

9a   9b

9a *Common approach to rendering projecting party walls allowing considerable water movement and thus promoting crystallisation.* **9b** *Modification incorporating dpc and coping.*

4.14 Outer layers of render should not be stronger than inner ones; generally the same mix can be used for all coats. Two coats are usual, though three should be used in severe exposures and on expanded metal and metal lathing. To avoid many of the recent cracking failures use cement: lime: sand

mixes with sulphate resisting cement where sulphate action shows:
- 1:2:9 for moderately exposed or sheltered walls
- 1:1:6 for severely exposed walls
- 1:1:6 for no fines concrete, expanded metal or metal lathing in moderately exposed or sheltered walls
- 2:1:9 for the above on exposed walls.

4.15 Mixes could be weaker on poorer walls but if adhesion is a significant problem use expanded metal or metal lathing. In severe exposures do not make the mix too strong. If local experience shows render is not sufficiently weatherproof, add a waterproofer to a first spatterdash coat. Keep a check on mixing and shelf life of waterproofer. Alternatively to a waterproofer, wet dash could be used, **5.01**. This is more durable and weatherproof.

4.16 *Workmanship*
Surface crazing is tolerable for weatherproofing if not appearance as long as more serious shrinkage cracks do not develop. Several steps help reduce such cracking:
- A coarser graded sand could be used.
- Drying should be gradual, slowed in warm weather by spraying with water or draping with damp sacks.
- Avoid overtrowelling the surface.
- If a strong base coat is used, top coats could be weaker. (This should not be necessary).

If the top coat is markedly crazed after drying out, a cementitious paint would help seal it. However, painting is not generally advised since it is an extra expense and tends to show dirt sooner than render, **11**. Do not render in frosty weather.

4.17 Stop off render above dpc level, making a bellmouth drip. Form the drip in the two/three coats. If it is vulnerable to damage it could be reinforced with expanded metal, **12**, or a galvanised trim used.

4.18 Refix surface pipes on new spacers to accommodate render.

5 Wet dash and dry dash

Selection
5.01 Wet dash (harling or roughcast) and dry dash should be more durable, resistant to cracking and weatherproof than render, though the quality of the finish depends a great deal on workmanship. Wet dash (harling) is traditional in Scotland but less traditional skill exists for dry dash and there tends to be flaking of the surface layer. It may be worth introducing these finishes, where sympathetic in appearance in areas of high exposure if skilled workmen are available.

Mixes
5.02 Use cement: lime: sand for all coats (except wet dash final coat) in severe exposure conditions:
- 1:1:6 for roughcast for all walls
- 2:1:9 for dry dash for all walls
- 2:1:9 for roughcast and dry dash for no-fines concrete metal lathing and expanded metal.

Mixes can be varied from these recommendations as in **4.15**.

5.03 Aggregates for the final coat of wet dash are graded up to about 12 mm to replace nine parts of sand. The coarsest may be crushed stone or gravel. The grading may come from varied crushing of stone or gravel plus sand. The proportion of coarse material (over 5 mm) to fine can range between 1:1 to 1:2 by volume. For dry dash, aggregate can be graded about 5 mm to 10 mm.

Use
5.04 Repair and lay on undercoats as for render. For wet dash, mix the graded aggregate instead of sand for the final coat and throw on. For dry dash, make the final coat wetter, throw on dash and press in with a float.

11

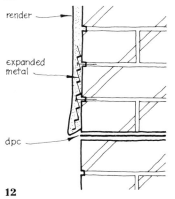

12

10 *Chimneys are highly exposed to the weather and to sulphates from combustion so that faces are blown off bricks, often by a combination of crystallisation and frost action.*
11 *Render dirt stained after little more than a year.*
12 *Reinforced drip in render above dpc.*

6 Further information
6.01 BS 5262: 1976 (formerly CP 221) External rendered finishes (Gr7).
CP 231: 1966 Painting of buildings (Gr9).
BRE Advisory service information: Exterior wallcoating, 1972.
BS 3826: 1969, Silicone-based water repellants for masonry (Gr4).
BRE digest 55 Painting walls: 1.
BRE digest 56 Painting walls: 2.
BRE digest 57 Painting walls: 3.
BRE digest 125 Colourless treatments for masonry.

Information sheet 5
Separate layers

Separate layers—slating, tiling and weatherboarding—are possible treatments to combat penetrating damp. But as render, wet or dry dash can be applied to most walls (see the preceding section) separate layers are usually chosen for other reasons as well as damp-proofing. For example, separate layers may be locally traditional, the use of battens and counterbattens can provide a space for adding insulation, and local contractors may be more skilled in fixing separate layers rather than surface treatments.

1 Selection

Timber, metal, plastic

1.01 Timber should only be used where essential in damp-proofing treatments, even though pressure impregnated. While render can be supported on metal if necessary, the battening and any counterbattening for slating, tiling and timber weatherboarding will need timber. This is more prone to decay than in most roofs (though akin to rooms in the roof) due to limited ventilation. This, plus a continuing commitment to repainting, makes timber weatherboarding inadvisable used primarily as a damp treatment. There may also be problems about surface spread of flame.

1.02 Pvc weatherboarding has at least freedom from such decay and low maintenance to recommend it, **1**. Some yellowing will occur after only a few years and there will be gradual creep and embrittlement. Life is difficult to estimate but may be 15 to 20 years based on past experience, though 60-year claims are made. There may be trouble getting standard sections for some old buildings to trim edges and openings and fitting it to irregular walls. Pvc weatherboarding is impervious, so any water in the wall or rising damp will dry out on the inside surface of the wall. Being impervious, it may also promote interstitial condensation.

Damage

1.03 Pvc weatherboarding, slating and tiling are all more vulnerable than render to impact damage. So avoid open situations such as ends of terraces adjacent to footpaths and car parking. A common tradition is to start separate layers above ground floor level, out of reach with render below.

Thin walls and insulation

1.04 Extension and other walls may be only half-brick thick, requiring both damp-proofing and insulating. Separate layers on counterbattens with insulation between, eg mineral wool batts or foam slabs could be used. This inhibits ventilation so damp walls will tend to dry out to the inside. An extra brickwork skin is more expensive, requiring new foundations, and is usually more trouble at openings.

1.05 If insulation, not damp-proofing is the problem, dry lining is generally cheaper than separate layers, though it may be expensive due to negotiating openings, and removing and refixing fittings. (For dry lining, see Technical study 6 Interiors). Dry linings provide a more rapid thermal response, more appropriate to intermittent heating.

2 Repair

Weatherboarding

2.01 Replace existing warped, split or decayed timber with new that is pressure impregnated and twice primed before fixing, **2**. (Exceptionally, timber is unpainted, eg oak boards,

1 *Pvc weatherboarding on exposed gable. Some rippling, probably due to creep or uneven substrate.*

2 *Timber weatherboarding cheaply done with butt joints leaking and very high U-value. Batts or slabs of insulation and a breather-type dpm would be needed behind new boarding.*

but an unobtrusive impregnation or surface treatment would still help.) If boards sag, extra vertical battens could be used to make say 1 m centres overall. Check for decay in battens (studs in timber construction) either when boards are removed or by prising up the bottom edges of lapped boards. If decay exists in battens, many boards will need taking down and cutting out and treating timber may be extensive (see Information sheet 7 Timber decay), **3**. It is worth considering a change of materials, eg pvc, render or tiles, where weatherboarding is a separate layer and not integral with the construction. Choice depends very much on local character and extent of decay.

Slating and tiling

2.02 Slates and tiles may be found on battens and counterbattens, just battens or fixed directly to walls. Slates and tiles may be vertically hung, nailed to common laps, say 25 mm-50 mm. To facilitate nailing to mortar joints walls may be in rat trap bond, producing a joint spacing of about 110 mm. (Bricks were laid on edge alternately headers and stretchers.) Instead of head nailing, slates may have been fixed on edge by clipping with nail heads, usually bedded on mortar, butt jointed and laid to courses, **4**.

2.03 *Defects*
Rapid run-off of water results in fewer of the defects associated with roofs such as frost and chemical attack (see Technical study 2 Pitched roofs). But slates and tiles are more likely to fall if only single nailed or if nails are rusting. And because they do not rest so heavily on each other as on roofs (except slates bedded in mortar) they are more likely to be rattled and broken by the wind, **5**, especially at corners. Bedding mortar for slates gradually decays and they fall away. As for pitched roofs, check flashing and any mortaring at edges and openings. Traditional corners are butt jointed or mitred with the joint plugged with mortars. Check that there are soakers underneath.

2.04 *Remedial work*
Where timber is decayed, replace with impregnated timber and treat masonry (see Information sheet 7 Timber decay). Brush treatments on site are less effective and cut ends are often neglected. Nail battens with galvanised or non-ferrous nails. Double nail every slate/tile; zinc for slates, aluminium for tiles. Repoint corners, installing soakers as necessary. Corner tiles may often be colour matched but tend to change the character of tiling. This may be an opportunity to improve some details, see para **3.03**.

2.05 For slates laid horizontally to courses, try to find replacements similarly weathered. Soak in water overnight, hack off any old mortar from the wall and bed the slate on a wetted wall with a fairly strong mortar. The limit on mortar strength is usually adhesion to the wall. A mix of 1 cement: 1 lime: 6 sand is suitable for most walls. If softer, use a weaker mix (eg 1:2:9). If very friable, galvanised nailed expanded metal or wire netting should be placed over the masonry before applying mortar. Nail as for the existing slates. If several are missing, say 10 per cent, without localised cause then life is limited to a few years and replacement will be necessary. Slates are expensive and bedding slates is not a highly durable treatment. Replacement could be coloured paint (the wall will be pattern stained), render or perhaps vertical slating on battens.

5 Recent tiling on exposed wall. Timber in good condition. White stains from birds nesting behind. Broken and slipped tiles probably due to single nailed or un-nailed tiles being rattled by wind (and perhaps poor quality tiles and/or workmanship).

3 Decay is likely from leakage at corners and where weatherboarding finishes in contact with masonry.

4 Slates, usually with mortar bedding are laid to courses with about 40 mm lap and butt jointed at their sides. There are two large headed zinc nails at each vertical joint and the whole joint is tarred over. Slates at centre and at roof line are nailed through rather than at edge.

6

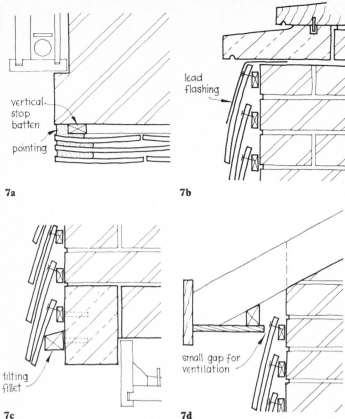

7a   7b

7c   7d

6 *Tiling may not be very durable even though relatively expensive, eg compared with render. Many tiles have already slipped out of line after a few years. A detail of the wall is shown in* **5**.
7a *Plan of mortar sealing of tile layers at opening.*
7b *Section below sill showing drop of dpc required to limit penetration.* **7c** *Section over opening incorporating tilting fillet. Fixing a fillet will require drilling and plugging into lintel.* **7d** *Section at eaves showing gap left for ventilation.*

3 New slating and tiling

Slates or tiles
3.01 Natural slates are expensive. The choice between asbestos slates and tiles is usually aesthetic since they are similarly priced as fixed, varying with quality, **6**. Cutting is expensive so choice of a stock size to fit the wall with minimum cutting would help, though such fine judgement relies on predictable (practised) site work. Increasing horizontal spacing can only make up about 20 mm per metre without detriment to weather-proofing.

Battens and counterbattens
3.02 Use pressure impregnated timber. Check that the wall is not too friable to support nailing of battens (say 50 × 25 mm). Non-ferrous nails are preferable because nailing into masonry scrapes off galvanising. Some masonry nails will be needed, as mortar coursing does not match gauge (batten spacing). If it is too friable or insulation is needed, fix counterbattens at, say, 400 mm centres. These may be nailed directly or, in friable walls, anchor bolts could be used or nails or bolts grouted in. The contractor will probably have a preferred method he can rely on. On site, check counterbattens are firm.

Detailing
3.03 *Insulation*
If insulation is added, eg mineral wool batts or foam slabs, there will be no wall ties to support it as in cavity walls. Staple wire netting or skewnail pieces of batten between the counter-

battens. Check that untreated timber is not used. Add a breather (ie vapour permeable) sheathing between counterbattens and battens. Twice nail all slates/tiles; aluminium for tiles, galvanised for asbestos slates and zinc for natural slates.

3.04 *Edges and openings*
If there are counterbattens, and no insulation, this helps ventilation so do not seal at top or bottom. Details for edges and openings are shown in **7a, b, c, d**. Stop off short of the dpc, using a tilting fillet as over openings, **7c**. If corners are butt jointed or mitred, nail a zinc soaker behind stretching about 100 mm either side of the joint.

4 Further information
4.01 Cecil C. Handisyde *Everyday Details*, The Architectural Press Ltd: London 1976.
6 Timber framed walls: dpc at ground level, p. 25
9 Tilehanging and timber cladding, p. 39

Information sheet 6 Condensation

Recognising condensation is important as a means of analysing sources of damp. But after damp-proofing, the problem is to anticipate where condensation may occur in future. This sheet notes likely sites of condensation.

1 Diagnosis

Signs of condensation

1.01 Ways of distinguishing penetrating and rising damp from condensation were given in Information sheets 1 Dampness in buildings and 3 Penetrating damp (para **1.02**). In several cases condensation may not be visible. Surface condensation does not usually form evident damp patches as readily as in new buildings since finishes are usually more absorbent, though mould may form without these evident patches. Interstitial (within materials) condensation, eg in solid floors, walls and roofs, is often not detectable. (It may be worsened, especially in walls, by the addition of damp-proofing finishes which are of reduced porosity or impervious, inhibiting moisture evaporation to the outside.) In any case, there may be few residual signs of condensation if it is intermittent, eg seasonal, or related to particular activities such as cooking.

Predicting condensation

1.02 Prediction is important to indicate likely sites of condensation in both existing conditions and after repair and maintenance. Remedial damp-proofing, stopping leaks, opening up ventilation such as blocked air bricks and windows, and changing heating (eg substituting for paraffin heaters) changes the problem. That is, to predict the likelihood of condensation after remedial work and so decide if further remedies are needed specifically for condensation. Calculation methods are available (see AJ 19.5.71 p1149, 26.5.71 p1201 and 2.6.71 p1265). More pragmatically, existing and remedied building can be compared with good practice. The following notes are of likely problems where practice needs improving.

2 Problems of condensation

Roofs

2.01 Construction of flat roofs and rooms in the roof is especially likely to be badly ventilated and insulated. It is worthwhile opening up roof coverings or ceilings to check for timber decay. Generally, roofspaces may be further ventilated by setting air bricks into flues no longer used for combustion exhausts. See Technical study 2 Pitched roofs and 3 Flat roofs.

Decorations

2.02 Decorations, especially wallpaper and emulsion paints, are liable to be stained or mouldered, **1**. Strip/clean off and wash with fungicide or bleach. New paint should contain a fungicide. Where there has been damp in chimneys, chimney breasts may have oily black stains. Cap the chimney to keep out rain but allow ventilation, eg cap pot with a half round tile. Cover breast with an impervious layer such as foil-backed paper, or replaster using a base coat of 1 cement: 3 sand.

1 *Condensation is almost always present where mould is found. 70 per cent relative humidity is needed for mould growth.*

Pipes

2.03 Pipes, eg in bathrooms, including under baths (remove side panel) and in kitchens, especially in cupboards under sinks, may have condensation on the surface which has dripped consistently, decaying timber. Keep surrounding spaces ventilated and treat timber—see Information sheet 7 Timber decay.

Fitted furniture

2.04 Fitted furniture, eg wardrobes and kitchen cupboards, especially against outside walls, is liable to condensation between wall and back panel or within. Allow air to circulate. For example, drill 25 mm diameter holes at 500 mm centres in back panels and tops to ventilate wall and contents.

Window aprons

2.05 Window aprons may be half-brick thick. An extra skin would require a lintel over the opening below. A dry lining would be more convenient—see Technical study 6 Interiors.

Blind windows
2.06 Blind windows are effectively a thinning of walls. An exterior coat of clear water repellant which helps to dry the wall, so keeping U-value down is usually enough. Thick external render (perhaps with insulation) or localised dry lining are usually difficult to integrate visually.

Windows
2.07 Windows are usually sash so adequately ventilated if not sealed up with paint, etc. Condensate drains to the outside (in a roundabout way). Hinged lights seal tighter but the cost of double-glazing is not usually justified for these and fixed lights. Weepholes could be made, eg **2**.

Room ventilation
2.08 There should be one air brick per room unless there is an open or vented fireplace. Airbricks are fine in principle, though often blocked up. Loose sashes may be more reliable. It seems arrogant to try to position air bricks out of sight or out of reach, but many people will not believe that their own respiration, rather than rising or penetrating damp, can be a prime cause of condensation. Where affordable, install forced ventilation to cope with bathing, cooking and laundry and use impervious finishes such as gloss paints, vinyl wallpaper and tiles. A rate of two air changes per hour is usually adequate with about half per hour for other spaces. Fixed lights could be made openable.

Heating
2.09 See heating study in section 4, Improvements and conversions. Background heating is safe but energy consuming. Try to provide some clothes drying facility. Greater ventilation and insulation are some compensations where heating plant, existing or affordable, is limited. (For example, public sector installations may now be only a radiant-cum-water heater in a living room plus one other radiator.) Try to provide enough heating and clothes drying facilities so that occupants do not need to use paraffin heaters; they produce a litre of water for a litre of fuel.

Underfloor spaces
2.10 Underfloor spaces frequently suffer from condensation. Leaking drains, lack of oversite concrete (despite regulations requiring it in the 1880s) and rising damp in walls may provide moisture. Frequently there is inadequate ventilation, **3a**, **b**. Dig out and add polythene sheet finished at least 150 mm below the underside of joists. Install air bricks to give say 3000 mm² of open area per metre run of external wall. Make sure some are positioned near corners. If sleeper walls are solid, rebuild honeycombed or knock out bricks.

Solid floors
2.11 Solid floors usually need treating for rising damp—see Information sheet 8 Basements and solid floors. This plus other general remedial work generally cures condensation. If necessary, a low U-value finish, such as cork tiles, can be added. Use adhesives tolerant of moisture.

Wall timbers
2.12 Bressummers, lintels and bond timbers are all vulnerable to interstitial condensation leading to decay. Where timbers are known to exist, break off some plaster to check for decay. Replace decayed timber with concrete — see Technical study 5 External walls, para **2.10**. Damp treatments may reduce porosity or make outer surfaces impervious, so interstitial condensation will increase unless walls dry out. Adequate damp-proofing and ventilation will inhibit moisture build up in walls.

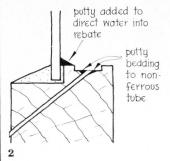

2 *One method of making weepholes, say 3 per metre. Cut 3 mm rebate in sill with plane, finishing with chisel. Drill through as shown to take non-ferrous tubing, eg copper microbore. Countersink top of hole. Prime top and bottom of hole. Cut tube as shown, thread in then seal at top with putty in countersunk space. Putty behind glass as shown to direct water into rebate. Prime and paint as normal.*

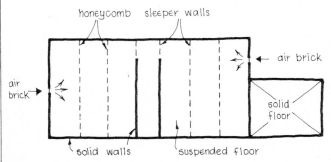

3a *Typical plan showing limited underfloor ventilation.*

3b *Common type of airbrick with small open area found in house illustrated on the plan.*

Cold bridges
2.13 Look for cold bridges anywhere there is a change of construction, such as a change of wall thickness at parapets, which may promote condensation in or on walls.

Information sheet 7
Timber decay

An unnecessary mystique often surrounds the hazards and treatments of timber decay. The main distinctions to make are between insect and fungal attack and, with the latter, between wet and dry rots. Distinguishing between wet and dry is difficult at some stages in their development. There is no substitute for being shown differences by someone experienced.

Though the first priority for treating rot is stemming dampness, drying out a damp building will take several months. Once established, dry rot survives in conditions not markedly damp. Direct treatment of decay is needed.

1 Timber decay

Location

1.01 Decay may occur in any timber eg joists, staircases, furniture. While rot (fungal attack) is directly associated with damp conditions insect attack is not, though some insects prefer wood already softened by fungi. Generally sapwood is attacked, **1**. It is necessary to go over all timber, making hatches into pitched roofs, opening up flat roofs from above or below and taking up floorboards at least where joists bear on walls. This includes sleeper walls. Bounce on floors to check for excessive 'give'. Be careful where floors are (or are likely to have been) damp eg at front doors. Energetic bouncers may disappear into cellars. If under-floor spaces are obviously damp and underventilated, eg in corners, adjacent to party walls and solid floors, a more thorough inspection will be needed, **2**. Inspect obscure corners such as eaves and under stairs.

General checks

1.02 Decay weakens timber; fungal attack leads to a general loss of strength while insect attack reduces strength by the amount of timber consumed. Look for dead beetles, bore dust and flight holes as signs of insect attack. Advanced rot is usually obvious but both rot and insect attack can become established with little surface disruption, especially behind paint. The insect workings or decay are soft and not resistant to probing with a screwdriver or other blunt instrument. Timber sounds dull if tapped. Any place where there is dampness is suspect (check skirtings and grounds).

Contractors

1.03 It is difficult to be sure that a treatment is successful. The guarantee of a specialist contractor is a commitment to return to treat any recurrence (if the contractor is still in business). Specialists are usually considerably more expensive than work done by a general contractor. (If the client requires a guarantee for any timber, it may be cheaper in ground floors to avoid the need for one by installing concrete.) If a guarantee is not required, still use a specialist contractor where you are not confident in diagnosis or the likely quality of site workmanship.

2 Fungal attack

General characteristics

2.01 Fungi need 20 per cent or more moisture content and grow faster at higher temperatures. For example, growth is twice as fast at 21°C as at 10°C. There may be visible growths on timber, shrinkage, discoloration, cracking, softening and a characteristic smell. The smell is similar to growing mush-

1 *Preferential attack of sapwood by insects.*
2 *Timber floor bearing on damp wall. Dry rot damage is aggravated by wood boring insects.*
3 *An extreme attack of dry rot with plates of fruit bodies conspicuous on door and skirting.*

rooms; not to be confused with the mustiness of mildew that is often present.

2.02 Fruit bodies usually form only when strands (*hyphae*) have formed into a considerable mass (*mycelium*). Cap fungi (toadstools) and brackets (jutting out from wood) are common fruit bodies outside. Plates (flat skins) lying on the surface are usual inside buildings, **3**. They grow where there is enough open air to disperse spores. These are like fine dust, released by the million.

Wet and dry rots

2.03 Classifying rots can be a sensitive subject with some experts. A common convention, adopted here, is to refer to *merulius lacrymans* as dry rot and other domestic fungi as wet rots. Dry rot usually but not always occurs in drier conditions than wet rot. The term 'dry', however, derives from the dessicated appearance once timber dries. Distinguishing features are cracking, spore dust, and spread and nature of *hyphae*. Fruit bodies are distinctive but need at least colour illustration, and preferably expert introduction on site.

First treatment

2.04 Whichever type of rot, the first step is to control damp and ventilation. Some preservatives have a lingering smell. Preservatives used for decay treatment are not generally the same as those used for new timber.

3 Dry rot
Characteristics

3.01 Dry rot usually attacks softwoods, though it may spread to hardwoods. Humid, unventilated places are needed for it to flourish; 95 per cent relative humidity and over 20 per cent moisture content of timber. Once established, it can affect dry timber by carrying moisture to it and depositing beads of moisture like tears (hence *lacrymans*). This noted characteristic is usually fairly limited in effect.

3.02 Rotted timber goes pale brown and develops deep cracks across the grain. The clear cut dramatic effect, **4**, may be obscured on site by grime and fungal attack, **1**. Spore dust is a rusty-red powder.

Spread

3.03 *Hyphae* combine into grey strands that can be as thick as a pencil lead. They become brittle when dried. They can carry water to dry timber in a limited way and spread through walls, often between plaster and masonry. This is unlikely to extend more than a metre or two. It does not depend on nutrient found. (A spread of 5 m has been recorded.) Dry rot may survive for a year in air dry conditions.

Treatment

3.04 Dry rot is tenacious, can spread quickly and is likely to recur if not completely treated. A specialist contractor is advised. Treatment needs to be reliable because drying out buildings may take several months. Treatment by general contractor could require the following steps:
- Stem damp and ventilate
- Cut out and burn all infected timbers including laths in ceilings, cutting back 750 mm beyond signs of rot. (Support or splice on structural timbers—see Technical study 4 Structural stability, para **4.16**)
- Vacuum out all dirt, shavings, spores, and so on
- Trace *hyphae*, stripping off plaster and raking out mortar joints
- Sterilise walls with a blow lamp, heating till wall is too hot to touch
- Where *hyphae* penetrate walls and blow lamp treatment will not reach far enough, they can be contained with a fungicidal (zinc oxychloride) render. A fairly infrequently used (and expensive) treatment is irrigation. A row of 200 mm deep holes, say 10 mm diameter, are drilled at 300 mm centres above the area of attack. Fungicide is poured into these through funnels or bottle attached to tubes until it appears in a row of similar holes below. Row spacing may vary from 250 mm to 750 mm; the smaller spacing requires less time but more labour. Irrigation will be used to protect valuable, unaffected timber, to avoid stripping off valuable plaster to trace *hyphae* or to guard against attack from neighbouring buildings.
- Apply fungicidal preservative liberally to walls to manu-

4 *Dry rot; deep cracks across the grain.*
5 *Hyphae of cellar fungus turning black.*

facturer's instructions
- Allow walls to dry out and brush off any efflorescence
- Paint all remaining timber with three full coats of proprietary preservative. Remove floorboards for painting. Check what paints will be compatible with it
- Use only pressure impregnated new timber.

Retaining infected timber

3.05 If a member is strong enough but expensive to remove, an in situ treatment by specialist contractor may be possible. This could involve drilling and feeding in preservative or applying a paste (mayonnaise) which diffuses into the timber or even simply drying out the construction.

4 Wet rot
Characteristics

4.01 The common rots are cellar fungus (*coniophora cerebella*) and various of the *poria* species. Conditions are generally (but not always) wetter than for dry rot.

4.02 *Cellar fungus*
Cellar fungus *hyphae* are thread-like, yellow at first but become brown or black, **5**. There may be little or no surface growth of fungus. Timber goes dark brown, rotting along the grain at first. Sometimes rot is internal, leaving an apparently sound surface. Later there is some cracking across the grain but cracks are shallower and closer spaced than those of developed dry rot.

4.03 *Poria*
Poria hyphae may combine as whitish threads, thicker than twine. They remain flexible when dried (dry rot goes brittle). The wood goes light brown and there is cracking across the grain which may not become as developed as dry rot.

Spread

4.04 Though dry rot *hyphae* may spread extensively, *poriae* cannot spread far beyond the dampness, and cellar fungus not at all.

Blue stain fungus

4.05 Blue stain fungi are disfiguring rather than damaging, requiring 27 per cent or more moisture content. There are blue patches, **6**.

Treatment

4.06 If you are *sure* that you have wet rot and not dry, then adequate drying, ventilating, vacuuming out and cutting out decayed timber will suffice. New timber should be pressure impregnated. Old surroundings timber should be painted with fungicidal preservative. Structural timbers can be supported as illustrated in Technical study 4 Structural stability, para **4.16** or in floors, extra sleeper walls built for joists, topped with a dpc. This allows separation of joist and wall during drying out and inhibits some structure-borne sound. Suggestions that drying out wet rot will lead to dry rot seem unfounded.

4.07 Rot, especially wet rot, may occur at junctions in window frames, **7**. Cutting out decayed timber, treating with fungicide and piecing in is usually cheaper than replacement. For slightly affected or damp joints, a proprietary injector can be used as a protective measure, **8**.

4.08 *Blue stain fungus*

Blue staining pales in time but does not disappear. Stripping off paint or varnish and painting with bleach can be effective but try in an inconspicuous place first, as the timber's colour may be changed too.

5 Insect attack

General characteristics

5.01 Insects eat timber, reducing the effective section, but do not otherwise diminish its strength. Attack can of course be extensive, **9**. Occasionally attack goes on just below the surface but usually there is bore dust around, dead beetles and exit holes. Exit holes are usually clean and sharp edged, as in the heartwood of **1** (except for weevils, see para **5.07**) so not easily confused with nail holes. Infestation sometimes dies out. Exit holes lose the sharpness of their edges and become dirty. There is usually no fresh bore dust, though old dust may be vibrated out by foot traffic. If in doubt whether attack has ceased, treat it.

Types of insect attack

5.02 Insects usually found are common furniture beetles, deathwatch beetles, Lyctus powder-post beetle, house long-horn beetle and wood boring weevils. Of these, the most frequently found are furniture and house longhorn beetles, **10**. See table 1.

6

7

6 *Blue staining of external door.*
7 *Wet rot in mullion and mullion to sill junction.*
8 *Proprietary injectors for timber installed at junction of frame.* **8a** *Frame drilled and brown injector hammered home (using white drift).*
8b *Preservative under pressure retained in joint by valve in injector. Injector end is chiselled off flush and painted over.*
9 *Tiling battens damaged by insect attack resulting in falling tiles and rain penetration.*

8a

8b

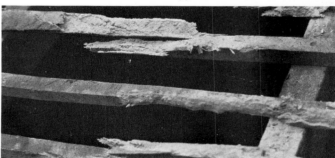

9

Table 1 Insects and their attack on timber

Insect	Colour	Sound	Wood attacked	Condition of wood	Exhit holes	Bore dust
Wood boring weevils	Red-brown to brown-black		Hard and softwoods	Decayed or very damp	Ragged edged, 1·5 to 2 mm across	Slightly gritty like fine sand
Furniture beetle	Dark brown		Sapwood of hard and softwood. Plywoods with natural glue	Dampness and incipient decay encourage attack	Circular, 1 to 2 mm diameter	Slightly gritty like fine sand
Powder-post beetle	Reddish brown		Sapwood of partly or recently seasoned hardwoods		Circular, 1 to 2 mm diameter	Fine, like talcum powder
Death watch beetle	Dark brown, sometimes mottled with lighter colour	Intermittent tapping, six to eight taps at short intervals in March-June	Old oak and other structural timbers. Occasionally spreads to adjacent softwood	Often found where moisture and lack of ventilation cause beams and other woodwork to decay	Circular, about 3 mm diameter	Gritty, like coarse sand containing bun-shaped pellets
House longhorn beetle	Black usually, sometimes brown. Head and first body segment covered with grey hair. First segment has two shiny black dots	Slight intermittent scratching sound of the large (30 mm) grubs, mostly heard in warm weather	Timber usually less than 50 years old. Seasoned softwood outside, eg fence posts. Inside, softwoods such as joinery and roof timbers	Develops quicker in warm and dry conditions. Often attacks leaving surface skin so timber may be near collapse with little external sign of attack	Oval, about 10 mm × 5 mm	Sometimes not expelled from workings. Powder and large cylindrical pellets

5.03 *House longhorn*

Sometimes no bore dust is expelled, but there may be tunnels underneath the surface not unlike the striations caused by sawing. These will collapse if probed. House longhorn is concentrated in the Surrey area but has been found in isolated attacks in a few other parts of the country. (See Building (Third Amendment) Regulations 1975, regulation B4, schedule 5 for areas at special risk. Attack has occurred elsewhere.)

Extent of attack

5.04 It is necessary to try to split away any surface that is suspected of concealing attack. There may be extensive workings behind a sound, thin surface layer. Once located, probe fairly widely. Often attacks are confined to a few timbers.

Treatments

5.05 If there is the opportunity, time treatment to precede flight of insects in spring or early summer. Replace weakened timber as necessary and burn it. A specialist contractor will generally treat by spraying (the smell of preservative tends to linger more than with brush application). Avoid creosote inside. Brushing is usually done by general contractors, though low pressure sprays will be needed if timbers are inaccessible, eg at eaves. Treatments should be preceded by vacuuming out dirt, dead beetles, and so on. The use of smokes (Information sheet 9 Insecticidal smokes) is generally confined to inaccessible timbers such as church roofs. For floors, all furniture usually has to be removed.

5.06 *Preservatives*

Use proprietary contact insecticides, eg containing chlorinated hydrocarbons. This should be at least 0.5 per cent concentration for lasting protection. Solvents are generally flammable. For furniture and exposed wood finishes use more expensive, clear, low odour treatments. Remove finish and replace soft timber such as back panels, drawer bottoms.

5.07 Preservatives are toxic so wear rubber gloves, overalls and goggles for brush application and a face mask for spraying. Check that preservatives will not react with surrounding materials. Some interact with metals. Some tar-oil preservatives stain plaster, paint, carpets (so lay on polythene) and some interact with linoleum. Some affect timber glues. Some affect pvc cable insulation. Ventilate building during and after treatment.

5.08 *Brushing*

Brush on preservative liberally to affected and surrounding timbers. Planed timber is less absorbent and should be retreated after two days. Work preservative well into all joints. Coverage is about 4 m² per litre. Where timber is inaccessible use a low pressure spray.

5.09 *Spraying*

This is usually done by specialist contractors. In floors all boards are usually removed so smell permeates wallpaper etc.

6 Further information

6.01 CP 98: 1964, Preservative treatments for constructional timber (Gr4).
Princes Risborough Technical Notes (free):
39 The house longhorn beetle
44 Decay in buildings; recognition, prevention and cure
45 The death-watch beetle
47 The common furniture beetle
BS 565: 1972 Glossary of terms relating to timber and woodwork (Gr9). (This equates decay with rot, ie decay is not taken to include insect attack.)

insect actual size   exit holes actual size   insect x3

10 *Wood boring beetles and their exit holes actual size and enlarged 3 times.* **a** *weevil,* **b** *furniture beetle,* **c** *death watch beetle,* **d** *powder-post beetle,* **e** *house longhorn beetle. Their size, shape and location should make them easily distinguishable from other domestic insects.*

7 Acknowledgement

7.01 Thanks to Princes Risborough laboratory for information supplied.

Information sheet 8
Basements and solid ground floors

There is a large variety of hot and cold applied materials and sheets that might form dpms. Unless a specialist contractor is used to apply asphalt or inject latex-siloconates, it is important to get familiar with particular products and work out details that exploit their properties (and are acceptable to local building inspectors). A party wall award or other notice to neighbours is a courtesy even where not essential.

Sample details, figures 7 (based on manufacturers' literature) 9, 10, and 14 were provided by JOHN BENSON.

1 Sources of defects

Floors
1.01 Floors are commonly of concrete or stone flags though some basements may have timber floors. Flags and concrete will not be waterproof (even where additives have been used in concrete). Hardly ever will there be a dpm. But check that floor dampness is rising damp, not condensation. Efflorescence is one sign of rising damp. Also, lay a piece of roofing felt on the floor for two days with the basement well ventilated but not intermittently heated. If the underside is damp, water is rising. Timber floors are usually decayed or vulnerable to decay even in a damp-proofed basement and it is often impossible to provide adequate floor ventilation. So timber is usually replaced by solid floors.

Walls
1.02 Walls are frequently damp from rising, and maybe, penetrating damp. Information sheet 2, 'Damp-proof courses' and Information sheet 3, 'Penetrating damp' can be used to distinguish the two. Often dampness is obvious. Check the outsides of basement walls: they may be open to the air, partially or wholly holding back earth. A basement may abut a semi-basement or no basement at all in an adjacent house. Light wells at back or front may be inadequately drained and/or built up above floor levels.

Vaults
1.03 Vaults under streets, common for Georgian houses, are usually damp. There are few services, little daylight and limited headroom. So they are often appropriate as stores, tolerating less stringent environmental conditions than for habitation.

Pipes
1.04 Service pipes may pass through walls/floors, badly fitted, allowing moisture penetration. Those fixed to surfaces or chased into them usually require repositioning on the dry side of damp treatments.

2 Selection of treatments

Improvement and conversion
2.01 Basement spaces have often been neglected or used for storage. If they are to change use, eg become habitable spaces, then damp treatments should be co-ordinated with improvement and conversion (see section 4 of the handbook). This may involve (re)moving or installing walls, openings, stairs, services, etc, and digging out floors and underpinning existing foundations.

Experimentation
2.02 Usually clients want quick, clear-cut damp-proofing. But if there is time to experiment, results may be adequate and cheap. A low U-value floor finish to inhibit condensation and adequate heating and ventilating could make a basement habitable. Ventilation alone might be enough for a store. Damp penetration could be limited by laying land drains and/or paving over adjacent soil (though effects of changing water paths are problematic in shrinkable clays). Usually though, treatments are needed at least to combat rising damp.

External treatment
2.03 As it is possible to continue floor dpms through walls there is a choice of treating walls internally or externally. Traditional external treatments may be found in slate, **1**. Now they would usually be found in asphalt. But while an outer asphalt layer is serviceable, **2**, inspectors generally want an extra protective masonry skin and the gap between masonry and asphalt grouted. So there would be the expense of running

1 *External slate damp proofing to a basement; tree root has grown under floor.*

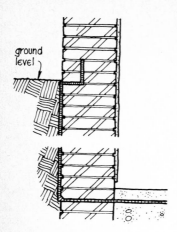

2 Two coat, 20 mm thick asphalt set into raked joints, linked with horizontal dpm through wall. Asphalt set into wall at top to avoid impact damage and by-passing by driving rain.

floor dpms through walls, digging out, shoring excavations, raking joints, asphalting, building skins, grouting and back-filling. This is an expensive treatment compared with some internal ones but has the prime advantage of not disturbing the interior. A somewhat cheaper alternative to asphalting would be to paint the wall with bitumen then render. Soil could be back-filled or a retaining wall built.

2.04 Obviously external treatments cannot be applied to party walls backed by earth or in semi-basements but they could pay off where there is a small area of external wall backed by earth, eg 1 m high. External treatments would be of similar height but internal treatments would generally need to be up to the ceiling. Since they are generally bulky a partial treatment would leave a step in the plaster finish.

2.05 Where an external wall is continuous with other buildings, beware flanking penetration. The use of external asphalt may be rendered impractical if the requirement for dpms to continue through walls as dpcs cannot be done consistently round the building. This is often not possible through party walls. If a chemical or electro-osmotic dpc is used, check with installers for asphalt-to-dpc details that do not infringe guarantees.

Water pressure and loading elements internally

2.06 Walls and floors in contact with damp earth are subject to some water pressure which could, were it great enough, disrupt waterproof linings. Though the effects of pressure tend to be over-rated this is not simple to predict with any accuracy, so common practice of inspectors' requirements are to play safe. Floors below ground require a 'loading' screed to weigh down the dpm, usually 50 mm. And asphalt wall membranes, difficult to key to masonry, especially if wet, require a separate skin of masonry set 20 mm away with the gap between grouted.

Protective layers internally

2.07 Most treatments are thick enough to produce some detailing problems at openings, services, stairs, etc. So the building of an extra masonry skin may not involve much extra disruption. Though required for asphalt it is advisable for all other wall treatments where they are liable to be punctured by following trades—plumbing, electrics, heating, etc—and by occupants' use—hanging pictures, fixing cupboards and shelving, and so on. Even with their protective layers, asphalt is more expensive. There is also the disruption of bringing a specialist contractor on site.

Latex-siliconate treatments

2.08 The injection of latex-siliconate to form dpcs and wall dpms solves several problems at once. There are no problems of negotiating openings, services, stairs etc except those normal to replastering or where pipes pass through walls. The plastered surface accepts the usual chasing and fixing from following trades and occupants' use. If only a dpc is installed,

damp in the wall is not dispersed immediately so has to dry out into the basement delaying replastering and often causing efflorescence. If walls are injected too, plastering (or rendering of a spalling surface) can be almost immediate. Specialist contractors generally require their own additive to be added to plaster or render. Latex-siliconate treatments are expensive though generally cheaper than asphalt tanking.

Tanking or drainage

2.09 The usual approach to damp-proofing is tanking (ie sealing the basement like an impervious tank). A simple though more space-consuming alternative is to allow water to penetrate through walls and to collect it, **3**. Here venting to the outside is crucial and may not be practical since there must be external walls. Many houses are deep and narrow on plan so that much of the party wall space cannot be thoroughly ventilated.

Services

2.10 Before installing damp-proofing it is advisable to relocate services that would otherwise be left on the wet side of dpms. Usually ventilation is reduced on the wet side of damp-proofing, promoting corrosion, and dpms are often difficult to patch when access is needed for maintenance, **4**.

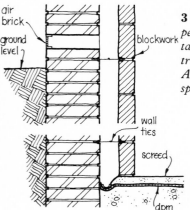

3 Gutter set around basement perimeter draining to sewer or tank for pumping (pump triggered by water level rise). Air bricks should vent damp space to outside.

4 Disruption of cork tiles on mastic asphalt. Asphalt expanded due to central heating pipe left chased into concrete slab.

3 Treatments

Damp-proofing solid floors

3.01 Where floors are at or near ground level, a loading floor (generally a screed) is not needed, the dpm can be the floor finish, generally mastic asphalt or pitch mastic. However, these are susceptible to impact damage by following trades and to indentation by heavy loads so should be laid as late as possible, just before the final finish of tiles, carpets, etc. The cost effectiveness depends very much on the costs of getting any specialist contractors on site. A group of houses, or ones where asphalters are needed for other jobs such as flat roofs are likely to be cheaper.

3.02 Mastic asphalt and pitch mastic can be laid on a well finished slab and perhaps used for evening it up a little. Two 10 mm coats should be used and the coating set into a 25 mm × 25 mm chase in the wall bonding with the dpc, **5**, or a dpc installed—see Information sheet 2, 'Damp-proof courses'. If the dpcs are installed by specialist contractors check compatibility of details with them. Where a new slab is cast (say 100 mm concrete plus 50 mm screed) the slab surface may be above existing dpc level unless the ground is dug out. Instead of digging, the dpc could be joined by the general contractor using flexible sheet dpm, **6**. Check that this dpm will bond with mastic asphalt or pitch mastic.

3.03 A compressible insulant such as glass fibre can be used though is not recommended by BRE (digest 54). Insulation board is preferable. There will be no bond of finish to concrete.

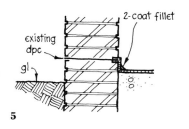

5

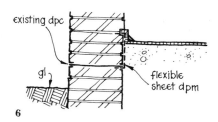

6

Screeded floor finishes

3.04 Except where an asphalt wall dpm is being used (highly effective but relatively expensive), there is little point in using asphalt as a floor dpm. There is a variety of hot and cold applied substances and sheets which can be used below a screed. Where insulation is also included, between screed and floor dpm, there is a danger of the screed cracking. Chicken wire reinforcement could be used with the screed a minimum of 65 mm thick for safety, though few problems are found without reinforcement. Where it is used it may not be very effective, depending very much on workmanship. So where a new slab is being cast it is safest to put insulation and dpm below the slab, **9**. The slab then also acts as a heat store. The main disadvantage is the long drying out time; about a month for each 25 mm.

3.05 Making laps and negotiating pipes and other projections need special care in flexible sheet dpms, **7a-e**.

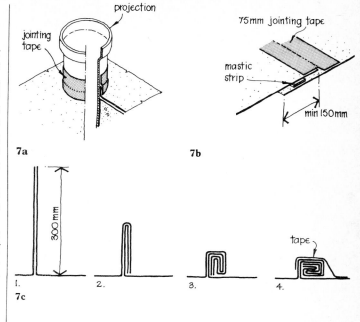

7a **7b**

7c

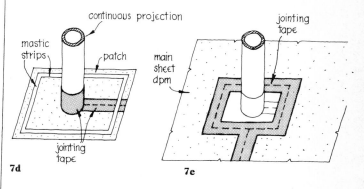

7d **7e**

5 *Fixing of finish to dpc at wall.*
6 *Flexible dpm sheet installed before laying slab to link damp proofing surface to existing dpc. An alternative is to paint the wall with a liquid dpm.*
7 *Details of proprietary clear sheet dpm. These could be adapted for heavy duty polythene.*
7a *For short projections cut a hole 50 mm less in diameter than the projection. Stretch the membrane over the top of the projection so that the membrane clings firmly to it. Press down flat to ground and seal upstand to projection with tape.*
7b *Where there is a level surface a lap can be made with mastic or mastic strip between sheets and the edge sealed with tape. Suitable for clean, dry and even conditions.*
7c *Where **7a** not suitable surface make a double welted fold. Hold down the fold with tape, sand, etc before concreting. For longer pipes and other projections use **7d** and **e**.*
7d *cut out a patch to allow 250 mm on all sides of the projection. Slit from side to centre, cut out the centre to allow 50 mm less than the diameter of the projection. Draw the patch round the projection to leave 25 mm upstand and overlap the slit. Seal slit and upstand-to-projection joint with tape. Apply mastic or mastic strip 50 mm from edge of patch.*
7e *Slit and tailor-make the sheet to overlap mastic by 100 mm. Make slit in different direction to slit in patch below. Press sheet onto mastic and seal edge and slit with tape.*

Slated walls

3.06 Slates can be refixed individually as found either externally, **1**, or internally, often laid to courses, in two layers, **8**. Or slates may be found nailed and mortared to laps as for roofs. Individual slates can be rebedded or the whole surface remade if the slates are in good condition and this is acceptable to the local inspector. It is too expensive to buy new and labour intensive. To fix slates, soak thoroughly, preferably overnight and lay in a strong mix, say 2 cement: 1 lime: 9 sand.

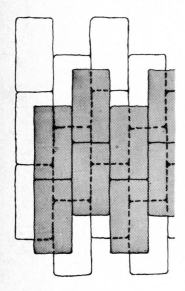

8 Pattern of laying slates to courses in two layers, with joints between layers staggered. Course may be horizontal or vertical.

Asphalt tanking

3.07 Asphalt is less used than it was, due to cost and the variety of effective substitutes that are now available for general contractors to install. Where asphalt is used plaster should be removed from walls and mortar joints raked out 25 mm. Asphalt will be continuous over floor and walls making a fillet in two coats at angles. If there is high water pressure from a high water table three 10 mm coats should be used on walls otherwise use two 10 mm coats overall. Joints should be staggered while spreading. A separate wall should be built 20 mm from the asphalt wall and a liquid grout mix (eg 1 cement: 3 sand) poured in the gap after every few courses have been constructed. If walls are 2·5-3·0 m high then bonding the new skin to the old wall will be needed. Before asphalting, cavities should be cut out of the existing wall large enough for the ends of stretchers to be mortared in after asphalting.

Other membrane methods of tanking

3.08 A variety of proprietary membranes for floors and walls are available. Since floor and walls are generally fixed conveniently in separable operations, there is no particular reason for using the same membrane for wall and floor. As a matter of convenience it is easy to use sheets for floors since they can be walked on during fixing and to use liquids for walls since they are easy to apply and do not have problems of support as do sheets. **9** and **10** are details of tanking in this way with **9** the minimum damp-proofing required and **10** incorporating an inner skin to protect against dpm puncture by following trades and occupants.

Latex-siliconates

3.09 These can be pressure-injected by specialist contractors to form dpcs and wall dpms. Any floor damp-proofing might be appropriate; check that it will not invalidate a guarantee given. All plaster will need removal at least inside external walls and holes will be drilled at say 100 mm centres, depending on the specialist contractor. Drilling at junctions of internal and external walls plus dpcs will usually be enough to isolate internal walls. Injection at corners inhibits flanking penetration from adjoining houses and from garden walls abutting

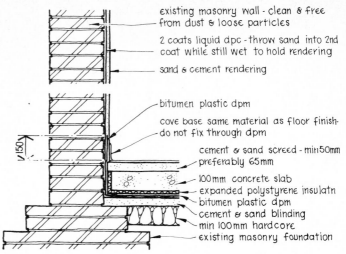

existing masonry wall - clean & free from dust & loose particles
2 coats liquid dpc - throw sand into 2nd coat while still wet to hold rendering
sand & cement rendering

bitumen plastic dpm
cove base same material as floor finish - do not fix through dpm
cement & sand screed - min 50mm preferably 65mm
100mm concrete slab
expanded polystyrene insulatn
bitumen plastic dpm
cement & sand blinding
min 100mm hardcore
existing masonry foundation

9 Tanking with dpm and insulation below slab. Blinding must protect dpm from puncture by hardcore. Proprietary liquid dpm to wall to manufacturer's instructions.

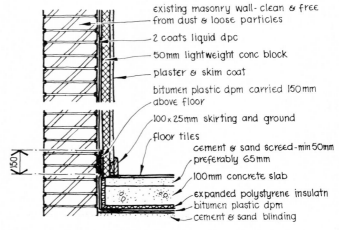

existing masonry wall - clean & free from dust & loose particles
2 coats liquid dpc
50mm lightweight conc block
plaster & skim coat
bitumen plastic dpm carried 150mm above floor
100 x 25mm skirting and ground
floor tiles
cement & sand screed - min 50mm preferably 65mm
100mm concrete slab
expanded polystyrene insulatn
bitumen plastic dpm
cement & sand blinding

10 Internal skin instead of render of 9 to protect dpm from puncture by following trades or occupants.

11 Plaster applied in two coats may be no thicker than existing plaster.

basements. Plaster (or render if the wall surface is crumbled) can be applied without delay; drying is rapid as pressure impregnation forces out water. There is an attendant danger that this brick-coloured water will be forced into an adjoining basement, staining plaster.

Pitch impregnated corrugated fibre
3.10 Being corrugated, pitch-impregnated sheet provides a good key for plaster, **11**, though it is not resistant to puncture by following trades or occupants. Fixing is recommended to give ventilation at top and bottom, though this is rarely done (either it is missed out or carpet often blocks the bottom, **12**). And it is not apparently very important since few other damp-proof treatments do this. The circulation of damp air is hardly beneficial to health and may leave a damp smell. (However, these are manufacturer's instructions and may be insisted upon by building inspectors.) But it is important to lead a floor membrane up the wall behind the fibre sheet to provide a 150 mm lap. If only a floor dpm and dpc are needed, corrugated sheet provides a base for plastering before the walls have dried (so ventilate). Corrugated fibre sheet is useful for keying plaster over large irregularities, **13**, though where a latex-siliconate has been used, expanded metal is more reliable. In this case an additive will help inhibit passage of salts to the surface of the plaster.

Renders
3.11 Renders with waterproof additives may be effective but are not always acceptable to inspectors. Treatment tends to be expensive. Check that specialist contractors offer guarantees.

Vaults
3.12 Vaults are usually unserviced, damp and lack headroom. So making them habitable will require damp-proofing, underpinning and permanent artificial lighting. The detail, **14**, is for damp-proofing and underpinning. The upper part of the detail, for vaulted roof and wall dpm, could be linked with a conventional floor dpm (**3.01-3.04**) where underpinning was not carried out. This detail assumes that vaults run only under pavements which can be taken up to put a screed and dpm over vaults. Where vaults run under roads an internal dpm will be needed, more resistant to water pressure, such as bitumen paint and render or asphalt.

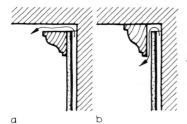

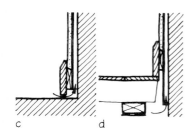

12 *Manufacturer's advice for venting at top **a**, **b** using coves; **c** ventilation for solid floors is often blocked by carpets; **d** for timber floors ventilation is more fail-safe.*

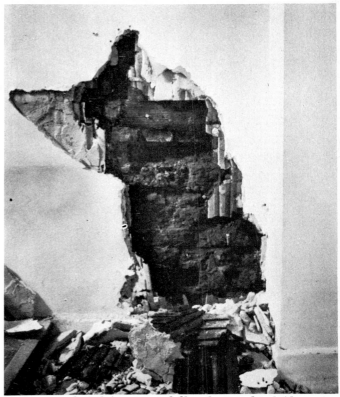

13 *Corrugated pitch impregnated fibre sheet used to bridge large losses in a brick wall before plastering: here cut away for inspection. The plaster is damp through flanking penetration from cross-wall to the left and possibly from poor detailing of floor-to-wall junction.*

14 *Detail of vault providing damp-proofing, involving opening up from pavement above. Underpinning is to provide adequate headroom for habitation.**

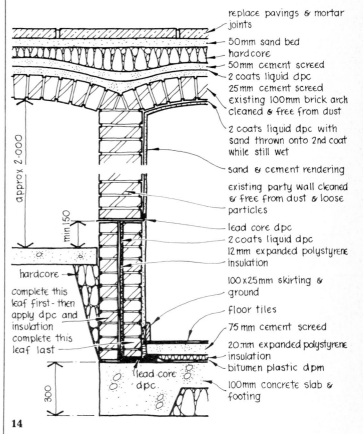

replace pavings & mortar joints
50mm sand bed
hardcore
50mm cement screed
2 coats liquid dpc
25mm cement screed
existing 100mm brick arch cleaned & free from dust
2 coats liquid dpc with sand thrown onto 2nd coat while still wet
sand & cement rendering
existing party wall cleaned & free from dust & loose particles
lead core dpc
2 coats liquid dpc
12mm expanded polystyrene insulation
100x25mm skirting & ground
floor tiles
75 mm cement screed
20mm expanded polystyrene insulation
bitumen plastic dpm
100mm concrete slab & footing

approx 2·000
min 150
300

hardcore
complete this leaf first - then apply dpc and insulation complete this leaf last
lead core dpc

14

* Notes to detail: underpin in sections maximum 900 mm. Slab, wall and footing all to be built in sections. It is essential that liquid dpm and lead core dpc be lapped and sealed. In some situations it may be possible to build the outer half of the wall only as underpinning. Then all dpcs could be installed continuously and finally the remaining leaf of the wall built. Check with local inspector.

Manholes

3.13 Where manholes are required inside buildings there must be a double cover and continuity of damp-proofing. **15** and **16** are details for solid and suspended timber floors. Some simplification could be achieved by bringing the cover to floor level though the edge strip would show or be uneven below floor coverings. For timber floors where joists are strong enough the manhole might be stopped below joists and the opening made self-supporting by trimming (cf at fireplaces).

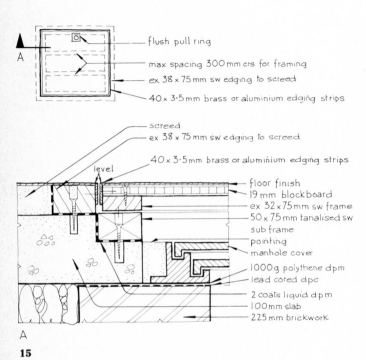

- flush pull ring
- max spacing 300 mm crs for framing
- ex 38 x 75 mm sw edging to screed
- 40 x 3.5 mm brass or aluminium edging strips

- screed
- ex 38 x 75 mm sw edging to screed
- 40 x 3.5 mm brass or aluminium edging strips

level
- floor finish
- 19 mm blockboard
- ex 32 x 75 mm sw frame
- 50 x 75 mm tanalised sw sub frame
- pointing
- manhole cover
- 1000g polythene dpm
- lead cored dpc
- 2 coats liquid dpm
- 100 mm slab
- 225 mm brickwork

A

15

15 *Manhole detail for casting integrally with new slab.*
16 *Manhole detail for suspended timber floor. A cheaper alternative where floor joists are strong enough would be to stop the manhole below joists and trim round the opening.*
Details 15 and 16 were produced by Levitt Bernstein Associates and Anthony Richardson & Partners.

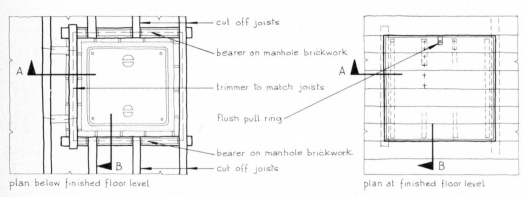

- cut off joists
- bearer on manhole brickwork
- trimmer to match joists
- flush pull ring
- bearer on manhole brickwork
- cut off joists

plan below finished floor level   plan at finished floor level

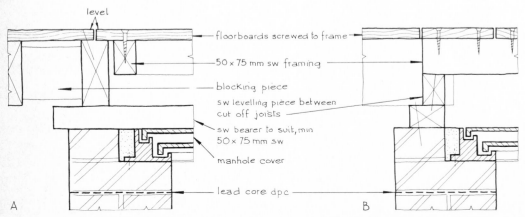

level
- floorboards screwed to frame
- 50 x 75 mm sw framing
- blocking piece
- sw levelling piece between cut off joists
- sw bearer to suit, min 50 x 75 mm sw
- manhole cover
- lead core dpc

A   B

16

Information sheet 9
Insecticidal smokes and vapours

Smokes and vapours may be cheap alternatives to application of liquid insecticides in open timbered spaces. Vapours are generally used in domestic roofs for furniture beetle (and maybe powder post beetle —see 1.03). Smokes are used in large spaces with inaccessible timbers—commonly churches and other historic buildings—for death watch beetle.
Both treatments kill emerging beetles, not larvae (grubs), so take several annual doses. For rot treatments—see information sheet 7 Timber decay. Information on Smokes was provided by G. R. Coleman of Princes Risborough Laboratory.

1 Insecticidal vapour

Selection

1.01 Dichlorvos vapour is released in a controlled way by being embedded in insecticidal plastic strips. Strips can be hung in domestic roofs (or other small timbered spaces) in May/June and replaced each year for five years. However, clients often prefer the secure feeling of direct treatment giving immediate results, and of course there is no written guarantee with vapour treatment.

1.02 Insecticide is released in minute concentrations over at least three months to kill emerging beetles. So roofs must be fairly well sealed to maintain concentration, eg felted, boarded or thoroughly torched tiles. Slating/tiling directly on battens is not suitable. Nor are markedly damp, usually fungus infected spaces, as strips break down too quickly. Insect attacks are usually localised, but if widespread and voracious, direct treatment is advised—see Information sheet 7 Timber decay, especially para **3.05** for specialist methods.

1.03 Strips have been tested for common furniture beetle (woodworm). They would probably also be effective for powder post beetles, but not for house longhorn. Nor are they likely to work in the customary open locations of death watch beetle or the damp conditions where weevils are usually found.

Treatment

1.04 Generally one strip is required per 28 m³ of roof space (check manufacturer's instructions). Strips should be hung freely fairly high up at about 3 m centres. Used as recommended, dichlorvos vapour does not contaminate water in storage tanks, but they could be covered.

2 Insecticidal smokes

Selection

2.01 Killing death watch beetles with smokes is useful because they are often found high up in inaccessible timbers (usually oak) of historic buildings. Though treatment can be done from the ground, inspection involves reaching timbers. Smokes are effective up to at least 10 m. Smokes are cheap and do not significantly disfigure surfaces but the disruption of building use by treatment annually for 10 years makes them applicable only to a limited range of buildings. In roof spaces over ceilings and other high spaces, cleansing after smoking will rarely be needed, but will be necessary for walls, floors and furniture that people may touch. (Smokes have been found less successful for treating common furniture beetle.)

Treatment

2.02 *Inspection*
Carefully inspect the structural condition of timbers, especially those embedded in masonry or otherwise inaccessible to smokes. Where timber is inaccessible to smokes use liquid treatments—see Information sheet 7 Timber decay. Whether it is worth treating all timbers directly or mixing liquid and smoke treatments depends on what proportion can be smoked and how easy it is for operatives to get at it. Replace structurally unsound timbers with treated ones.

2.03 Exit holes may stay clean for a few years in some buildings. Bore dust may be shaken out by foot traffic or the impact of ladders. So it is difficult to be sure of the state of attack. To check that attack is lessening, a 'beetle census' can be carried out before and after treatments. This consists of weekly collecting, counting and mapping of beetles that drop from the roof throughout the emergence period—late March to early June. A thorough search is required, paying special attention to undersides of carpets and rugs, hassocks in churches, and so on. Carry out treatment in late March, **1**.

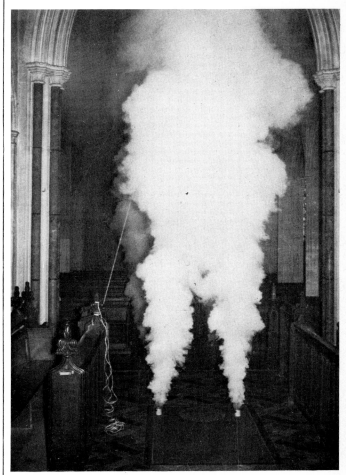

1 *Smoke treatment for death watch beetle, released in a church nave and choir at the beginning of the emergence period in late March or early April.*

2.04 *Mapping*
Beetles fall almost vertically from timbers and then move little, so positions can be plotted on a plan after each collection. After the emergence period the plan will indicate beetle distribution and activity, aiding decisions on treatment for the following year.

2.05 *Precaution*
Fire services and police should be notified because some smoke leakage may be mistaken for a fire by passers-by.

2.06 *Insecticides*
Insecticides, in pellets or canisters, are combined with an oxygen generator and fuel. Insecticides are vapourised during combustion then condense into a dense smoke. Gamma HCH is usually used. Some products also contain Dieldrin which is potentially hazardous to health and is better avoided. An HCH-Dieldrin composite should only be used in unfrequented spaces.

2.07 *Environmental conditions*
The following conditions contribute to an efficient treatment (the first is the most critical):
● Reasonable sealing to prevent draughts
● Still weather
● Cool conditions within the building, preferably not over 15°C.
● Absence of marked temperature gradient, rising from floor to ceiling, which would tend to check the ascent of warm smoke columns. So treatment of roof timbers is best carried out early in the day.

2.08 *Application*
Follow the manufacturer's instructions carefully (but ensuring the following dosage is achieved). If in doubt contact Princes Risborough Laboratory (Princes Risborough, Aylesbury, Bucks, 08444 3101). Use 1 g of gamma HCH per 7·5 m³ of space. Usually 20 g canisters are used except where more than 30 are required, then use larger ones. Operators cannot ignite more than 30 canisters safely before retiring from the building.
2.09 After ignition, the building must be vacated and locked. Post notices at all entrances that a toxic insecticidal treatment is in progress. After 24 hours open up and allow the building to ventilate for three hours before entering. Anything that people may touch—floors, walls, furniture—must be washed, changing water frequently. Then dust with a dry cloth. Cleaners should wear overalls, rubber gloves and simple face masks. It is essential to wash thoroughly afterwards.

2.10 *Monitoring success*
A successful series of treatments will show a steady continuing decline of emerging beetles at each beetle census after the second or third year of treatment.

3 Further information

3.01 Princes Risborough Laboratory technical notes (free): 7 Insecticidal smokes for control of wood boring insects. Several details of practice and effectiveness outlined in this note (1975 revision) are superseded by information in this sheet.
58 Woodworm control in domestic roofs by dichlorous vapour.

2

3

2 *Inaccessible timbers often lack regular maintenance. There may be advanced fungal as well as insect attack.*
3 *For death watch beetle, more common in conservation than rehabilitation, expensive routine inspection forestalls such much more expensive repair.*
4 *Death watch beetle actual size with exit holes, and enlarged three times.*

4

Section three: Case Studies

Introduction

This third section of The Housing Rehabilitation Handbook, shows projects as a whole, exemplifying a variety of approaches. The purposes of case studies are outlined below followed by an introduction to the first study of ASSIST, a community based design practice.

1 Case studies

1.01 Rehabilitation requires a close integration of the constructional and the organisational very different from that of designing new housing. There are changed constraints and opportunities when starting with existing, often delapidated, buildings that may have been poorly designed. Often relatively little time is spent at the drawing board. But much greater time and familiarity with the site is needed. Contractors are generally much smaller—down to one man, a barrow and a dog. Architects starting in rehabilitation will have little appropriate documentation among what they have built up for new work. And so on.

1.02 The case studies take rehabilitation as a whole, from inception to completion, illustrating this characteristic makeup of rehabilitation jobs. And they provide a context for the later sections of the handbook, 4 Improvements and conversions, and 5 Administration. The studies were chosen partly to provide an overview of housing rehabilitation and partly to show schemes and ideas which span several sections of the handbook.

1.03 Studies show the running of jobs with their design, documentation, costing, etc. Community based housing associations, organisations that will be new to many architects, are introduced. One study deals with a problem neglected by nearly all associations and local authorities, and by government too—rehabilitation for the disabled. Studies incorporate various strategies for rehabilitation. In this respect three articles from previous AJs are especially relevant:

● Gradual renewal, AJ 5.2.75 pp275-278 (see also Astragal AJ 19.2.75 p383).

● Lash up in Camden, AJ 23.4.75 pp865-868.
● Macclesfield: the self-help GIA, AJ 12.11.75 pp995-1002.
The first study is of ASSIST in Glasgow.

1.04 Perhaps it is inevitable that architects rehabilitating houses will be more involved with users than they would be in new schemes. Landlords, owner-occupiers and tenants are often known at inception. Indeed work may be done with occupiers resident, though this is more common in interwar dwellings. However, there is a big difference between the architect tacitly accepting this involvement and positively making it an occasion to bring people more fully into design.

1.05 ASSIST is a community based design practice in Glasgow which serves as one model for involving people in their own housing. Without in any way denigrating Rod Hackney's design philosophy in Macclesfield, it is significantly different from ASSIST's more generally applicable approach. ASSIST is a viable practice with a long term commitment to making control of the housing process accessible to the housed. Rehabilitation is a way of promoting this. Significantly the ASSIST case study begins at a stage in project planning before areas have been designated for rehabilitation; a stage usually the province solely of housing management.

1.06 The first part of the ASSIST case study sets out the opportunities and problems of a community based approach to rehabilitation. The second part illustrates in detail how ASSIST is involved in this in Glasgow. The third part deals with the practicalities of rehabilitating tenement buildings. This latter is not of such specialist interest as it may seem. There are general lessons to be drawn, eg about multi-occupied dwellings, very tight planning, organising work on site and by inference, the rehabilitation of interwar flats.

Area of multiple stress: what is the architects' role?

Case study 1: ASSIST, a basis for tenement improvement in Scotland

ASSIST works in a context of interrelated organisations: Glasgow District, Housing Corporation and several community based housing associations. This first part of the case study describes the opportunities ASSIST have found and created for a community based approach to rehabilitation.

1 Improving tenement housing

Organising improvement

1.01 This case study focuses on the rehabilitation of Scotland's, and in particular Glasgow's, tenement housing. It is estimated that there are about 160 000 substandard houses in Scotland; the largest single concentration occurring in Glasgow where there are approximately 50 000, almost all in tenement properties. (The figures for other towns are: Dundee 10 000; Aberdeen 8500; Renfrew including Paisley 6000; Edinburgh 5500), **1**.

1.02 The majority of Glasgow's tenements were constructed in a massive burst of building which threw up a ring of working class housing around the city centre at about the turn of the century. The local authority are now promoting a programme of improvements covering about half of the 50 000 substandard houses in the private sector. The remainder are to be demolished. The programme is being implemented on the ground by nineteen community based housing associations which have been formed in areas such as Govan, Govanhill, Dennistoun, Tollcross, Shettleston, Springburn, Maryhill, Partick and Linthouse. The housing assocations receive support from the Housing Corporation, which has set up an office in Glasgow with the broad aim of improving housing conditions generally in the tenement areas of the city.

ASSIST's role

1.03 ASSIST is a unit of the Department of Architecture and Building Science at the University of Strathclyde. The unit was formed in 1972 as an action-research project to examine the feasibility of the voluntary improvement of Glasgow's tenement housing. After an initial assessment, the project concluded that, despite all the problems facing low income owners living in tenements, voluntary improvement was possible and preferable to the then Glasgow Corporation's policy of improvement by compulsory purchase. But a voluntary approach implied:
• A reappraisal of the roles played by residents and the local authority. This involved the creation of community organisations to manage the improvement programme on the ground.
• Such community organisations required locally based technical and administration services.
• The technical problems of improving multi-storey tenements, and associated problems of cost, required innovative architectural solutions.
ASSIST set out to prove these points resulting in the rehabilitation of 200 houses and the rebuilding of the back-court in a tenement block in Govan (see AJ 10.1.73 pp60-62).

Locally based improvement

1.04 The Unit's first local office, a converted bicycle shop in Govan Road, closed in 1976. ASSIST now operates in a number of areas in Glasgow, working in local premises from which it provides a variety of services, both to community based housing associations in the area, and direct to local residents. ASSIST has also carried out a 2-year study in

Ferguslie Park, Paisley, a huge and largely dilapidated area of inter-war housing, in conjunction with the only Scottish Community Development Project and Renfrew District Council.

Other projects

1.05 ASSIST's staple diet has always been house improvements. However, other schemes have also been carried out by the various offices. These include small projects such as colour schemes for pre-school playgroups and the conversion of shops or ground floor tower block units into community information centres. Larger projects include many backcourt environmental improvement schemes, work for Glasgow Free School, a feasibility study for the Dixon Halls Old Peoples Day Centre, and the conversion of temporary school classrooms into a Community Centre financed by the Job Creation Scheme. ASSIST's first new build project, amenity housing on an infill tenement corner site, is at the design stage.

ASSIST's finance

1.06 ASSIST's main income derives from architectural fees. Any surplus, after salaries and overheads, is put into research or used for non-fee earning work for community groups. The other source of income is from specific research projects. Recent and current projects include the computerisation of ASSIST's Tenement Improvement Procedures sponsored by the Scottish Development Department and a reappraisal of plumbing and other services in relation to house improvements. ASSIST also runs community design and housing courses at the University of Strathclyde. The Unit normally has between 15 and 20 members (with various architectural, planning, sociological, administrative and other backgrounds) who run the project on a fairly co-operative basis; no mean feat considering the dispersed nature of the small organisation.

1 *Glasgow inner city tenements. They are usually built up to the pavement. Flats, of few rooms, may be in any tenure: local authority, privately rented or owner occupied.*

Community based housing associations

1.07 As part of the original project's work in Govan, Glasgow's first community based housing association was formed. Central Govan Housing Association was set up to purchase from landlords and other owners who did not wish to improve their property and so could have stood in the way of the rehabilitation scheme, unless they were bought out. ASSIST ran Central Govan Housing Association on a shoe string on behalf of a management committee composed of people who lived or worked in Govan (see **2.08** for further details of associations).

1.08 The Housing Corporation took the example of Central Govan Housing Association, and came up with a solution to the problem of improving Glasgow's tenement housing on a city wide scale. Community based housing associations have now been set up throughout Glasgow not only to act as purchasing agents, but also to provide the administrative and technical services which ASSIST brought to Govan. The new community based associations are well financed. Coordination of the programme is largely handled by development officers employed by the associations. Technical functions, such as architectural and quantity surveying services, are at present supplied by outside consultants. ASSIST is unusual in that it can not only provide technical and administrative services if required but also prefers to work locally.

1.09 The improvement agencies, the community based housing associations, are answerable, through their members and elected management committees, to the areas in which they operate. Glasgow District maintains control of the overall programme by designating Housing Action Areas (HAAs), but the responsibility for implementation has passed to the community based housing associations who are supported financially and in many other ways by the Housing Corporation's Glasgow office.

Technical problems
Standards

1.10 Tenements are sometimes three storey properties, but generally four with a common entrance (the close) leading through to the backcourt passing the bottom of the internal stair, **2**. There are two or three houses (flats in English parlance) per floor. While apartment sizes can be reasonably generous the average number of apartments is small except in the better off districts of the city where the well appointed houses are graceful and spacious. But, in areas such as Govan, the majority of the houses have only two or, at the most, three apartments, **3a, b**.

1.11 Cooking facilities are meagre and are confined to a small scullery, **4**, or are located in the kitchen which doubles as a living room and, often, as a bedroom. Storage is minimal. Toilets are situated within the house, sometimes venting over the sculleries, or are located off the stair where they can be shared by the houses on each landing. In the latter circumstance, it is not unusual for up to twenty people to be sharing one toilet. Hot water, if any, comes from geysers. There are few bathrooms but some ingenious attempts have been made to install showers. The front street facades of grey or red sandstone are impressive, in contrast with the backcourts which are often in appalling condition, **5, 6**.

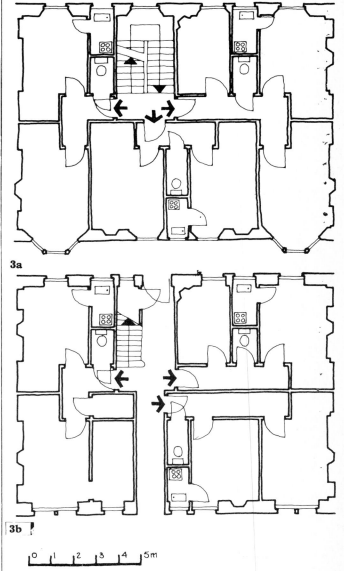

3a

3b

3a *Upper and* **b** *ground floor of Glasgow tenement. Tenement plans are mostly similar. There are few apartments (rooms) per house. The scullery is little larger than a cupboard (see also* **4**). *There is a bed recess (about* $1 \cdot 8 \times 1 \cdot 2$ *m) at the back of each apartment.*

2 *A close entrance in Govan. Its upkeep is shared by all owners.*

4 *Existing scullery photographed from doorway. Plans* **3a, b** *give a clearer idea of size.*

5 *Front facades can be impressive in an appropriate setting.*

6 *A no-man's land of backcourts.*

1.12 The local authority has a statutory duty to deal with substandard properties, either by demolition or improvement. In Scotland the measure of fitness is the Tolerable Standard as set out in the Housing (Scotland) Act 1974, S14. A house is said to meet the Tolerable Standard if it:

(a) is structurally stable

(b) is substantially free from rising or penetrating damp

(c) has satisfactory provision for natural and artificial lighting, for ventilation and heating

(d) has an adequate piped supply of wholesome water available within the house

(e) has a sink provided with a satisfactory supply of both hot and cold water within the house

(f) has a water closet available for the exclusive use of the occupants of the house and suitably located within the house

(g) has an effective system for drainage and disposal of foul and surface water

(h) has satisfactory facilities for the cooking of food within the house

(i) has satisfactory access to all external doors and out-buildings.

1.13 It will be noted that the Tolerable Standard does not include a bathroom. However, where a HAA is declared for a life of more than 10 years, S16 specifies that houses:

(a) shall meet the tolerable standard

(b) shall be in a good state of repair having regard to the age, character and locality of the houses and, where the houses have a future life of not less than 10 years, the local authority may specify that all the houses be provided with the standard amenities which include a bath, or shower, with hot and cold running water.

National problems

1.14 Measured against the above criteria, the scale of the problem in Scotland is monumental. About 10 per cent of the total housing stock is substandard and local authorities individually estimate that more than 100 000 houses need to be improved. Central government's response to the problem is embodied in the Housing (Scotland) Act 1969 and the Housing (Scotland) Act 1974. The 1969 legislation introduced the concept of Housing Treatment Areas for Improvement—designated areas of all types of properties where the owners were obliged to improve their houses under the threat of compulsory purchase.

1.15 In the period 1969-74 approximately 140 Treatment Areas were declared throughout Scotland covering about 8000 houses. Probably less than 1000 were subsequently improved. The main bulk of house improvements during this period were individual house improvements carried out with the aid of 75 per cent grants (which at that time were available throughout Scotland). There is evidence that many of these grants were given to better off owners to carry out fairly incidental improvements such as rewiring and upgrading existing facilities in their villas rather than to worse off owners for more fundamental improvements such as installing an inside toilet or bath in their tenement houses.

1.16 The Housing (Scotland) Act 1974 attempted to redirect resources into improvement of tenements by allowing 75-90 per cent grants to be made available only to owners living in the new Housing Action Areas for Improvement, similar to the old Treatment Areas for Improvement (with only 50 per cent grants available elsewhere in Scotland). Why spontaneous improvements should occur in HAAs simply because house improvement grants are restricted elsewhere is difficult to understand. So it is hardly surprising that not only has there been little improvement in HAAs but improvement grants elsewhere have slumped. Even in Glasgow, the well organised programme of improvements is overshadowed by the sheer size of the city's problems.

Tenement problems

1.17 Local authorities are now obliged to publicise their intentions and consult residents in HAAs where there are some cash incentives to improve property. However, residents, particularly low income owner occupiers who, along with the landlords, are expected to carry out the work, are in no better position than they were in the old Treatment Areas for Improvement. They still live in tenement houses and therein lies the main problem. By and large terraced houses, which predominate in England and Wales, can be improved independently without disturbing adjacent houses or other occupants. This is not possible in tenement properties where each house is stacked one above the other and all the houses share the same foundation, roof, stairs, external walls and plumbing.

1.18 There is little space for the installation of a bathroom in a tenement house. Cost limitations and the problems of restricting daylight preclude the construction of rear extensions. Normally the best location for a new bathroom is in a bed recess (approx $1 \cdot 8 \times 1 \cdot 2$ m) at the back of each apartment (originally double beds were built into the bed recesses and were curtained off from the main living area), **3b, 7**. In this way it is possible to avoid encroaching overmuch on the main living spaces, or taking up valuable space adjacent to windows which could be better used for kitchenette improvements. Bathrooms are therefore internal and require artificial ventilation. Sanitary inspectors are reluctant to see long runs to waste pipes on the face of the building and prefer artificial ventilation to discharge above roof level rather than on the face of the building near to kitchenette windows.

1.19 There is also little space for new cold water storage and associated hot water cylinders within each tenement house.

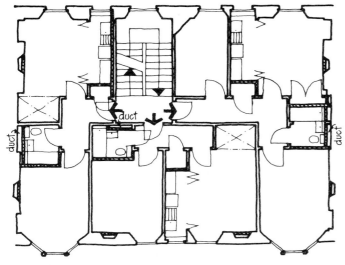

7 *Improvement to upper floor houses (compare similar existing houses, 3b). Toilet and scullery spaces are combined as a kitchenette behind folding screen, with store cupboard opening onto hallway. Bed recesses are used for bathrooms. New half hour fire check doors with georgian wired glass fanlights face staircase.*

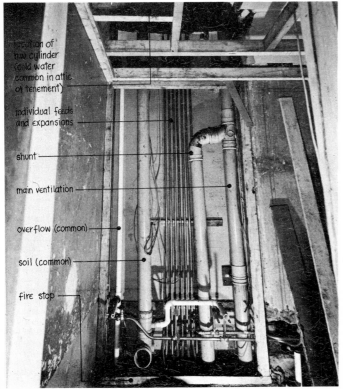

8 *Internal duct providing shared services to houses.*

An alternative is to locate common water storage in the roof space which in turn introduces the problem of long runs of expansion and feed pipes. Whichever solution is adopted, in most cases it will be necessary to install a duct at the back of each bathroom with vents above roof level and connections to the drain in the street. Most significantly, it has to pass through each house in the relevant stack of bathrooms.

1.20 If the waste pipes for internal bathrooms are located on the face of the building there are difficulties of locating rising mains and providing satisfactory ventilation, as well as the obvious problem of backventing the soil stack. These problems are rarely if ever solved by locating the bathroom near to the external wall, adjacent to the stack on the face of the building, because of the associated problem of restricting daylight which is at a premium to the rest of the inside of these narrow fronted houses.

1.21 Therefore the solutions that have usually been adopted to date are internal stacks of bathrooms with a complete tenement of up to 12 houses (2 or 3 stacks) being improved together. In this way the owners share the cost of the pipes and all the residents are inconvenienced at the same time and for as short a time as possible (about 10 to 12 weeks), **8**. An alternative incremental approach has been suggested which would involve a three-stage operation:

- Common repair work: roofs, external walls, gutters etc
- Common improvements: new plumbing stacks, close doors etc
- Internal repairs and improvements: individual bathroom, kitchens etc

This would allow individual owners to improve their houses in their own time. Such an approach, however, raises the problem of initial investment in repairs and services and could lead to more inconvenience to the residents who might have to put up with building operations spread over a number of years.

Social issues

Shared technical problems

1.22 The main problem in improving tenements is to persuade residents as a group to agree to a technical solution that is already limited by house planning and plumbing constraints. Tenements are usually of mixed ownership, containing both owner-occupied and tenanted houses, the latter owned by a multiplicity of trusts and landlords, some more absent than others. Furthermore, while the ownership of the separate houses is vested with the individual owner occupiers and landlords, the common parts (the roof, stair, close, foundation, fabric of the property, and backcourt) are owned jointly by all the proprietors. Tenement law can be complex. A system of property management (factoring) has developed whereby the factors, paid by the owners, manage the properties, including collecting rent and organising repairs, on behalf of all the interested parties. As this has not usually been successful there has been a general lack of maintenance.

Conflicting aims

1.23 As would be expected, the interests of the owner occupier are different to those of the landlord. The owner occupier may weigh up the decision to improve in terms of secure investment. The landlord is worried about investment too but is also more immediately concerned about return in terms of rent after improvement—and rent level obviously concerns tenants, though from a different point of view. The tenant will consider whether he or she is getting value for money; the landlord will be hoping for maximum return, from minimum outlay, within the constraints of the Rent Acts.

1.24 Apart from different financial priorities it is possible to identify other housing matters which influence residents' views of house improvement and are a product of cultural influences, family circumstances, and tenure preferences. Glasgow has the highest proportion of municipal housing of any city in Britain. The great majority of residents in substandard houses see a council house as desirable, but at the same time usually want to remain in the same area of the city. The relatively few, good-quality, inner area council houses are highly sought after, and a rehabilitated tenement is, therefore, often an attractive and more easily available alternative.

1.25 Many owner occupiers, particularly young families, are forced into buying a tenement house as they do not have the right qualifications for a local authority house. Owner occupiers in this group would prefer to sell their houses and, if necessary, rent them back improved rather than improve it themselves if they were not able to obtain a corporation house of their choice. Like tenants generally, they wish to see the rented house improved to the highest possible standard, including the provision of additional space.

1.26 Some owner occupiers wish to remain owners. The standard of improvements they like to see depends on the cost of the work in relation to their own financial commitments. Most owner occupiers in this group at present find it difficult to pay for anything but the most basic schemes and would be very reluctant to see any existing partial improvements they have already made removed as part of a more comprehensive improvement scheme. It should be appreciated that very few tenement houses still contain the original range, gas lighting and distempered walls. Showers have been squeezed into toilets, cupboards built into bed recesses, and polystyrene tiles stuck to the ceiling. Few of these improvements have been grant aided. Residents are obviously reluctant to see their houses disturbed unless they think the end product worth the money and feel that they have the ability to pay, either as tenants paying increased rent and rates or as owner occupiers paying off home loans (after grant) and rates increases.

A chance to move

1.27 Other owner occupiers will wish to sell their present house and buy a house in another area. A few households will be uncertain as to the exact timing of the move. They may be weighing up decisions about schools, job opportunities, pay and so on. These owners would prefer to sell, banking the proceeds of the sale, and rent their present house, improved or unimproved, until they have seen a suitable alternative. Finally, a small group of owner occupiers will wish to move immediately. They will not be interested in improving their present house but will want to find someone to buy their house soon. This will be difficult as prospective buyers may be put off by the improvement proposals, hence the need for early establishment of a local agency (the community based housing associ-

ation) willing to purchase, and improve, from owners who wish to sell, **10**.

Intervention by housing associations

1.28 As can be seen, many owner occupiers want to sell their houses whether or not they decide to stay in or leave the area in which they presently live. There is a danger that the purchasing activities of housing associations will seriously reduce the stock of low income owner occupied housing. By purchasing now from the owner occupiers, individual housing associations may solve particular local problems but, taken together, may create other city wide problems unless they themselves undertake to house those groups of people, such as young couples, who were forced into becoming owner occupiers in the first place.

1.29 At present, most community based associations require all their empty houses to provide temporary accommodation for their own tenants during improvements, and are not able to open housing lists. Even when houses are available for rent, associations are likely to be constrained by nomination agreement with the local authority as to who the tenants shall be. Thus there may be a case for setting up community estate agencies which would put sellers in touch with buyers in HAAs thereby maintaining the stock of low income owner-occupied houses in the city.

1.30 Landlords as a group do not need to be protected in quite the same way as low income owner-occupiers. Most landlords would prefer to sell, and community based housing associations are willing buyers. What cannot be ignored are the rights and aspirations of the tenants. It is often claimed that tenants are rarely interested in their own housing. But the reason for this alleged apathy may be that in the past tenants have been stripped of fundamental rights. The only way to restore confidence is by involving tenants in improvement work right at the beginning and by giving them complete power to run their own housing, as individual owners, tenant co-operatives, or through the management committee of a community based association.

A wider view

1.31 It follows that tenement improvement is not simply a technical problem like installing a new bathroom. Because of the inter-related, communal nature of tenement living everybody is affected to a greater or lesser degree by a house improvement scheme. Technical problems throw up a whole range of social issues. When one person can affectively veto a scheme, even the most Machiavellian operators have at least to recognise that not everyone shares the same commitment

9 *Reidvale Street, Dennistoun. While improving such tenements is obviously desirable, there are disadvantages inherent in the building type such as difficulties with children's play (common to several storey, flatted housing).*

10 *Employment is one main factor in wishing to move. The tenement areas are not generally thriving industrially. Govan Shipbuilders, formerly Upper Clyde Shipbuilders, is the last remaining up-river yard.*

to house improvement. Tenement improvement raises the whole question of housing choices: attention is focused on the housing process rather than housing products, both at planning and implementation stages. Residents can be expected to question house improvement schemes not simply in terms of installing bathrooms but in terms of their own general housing aspirations. Only when these matters have been resolved can discussion take place about the details of the house improvement programme on the ground.

1.32 Such discussion will be in both technical and non-technical terms. Questions as to whether existing refrigerators can fit into the new kitchenettes are interspersed with inquiries about decanting, meter reading, choice of wallpapers and so on. Therefore a whole host of matters need to be sorted out before building work can start. Houses have to change hands. Residents have to be rehoused, permanently or temporarily, round the corner in a housing association house or across the city in a local authority house. Legal questions have to be resolved; grant applications applied for; home loans arranged and rent increases discussed. Meetings are held in people's houses to explain the process; information is sent to each family.

1.33 These problems are rarely fully resolved before the architect becomes involved. During the survey, design and building stages there is a constant interaction between technical and social matters. This case study must look at both the social and technical aspects of house improvement.

2 Background to a house improvement programme

The community approach

2.01 There is little point in undertaking a tenement rehabilitation programme unless there is a substantial number of residents in favour of house improvements. Ideally residents should be able to instigate and control their own programme of improvements. Unfortunately, the Housing (Scotland) Act 1974 does not provide an equivalent Section to 36 (1) of the English legislation which allows the local authority to declare a HAA on the recommendation of a report submitted by 'a person or persons appearing suitably qualified'.

2.02 However, this does not preclude community groups making a case for their area to be included in a HAA. For example three years ago it became clear that some residents in a small area of tenements in Springburn, perched high up on an escarpment overlooking the city, were finding it difficult to sell their houses as Corporation loans were not being made available to prospective buyers. They discovered that their houses were included in a Comprehensive Redevelopment Area (CDA), the boundaries of which ignored the 50 metre drop at the back of the tenements but ran right through the middle of St Monance Street. Houses on one side of the road were to be demolished while identical houses on the other side were to be retained.

Residents organisation
2.03 Residents held meetings which 60 or 70 people attended each month. (They served cups of tea and biscuits, charging 10p—the money mounted up.) They persuaded the planning department to amend the CDA proposals but not before the residents association had successfully served, at great expense, a notice restraining a notorious property owner from carrying out substandard improvements. The residents association also bought and rented out a house which was later sold to the sitting tenant. The residents carried out their own survey to establish the condition of the houses and submitted the results to Glasgow District requesting them to declare a HAA. The HAA has now been confirmed, another house has been taken over as an office, and the residents have measured up the back-courts and produced an environmental improvement scheme for the area. The Mansell-St Monance Housing Association

was formed to manage and co-ordinate the house improvements.

2.04 When improvement is contemplated some residents may campaign to have their houses included in a HAA. Others will find that their houses have been included whether they like it or not. If so there has probably been very little consultation by the local authority with the residents. Some authorities are still considering compulsory purchase as the means of implementing house improvements. In these circumstances the residents have to produce evidence of a willingness to improve before the local authority finalises its plans, as happened in Govanhill. Here, in 1973, the then Glasgow Corporation declared 5 Treatment Areas for Improvement. This required the owners to improve their houses, or sell immediately or be bought out later by the local authority.

2.05 Govanhill residents were expected to make their choice but access to informed advice was haphazard. For example, one resident, Miss Mearns, had heard of ASSIST's work in Govan and visited the office for advice. ASSIST confirmed that it would be technically possible to improve her house but that it could not guarantee that the house, even if it was improved, would not be compulsorily purchased later in order to facilitate the overall scheme. Instead ASSIST referred Miss Mearns to The View, a local information centre, who put her in touch with the Govanhill Action Group. To explain the possibilities the group organised a meeting for residents in a scout hall.

Making a case for improvement
2.06 ASSIST staff and the secretary of the residents association in Govan explained how the house improvements had been carried out in the Govan (Taransay Street) Treatment Area, **11**. A bus run was organised and the residents of Govanhill were shown round the houses in all stages of improvement by the Govan residents. A report was produced by ASSIST, based on information from a residents' survey, making out a case for voluntary improvement. The Corporation eventually agreed to this approach and subsequently made a grant to

11 *Taransay Street Treatment Area; impressive,* **5,** *or oppressive depending on the setting and the weather. There is little of the sense of brightening up the street that often occurs with improving brick terraces; changes here are internal or to backcourts.*

allow the residents to set up their own housing association. Govanhill Housing Association now owns over 600 houses, 300 of which have been improved with a current programme of 200-300 improvements per year.

2.07 This approach has been formalised in Glasgow in an attempt to deal with the numbers of houses that required to be improved. A number of community based housing associations have been formed throughout the city, with the support of the Housing Corporation, operating effectively as agencies for the district council who are responsible for declaring HAAs.

Community based housing associations
Formal organisation
2.08 Housing associations are non-profit making organisations that purchase (or construct) houses for renting. They are registered with the Registrar of Friendly Societies and have as their constitutions model rules drawn up by the National Federation of Housing Societies or, more recently, by the Housing Corporation. Housing associations are run by management committees elected from the members who take out a nominal non-returnable £1 share in the organisation. The management committee and other sub-committee members give their time on a voluntary basis. Under the 1974 Housing Act stricter controls on housing associations have been introduced whereby all housing associations financed through the Housing Corporation have to be vetted for registration purposes. For instance consultants working for an association, such as architects or other professionals, are no longer permitted to be members of the management committee.

Community base
2.09 Community based housing associations in Glasgow have a special local outlook. They have often been set up by established community organisations such as the New Partick Society or Govanhill Action Group. The most successful associations have often had a background of community development. For instance, the Reidvale Residents' Association was set up with the support of the Young Volunteer Force Mile End Project in Glasgow. For the first two years they campaigned to increase residents' awareness of their living conditions. A local newspaper was launched and ASSIST, with help from architectural students, prepared backcourt schemes. A planning exhibition summarised the problems and possibilities. Local planning proposals were produced by Glasgow District in conjunction with the residents groups through the medium of the Community Planning Working Party convened by Glasgow District. The residents' association set up a sub-committee to look at the possibility of house improvements which led to the formation of the Reidvale Housing Association.

2.10 The management committees comprise residents living in the parts of the city covered by the individual community housing associations. They employ their own staff to organise the administrative and promotional function of the association's work. Consultants provide architectural and quantity surveying services although some associations are beginning to employ in-house staff. The community associations have local offices, converted shops or ground floor houses, where residents can drop in any time of the day.

2.11 The community housing associations purchase from landlords and owners who do not wish to improve their property, but prefer to sell. Associations improve the property they purchase and offer a package deal to owner-occupiers. Associations promote and manage locally the whole improvement programme, arranging publicity, finance, rehousing, decanting and so on. They also provide architectural and quantity surveying services and sign the contracts with the builders, having reached agreement with owners and all other interested parties.

Housing Corporation
2.12 The Housing Corporation interprets its remit as being wider than simply arranging loan finance, its primary task. It promotes and monitors housing associations, and approves all schemes at area and specific project level. It also advises on staffing, management, accounting, and also provides a house acquisition service for the community associations, liaising with the district valuer, lawyers and the associations' staff over the purchase of property from the major property owners. In partnership with Glasgow District, the Housing Corporation acts as co-ordinator of a city wide programme of improvements, **12**.

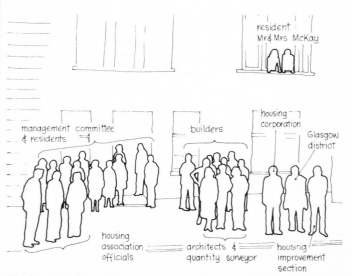

12 *A range of people whose co-ordinated effort leads to improvement (some landlords are absent).*

Local responsibility

2.13 The housing associations, acting as area co-ordinators, remove a great deal of uncertainty which previously blighted tenement improvement. On completion of the promotional and development work they also take on housing management functions, including a repair service. They are responsible to the community in which they work for the house improvement programme which to a large extent has been devolved to the local areas. Within the inevitable constraints of legislation, and given the co-operation of the local authority and the Housing Corporation, the feasibility of a community-based improvement programme has been clearly demonstrated in Glasgow. This devolution of responsibility can be criticised on the grounds that local people are merely doing the local authorities' work at much less cost, and that the residents directly involved will bear the brunt of the blame from their neighbours if anything goes wrong. These criticisms are refuted by those who argue that the short term gain of improving living conditions, and the long term possibility of significant power passing to the community make the risks and the compromise worthwhile.

The local authority's role

2.14 The local authority has a statutory duty to identify unfit housing and to deal with the problem either by improvement or demolition and rebuilding. In Glasgow the local authority has commissioned a survey covering, initially, 12 000 houses to assess their potential for improvement and the likely costs. After consultation with the Housing Corporation and the community housing association, if it exists, the local authority will publish a draft resolution of the HAA and circulate the report to all the householders. The draft resolution must contain:

(1) those buildings to be demolished (if any)

(2) the standards of improvement specified by the local authority

(3) the houses that are below the specified standard

(4) the houses, which cannot be improved as they stand and which are to be integrated, and the tenements in which the integration occurs. (This last provision refers to the problem of tenements where centre houses, usually single apartments, are considered too small to be improved and therefore can be integrated with the adjacent house to create fewer but bigger house units, **13a, b**.)

2.15 At the time of the draft resolution, Glasgow District will nominate a housing association to co-ordinate the improvement work on the ground. A two month representation period follows, during which the residents can comment and make suggestions before the final resolution. This procedure puts the onus on the community to organise itself prior to HAA declaration. Furthermore, the viability of an improvement programme, locally, rests with the housing association. This emphasises the need for the community housing association to be very much part of, and controlled by, the community it serves.

2.16 Unfortunately, other local authorities still declare HAAs in the belief that this will promote spontaneous improvements by owners. Others instigate compulsory purchase procedures at the outset. Past evidence from Glasgow indicates that neither method is effective technically and can be extremely disruptive socially. Present evidence from Glasgow suggests that the alternative community based approach will be more successful.

Finance

2.17 The Housing (Scotland) Act 1974 provides for grants to cover improvement work for owners. Outside HAAs the grant can be 75 per cent of approved expenditure up to the value of £5500 in certain cases (see SDD Circular 48/78). In HAAs the grant can be from 75 to 90 per cent of approved expenditure up to £7000 depending on family income (ie the maximum possible grant is between £5250 and £6300). These figures may be updated from time to time and details of the grant schemes vary among local authorities. The balance of improvement costs, after grant, must be borne by the owner.

2.18 A local authority loan may be available which, taken with any other home loans, for instance for the initial purchase of the house, will be up to the improved security value of the house.

Thus if the total cost of improvement work is £8000
Grant (75 per cent of £7000, maximum) £5250
Therefore owner's share is £2750
Or with a 15 year loan at 10·5 per cent £31·45 per month
(Tax allowances will further reduce the weekly payments).

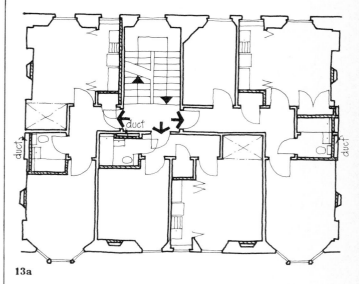

13a

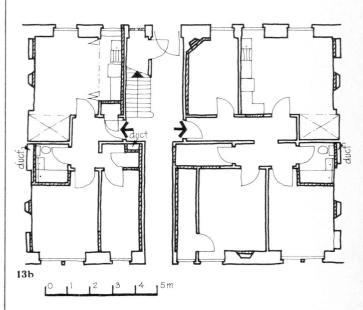

13b

|0 |1 |2 |3 |4 |5m|

13a *Upper and* **b** *ground floor showing conversion of three houses (* **3a, b** *) to two. The three ducts at the back of bathrooms shown in* **7** *must be continuous so a duct passes through floors converted to two houses in position of former centre house without connection.*

2.19 The Housing (Scotland) Act 1974 provides for finance to be made available to housing associations for the purpose of purchasing and improving property. Capital costs are covered by Housing Corporation loans; the loans being paid off almost immediately by housing association grants administered by the Scottish Development Department. The management and maintenance of property is paid out of income received from fair rents fixed by the rent officer. Any shortfall is covered by a Revenue Deficit grant cleared at the end of each financial year, if advance approval has been given by the Scottish Development Department; hence the need for associations to produce annual budgets. Bridging finance is obtained from guaranteed bank overdrafts. Finance is also available in the form of allowances for the administration of the improvement programme.

3 Developing a brief

Initial soundings

3.01 While the statutory responsibility for declaring HAAs rests with the local authority, the local community can very much influence the course of events. As mentioned earlier (**2.04**), the residents in Govanhill responded to what they saw as a threat by the local authority. On the other hand in Reidvale the residents initiated action where none had existed before (**2.09**).

3.02 In both cases it was felt advisable to test local opinion before launching into a full scale publicity campaign. This could have done more harm than good if ultimately the improvements did not materialise. There might be a lack of local support, or insufficient backing of a wider more political nature, or both, as is often the case. The residents group (or the community based housing association) has to establish that it has local support for its proposals. And it may wish to demonstrate this support to the local authority or funding authority.

3.03 Before ASSIST becomes fully involved with any group it may ask the residents to carry out their own survey. ASSIST has helped prepare surveys by typing and duplicating if necessary, and putting residents in touch with other groups who are carrying out the same work. The aim has always been to build up residents groups in the residents' own eyes, to let the committee gain their own confidence so that they can control consultants rather than vice versa. For the same reason ASSIST sometimes asks its clients to measure up their existing back courts and prepare their own proposals before discussing the scheme with the architects.

Sampling opinion

3.04 Returning to the residents' survey, the questions should be short and general. For instance:
● do you like living in the Govanhill area?
● do you think any improvements could be made to the house?
● Would you be prepared to come to a meeting to get further information?

3.05 Although it has been suggested that such questions are too general to be useful and are so non-controversial that they are bound to elicit support, in practice the surveys do seem to give a very good indication of residents' general feelings about their housing. Low response rates and few people in favour of house improvements will usually be followed by hostile public meetings. The natural response to anybody asking questions about important issues such as housing is one of suspicion, especially in potential clearance areas. (How many architects find themselves obliged to bring their own houses up to standard, as opposed to the number of architects who purchase substandard property to improve with the aid of a grant.

3.06 So a favourable response to the residents' survey suggests that the support is strong enough to break down these suspi-

cions. A letter or news-sheet can be sent with the questionnaire maybe delivered by children big enough to reach letter boxes. Completed questionnaires can be returned to a dairy (corner shop) or picked up by residents who sent it out. Collecting replies gives residents the opportunity to identify themselves and explain their ideas as they go around the houses.

Publicising house improvement

3.07 If the survey results are favourable a publicity campaign will be needed to explain the detailed implications of house improvements. In these campaigns ASSIST has helped with the presentation of material and has also been able to draw on the resources of Strathclyde University for support by providing film projectors, exhibition screens, or headed notepaper printed by the stationery department. There is a clear need for community resources centres to provide this type of back-up for residents groups who cannot afford expensive equipment and lack access to typing and duplicating services. (Many of these exist in schools and colleges, though are not made available.) A publicity campaign should be run by residents. It can include a variety of approaches, outlined below.

Public meetings

3.08 Public meetings publicise the survey results, introduce the campaign organisers, and provide an occasion to see films (Glasgow district has produced its own film, *If only we had the space*, and a Strathclyde student is making video tv films of back-court improvements.) Perhaps the best method of explaining improvements is to hear from residents who have been improving their houses in other areas of the city. This is also a good opportunity to enlist more helpers.

Close meetings

3.09 Close (the common entrance) meetings are far more productive than public meetings. The unit for improvement is effectively the close and ultimately it is collective action by residents in any close that determines when and how the houses in the property are to be improved. The close meeting emphasises the collective nature of tenement improvement and allows far more information to be passed between residents.

Exhibitions

3.10 Models are better than plans (as long as the models are as representational as possible—as detailed as a doll's house), **14**. If plans are to be used they should include furniture, be handed and supplemented with photographs. Models and plans should be of specific house types most prevalent in the area being covered. Each house in the area must be clearly identified. Ideally, any resident attending the exhibition should be able to locate their own house, see its existing layout and a variety of improvement proposals for that house type. Similarly, photographs and plans of existing backcourts and models of proposals could be on display. It is best to have someone who has been directly involved in mounting the exhibition in attendance to explain any points brought up by visitors.

Show houses

3.11 A show house is better than a model. It should be possible to construct the real thing rather than a mock-up. There is nothing more disappointing than an unlived in new house, with exotic furniture supplied courtesy of the largest departmental store in town, and no water coming out of the taps. The lady of the house is much the best person to explain the house improvements, **15**.

3.12 An alternative approach is for the show houses to double up as offices for the architects working in the area (for instance ASSIST used the Reidvale Housing Association show house

How can a house be improved?

This Room and Kitchen originally had an inside toilet and a scullery It now has a bathroom, kitchenette and extra storage

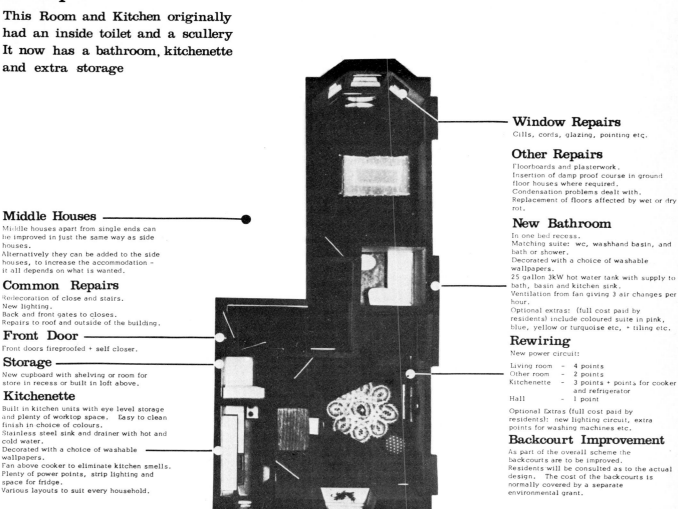

Middle Houses
Middle houses apart from single ends can be improved in just the same way as side houses.
Alternatively they can be added to the side houses, to increase the accommodation – it all depends on what is wanted.

Common Repairs
Redecoration of close and stairs.
New lighting.
Back and front gates to closes.
Repairs to roof and outside of the building.

Front Door
Front doors fireproofed + self closer.

Storage
New cupboard with shelving or room for store in recess or built in loft above.

Kitchenette
Built in kitchen units with eye level storage and plenty of worktop space. Easy to clean finish in choice of colours.
Stainless steel sink and drainer with hot and cold water.
Decorated with a choice of washable wallpapers.
Fan above cooker to eliminate kitchen smells.
Plenty of power points, strip lighting and space for fridge.
Various layouts to suit every household.

Window Repairs
Cills, cords, glazing, pointing etc.

Other Repairs
Floorboards and plasterwork.
Insertion of damp proof course in ground floor houses where required.
Condensation problems dealt with.
Replacement of floors affected by wet or dry rot.

New Bathroom
In one bed recess.
Matching suite: wc, washhand basin, and bath or shower.
Decorated with a choice of washable wallpapers.
25 gallon 3kW hot water tank with supply to bath, basin and kitchen sink.
Ventilation from fan giving 3 air changes per hour.
Optional extras: (full cost paid by residents) include coloured suite in pink, blue, yellow or turquoise etc, + tiling etc.

Rewiring
New power circuit:

Living room	– 4 points
Other room	– 2 points
Kitchenette	– 3 points + points for cooker and refrigerator
Hall	– 1 point

Optional Extras (full cost paid by residents): new lighting circuit, extra points for washing machines etc.

Backcourt Improvement
As part of the overall scheme the backcourts are to be improved.
Residents will be consulted as to the actual design. The cost of the backcourts is normally covered by a separate environmental grant.

14 *Exhibition panel used by ASSIST to show possible improvements. The model illustrated is also on show.*

as its local premises in Dennistoun). This at least ensures that the architects have to work if not actually live in the houses they are improving. In all cases show houses should be located on the ground floor or first floor.

3.13 Improvement of a show house has to be organised well in advance of the publicity campaign (at least six months). In many cases show houses are atypical, often being one-off improvements and are likely to be more expensive than the normal improved houses. The improvement of the show house does provide the opportunity for the consultants or housing association staff to get to know the problems of improving the houses in any particular area and also allows the committee to test out its relationship with consultants or officials. The effect of improving a show house can be considerable. It proves to residents that houses can be improved and it proves to the residents committee that it can improve houses.

Bus runs
3.14 Where a show house cannot be improved and opened, a good alternative is to organise a bus run to visit other groups who are improving their own houses. An added advantage of the bus run (apart from the likelihood that it will turn into a pub run) is that the visitors can watch the work in progress rather than just see the pristine end product. In this way it will be possible to talk to people who have been through the

difficulties of house improvements and learn about the problems and pitfalls. In the end ASSIST has always found it much easier when explaining house improvements to say to a resident that 'such and such a kitchenette is like the one with louvred doors you saw in Govanhill' than to laboriously simulate reality with plans and models.

Information sheets and newsletters
3.15 Information sheets and newsletters can be circulated to all residents to explain what can be done in each house and to set out very carefully the financial implications of the proposals both for tenants and owners. Information sheets have to be carefully worded if they are to be done well (what would you think if you got a letter telling you that your house should be improved?), **16**. Duplicated sheets are cheap but rarely look interesting; litho can look better but is more expensive—the same goes for posters.

3.16 Another variation on information sheets is newsletters which are often difficult to sustain: two newsletters do not make a newspaper. It is also difficult to avoid making information repetitive and too vague. Most people will want to know the cost of improvement, and when the work is going to start which is difficult to predict when there are so many inter-related technical and administrative problems to resolve. If this type of information is not given people will not read

Home Improvers

Mrs Sinclair

"I rent my house - it's a room and kitchen 3 up.

Before improvements I only had an inside toilet and the usual small scullery.

After improvements I have a fully fitted bathroom. My scullery has been modernised, with hot water to a new stainless steel sink. I had a choice of colours for the kitchen units - I took blue in the end. The house was also rewired and my windows repaired.

Mind you the best thing about the improvements was that I got a large cupboard built in where I can put my ladders and all the other things I've collected.

I was terrified by the thought of the mess that would be made when the work was carried out. Actually it turned out to be not half as bad as I expected. The builders were very quick. You soon forget about it when it's all over. I've had my house decorated as well.

The rent has gone up but it was worth it. Anyway, I'm an OAP so the increase gets covered by the supplementary pension.

It's marvellous having a bathroom after all these years."

Scullery before
Kitchenette after

Mr & Mrs Hamilton

"We bought our house 3 years ago and had it improved last spring as part of a co-ordinated scheme. That way we were able to share the cost of the pipes with our neighbours.

A bathroom makes a tremendous difference when you've got two children in the house as we have.

We were worried that we would lose too much space. (As we are on the ground floor it wasn't possible to get an extra room.) They put the bath in a bed recess and now you hardly notice it. Anyway, you've got to lose something if you want your house improved.

On the other hand we now have a much bigger kitchenette and extra storage so it seems that we actually gained space.

The kitchenette is really marvellous - better than you get in a lot of new houses.

We got a 75% improvement grant and the rest was covered by a Corporation Home Loan. We didn't have to start paying a penny until the work was completed.

All in all the house improvement was very good value for money."

Toilet before
Bathroom after

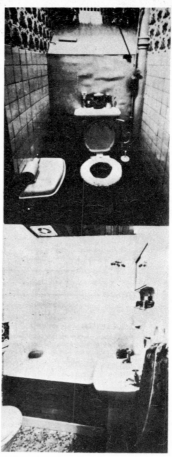

15 *Display panel is used in conjunction with show houses. Residents' experiences are recounted in a fairly anecdotal way, dealing with issues important to others contemplating improvements.*

What do you want to do?

If you are a tenant you can

either a) <u>stay</u> and have your house improved
or b) <u>move</u> to another house in the block or nearby
or c) <u>be rehoused</u> by Glasgow District Council (please note that the chances of getting the house you want locally are small).

If you are an owner occupier you can

either 1) <u>stay</u> and improve your house (the Housing Association will offer you its "improvement service")
or 2) <u>sell</u> your house to the Housing Association
    and a) <u>stay and rent</u> your house back from the Association
    or b) <u>move and rent</u> another house in the block or nearby
    or c) <u>be rehoused</u> by Glasgow District Council (please note that the chances of getting the house you want locally are small)
    or d) <u>rehouse yourself</u> privately.

Before the builder moves in

The Housing Association may be able to provide residents with <u>temporary storage space</u> for large items of furniture and <u>temporary accommodation</u>. We would strongly recommend that where possible you stay in your house while it is improved - the occasional brush out makes all the difference, and you can keep an eye on what is happening to your house.

Remember

Glasgow District Council requires that all the houses are brought up to a modern standard. Even if your house already has a bathroom, there may be other improvements and repairs needed. Most people prefer to stay in Govanhill and improve their houses. Something has to be done if Govanhill is still going to be a pleasant place to live in next year - and the years after. Something <u>can</u> be done.

What happens next?

Please think over the options. A survey will be carried out to establish <u>your preferences</u>. We hope you won't just say "I'm leaving" or "I'm not interested" and shut the door. The Housing Association is here to help you get what you want - where you want. When we find out what you want to do the rolling programme can be launched. We will keep you fully informed. If you need any further information or wish to know what is happening at any time call round to the Housing Association offices at 172 Butterbiggins Road - someone there will be able to help.

Improve your home with the Govanhill Housing Association

Govanhill is an area undergoing considerable change. Living conditions will deteriorate unless action is taken to improve the houses, the backcourts and the surrounding streets. Glasgow District Council have decided that houses in certain areas of Govanhill must be brought up to a modern standard.

The following information shows how house improvements can be carried out by residents with the assistance of the Govanhill Housing Association.

Govanhill Housing Association, 172 Butterbiggins Road   (Tel: 424 3700)

16 *Information sheet carefully setting out options and anticipating some residents' concerns.*

BOYD STREET AREA NEWSLETTER No. 3

4th October 1976.

In the last two weeks a great many people have contacted me to ask about improvements generally, and their own houses in particular. I very much appreciate all the interest that has been shown, and all the cups of tea and coffee I have been given! I will always be happy to explain things, so far as I am able.

Various questions have been asked, and the answers are of general concern, so I am circulating some of the answers in this newsletter.

Question: Specifically which closes are involved in the Action Area declaration?

Answer: Although the area has been referred to as the 'Boyd Street Area', it includes parts of Allison Street, Cathcart Road and Dixon Road as well as Boyd Street itself. It is the tenement buildings forming two blocks that are involved, excluding the council-housing that is separated from the main buildings, as shown in the diagrammatic map below:

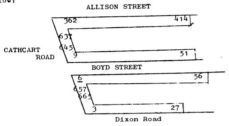

The specific addresses are:

Allison Street - 362, 366, 372, 378, 384, 390, 396, 402, 408, 414

Boyd Street - 6, 9, 15, 16, 21, 22, 27, 30, 33, 36, 39, 42, 45, 50, 51, 56

Dixon Road - 3, 9, 15, 21, 27

Cathcart Road - 637, 645, 657, 665.

Question: Will people in middle houses have to move out?

Answer: No. In some areas of Glasgow the middle houses of tenements have been single-ends, and it has not been possible to put a bathroom and kitchenette into the space available, so the middle house has been amalgamated with the side houses. However in Govanhill we have found most middle houses are two-apartments, and this is certainly true of the Boyd Street area. Middle houses can be improved as they are, and no-one will be pushed out of middle houses who wants to stay. However, if a middle house was empty P.T.O.

17

IMPROVING YOUR HOME AS AN OWNER OCCUPIER WITH GOVANHILL HOUSING ASSOCIATION

For owner/occupiers who want to improve themselves. Please read carefully.

As an owner/occupier there are two main choices open to you, as regards house improvements:

(1) you can stay and improve your own house

(2) you can sell your house to the Housing Association, and become a tenant or move away from the area.

You have chosen to improve your house yourself, with the aid of grants. This pamphlet is intended to explain what will happen now you have made this choice. It is, of course, still possible for you to change your mind at this stage.

The Housing Association is willing to offer its "improvement service" to all owners who wish to join an overall improvement scheme. It is in your interest to join the scheme as this will help keep costs down. The service offered will cover:

(a) design proposals and obtaining building permission

(b) advice about costs, grants and loans

(c) paperwork, such as grant, home loan applications, and final accounts

(d) organisation of the building contract and supervision of the work

(Fees for this work will be included in the improvement grant application).

You will be entitled to a 75% Improvement Grant on all "approved" work carried out. (e.g. Glasgow District Council will not approve the extra cost of a coloured bathroom suite over the cost of a white one, nor the cost of complete house redecoration). This means that you will have to pay 25% of the "approved" costs of improvement work. An example might explain this clearer. Costs for a 1 Room and Kitchen are likely to be as follows:

Cost:		
	Bathroom	1200
	Kitchenette	770
	Preparatory work	150
	Storage	150
	Repairs(windows,doors,etc)	250
	Rewiring	300
	Share of common repairs	400
	Cost of work	3220
	Professional fees (14%)	450
		£3670 Say £3,700

The costs listed are approximate, but are reasonably accurate at the time of printing (September 1975). Remember that costs are rising all the time.

If all of this work was approved by Glasgow District, then 75% of this would be paid by a House Improvement Grant. This would leave you as an owner to pay £925 (or 25% of the approved costs). The cost of any work over the £3,700 Grant limit must be borne by individual owner/occupiers. There is no 75% for any costs over £3,700.

18

---

newsletters. But if starting dates are given then people will be disappointed and angry when almost inevitably programmes have to be altered. As one resident put it, 'what you planners call flexibility we call uncertainty'.

3.17 The policy adopted by many housing associations in Glasgow has been to produce a few newsletters and information sheets covering specific topics, eg *House improvement and what it means for tenants*, **17**, **18**. Details of programming can be covered on a notice board, updated every day if necessary. The Govanhill notice board gives details of all the houses that are in HAAs (thus warning the residents of the possibility of their houses being improved) but only gives firm start dates when these are definitely known.

Local premises

3.18 The best way to keep everybody in touch is by simply being in the area and being available. In 1976, Matt Bruce, a member of ASSIST, moved into a tenement house in Springburn for two-month spell to carry out initial survey work. The house doubled as an office and temporary home enabling him to visit residents who were only available in the evening. On another occasion an ASSIST architect was dragged out of bed at 2.00 am by an irate resident in Govan whose bed recess ceiling had collapsed following the testing, and failure, of a new stack of plumbing. The architect was instructed by the resident to clear up the mess.

3.19 All the community based associations in Glasgow have local premises. Apart from office space for their staff they provide room for exhibitions, evening committee meetings and so on. Residents can drop in any time of the day to find out what is happening, or to complain about what is not happening. Likewise the staff find it easy to visit residents who live just round the corner from the offices. (See **5.01** for a full discussion of local offices.)

Residents' preferences

Preference survey

3.20 Once sufficient information about the house improvements has been given to all the residents and everybody has had time to digest the facts and alternatives it is possible to carry out a preference survey. It is most important that residents are not rushed into what is going to be a major decision in their lives. The preference survey differs from the earlier sounding out survey which sought only broad information to establish general feelings about the idea of house improvement. The preference survey is asking for specific and detailed information to establish exactly what each household wishes to do. The main areas covered are ownership, occupancy, and housing choices, as well as obtaining useful information such as telephone numbers, and times when people are usually at home.

3.21 As indicated under *Social issues* (para **1.22**), the main problem of rehabilitating tenements is to obtain common agreement for an improvement scheme to suit a particular property. It has to be appreciated that some residents are more enthusiastic about house improvement than others. House improvement is only one of a number of housing options that may be available. So it is not sufficient just to identify those people who wish to improve their house but also those people who do not. The preference surveys should identify those who wish to be involved in the house improvements and how they wish to participate, **19**.

3.22 Residents can be offered a number of housing options. If they are owners they can:

● sell (to, say, a housing association which will improve the house)

17 *Newsletter dealing with specific issues with each house clearly identified.*
18 *Information sheet for owner-occupiers intending to improve their houses.*

TIP PREFERENCE SURVEY
HOUSE FILE: GH1
DATE OF FIRST CONTACT: 8.7.75

	ANSWER I			ANSWER II			CODE
	Y/N	C	E	Y/N	C	E	
ADDRESS:							
CLOSE 167 LANGSIDE ROAD	167 L						
HOUSE	1/1						C
POSTAL CODE							H
TELEPHONE	424 3010						
HOUSING ACTION AREA	TA 2						
Do you own or rent this house?	OWN						
BEFORE IMPROVEMENT							
OWNER	MARTIN						OWB
OCCUPIER	MARTIN						OCB
FACTOR	MACHIE						FAB
SIZE OF HOUSE	1 R, KST						SIZB
SIZE OF FAMILY: ADULTS MALE	1						
FEMALE	1						
CHILDREN (10 AND UNDER) MALE	1						
FEMALE	1						
IS HOUSE SECURITY FOR A LOAN	NO						
a) CORPORATION	–						
b) BUILDING SOCIETY	–						
c) OTHER (STATE)	–						
DOES OWNER HAVE A SOLICITOR	YES						
NAME, ADDRESS, WHO DEALS WITH HUGH T. MCCALMAN NO HOPE ST							
TITLES HELD BY	SOLICITOR						
AFTER IMPROVEMENT							
OWNER	GHA						OWA
OCCUPIER	MARTIN						OCA
FACTOR	MACHIE						FAA
SIZE OF HOUSE	1 RK B						SIZA
SIZE OF FAMILY: ADULTS MALE	1						
FEMALE	–						
CHILDREN (10 AND UNDER) MALE	–						
FEMALE	–						
SOLICITOR (NAME AND ADDRESS)	–						
TITLES HELD BY	–						
ACCESS BEFORE 10 00 AM							
NOTES DO YOU BUY WITH VACANT POSSESSION ON WITH SITTING TENANT? BROTHER IS A PLUMBER							

OWNER	ANSWER I			ANSWER II			CODE
	Y/N	C	E	Y/N	C	E	
DOES OWNER WISH TO IMPROVE HOUSE	Y						
OWNER IMPROVING H.A.							
DOES OWNER WANT AGENCY TO PREPARE SCHEME							
WILL OWNER REQUIRE IMPROVEMENT GRANT							GRAEN HIRE?
WILL OWNER REQUIRE HOME LOAN							
WILL OWNER REQUIRE OTHER FINANCING (STATE)							
DOES OWNER WISH TO EXTEND HOUSE							
(1 EXTRA ROOM? 2 EXTRA ROOMS?)							
DOES OWNER AGREE INITIALLY WITH PROPOSED LAYOUT AND PRICE							OWAGR
DOES OWNER CONFIRM APPROVAL OF LAYOUT AND PRICE							REAIN
OWNER NOT IMPROVING							
CAN/DOES HOUSE REQUIRE IMPROVING	Y						
DOES OWNER WISH TO SELL H.A. PERHAPS	Y						OWSEL
DOES OWNER WANT OFFER FROM AGENCY	Y						
DOES OWNER WISH TO SELL PRIVATELY							
DOES OWNER WISH TO STAY AS TENANT H.A.	Y						
DOES OWNER WANT TENANCY OF ANOTHER AGENCY HOUSE							PIPAS
WILL OWNER ALLOW ACCESS FOR PIPES							OWIMP
DOES OWNER WANT TO IMPROVE NOW							
OCCUPIER							
IS HOUSE EMPTY	N						HOUEMP
DOES OCCUPIER WANT HOUSE IMPROVED	Y						OCCIMP
OCCUPIER IMPROVING							
DOES OCCUPIER WISH TO EXTEND HOUSE	N						
(1 EXTRA ROOM? 2 EXTRA ROOMS?)							
DOES OCCUPIER WISH TO MOVE TEMPORARILY	N						MOVETM
a) BY HOUSING ASSOCIATION							
b) BY SELF							
c) BY OTHER (STATE)							
DOES OCCUPIER WANT FURNITURE STORED	Y						STORE
a) ALL							
b) SOME							
OCCUPIER NOT IMPROVING							
CAN/DOES HOUSE REQUIRE IMPROVING							OCPIP
WILL OCCUPIER ALLOW ACCESS FOR PIPES							MOVEIM
DOES OCCUPIER WANT TO BE REHOUSED a) BEFORE IMPROVEMENT							RHA
b) ANY TIME							
a) PRIVATELY							
b) BY HOUSING ASSOCIATION							
WHERE							
WHAT SIZE							
c) BY GLASGOW DISTRICT (FILL IN REHOUSING FORM)							
d) BY OTHER AGENCY (STATE)							
COMPENSATION – How long has occupier lived in this house?							
DOES OCCUPIER QUALIFY FOR							
HOME LOSS PAYMENT	Y						
DISTURBANCE PAYMENT	N						
PROGRESS: IS THE WORK PROBABLY COMPLETE							WKCOM
IS THE WORK PRACTICALLY COMPLETE							PRACOM
ARE ALL THE DEFECTS MADE GOOD							DEFMG

WEIGHTING

INIT	OWN	RES	SURVEY	LEGAL	APPNS	BUILD	TRUB	COUNT

19 *Preference survey form laid out for computer processing (see para **4.05**).*

● improve their property
And anyone, tenants or owner occupiers, can:
● stay in their own improved house
● be rehoused by the local authority
● rehouse themselves privately
● move up or down the stair or round the block to a smaller or larger house.

Compromise solutions
3.23 Sometimes residents wish to do nothing. The problem is to balance the individual's preferences against the preferences of the rest of the residents in a tenement. It is difficult for residents as small groups to resolve this problem internally because of the likelihood of a few residents being isolated from their neighbours and therefore adopting an intransigent position. In these cases the improvement agency can negotiate between the parties concerned. By offering residents housing choices the possibility of an individual vetoing the improvements is greatly reduced. Where somebody does not wish to improve, perhaps for health reasons, the final solution is to persuade that person at least to allow the common pipes to pass through his or her home thereby letting people above or below improve their houses.

Increasing choice
3.24 Agreement between residents has to be reached because of the comprehensive nature of improvements. Allowing pipes to pass through a house points to an alternative technical solution whereby pipes are installed as a common service onto which bathrooms can be added at a later date, thus encouraging spontaneous, self-help schemes. Experiments have been carried out with this idea in Springburn where a publicity campaign tried to get people to accept pipes passing through their tenement houses as a normal occurrence.

Carrying out a survey
3.25 Probably the best way of carrying out a preference survey is to visit each household, **20**. An alternative is to ask residents to fill in and return their own forms. If there are any problems the residents should ask someone to visit. The difficulty with the house to house survey is that in a large area it poses a huge logistical exercise. The difficulty with the postal-type survey is that the information is inaccurate. There are also general problems of information altering over time, for instance building prices, and residents changing their minds as the improvement programme progresses. It is most important that the improvement agency remains in close contact with the residents all the time.

20 *Conducting surveys by door to door visits produces a better response than by post and improves personal contacts with other occupiers.*

4 Establishing a rolling programme

Dealing with delays

4.01 Having analysed the information from the preference survey it is possible to identify those closes where there are relatively few difficulties or conflicts of interest and those closes where there are considerable problems and little common agreement. Attempts can be made to rank the closes in order of difficulty and to concentrate on resolving the few remaining problems in the easiest closes while at the same time working on the closes where there are likely to be lengthy delays unless some action is taken.

4.02 Major delays can occur over ownership, particularly when missing owners have to be traced. They may be as far away as Alice Springs or Calgary, symptomatic of the number of people in Scotland who have emigrated. On one occasion ASSIST improved a house where the transaction had not been finalised. Unfortunately a trustee came out of retirement and chose to inspect the trust's property only to catch ASSIST in the act of installing a bathroom. His lawyer was moved to write that 'some of the formalities required by the law appear to have been a bit hurried over'.

Keeping track of changes

4.03 The information is constantly changing. Ownership is altering, residents are leaving the area, moving to houses round the block, people are changing their minds and so on. Information can be kept on the walls of the office, plotted onto close charts. Close charts are diagrammatic sections through the tenement showing the vertical relationship between houses, so necessary to understand if service pipes are to be shared. The close charts give an overall view of the houses in each close as well as a picture of all the closes' programmed for improvement, **21**.

```
CLOSE   305A  13 JUNE 1975
-------------------------
------------------------------------------------------------------
        :                     :
GDC      -ACTION-: GDC        -ACTION-: GHA       -ACTION-
EMPTY    *OWN    : GALLAGHER  *OWN    : MILLS     *RES
MACFIE           : MACFIE     *ANSWERS: MACFIE    *SURVEY
1RKST            : 1RKST      :         1RKST     *LEGAL
        :                     :
GHA      :         GHA        :         GHA       :
*        :       * :        *  :
MACFIE   :         MACFIE     :         MACFIE    :
*        :       * :        *  :
        :                     :
*?       :       *? :        *? :
NO       HOUSE 3/1 : NO       HOUSE 3/2 : YES      HOUSE 3/3
------------------------------------------------------------------
MEARNS   -ACTION-: GDC        -ACTION-: KELLY     -ACTION-
MEARNS   *SURVEY : EMPTY      *ANSWERS: KELLY     *SURVEY
MACFIE   *LEGAL  : MACFIE     :         MACFIE    *LEGAL
1RKST    *ANSWERS: 1RKST      :         1RKST     *ANSWERS
        :                     :
MEARNS   :         KELLY      :         KELLY     :
MEARNS   :         KELLY      :         KELLY     :
MACFIE   :         MACFIE     :         MACFIE    :
1RKK+B   :         SPLIT      :         3RKK+B    :
        :                     :
*?       :       *? :        *? :
YES      HOUSE 2/1 : *?       HOUSE 2/2 : YES      HOUSE 2/3
------------------------------------------------------------------
GHA      -ACTION-: GHA        -ACTION-: GHA       -ACTION-
WATSON   *SURVEY : SIMPSON    *SURVEY : COURTNEY  *SURVEY
MACFIE   *LEGAL  : MACFIE     *LEGAL  : MACFIE    *LEGAL
1RKST    *ANSWERS: 1RKT       *ANSWERS: 1RKST     *ANSWERS
        :                     :
GHA      :         GHA        :         GHA       :
WATSON   :         SIMPSON    :         COURTNEY  :
MACFIE   :         MACFIE     :         MACFIE    :
1RKK+B   :         1RKK'B     :         1RKK+B    :
        :                     :
*?       :       *? :        *? :
YES      HOUSE 1/1 : YES      HOUSE 1/2 : YES      HOUSE 1/3
------------------------------------------------------------------
MCLAUGHLIN -ACTION-:          : GDC      -ACTION-
MCLAUGHLIN *SURVEY :          : *        *OWN
MACFIE   *LEGAL   :          : MACFIE   :
2RKST    *ANSWERS :          : *        :
        :                     :
MCLAUGHLIN :                  : GHA      :
MCLAUGHLIN :                  : *        :
MACFIE   :                    : MACFIE   :
2RKK+B   :                    : *        :
        :                     :
*?       :                    : *?       :
YES      HOUSE 0/2 :          : NO       HOUSE 0/1
------------------------------------------------------------------
```

21 *Close chart; a computer printout of a diagrammatic section through a tenement showing current information on each house.*

4.04 ASSIST, with a grant from the Scottish Development Department, has developed two computer programs TIP—Tenement Improvement Procedures—an administrative aid, and CAP—Cost Analysis Procedures—a billing and analysis programme.

TIP program

4.05 In TIP the information from the preference survey was programmed to provide a prompting service specifying which administrative tasks should be carried out next in order to minimise overall delays. The program can also provide a checklist of activities and can assess the relative progress of each close. The output can either be printouts of the close charts, prompt sheets, or bar charts. The information is circulated and updated approximately weekly. So that the architects, for instance, are asked weekly to confirm that they have applied for building permission or have issued interim certificates, **22, 23**.

CAP program

4.06 CAP is a library containing a range of work items that normally occur in tenement improvement work. The work items can be called up as necessary to form a bill of quantities which in turn can be easily analysed into the various cost categories required for loan and grant approval.

Work sequence

4.07 Eventually closes where nearly all the administrative problems are solved will emerge at the top of the programme and can be considered for surveying and including in a building contract. However, a single close contract tends to be expensive both in terms of the contract amount and administrative overheads. Continuity of short 12-week contracts is difficult to maintain, leading to a stop-go improvement programme. Ideally, contracts should cover a number of closes which follow one after another in a rolling programme of improvements. In practice this is difficult to establish because of the uncertainties of obtaining a sufficient pool of closes to form a reasonable size of contract without the clients—the residents who are on the management committee —running the risk of claims against them under the contract for damages as a result of delays in handing over closes to the contractor for improvement.

4.08 Unfortunately, if it was a matter of waiting for all the problems to resolve themselves before letting contracts there would be little or no improvement work carried out. No area is static and there will always be problems. Therefore the alternative is for the improvement team, working closely together, to build up the number and size of contracts as the closes emerge either singly or in runs as the position on the ground alters.

4.09 One of the major contributions to keeping a programme going is the impetus of the programme. Once work has started residents can see that house improvements are possible, and are happening, which helps them make up their minds about what they want to do. Once a builder arrives in an area any break in the work in a sense represents a failure. Finally there are clear financial incentives in keeping a programme rolling with administrative allowances (to housing associations) and fees (to consultants) becoming payable when the work is on site or completed. Thus it is impossible to avoid taking risks, and the pressure to succeed both to please the resident clients and to obtain payment in fact encourages risk taking.

5 Local offices

Contact with locale and site

5.01 Risks in programming can be minimised through having complete knowledge of the state of every close and by being aware of and involved with the problems facing residents and

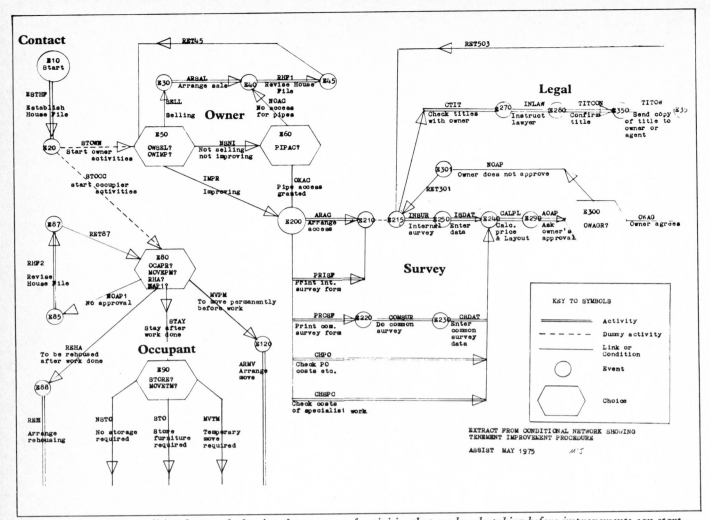

22 *Extract from TIP conditional network showing the sequence of activities that need undertaking before improvements can start.*

```
NAME OF PROJECT?GH1


YOUR WISH IS MY COMMAND?CLOD-SE ,30SA,HOUSE,1/2,PROMPT


CLOSE   30SA HOUSE   1/2
--------------------------

DO THE FOLLOWING:
SURVEY    CHSPC    CHECK SPECIALIST COSTS
SURVEY    CHPO     CHECK PO COSTS ETC
SURVEY    PRCSF    PRINT COMMON SURVEY FORMS
LEGAL     CTIT     CHECK TITLES WITH OWNER
SURVEY    ISDAT    ENTER INT SURVEY DATA

FIND THE FOLLOWING INFORMATION:

OCFIP    MOVEPM    RHA

Y.W.I.M.C.?
```

23 *TIP provides a prompting service specifying which routine administrative tasks should be carried out next.*

the other members of the improvement team. Concentrating on one professional task (say architecture) is too narrow a base for programming. As a successful programme depends ultimately on goodwill between the residents, officials and builders it is particularly important that all the participants work closely together. Immediately the people involved in improvement work move apart, programmes become institutionalised, depending no longer on goodwill but protocol for impetus. House improvement in multiple-owned, high-occupancy areas require the seizing of every opportunity as it arrives to speed up the programme.

ASSIST feels that only by working in the area which is being improved can this type of approach succeed. There will probably be greater accountability through working locally;

problems cannot be out of sight and therefore out of mind. And there are other real advantages, not least that all the clients become people and often friends. Also the builders cannot ignore the fact that the architects are working with them on site and sharing the problems and some of the privations of improving houses in difficult conditions. In this way the builder is drawn into the improvement team and becomes equally involved both in broad issues such as programming or details such as installing tenants' gas refrigerators.

Taking on wider responsibilities
5.02 In ASSIST's first project in Govan the staff acted as architects, administrators, community workers, housing visitors and clerk of works. None of the young staff were experienced in any of these fields—it was the combination of roles that counted. The residents had only to deal with one person in the shop whether it was about colours of bathroom suites or rents. The residents did not see any particular distinction between these problems; it was all to do with house improvements and the staff responded by refusing to box themselves professionally.
5.03 The building programme was extremely flexible and both the residents and the contractor were willing to accommodate changes at the last moment. The residents effectively were in control of the programme because as the improvements were confined to one tenement block, progress could be checked by watching out of the kitchen window. The direction of the programme was the clear result of residents in each close agreeing to the work going ahead.
5.04 In a 22-month period 180 houses were improved and the contractor was never off the site despite at one stage being owed £34 000 (because of general delays in payment of house improvement grant but especially because lawyers were very

slow to arrange and eventually release home loan payments to their low income clients). ASSIST, who was legally the client under the contract but had little enough money to pay its staff came to dread weekly site meetings with the contractor. In retrospect, it was remarkable that there were no major disasters and it is still a source of some amazement to ASSIST that a survey carried out 18 months after the houses were improved showed that 85 per cent of the residents who had their houses improved in Govan were satisfied with the work.

Growth of improvement organisations

5.05 As an improvement programme expands in size it is difficult to avoid specialisation taking place. This has happened in Govanhill where ASSIST originally provided a complete architectural and administrative service to the housing association during its development stages. It now gives a mainly architectural service though one member of the ASSIST staff still works entirely on housing association administration. The potential problem of fragmentation is overcome by ASSIST and the housing associations sharing premises. ASSIST currently shares with three associations which reduces overheads—very important when an organisation is dispersed in several areas. But this is at the expense of staff having no place to work where they are not continually interrupted by visits from residents or questions from other members of the improvement team. Adequate premises are needed to allow for expansion.

5.06 ASSIST has never had sufficient space. In Govan the staff worked on top of each other in a back shop while the secretaries shared the front shop with the Community Information Centre. 25 Community Industry boys operated from the basement and a student worked in a storage loft. In Govanhill, staff are still overcrowded despite taking over a large corner shop and two ground floor houses. Architectural shops are a myth. Something larger is required, less concentrated on one use or profession.

5.07 In Dennistoun ASSIST carried out a feasibility study for Reidvale housing association for taking over a vacant factory for use by the association and ASSIST together with small local industries. The scheme proved abortive but the association is now converting, in close collaboration with the local community, a disused building college for use as a neighbourhood centre, which will also provide offices for the association and a local medical practice. The Centre will provide space for a pensioners club, playgroup, a small games hall, public restaurant and meeting rooms for local organisations. Competition for the available space was so intense that ASSIST was unable to obtain an office there!

Costs and benefits of working locally

5.08 Conventional architectural practices which move into local offices may find that their overheads and travel time are reduced but are likely to find too that such offices concentrating on improvement work are less profitable. This reflects the labour intensive character of rehabilitation work, which if carried out well requires a close attention to detail and much supervision. By being close to site the standard of supervision can be high, an important factor in improvement work where unexpected problems have to be resolved quickly and when contract times are short. And there are benefits for residents too, especially if, as ASSIST feels, every resident should be treated as a client. The community will demand a full-time service simply because for the first time the architects have made themselves available to meet such demands.

The longer term view

5.09 The main advantages of local offices are not so much financial or practical but, rather, ethical. By working in the areas of houses to be improved the architects become more accountable to the residents for whom they are working. There is no greater spur to good detailing than being reminded day after day about a design fault by an angry housewife who is having to put up with the mistake.

5.10 Many architects working on new housing complain that they do not know the occupants of the dwellings they are designing. When architects have the opportunity to get to know their clients, as they do in improvement work, it is difficult to comprehend why more local offices have not been set up. If architects operate from local premises they would understand far more the needs and requirements of their clients and the clients would start to understand the architect's and builder's problems, 24.

In-house architectural staff

5.11 An alternative to the establishment of local offices by private practices is for community organisations such as housing associations to set up in-house architectural services. This has been a popular approach in England but there is little evidence that the communities rather than the organisations have always benefited from such an approach. The tendency in the past has been for community organisations such as housing associations to use the surplus fees after salaries for their own administrative uses or expenses rather than feeding the money directly into the community. And if the surplus is fed back there is a danger that some members of the community paying fees, particularly low income owner occupiers, will simply be subsidising other people who may be better off in another part of that same community.

5.12 The argument is often put forward that the employment of in-house staff cuts fees to low income owner occupiers but can one be sure that this benevolent redistribution is equitable say between these and tenants paying rent? This is less tendentious when an external agency, say central government, is paying the fees and not the individual in the community though even this approach can be criticised on the grounds of national economy. There seems no really equitable principle for distribution though giving any surplus to a community centre or other shared facility may be accepted.

Acquiring architectural services

5.13 The self-help school argues that all professionals, not just architects whether in-house or in private practice, are developing technical and administrative solutions which because of their complexity require specialists to be paid for their design and supervision. While the purist may reject anything less than complete self-help, the community may prefer to pay for certain services especially if they can have some real measure of control over their nature. This is obviously difficult for communities starting out with no conception of what such services could be. Hence the need for community development which ASSIST has always seen as part of its task.

5.14 There have been some problems in applying the RIBA/RIAS fee scale to tenement rehabilitation, particularly in respect of the abatements for repetition (Conditions of Engagement para 3.4). The RIAS has issued a Practice Note in February 1978 which clarifies the situation. The Housing Corporation have agreed to pay fees up to RIBA work stage D (35 per cent of total fee) when detailed design and cost estimates are submitted (ie the submission of Housing Corporation form SHC/2) which considerably helps the consultant's cash flow.

5.15 These arrangements do not, however, relieve the underlying pressure from the Housing Corporation and some community-based associations to limit the proportion of total improvement cost taken by professional fees. Allowing for a normal amount of repetition, architectural fees are often around 8 per cent (although this may have to be increased for one-off corner closes or if there is a high proportion of owner-occupiers). Add to this 5 per cent for QS, one per cent for Clerk of Works and perhaps 0·5 per cent for Structural Engineer, and you approach the 15 per cent ceiling acceptable to SDD and the Housing Corporation. Attempts to reduce this take a number of forms. There is a marked reluctance to countenance the appointment of Structural Consultants (whose advice is often essential if there is evidence of structural movement or decay, particularly as Building Control Officers are increasingly insisting on detailed calculations). Some associations attempt to lower fees by negotiating 'packages' of, say, 10 closes in a defined time, ensuring continuity of work to consultants.

5.16 Arguments are sometimes made that more standardisation in rehabilitation schemes would both save on professional fees and cut tender prices. This can be a seductive argument but only if one loses sight of the fact that the *process* of improvement is as important to the overall success of the project as the end product. Attempts to shoe-horn residents into standardised schemes can be as socially disruptive as large scale clearance and redevelopment, but there is a real dilemma here; how far should one sacrifice the ideal that each close should be tailored to its occupants' needs to the pressures to expedite the programme for the sake of those still waiting in sub-standard accommodation, and to spread the available funds as widely as possible?

24 *Not the idyllic office site but a closeness to the project that has social, political and technical advantages.*

6 Design

Initial scheme

6.01 When it has been decided which closes are to be included in a contract the architects will receive an up-to-date close chart for the property. The close chart will say who is staying after improvements, which houses will be empty and 'the residents' preferences for house size and location. In effect the close chart becomes a condensed brief for the property and apart from giving the details described previously will also provide more informal information such as 'Mrs Nicholson prefers the bath in her room bed recess—she's an OAP who lives in her kitchen' or 'Mrs McKay has a large Alsatian'. The architect working from a local office will probably know many of the residents already. With this information ASSIST prepares a quick *ideal* scheme, giving the best technical solution which tries to maximise the sharing of services and so on, thereby giving optimum value for money. At this stage the scheme is unresolved. Not all the residents' requirements may be met in the initial solution. But neither will all residents have decided what they wish to do.

Cost limits

6.02 Unfortunately, adjusting a scheme to obtain the best subsidy is a technique that cannot be ignored. At present (January 1980) the cost limit categories for rehabilitation of tenement houses by housing associations in Glasgow are:

1 person house—£6900 (works only including VAT + fees)
2 person house—£7700
3 person house—£8400
4 person house—£8800
5/6 person house—£9200

These cost limits do not relate to the amount of repairs

required which varies from close to close depending on the past history of maintenance. (Theoretically the purchase price should reflect the state of repair of the property as a whole but in practice the value relates to the interior of each house.) Furthermore, the cost of repairs will vary by location. A corner close is invariably more expensive to improve than a mid-terrace tenement because of the complex plan types found in corner closes and the larger roof and wall area. Also there is little financial incentive to create bigger units. There is proportionately more money to improve 12 small houses than 8 larger houses, especially when the cost of common repairs can be spread between more houses thus reducing the overall repair cost per house.

6.03 The Scottish Building Regulations lay down specific minimum areas for houses but, fortunately, in Glasgow Building Control Officers and The Housing Corporation recognise that existing tenement walls cannot be moved at will to give each room a correct relative size. In tenements new kitchens or kitchen/dining areas tend to be small, being squeezed into existing toilet spaces, bed recesses or small rooms, **25, 26**. If the existing kitchen living room in a tenement is converted into a kitchen/dining room the room size as newly defined is too large.

25 *Making a kitchen space. Closed volume to left of space is new cupboard opening onto hall.*

26 *New kitchen. Cooker on plinth to match worktop height. On later designs the cooker does not abut sink.*

6.04 There is also an assumption that existing residents will be prepared to move anywhere to accommodate an architect's scheme designed to meet all modern day standards laid down by the loan authority and the building regulations. But a family who have had to live for 20 years in a small room and kitchen are unlikely to be impressed when they are told to move because the authorities have suddenly decided they are overcrowded. The cost limits therefore should be split between improvement and repair work (at present all schemes have to be analysed by these categories anyway). The cost limits for improvement work should encourage the creation of larger units and the repair cost limit should be on a sliding scale to take into account varying conditions and size of property.

6.05 Furthermore, the owner occupier has a particular problem as his cost limits may vary from those of the housing association which is co-ordinating the scheme of improvements. Unless the housing association is careful it will improve to a higher standard than the owner occupier can afford to pay for. At the same time, the housing association has to persuade the owner occupier to carry out common repairs that affect the condition and visual appearance of the whole property. There appears to be a strong case for raising the level of improvement grant in HAAs where owners are being obliged to improve their property to a standard that is effectively imposed on them by an improvement agency. This would also help to overcome the problem of the individual landlord who does not have the same resources as a housing association but wishes to improve rather than sell his property. In these cases at present, landlords are attempting to get away with a lower standard of improvement than that of a housing association, while at the same time charging tenants approximately the same rents.

Discussing the scheme
6.06 When the *ideal* scheme has been prepared a close meeting is organised. All the neighbours meet in one house to discuss the scheme and how it will be implemented. Tea and buns are usually served. The architects explain their scheme by walking round the housing, standing where the bathroom could be positioned, demonstrating how a kitchenette might be fitted in, etc. As long as the residents have seen some improved houses there is little need to use plans or models, which only tend to confuse. However, when the scheme is agreed, a plan is useful for everybody to keep a record of what is to happen to their house. Dimensioned plans also allow people to take measurements for new carpets, **27**.

27 ASSIST staff discussing scheme with residents. It should not be assumed that the media of models and plans are self explanatory or even easily comprehended.

6.07 Now follows the most interesting part of the design process. The whole scheme is in a state of flux as residents assess the proposals, work out the implications on their lives, take up bargaining positions, make suggestions and alterations. All the participants realise that the time has finally come to make decisions and also that there is a certain inescapable interdependence between neighbours' individual decisions. The outcome of the close meetings is unpredictable and the design problem is usually resolved not so much by a technical solution but rather by someone who, prior to the meeting, had been undecided making up his mind about his housing preferences. The ingenious technical solution usually causes more trouble than it is worth at the billing and permissions

stages and on site. It is best to juggle a few simple well tried elements to arrive at the final scheme:
- the position of a standard bathroom
- the position of a standard kitchenette
- the size of the house (whether it is to be twinned or not).

6.08 A whole lot of non-architectural matters which are more easily answered by the housing association staff come up at the close meeting. But it is impossible to divorce the design and the process by which the design is finalised from the administrative problems such as rehousing, decanting and other matters.

6.09 At the end of the meeting the architects arrange times with residents to survey their houses. Also the residents are given catalogues of the kitchen units for choosing the face and worktop colours. This information along with choices of heating, colours of bathroom suites, planning and storage will be picked up by the architect when the surveys are being carried out.

Surveys
6.10 After the close meeting the architects adjust their scheme to suit the residents' preferences. The surveys of the individual houses are then carried out. These surveys are an important part of the design process. The residents have another chance to discuss the proposals and are able to point out specific faults which have caused trouble in the past. The architect will also be able to measure up cookers, refrigerators and other appliances to check that they will fit into a standard kitchen layout. If, as sometimes happens, refrigerators are too large to fit under worktops the standard schemes have to be modified. Later after the contract is off the ground the wallpaper book will be circulated among the residents who can work out the decoration of their houses. Once the surveys are completed, the residents will be given a record of what their house will contain after improvement. The residents can also drop into the shop at any time to discuss the scheme.

Sponsor clients and user clients
6.11 ASSIST tries to treat every household as a separate client, and make a distinction between the *sponsor client* (the housing association) and the *user client* (the residents). This means that a high level of service can be given to everybody and that all the residents are equally involved in the improvement. It also means that individual problems that could potentially hold up the improvements can be identified and resolved. For instance, recently one owner occupier in Govanhill was worried about the cost of the improvements and the amount of space he might lose. ASSIST was able to work out a solution for the owner occupier that allowed him to build part of the bathroom in advance of the contractor arriving. Also with his friends he gutted the house, repaired the windows and carried out the replastering. Similarly, it is not possible simply to ignore the fact that a tenant has installed a large fire surround that covers the normal location of a new plug or has put a light fitting on a wall.

6.12 Difficulties are encountered with this approach when the sponsor client is trying to establish building standards that will apply to all the houses. For instance, a tenant's glazed inside doors may be in a bad state of repair and the housing association would prefer to replace them with solid doors. The tenant likes the doors because they make the house look modern and let in more light. The housing association considers the doors too dangerous and if they are left the association may be faced with a claim for damages and will certainly be faced with a substantial repair bill at some stage. These problems can never be entirely resolved and the only way to reduce the problem is to have a building sub-committee consisting of residents who will lay down the standards and consider appeals against the architect's decision where necessary. This puts the onus on the architect to explain exactly what he is doing and why.

Educating the user client

6.13 It is for these types of reasons that ASSIST takes the building committee through improvements stage by stage and instructs members on how to survey a house. Recently the members of the Building Sub-Committee of the Govanhill Housing Association held three meetings to cover the Standard Form of Building Contract so that these sponsor clients could understand and grasp their responsibilities under the contract.

Residents' backcourts schemes

6.14 When backcourts are designed a similar process is followed. Last year the Calder Square Residents Association asked ASSIST to prepare a backcourt scheme. ASSIST accepted only after the residents undertook to survey their own backcourt and prepare their own scheme first. After a month ASSIST was called to a meeting and shown the existing plan of the backcourts as drawn up by the residents. It was only at the end of the meeting that the residents plucked up courage to produce their own scheme to show to the architects. The scheme designed by the residents laid great emphasis on rubbish disposal, which at that time was non existent. ASSIST prepared further alternative schemes round the proposal to put the rubbish out of sight and came back to three further meetings at which the plans were drawn up with the residents present so that they could start to understand how plans work.

6.15 Eventually a scheme which provided equal drying areas and similar carrying distances for rubbish was agreed on and a model built. The model showed the position of new bin shelters, the areas of the individual drying areas, and the line of the fences. Meetings were arranged in every close. The model and a sample panel of materials (photos cut out of the AJ Hard Landscape handbook) were taken to each close. Detailed designs for individual backcourts were worked out at the close meeting and incorporated into the overall scheme. The result was that each backcourt area was different and had its own individual mark, whether it was crazy paving or ordinary slabs; metal fences or concrete patterned screen walls; lawns or planting areas, **28**.

28 *Backcourt design by Calder Square Residents Association and ASSIST. Residents and architects removed the back wall and bin shelters to cut costs.*

6.16 The new backcourt almost proved too costly to build, so in order to execute the scheme as designed by the residents and the architect, the residents decided to do their own demolition. One weekend the whole backcourt was cleared. Residents of the tenement block, children as well as old people, working with their architects, threw the rubble into 12 skips. As one old lady said, 'it's just like China'.

7 Building

Billing

7.01 The Housing Corporation has a 4 stage pre-contract approval system. The first stage is a sketch design for the close which can be submitted after consultation with residents but before detailed dilapidation surveys are carried out. The second stage requires detailed plans and cost estimate on an elemental basis (see para **12.09**). On approval of stage 2, drawings and surveys can be sent to the QS for billing. Stage 3 consists of approval of the tender list, and stage 4 is the tender approval. The submission for this stage includes an analysis of the lowest tender comparing it with the estimate approved at stage 2.

Decanting

7.02 In Govan the residents stayed in their houses during improvements because the work was not very extensive and there were no financial arrangements for providing temporary housing. This made it very easy to get onto site quickly but it was nevertheless very difficult for the residents who braved dirt and upset with great fortitude, **29**. The only advantage of such a scheme is that the housewives can make good clerks of works (as long as they are not continually on the back of the tradesmen) and they get to understand exactly how their house improvements work. But overall the problems of dirt and disturbance far outweigh the advantages. (In Govan some residents would go and live with relatives nearby and in one case an old person was sent on holiday.)

29 *Obvious reasons for decanting.*

7.03 In the later schemes everybody has been decanted, usually to houses in the immediate neighbourhood to avoid upsetting work, school and shopping routines. Being nearby means that residents can still check progress on their houses. Though less trouble than staying, moving twice in twelve weeks can be a traumatic experience and great care and attention is required if the difficulties are to be minimised. Everyone, including the architect, should help during this period of the removals.

Contract period

7.04 From the residents' point of view the contract goes well except when they want to change their minds after materials and units have been ordered or the builder experiences delays in supplies. It is important to fix a date after which changes should not be made, although a few are inevitable. It is also important to go over with owner occupiers precisely what is to be done to their houses, and agree how much authority the architect has to order variations. Particular attention has to be paid to tenants' fittings which cannot be easily moved (although where possible the tenants should be encouraged to remove all their possessions from the houses). Ultimately it is attention to detail which makes the scheme successful; boxing up telephones, saving the tv aerials, rescuing a clothes pulley from a skip and handing it back to the resident who inadvertently left it behind.

7.05 The houses should not be handed over until they are completely finished. During a rolling programme of work there are considerable pressures to do otherwise which should be resisted if possible. When houses are finally handed over it will be necessary to establish a complaints procedure to cover snags that emerge during the defects liability period. A final survey should be made with each owner occupier to check that the work which is to be paid for has in fact been done and to go through the variations. The final accounts should be prepared immediately, before owners start to forget what work has been carried out. ASSIST also carries out a third close meeting at which someone other than the architect goes through the improvements with residents to pick up complaints which residents are reluctant to make directly to the architect, so that future improvements can proceed more easily, **30**.

30 *Govanhill house improved . . . and, perhaps, a greater sense of control over one's own housing.*

8 Postscript

Community based organisation

8.01 To some extent this has not been so much a case study of ASSIST as of Glasgow. It is the possibility of improving all the houses in the city which is fundamentally interesting. This city has recognised problems but its solutions have not always been praised. In the field of tenement improvement, however, Glasgow deserves both recognition and praise. The original ASSIST project in Govan improved living conditions for only relatively few people. By itself, and at that time, it could do little to solve the overall problem of Glasgow's tenement housing. It is the community based housing associations supported by the Housing Corporation and Glasgow District that have now started to solve the problem and will continue to do so as long as central government support is forthcoming.

8.02 The contribution of the ASSIST project in Govan was to provide an example which was emulated and improved upon by the community based housing associations. It has provided administrative and technical support for two community based associations and architectural services for two others. Ex-members of ASSIST have gone on to work in other practices, and in the Housing Corporation and the NBA. One has become the first in-house association architect in Glasgow. ASSIST also continues to carry out research and development in the field of tenement improvement.

New approaches to improvement

8.03 But the changes that have occurred in Glasgow over the last two years have depended on the contribution of many other people and organisations, and a little bit of luck—not least in the strange conjunction of English/Welsh and Scottish housing legislation. The English/Welsh legislation provides the money needed to finance the community based housing associations; Scottish legislation provides the means for the local authority to designate the areas and finance the owner occupiers. On the one hand the chance success of these two pieces of legislation supports the case for a much more diverse body of housing legislation which allows alternative approaches to be tried out and tested. On the other, one cannot rely entirely on luck to solve housing problems which suggests that new legislation aimed specifically at improving Scottish housing, particularly the tenement, is required. Even with specific tenement legislation little can be done unless a large number of people work together.

ASSIST's aims

8.04 ASSIST takes an approach which is different from that of many normal architectural practices. First, ASSIST tries to treat every person as an individual client and to involve him fully in the process of improving his home. This is difficult to do on a large scale. Second, ASSIST believes in working for community organisations comprised of its individual clients and recognises that these organisations do not necessarily require merely architectural services. Third, it is ASSIST's view that the process of improvement based on housing choices is far more important than the basic technical solution.

8.05 In a sense ASSIST is like a small provincial practice except that there are many more clients. However, it is a pity that in cities it takes an extremely difficult housing problem, such as improving tenements, to provide the impetus for such an approach. It should and could be adopted as part of any housing programme be it redevelopment, improvement or both.

Final part

The final part of this case study will cover technical aspects of tenement improvement and will be published in the new year.

9 Documentation

Background

9.01 Before commencing detailed survey work of individual houses it is useful to identify the range of tenement types in an area. The more usual sources are original plans submitted for Dean of Guild approval sometimes available from the city archivist, or pre-HAA designation surveys, or, if necessary, a house-to-house survey. Although a 100 per cent survey is time consuming, it provides a great deal of information on how houses are used. This gain can be balanced against the disturbance of residents by repeated surveys. Plans of individual houses have usually been drawn at 1:100, which is suitable for surveying, but 1:50 is better for site information.

9.02 At the same time, a range of bathroom and kitchenette solutions can be developed and some tested by improving a stack or even a close of show houses. This will also provide costing information.

9.03 As explained in **4.03**, the client may provide details of residents' requirements in the form of a close chart, a cross sectional representation of the tenement. Using the range of solutions already developed, the architect can quickly prepare an 'ideal' scheme which can be speedily adapted during a close meeting with residents. The plans are finalised and arrangements made to survey houses with residents at home.

Survey

9.04 Surveys are carried out on a twelve-page form. The first sheet includes a plan of the house and records information on the size of the existing appliances, **31**. This sheet also details the bathroom and kitchenette types to be used and specifies the colour of bathroom suites and kitchen unit catalogue number. The builder can use the front sheet for ordering the sanitary fittings and kitchen units at the outset of the contract in order to avoid delays in deliveries of these critical items. The first four sheets, covering major downtakings and alterations, are not broken down on a trade by trade basis because of the difficulty of quantifying the separate parts at the survey stage. However, the remainder of the form is split up by trades—plumber (gas only), electrician, joiner (windows, doors and other repairs), plasterer and painter. Rooms, windows and doors are located by a code to the house plan on the front of the page. Common repairs are described in long hand on a separate schedule.

9.05 The reliability of the survey is influenced by the rapport or otherwise that is created between the householder and the surveyor and the ability of the surveyor to be painstakingly thorough despite well intentioned interruptions from the householder. Windows are undoubtedly the hardest items to survey (especially at night) as access is often impeded by furniture, blinds and curtains. It is in this area that the largest number of errors occur. But the survey is the basis of the entire contract and has to be comprehensive if the final account is to resemble the contract sum. Very few items, perhaps only plasterwork, should be measured provisionally if accurate costs and tight programming are the main aims.

Billing

9.06 The completed survey forms and drawings are sent to the quantity surveyor who will already have the main 'compendium' items such as bathrooms and kitchenettes broken down into work items on a trade by trade basis. A 'master document' containing and describing theoretically all possible work items as opposed to a full bill of quantities has also been prepared. The master document, which contains the contract conditions as well as sections covering specification, materials and workmanship by trade, is updated from time to time. The work items described in the master document are coded and cross referenced to the survey form. The coded items are consolidated into a 'schedule of works' for each close which in turn cross references with the master document, **32**.

9.07 In this way information sent to the quantity surveyor on a house by house basis (the unit for surveying and cost analysis for owner occupiers) can easily be billed on a close by close basis (the unit for pricing), thus avoiding bulky documentation and pricing on a house by house basis which is an estimator's

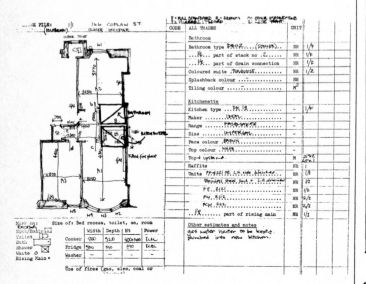

31 *First sheet of survey form recording existing layout, fixtures and fittings to bathroom and kitchenette.*

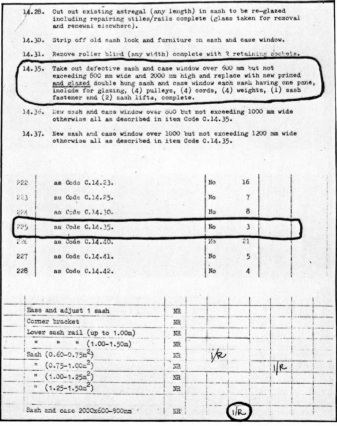

32 *Billing a repair item. Top, item described in master document with code. Middle, consolidated as code in schedule of works. Bottom, noted on survey form.*

nightmare. By clearly establishing rates, this approach facilitates easy remeasurement and accommodates renegotiations for the continuation of contracts, but can present real difficulties on site unless enough clues are given in the schedule of work as to the nature and location of the work items. This method of surveying and billing has been adopted by a number of architects and quantity surveyors in Glasgow and lends itself to being computerised (see **4.04**).

Contract

9.08 The contract normally used is the Standard Form of Building Contract, private edition without quantities, and incorporating the Scottish Supplement (with the latest revisions). A number of additional clauses are also added to conform with the requirements of the lending authorities (eg the fair wages clause) and also to cover the special circumstances that are met in tenement improvement. The Housing Corporation issues guidance notes on the additional clauses to be incorporated. Of general note in improvement work is the normal practice of the client taking out insurance against fire etc under clause 20 (c) rather than the contractor under clause 20 (a). It may also be worth incorporating clause 19 (2) (a), insurance against damage to neighbouring property.

Site information and procedures

9.09 Detailed drawings are issued to site (in fact the same as those used for pricing and building permission and loan approval), plus schedules covering joiner repairs and decoration, **33**. (There is potential duplication of effort caused by the varying information requirements for surveying, pricing and site work.) Some contractors also like to be issued copies of the original surveys although these do not form part of the contract documentation. It is possible to run a contract by only referring to and amending the survey form as is necessary, issuing blanket architect's instructions at the beginning and end of the contract. Normal procedure is to issue architect's instructions as and when appropriate, though there are dangers that short programme contracts will become overloaded with paper work.

9.10 This problem can largely be overcome by working from local offices and acting effectively as site architects. A march-in is carried out at the beginning of the contract checking the condition of the empty houses against the survey forms. With programming being so tight, site meetings are held every two weeks and progress meetings at the end of each week.

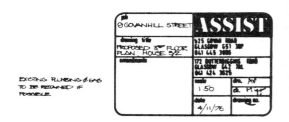

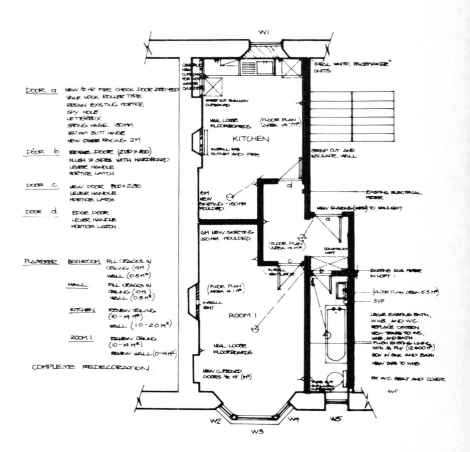

33 Plans can be combined with repair schedules, reducing the number of pieces of paper in circulation.

months

| 1 | 2 | 3 | 4 | 5 | 6 | 7 | 8 | 9 | 10 | 11 | 12 | 13 | 14 | 25 |

pre-contract programme ← → ← on site →

preparatory work by housing association development officer — close meetings + scheme design — shc/1 submission — housing corporation approvals — surveys + detailed design — cost plan — shc/2 submission — housing corporation approvals — production dwgs. — building control — shc/3 submission — billing — tender — tender analysis — shc/4 submission — housing corporation approvals — contractors pre-site preparations — defects liability period + final account

34 *On-site time is a relatively short part of the overall rehabilitation programme. Note that the 9/10 months period up to tender approval is governed to a large extent by the time required by Housing Corporation approvals.*

9.11 There are two difficult periods in the contract. One occurs in the middle when all the downtakings and roughings should be completed but the finishings have not started. Morale is low because it does not look as if the work is getting anywhere. The second difficult period occurs towards the end of the contract when, because of the pressure to maintain the momentum of a rolling programme and the need to make arrangements in advance to move residents back, clients tend to want to take possession of the houses before the work can be said to be practically completed. This only leads to problems of gaining access to complete outstanding work and causes a great deal of resident dissatisfaction.

Alternative documentation

9.12 The documentation described above was developed to meet the requirements of government departments concerned about public accountability, the funding authorities who require the costs to be broken down into various categories (see **12.09**) and the estimators who want a slim and easy to price bill. The above approach assumes conventional contractual arrangements and full architectural and quantity surveying services. However, it might be preferable to adopt the English house improvement practice of pricing on only drawings and specification, with the client employing a contracts manager to co-ordinate the separate trades. In this way builders' percentage mark up, preliminaries and fees could be reduced, bringing down the overall cost of improvement work. Unfortunately the RIBA Agreement for Minor Building Works cannot be used in Scotland. So the problem of cost analysis (particularly for the owner occupier) needs to be overcome. It is also not proven whether this form of documentation is suitable for say £200 000 four close contracts. Because of the unknown nature of improvement work such contracts will inevitably be subject to changes and subsequent financial adjustments which are normally based on rates derived from a priced bill.

Programming of information

9.13 The three months on site only form a small part of the overall programme, **34**. At the quickest it normally takes about nine months to get a scheme onto site (assuming background work has already been done) and the overall time from surveys to final account can be up to 2½ years. This assumes that application for building permission will occur at the same time as the information is sent to the quantity surveyor for billing. So the architect has to have established in advance, as part of the preliminary work, what standards and designs are permissible. Apart from the contract period itself, the most critical period is the fixed period for the acceptance of the tender.

9.14 The analysis and application for loan approval should be made as quickly as possible. Any savings exercise will cause delay and therefore again it is worth establishing, before survey work commences, the exact nature of the standards that the client and the loan authority require. The loan authority will need as much time as possible to vet the scheme and the price, which should ideally be accepted one month before the tender period elapses.

9.15 The tender acceptance period should also be used for making grant and home loan applications on behalf of owner occupiers. Draft final accounts (or interim accounts) should be drawn up as soon as possible on the completion of the scheme to allow the housing association client to apply for a housing association grant and in order to agree the details of the completed work with the owner occupiers before everybody forgets what has been done. (Architect's instructions or certificates will not necessarily be accepted as evidence of work having been carried out. It is best to check the house over with the owner occupier immediately on completion and follow the visit up with an account, which can be difficult if the builder takes time to complete his paper work.)

10 Improvements

10.01 Work of improvement is described separately from repairs as cost analyses (see **12.01**) require work to be classified in this way.

Layout improvements

10.02 In most cases tenement houses can be improved as they stand. Alternatively, some houses, usually centre houses, can be amalgamated with adjacent (side) houses to create fewer but larger units, **3, 13**. Single apartment houses are rarely improved and therefore require to be amalgamated. For amalgamation to take place, there should be agreement on the part of all the owners and occupants, especially when the proposal would result in the displacement of a household.

Bathroom improvements

Shared cold water storage systems

10.03 Tenement plumbing systems fall into two categories: plumbing stacks with shared or individual cold water storage. Shared cold water storage is located in the roof space, in 227-litre tanks breached together with feeds to individual 115-litre hot water cylinders located in the ceiling void above the bathrooms on each floor. This may necessitate placing the cylinder on its side which in turn requires a spreader fitted at the cold water inlet. Grade I cylinders should be used on the lower two floors. There are long runs of feeds and expansions but all the components can be obtained ex-stock and showers will operate on gravity.

10.04 An alternative approach is for cold water from common storage to feed down to an instantaneous gas water heater rather than an electrically heated water cylinder. There is a strong resident preference for gas heating and cooking and this would be a popular solution. The gas heater can be located at the kitchenette window. A further possibility is to use a combined gas room and water heater, venting into an existing flue. In this case, the common cold water storage could in theory be eliminated altogether, although there is strong resistance to this by the water boards. There are also good practical reasons for retaining the storage apart from the fact that supplies can be cut from time to time. Water in storage is warmer than water straight off a rising main, thus reducing the likelihood of condensation forming on wc cisterns and cutting down costs of heating water.

Individual cold water storage systems

10.05 Cold water storage, located within each house, feeds a low level hot water cylinder (often a Dublotank) placed on or near to the floor. The 3 m high rooms provide sufficient head although pumps are needed for showers. In this way most of the secondary plumbing, ie excluding the waste, common overflows and sludge plus ventilation duct, will be within each house. (Some inspectors will even allow the overflows, sludge and ventilation to be taken to the outside face of the building at each floor.) The necessary components can be obtained ex-stock and where the hot water cylinder is located outside the bathroom compartment, the opportunity exists of forming an airing cupboard, a facility practically unknown in most tenements. However, in most cases this system is installed as two part plumbing frames, within the bathroom, backing onto and becoming part of the common ducts, **35**. Factory-made combination tanks are rarely installed in tenements although there should be no objection to their use.

10.06 Most new bathrooms are located in a bed recess. The layout can be conventional with all the fittings backing onto the common, accessible duct. Alternatively, the bath can be positioned parallel to and across the duct, thus reducing the encroachment by the bathroom onto living space by 150 mm. In this arrangement, the waste pipes pass into the void above the bathroom ceiling of the house below, which is less than satisfactory for access to repairs and fire protection. A further possibility is to raise the bathroom floor, which creates space for the pipes but increases the cost and is not always approved by the building inspector.

Firestopping ducts

10.07 The firestopping of the duct is a major worry. In some schemes, cast iron wastes and lightweight metal ventilation ducting have been used to prevent fire spread (the ducting may rust over time). In other schemes the wastes and ventilation have been installed in PVC. Tests have shown that PVC systems (which carbonise and tend to self-seal in conditions of fire) perform no less satisfactorily than metal systems in preventing fire spread. The major contributory factor in preventing fire spread is the firestopping of the duct at each floor (plaster on expanded wire lath with a plasterboard shutter).

Other stack arrangements

10.08 Bathrooms described so far are part of a new plumbing stack that will have to pass through each house. An alternative is to attach the new bathrooms onto the old toilet stack, although there are inherent planning problems with this method as the old toilet compartments are rarely big enough to allow a bathroom or even a shower to be added without creating tortuous circulation around the fittings. Also the old 4-inch pipe may be rotten or furred.

10.09 An alternative is to erect a new stack on the face of the building at the rear of the property with the waste pipe from the bathroom to the external stack passing between the joists. This approach, which allows individual houses to be improved, has been used with success in Aberdeen and may be worth adopting more widely. However, the extra cost of the installation, the distance from the toilet to the stack and the sub-optimal location of the bathroom in the kitchen recess do not make it as attractive as it might seem on first sight.

Kitchenette improvements

10.10 In the past, kitchen and living space were combined. Where a house cannot be substantially increased in size this pattern of living will have to remain, so it is better to make the new kitchenette directly accessible from the living room which will be doubling up as the dining area. At the same time it is important that the kitchenette area can be closed off from the living area, **26**.

35 *Plumbing frame. Cold water storage feeding down to hot water cylinder behind basin. Note access hatches to stop cock.*

36 *Cold wall strapped out awaiting insulation, dpm and plasterboard. This provides for wiring and good fixing for wall units.*

10.11 Kitchenettes can be located in old toilet compartments, nearly always adjacent to the old kitchen/living room, or even in old bathrooms, where new bathroom stacks have been installed in a bed recess. Alternatively, the bed recess itself can be used or the space created by dividing a large room into two. Where a larger house is being created (by amalgamation) an open kitchen/dining arrangement can be planned.

10.12 Residents' existing appliances can cause problems. Either cookers that are too low in relation to the worktop or refrigerators that are too high. The provision of a ventilated food cupboard causes the architect endless frustration but the difficulties are rarely insurmountable, as the building inspectors are quick to point out, if a little costly. Where a kitchenette abuts a cold wall (for instance a $4\frac{1}{2}$-inch brick wall onto the stair) the wall should be strapped and insulated, which provides fixings for the units, space for the wiring and reduces condensation. All other cold walls (for instance close walls) should be treated in a similar manner, **36**.

Storage improvements

10.13 Tenements have little storage space and potentially less after improvement. Lofts can be built above the bed recess, although these are difficult for old people to use. Bed recesses can be converted into walk-in stores as can old toilet and scullery compartments. Existing wall presses (shelved recesses in thickness of wall) can be retained or rebuilt. However many residents would like the presses to be taken out and the walls flushed. It is considered more modern-looking.

Other improvements

10.14 Other house improvements include the upgrading of entrance doors to give half-hour fire resistance. Current concern about the use of asbestos and labour involved in upgrading floors may make the installation of a new front door a more attractive proposition. Most houses will need rewiring or at least to have extra power points added. Housing association houses require one fixed fire appliance. Old fireplaces are being stripped out to create more floor space. Common improvements might include the insulation of the roof space, the installation of a communal tv aerial (thus reducing the damage to the slates caused by loose cables and men walking on the roof), insertion of a damp proof course where none previously existed, and the erection of a gate or door at the close entrance, **37**.

11 Repairs

House repairs

11.01 House repairs can be so open-ended that before the architect knows what has happened he has rebuilt rather than improved the houses. The two major areas are joinery work and plaster work, and in both cases a decision has to be made as to whether it is best to patch or replace. This decision, to a certain extent, depends on how the work is priced and in early contracts it may be worth considering including dual specifications. Replacement may be more expensive than patching and can also lead to expensive side effects. For instance, if a case and sash window is replaced, the ingoes (reveals) and framing will also have to be stripped out and rebuilt. The end product is to a high standard of finish and overcomes the problem of painting old skirtings and facings that may in fact necessitate the burning off of old paintwork, an expensive solution in itself. It may be difficult to match old and new timber sections without resorting to special runs.

11.02 Plaster repairs are difficult to estimate (particularly before the wallpaper has been stripped off) and care should be taken not to underspecify on the ground floor walls and top floor ceilings, both of which are vulnerable to damp. Generally, repairs require clear standards being set before the survey work is carried out, thorough surveys prior to billing and careful examination, especially of plasterwork, at the 'march-in' stage.

Common repairs

11.03 The major common repair items, apart from remedying severe structural failures, **38**, **39**, will be the repairs carried out on the roof. These can include an overhaul of the roof or the replacement of existing slates with interlocking tiles. The latter solution may require readjustment of the rones (half round eaves gutters) and reforming of flashings. Ridge pieces will be repaired or renewed, **40**, and the skews (raking top of

38 *Cracking due to subsidence. Steel lintel to be inserted behind facade.*

39 *Reconstruction of bay (4 floors). New concrete cranked beams tied into stonework at each floor.*

37 *New gate, tiling, floor and steps. There are usually existing gates and tiles, sometimes in good enough condition to retain.*

40 *Ridge piece needing renewal. Valley gutters, vent pipes and slates may need repair or overhaul. Note new glazed roof light/access hatch and reduced chimney height.*

gable) reblocked. Timber access hatches are best replaced with glazed rooflights. The lead coverings to the oriel may need repatching or a complete recovering (probably not in lead). Dangerous chimneys should be taken down and rebuilt where necessary, **41**. The ogee-shaped rones to the front of the property which rest on a moulded plinth course can now be replaced in glass fibre. The half round rones at the rear are best replaced in cast iron which is less affected than plastic by the high exposure to the wind on tenements. Bitter experience has shown a number of housing associations the folly of merely patching 80 year old roofs, and policy now tends towards complete re-roofing.

11.04 The rainwater goods and any soil vents on the face of the building can be replaced in plastic except for the bottom 3 m. A damp proof course may have failed, and the solum need treating and vents replaced. Some lintels may have to be reinforced and spalling stonework hacked back and refaced in render to match existing stonework. Repointing and re-rendering may also be carried out. Ideally, the stone should be cleaned which would greatly enhance the front of the buildings and transform the previously gloomy backcourts.

11.05 As much work as can be afforded should be carried out while the tenement is scaffolded. Individual repairs at a later date will be proportionally more expensive.

11.06 Internally daylights, hatches, and stairhead windows may need repairs, plasterwork carried out and the close and stair redecorated. The closes were originally tiled. If the tiles are of good quality and condition they should be retained. ASSIST's policy is normally to retile which gives a marked visual boost to the close. Badly damaged tiles can be sprayed, replaced (although it is difficult to obtain frost-resistant tiles) or hacked off and the wall rendered and painted. The close is relaid and the stair treads are sometimes resurfaced. Banisters and balustrades should be checked over.

11.07 The rendered walls below the dado can be painted in gloss but there are particular problems in handling the old lime washed walls above dado height. These can be either stripped and replastered which is very expensive or, alternatively, scraped, filled in and treated with a sealer and painted an eggshell finish. Alternative wall finishes include fleck paints which can look institutional. The internal scale of the tenement was originally humanised by differentiating between the upper walls which reflected the light and the dark hard wearing lower walls divided by a dado band, sometimes with stencilled patterns. It is a good opportunity to modernise the stairhead lighting and some architects prefer to cover the electrical and gas services located on the stairs, **42, 43**.

41 *Chimneys are highly exposed some 15 m above the pavement and may well need replacing. Here the stack height has been reduced with gas cowls set in. It will be rendered to match the stonework of the tenement front.*

12 Costs

12.01 Building costs
Assuming normal pricing and conventional documentation, house improvement costs, as illustrated by table I, are influenced primarily by standards and specification, building control, the existing condition of the property, apportionment of common repairs and cost limit.

Standards and specification
12.02 Only after a few houses have been improved can the building committee of the housing association effectively tackle the problem of standards of facilities to be installed and specification of materials and components. Nevertheless, in order to ensure equality of housing provision for tenants and to ease the maintenance burden later, it is necessary to establish standards and specification as soon as possible in the improvement programme. Some guidance notes are provided

42 *Existing stair with change of decoration at dado height. Existing GPO, gas electricity on stairs plus contractor's temporary water and electricity.*
temporary water and electricity.

43 *Renewed services covered in bulkhead duct. New stair head lighting. Half hour firecheck doors with wired glass fanlights. Traditional decoration retained on wall to right.*

Table I Fixed price contracts, Govanhill—July 1975 to September 1976							
Tender submission	*July* 1975	*October* 1975	*November* 1975	*March* 1976	*May* 1976	*June* 1976	*September* 1976
Number of closes	1	2	1	1	1	1	4
Number of housing association houses	7	21	9	7	9	7	32
Average cost of housing association house	4650	5360	5080	6140	5550	5680	5880
Number of owner-occupied houses	3	0	1	2	1	0	0*
Average cost of owner-occupied house	3890**	—	3540	3640	3680	—	—

* Originally two owner occupied houses at average of £5210.
** Including one twinning.

by the National Building Agency, the Housing Corporation and Scottish Development Department (see **15.01**).

Building control
12.03 It is difficult within current cost limits to meet the Building Standards (Scotland) (Consolidation) Regulations 1971. Notable problems include the requirement to permanently ventilate single aspect (middle) houses, common in tenements. By and large, designers have to accept the layout and dimensions of the existing rooms which do not really fit into the current space standards drawn up with new housing in mind. There is either too much or too little storage. And furthermore, it is not always easy to prove that some parts of the existing building are still performing adequately (eg the flues), particularly while the tenement is still occupied.
12.04 The solution is to apply for relaxation of building regulations but there is a marked reluctance by both architects and some building inspectors to make an issue of the problem, relying on a commonsense approach instead. This is an uneasy position for all the parties and there have been moves, in Glasgow anyway, to reach common agreement between building control and the housing associations on the standards required for tenement improvement work. Unfortunately, these discussions have not borne fruit as yet and many architects (and building inspectors) still need guidance, perhaps in a Scottish Development Department circular.

Existing condition of property
12.05 The existing condition of tenement property depends on age, quality of original construction, past maintenance, and orientation. Furthermore, corner closes with their complex plans and large areas of external wall and roof inevitably require more work than a tenement in the middle of a straight terrace. Unfortunately, the current cost limits do not take these differences into account, with the result that there is a danger that internal standards are cut to permit essential repairs.

Apportionment of common repairs
12.06 Common parts of a tenement—roof, walls, foundations, circulation, are jointly owned by all the proprietors for each property. The costs of these common repairs are set against each house. As can be appreciated, the cost of common repairs is proportionally less per house where there are, say, twelve houses rather than eight houses in each property. Again, at present this is not taken into account in cost limit calculations. The exact details as to the items classified as being common repairs can be checked by reference to the title deeds of the individual properties.

Cost limits
12.07 Current housing association works-only cost limits in Glasgow are given in **6.02**. These fixed limits have come in for some criticism, especially as their operation encourages the retention of the maximum number of small houses rather than amalgamations to form the larger units often desperately needed by the existing population of the area. An alternative procedure to using these fixed limits would be to carry out an assessment of houses in a specific area, forecasting costs, taking into account standard specification for improvements, varying repair costs and differing apportionment of common repairs. These forecast costs, which overcome the problems described above, could then be agreed with the funding authorities and so form the basis of the authorities' cost limits for that area.
12.08 Until 1976 the owner occupiers and landlords cost limit has effectively been £3700, the maximum building cost eligible for 75 per cent-90 per cent improvement grant. This cost limit can be seen from table I where the owner occupiers' schemes were subject to quite drastic savings exercises to bring their building costs within the effective cost limit. The maximum building cost eligible for improvement grant has been raised to £7000 in tenement areas only (see SDD Circular 61/1977).

Cost analysis
12.09 Housing cost breakdown may vary between the Housing Corporation and local authorities. The Housing Corporation's SHC/2 form has an elemental breakdown of the estimated costs, divided broadly into four sections:
● house improvement/conversion costs
● house repair cost
● common improvement/conversion cost
● common repair cost
12.10 Local authorities may require a different breakdown and it is important that the relevant categories are established early, and identified at the survey stage, in the information sent to the QS for billing and on the architect's instructions issued during the contract. (Again these categories lend themselves to computer analysis, see **4.04**.) An example of an owner occupier's cost breakdown into the five categories required by Glasgow District Council is given in Table II (September 1976 prices).

Table II Example of owner occupier's cost-breakdown				
	Full standard	Tolerable standard	Repairs	Non-grant earning work	Other improvements
Bathroom	626·76	—	—	—	—
Stacks	187·03	—	—	—	—
Drainage	117·04	—	—	—	—
Kitchenette	695·67	—	—	—	—
Kitchen fitments	—	265·53	—	—	—
Underground water	13·29	—	—	—	—
Rising main	69·25	—	—	—	—
Downtakings and alterations	550·85	—	—	—	—
Gas work	—	—	—	—	51·66
Electrical	232·68	118·72	—	—	—
Joiner repairs	—	—	307·13	—	—
Plaster repairs	—	—	31·53	—	—
Painter work	45·00	—	—	—	—
Common improvements	7·88	—	—	—	—
Common repairs	—	—	408·42	—	—
	£2545·45	£384·25	£747·08	—	£51·66
Proportion of preliminaries	203·64	30·74	59·77	—	4·13
Proportion of dayworks and contingencies	128·93	19·46	37·84	—	2·62
	£2878·02	£434·45	£844·69	—	£58·41

Total tender cost   £4215·57
Architect's and qs's fees 542·11
VAT on repair items   67·58
                        £4825·26

Grant (75 per cent)   3618·94
Net amount   £1206·32
Monthly repayments over 10 years at 7·4 per cent (option mortgage)—£14·55

13 Site
Access
13.01 Access both to and from most tenement sites is usually restricted. Many tenements are completely enclosed which results in difficulties in hutting, storage and plant, and leads to increased prices. Lack of access can cause particular problems in environmental work to completely enclosed backcourts (see **15.01**). Even when access can be gained from the rear it is often necessary to demolish boundary walls. Access is further restricted by scaffolding, work on drains, the presence of skips and other plant and the bulk storage, even temporarily, of sand and other materials on the pavement. For these reasons, most tenement sites are serviced from the front of the building, often from busy roads with limited space on both the road and pavement.

Accommodation and storage
13.02 On small contracts, site accommodation is usually located within the tenement being improved, or in one adjacent. The house that is used as the builder's howff inevitably suffers a considerable amount of wear and tear, and the storage of materials 'on the job' limits access and causes further damage. Thus the site accommodation is rarely ideal for the workforce and it is difficult to ensure that the Health and Safety regulations are being adhered to at all times. Again

storage of materials limits access and causes damage both to the houses and the materials.

13.03 On larger contracts these problems can be overcome by bringing in huts and setting up compounds, although it may be necessary to crane units over the buildings. Other approaches in Glasgow include running contracts from a fleet of pantechnicons, dumping bulk containers on site or using the old wash houses in the backcourts. The cheapest and most effective method is to arrange access for the builder to a tenement near to the site. This could be awaiting improvement or be due for demolition and preferably empty to avoid disturbance to residents. In this way it is possible to influence the levels of preliminaries and it is certainly worth discussing the problems with contractors at the pre-tender stage and including details of site accommodation in the tender document.

Plant

13.04 Plant for improvement work is small compared with even modest new build schemes. Most of the equipment is comprised of hand tools, or lightweight machinery. Mechanical hoists are rarely worth the trouble of erection but rubbish shutes, straight to skips, overcome the potential danger of killing off an already restricted site with rubbish, **44**.

13.05 The largest single element is scaffolding. Some jobbing builders still try to get away with carrying out roof work without scaffolding; their men are at best 'protected' by ropes attached to a chisel driven into the ridge piece. This method is unsupportable. Scaffolding attracts children and one solution is to hang scaffolding from the upper floors.

13.06 Before work starts on site the Electricity Board and Gas Board should remove meters and cut supplies. The GPO will disconnect phones. It is not unusual for some builders, two weeks into the contract, to find themselves without light, heat, power or water and unable even to telephone for these services to be temporarily installed. It is sometimes necessary to remind builders to arrange for site services in time for the start of a contract, although this is difficult when the contract is signed at the very end of the acceptance period because of delays by the client in obtaining financial approval.

Security

13.07 The need for security against theft and vandalism varies from district to district and is symptomatic of economic and social conditions in any area. The problems also vary according to the approach adopted by the improvement agency. It appears that clients, builders and architects who advertise their presence from scaffolding attract trouble, as does property that has been left empty. Children are often caught but the main offenders are the scrap merchants and others who move into improvement areas and offer the children rates for stripping out newly installed pipework, kitchen units and other fittings.

13.08 The responsibility for security during the contract lies with the builders. A watchman is essential though he will have difficulties if he has to watch several closes at one time. A sensible precaution is to put plywood shutters over ground and first-floor windows. Scaffolding is a major security problem. Not only does it give access to the upper floors and roof of the close under improvement but often to adjacent occupied closes as well. Work requiring scaffolding should be tightly programmed so that it can be removed as soon as possible.

Programming site work

13.09 Tenement contracts are short and fast, between eight and twelve weeks per close; about one home per week. This must be made clear to the contractor at the outset and an overall programme of work included in the tender document. The contractors should be invited to submit their own detailed programme as part of the tender, although most are reluctant to do so. It is the devil's own job obtaining one later. On site each small delay can totally disrupt progress as it is vital to keep the work moving in the correct sequence. There is no space to flood a tenement site with extra labour. Hence the need to have close site supervision, preferably with architects working from the site, and a constant review of progress. Inevitably the desire for speed has in-built problems, eg, drying out of plasterwork, especially in winter (table III).

13.10 Considering the specialist nature of tenement work, a better service might be obtained if, say, the medium to large contractors were chosen by tendering for rates with the programme and the mode of operation being open to discussion and negotiation between the client, architect, quantity surveyor and contractor. With the increasing amount of information on prices, approved cost limits, and controls on standards and specification, there should be no difficulties in terms of public accountability. There may also be a case for encouraging smaller builders to take on individual homes or stacks of houses with slimmed down documentation (see **9.12**). In any event, there is a need to examine the present methods of programming house improvements and to involve the contractors in this reappraisal.

14 Backcourts

Finance and programme

14.01 The finance for environmental improvements to backcourts is separate from the finance for house improvements and is obtained under section 58 of the Housing (Scotland) Act 1969. The effective cost limit of £500 per house. This grant is normally administered by the local authority, but SDD Circular 77/1978 makes provision for housing associations to claim the grant directly for houses in their ownership in HAAs—though for no apparent reason the grant limit in this case is only £400 per house. This allocation of finance on a house by house basis discriminates against those closes with a few houses, for instance two houses per floor, and where shops rather than houses appear on the ground floor. It also encourages the preparation of schemes before house improvements are carried out if twinning will reduce the number of houses, although contractually it may be better to carry out the backcourt work immediately on the completion of improvements.

44 Rubbish shutes. Skips would have been better placed beneath but there are problems of damage to pavements and permission from local authority.

14.02 Ideally, an incremental approach could be adopted although this is likely to increase the costs where access is limited to the closes, thus restricting the use of large pieces of plant, but also leading to damage to improved closes. Alternatively, if backcourt work is carried out before or during the house improvements, there may be a problem in co-ordinating two or more contractors and the possibility of landscaping being damaged by house improvements at a later date.

14.03 Thus a strong case emerges for carrying out all the external repairs to the houses and the backcourt environmental improvements before internal improvements commence. Because of the size of contract, this would give the cheapest price both for the repairs to the houses and the backcourt work. The residents would be encouraged both by the major repairs to the roofs and more particularly by the appearance of a new backcourt, the most obvious signs that house improvements are taking place. Unfortunately, at present such an approach is almost impossible to finance on a large scale, although paradoxically it has been made theoretically possible outside HAAs by the new repair grant legislation. However the need for individual grant applications from each separate owner, and the need for owners to contribute 50 per cent or more of the building repair costs, will make such schemes extremely difficult to organise. On balance it is probably better to carry out backcourt work prior to house improvements, designing the scheme in such a way as to allow areas to be easily lifted and relaid close to the back of the property and by including a large element of protection in the house improvement work. Certainly because of the likely delays in obtaining financial approval it would be advisable to draw up and submit proposals for backcourt work before commencing detailed surveys of houses.

Schemes

14.04 The procedure is for the scheme to be prepared with maximum of involvement of residents (see **3.06**). Indeed one of the conditions for approval is that the residents contribute either financially or in kind, for example by organising the application. Evidence of the existing poor state of the backcourt, a sketch scheme of the proposals and outline costs and the written consent of all the owners are sent to the district for outline approval. The district then submits the scheme to the Scottish Development Department which requires the cost to be broken down into elements attributable to eligible (ie improvement) work or ineligible (ie repair and replacement) work. The costs should be totalled for each of these categories and a cost per house given (inclusive of fees, VAT, etc).

14.05 When approval is obtained the detailed scheme is put out to tender and the costs, including any savings required and a priced document, are re-submitted to the district for final approval.

14.06 There is no space for a detailed description of backcourt designs except to make a few obvious points. Most residents seem to want the railings restored so that each close has its own back green. A drying area has to be provided as do bin shelters. There is currently a move back towards individual small bins for each house rather than shared Paladins. Although the £500 per house appears generous, the problems of access and the need to rebuild entire backcourts, often including the drainage mean that there is rarely an opportunity for designing exotic schemes.

15 Further information

15.01 Gourlay, C. *Elementary building construction and drawings for Scottish students (tenements)* 1903.
Jaggard, W. and Drury, F. *Architectural building construction* Volume 1. 1932.
McKay, W. *Building construction* Volumes 1 and 2. 1944.
Pride, G. L. *Glossary of Scottish building* 1975.
SDD Circular 72/75: Housing (Scotland) Act 1974: *requirements to be met by houses improved with the aid of grant.*
Housing Corporation Scottish Practice Note 2/78 (Working Draft) *Improvement/conversion/repair of existing property—technical brief for housing association property.*
SDD Circular 71/78: Housing Act 1974: *Housing association grant: Cost limits for improvement projects.*
SDD Circular 48/78: Housing (Scotland) Act 1974: *House improvement grants; percentage of approved expenditure for improvement grants etc.*
SDD Circular 47/77: Housing (Scotland) Act 1974: *House improvement grants. Approved expense limits and rateable value limits affecting house improvement grants.*
SDD Circular 61/77: Housing (Scotland) Act 1974: *House improvement grants; limits of approved expense and of rateable value.*
SDD Circular 35/78: Housing (Financial Provisions) (Scotland) Act 1978: *House improvement and slum clearance.*
NBA Technical Notes Nos 1-8 (obtainable from NBA, Mercantile Chambers, 53 Bothwell St, Glasgow):
Timber treatment
Stone cleaning and repair
Thermal insulation and condensation
Damp proof courses
Gable end treatments for tenements
Mechanical ventilation in tenements
Heating and hot water services in tenements
Survey techniques for dilapidated properties

Acknowledgement

Thanks to D. L. Brice & Partners (architects) and the staff of the NBA in Glasgow who helped in preparation of the case study (and for illustrations **35** and **43**); John Gilbert and Jamie O'Haire who took most of the photographs; and especially the McLaughlin family, Mr and Mrs Shaw of Govanhill and Mrs Lovatt whose homes mostly feature in the photographs.

Table III House Improvement programme for one close—building activities in sequence (including common repairs)

Week	Labourers bricklayers	Electricians	Plumbers	Joiners	Plasterers	Painters	Roofers
1	Clean out debris	Temporary power		March-ins	March-ins	Strip walls and ceilings	
2	Remove doors, ceilings, flooring, plaster, facings, old services as agreed at march-ins; work to chimneys						
3	Structural alterations, beams, new walls	1st fixing		Rot eradication			Strip and re-roof
4	Build ups, slappings; take up G/F	1st fixing	Roof, gutters and flashings	Stud walls	Plaster ceilings		Strip and re-roof
5	Main drainage	1st fixing	1st fixing	Strap existing walls			
6			1st fixing	Re-size door frames			
7	Lay new G/F			Windows	Plaster repairs to walls		
8				Floor repairs			
9		2nd fixing	2nd fixing	Facings, skirtings			
10	Finish drainage	2nd fixing	2nd fixing	Kitchen units	Work in common close	Paint houses	
11				Glazing	Scraping old plaster		
12	Snag	Snag	Snag	Snag	Snag	Paint close	
13	Snaggings completed, commission handover						

Case study 2:
Initial repairs at
Haringey, London

Initial repairs, the repairs needed to make Haringey's newly acquired dwellings habitable, provide accommodation quickly while keeping houses in reasonable repair until they are fitted into the full rehabilitation programme. Initial repairs are of interest partly for the role they might play in a strategy of gradual renewal. Initial repairs are the minimum works, hence least disturbance needed to make dwellings habitable. This section concentrates on organisation.

1 Housing need

1.01 The London borough of Haringey has a varied, somewhat ageing housing stock. To the west are very large three-storey houses set in quarter-hectare plots with 12 to 18 rooms, sometimes more. Then there are large terraced family houses ranging through to two up-two down terraced houses sometimes with a back addition, in the east of the borough. It is by no means generally poor but some owner-occupiers of larger houses are finding it increasingly difficult to afford necessary maintenance, **1**.

1.02 Such owner-occupiers who approach Haringey wishing to sell plus compulsory purchase of vacant properties make up most of current acquisitions, around 250 a year. (There must of course be a housing gain. Buying fully occupied houses is of no real interest unless other considerations also prevail.) Once purchased, the varied size of houses provides opportunities for conversions to suit a variety of housing needs; not just three-bedroomed family accommodation but small and single parent family units, units for single people and the old. Also, at the moment, Haringey is especially in need of accommodation for two-person and three-person families.

2 Purchase

Financing initial repairs
2.01 The current rate of acquisitions is partly of Haringey's own making through its purchasing of vacant properties, etc.

Owner-occupiers, however, approach the council without it advertising its willingness to buy. The sum of these acquisitions makes considerable demands on existing rehabilitation resources. Initial repairs provide one way of helping to smooth out the rehabilitation workload. Initial repairs make houses habitable for up to 15 years prior to full rehabilitation and are financed through DOE as part of acquisition. They are not paid out of rehabilitation (section 105) funds. Currently of 250 acquisitions around 150 are initially repaired: the remainder are in too bad a condition and are fully rehabilitated.

Purchase
2.02 DOE Circular 33/76 *Municipalisation—arrangements for the financial year* 1976/77 provides a series of categories for which compulsory purchase requires no special permission:
● acquisitions made in pursuance of a confirmed compulsory purchase order or to meet a statutory obligation to acquire a particular property (for example a resident landlord may be served a repairs notice by the public health department to bring a house to habitable standard. Instead of repairing, the owner may wish the council to buy and serve a purchase notice under section 101, Housing Act, 1974.)
● acquisitions of any dwellings in HAAs, PNs and GIAs declared and notified to the department to meet the objectives of those declarations;
● acquisitions of properties which have been standing empty for at least two months in areas where there is a serious overall shortage of housing or where the purpose of acquisition is to

1 *Large houses, many with elaborate enrichments, are expensive to maintain. Subletting helps finance upkeep.*

relieve homelessness (this is the category under which property in vacant possession is bought. Borough officers constantly keep an eye open for these).

- re-acquisitions of houses previously sold by a local authority;
- acquisitions of properties for use as hostels.

Purchasing from owners

2.03 Houses offered by owners outside 33/76 provisions require special permission to purchase from the DOE. With increasing financial stringency, greater housing gains are required from purchase for DOE approval. One or two bedspaces are unlikely to be enough to justify taking on the repairs of a whole house, unless medical or other special considerations apply.

2.04 An investigation report is completed for a prospective seller including how much of the house is used (it must be underused for there to be a housing gain) what facilities are shared, details of other tenants, income details for potential rent and rate rebates and what new accommodation the seller would accept if required. Owners do not in practice particularly want to stay in the same house but this can be agreed if initial repairs will produce a suitable unit in the house for continued occupation.

2.05 A borough valuer agrees a price mainly from the viewpoint of the house as a piece of property. The valuer is advised by the housing department concerned with the house as a useful addition to the housing stock and by the lettings department concerned with accommodating the displaced owner and with the council's existing housing needs.

First valuation

2.06 The valuer, together with an officer from the housing department, draws up a list of initial repairs and an estimate of their cost. The housing department has an outline set of costs to form an estimate, such as £50 for bricking up a fireplace or £250 per room for serious timber infestation.

2.07 The purchase and repair costs are subject to DOE approval. However, they cannot be very precise because the works are not detailed at this stage and a final decision on what units will be may not have been taken. This is not easily done because of difficulties of access to occupied property. So, for example, table I shows first valuations of initial repairs for two houses based on their becoming single family houses. Inderwick Road was used in this way but Middle Lane was subsequently used as bedsits for young people sharing facilities. Haringey did not need to go back to DOE because the repair work was done within the £5250 originally estimated, **2, 3**.

3 Schedule of works

3.01 On completion of purchase, which usually takes about six months for owners, the housing department surveys the house's repair and potential. The lettings department is consulted on types of accommodation in demand. Natural conversions, respecting existing building form as much as possible, are inevitable since initial repairs funding is essentially for repair and replacement and not for improvement and/or conversion into units.

2 *Inderwick Road (centre) makes a large family house with its two-storey back addition. One bedroom has to be provided downstairs.*

3 *Middle Lane (first from end) also has a two-storey back addition. It is being repaired for use as five bedsitters with two communal kitchens and a communal bathroom.*
Bedsitters are all high-ceilinged but vary considerably in floor area. The house is in generally good repair. The schedule of works does not include a major item for plastering.

Standards

3.02 Haringey used to have various standards for different accommodation but now has only one. Though initial repair involves a limited range of works, each is to as high a standard as possible, giving for a life of 10 to 15 years where appropriate. (Repairing for a shorter life is anyway problematic. Camden's Lash Up programme—see AJ 23.4.75 pp865-868—involving more temporary patching for a shorter life has resulted in roofs

Table I First valuation of initial works: two examples	
135 Inderwick Road	**118 Middle Lane**
Overhaul all wiring	Overhaul roof
Overhaul internal decorations	Rewire
Overhaul joinery	Refit kitchen
Possible woodworm treatment and new flooring required by ground floor bay	Refit bathroom
	Redecorate internally and externally
Renew ceiling in ground floor rear room	Renew gutters and downpipes
Some minor repointing required	Repair plasterwork as necessary
Overhaul stone sub-sills	Rearrange back addition kitchen/wc
Overhaul roof slopes	**Valuation £5250**
Overhaul main chimney stack	
Remove defective chimney pots on back addition stack	
Repoint party parapet walls	
Some external redecoration required	
Overhaul rainwater goods	
Valuation £2400	

leaking after less than five years.)

3.03 Circular 33/76 (see **2.02**) states that initial works are defined as repairs necessary to make dwellings reasonably habitable including the initial provision of standard amenities as defined in schedule 6 of the Housing Act, 1974. In practice this may involve damp and timber treatment, repair or replacement of roofs, door/window/plaster and other fabric repairs, decoration, heating (not central), rewiring, plumbing and sanitaryware to schedule 6:

- a bath or shower;
- a hot and cold water supply at a fixed bath or shower;
- a wash-hand basin;
- a hot and cold water supply at a wash-hand basin;
- a sink;
- a hot and cold water supply at a sink;
- a water closet.

(Wc at least readily accessible, if not self-contained.)

3.04 For multi-occupation initial repairs do not provide for alterations to make self-contained units. But they should meet means of escape requirements, fireproofing doors, floors and stairs, **4**, plus basic requirements for each unit (from schedules 15 and 16, Housing Act, 1961):

- natural and artificial lighting;
- ventilation;
- waste supply;
- personal washing facilities;
- drainage and sanitary conveniences;
- facilities for storage, preparation and cooking of food and for the disposal of waste water;
- installations for space heating or for the use of space heating appliances.

3.05 These standards are elaborated and priorities set in Haringey's internal standards document. This gives more detail on the balance of qualities to be achieved and on various individual items such as soundproofing.

Documentation

3.06 Initial works to these standards are prepared by the housing department as a schedule of works. Checks are made with public health, means of escape, etc. Since works are generally repair and replacement, positions of fittings are obvious and fairly well established over time. Drawings are used infrequently. Any uncertainties are cleared up on site, **5, 6**.

3.07 More formal contracts are drawn up for large items going out to tender: complete roof renewal, timber treatment and damp proofing including attendant replacements, replastering, etc. Representatives for water, gas and electricity are met on site, instructions issued and confirmed in writing. In these cases there are detailed costings.

Personal choice

3.08 The schedule of works is usually drawn up for types of accommodation; rarely is the specific tenant known. So there is usually no personal choice of tiles, paper, paint, kitchen units, etc. Occasionally a tenant is known, and in one case, for example, is paying extra costs for better kitchen cupboards and heating installation.

Examples

3.09 Tables II and III give schedules of work for Inderwick Road and Middle Lane. Inderwick Road is a two up-two down two-storey house with a two-storey back addition for use as a large family house. Middle Lane is three-storey, two rooms per floor with a two-storey back addition. It is repaired and occupied as five bedsitting rooms with tenants sharing the two existing kitchens, one bathroom and two wcs.

4 *The spaciousness of houses means that fireproofing to floors and circulation spaces is extensive.*

5 *Initial repairs are necessarily simple to come within an initial works budget in this bedsitter: blocking up fireplace, rewiring, installing basin and eventually redecoration. This large first floor front room at Middle Lane has open views to Alexandra Palace, but will be less of a joy to heat.*

6 *Similarly limited repairs at Inderwick Road.*

Table II Schedule of works for 135 Inderwick Road

Carpenter
FFF, FFM, FFB, GFF, GFM, GFB*
Overhaul double hung sashes. Renew beads, cords, and fasteners as necessary.
Ease and adjust entrance doors. Supply and fix new rim locks and furniture.
Match up skirtings after removal of fireplaces.
FFM
Remove small cupboard on chimney breast. Remove cupboard above wardrobe.
FF Landing
Ease door to cupboard on landing
FFB
Strut up ceiling, take down timber, lath and plaster partition affected by wet rot.
Treat timbers in ceiling and floor to prevent fungus growth spreading.
Build new 100 × 50 mm framing. Supply and fix Gyproc boards both sides. Tape joints.
GF cupboard under stairs
Ease and adjust doors. Supply and fix new catches.
All rooms
Refix floorboards lifted by electricians rewiring property.
Rear garden
Renew fence between numbers 133/135. Replace with similar fence and same height as fence between 135/137.

Plumber
FFM
Take out sink unit, disconnect services and waste.
Take down sink water heater, disconnect and remove water and gas services, cap off below floor.
FF bathroom
Take down gas water heater and wash-hand basin prior to removal of partition wall between bathroom and back room.
Refix wash-hand basin and gas water heater to new partition wall. Remove old hot water tank and flow and return pipes, service pipes.
GFB
Renew old back boiler and service pipes.
GF kitchen
Repair leak on supply to gas water heater.
General external
Overhaul gutters and rwps. Renew as necessary.

Bricklayer
FFF, FFM, FFB, GFF, GFM, GFB
Take out existing fireplaces, brick up openings allow for 225 × 225 mm terracotta airbrick to centre of fireplace.
External rear flat roof
Repair back addition roof

Plasterer
FFM
Take down wall tiles. Make good wall plaster as necessary.
FF Bathroom
Make good wall plaster after removal of hot water tank.
FFF, FFM, FFB, GFF, GFM, GFB
Remove and set new brickwork to marry up with existing wall plaster.

Decorator
FFF, FFM, FFB, GFF, GFM, GFB, Staircase
Strip walls, wash down ceilings, walls and woodwork. Line and emulsion ceilings.
Repaper walls, paint woodwork two coats oil colour.
FF Bathroom, GF Kitchen
Wash down ceilings, walls and woodwork, paint ceilings and walls two coats eggshell, paint woodwork two coats oil colour.

* FFF: first floor front. FFM: first floor middle. GFB: ground floor back.

Table III Schedule of works for 118 Middle Lane

Electrical (in conjunction with EEB)
GFF, GFB, FFF, SFF, SFB*
To form five bed sitting rooms with: 1 lighting point, 1 twin socket outlet, supply and fix 1 two bar wall fire, supply and fix 1 electric water heater (sink). Each unit to have quarterly EEB meter.
FFB, GF back addition
To form communal kitchens with: 2 cooker points, 1 lighting point, 3 socket outlets, 1 Wolf heater point.
FF back addition
To form bathroom: 1 lighting point only.
Staircase, hall, landing
2 lighting points (on 2-way switch), 1 socket outlet (hall), 1 socket outlet (FF landing).
Common parts to be on landlord's quarterly meter

Plumber
Strip out existing water mains, run new mains in copper with branches to form the following supplies:
GFF, GFB, FFF, SFF, SFB
To form five bed sitting rooms: supply and fit 400 mm wash-hand basin complete with backboard brackets, taps and waste; connect to new water mains. Cut hole through 225 mm wall to connect waste to new soil stack.
FF back addition
To form bathroom: new bath, services and fittings. Supply and fix 400 mm wash-hand basin complete with all fittings.
GF back addition, FFB
To form kitchens: supply and fit new 1065 mm (42in) sink unit complete with services taps and waste—cut hole through external wall to discharge waste into existing soil stack.
GF wc
Overhaul existing wwp, renew if necessary.
FF wc
Renew wc pan, renew wwp.
F elevation
Run new soil stack to take 3 sink wastes down to new back inlet gulley—connect gulley to nearest soil run in garden.
Check and repair as necessary gutters and rwps.
R elevation
Break into existing soil stack for 2 additional sink wastes.
Check and repair gutters and rwps.

Bricklayer
GFF, GFB, GF back addition, FFF, FFB, FF back addition, SFB, SFF

Remove fireplaces, brick up opening, allow for 225 × 225 mm terracotta air brick to centre of opening, render and set to match existing wall plaster.
SF storeroom
Remove old sink and services, make good brickwork and replaster walls as necessary.
Staircase
Hack off loose wall and ceiling plaster, renew as necessary.
F and B elevations
Overhaul main and back addition roofs, replace broken ridge tiles, make good cement fillets.
F elevation
Form small manhole in front garden. Run new drainage and back inlet gulley for new sink wastes on front elevation.

Carpenter
Front entrance door (main entrance)
Renew entrance door. Yale lock—supply 12 yale keys.
GFF, GFB, FFF, SFF, SFB
Renew rim locks and furniture. Supply and fix yale locks to each door (2 keys)
GF back addition, FF back addition
Supply and fix 2 × 2 door wall cabinets. Supply and fix 1 × 2 door, 2 drawer free standing kitchen cabinets.
GF back addition, GF bathroom, FFB, FF back addition
Renew rim locks and furniture. Lay hardboard to floors as necessary. Supply and lay thermoplastic tiles.
General items
Overhaul all sashes, renew sash cords, beads as necessary. Supply and fit new fasteners. Leave in good working order.
Replace and refix flooring as necessary after rewiring and re-carcassing for gas and water pipes.

Decorator
GFF, GFB, GF back kitchen, GF back lobby and cupboard, GFB wc, FFF, FF kitchen, FF wc, FF bathroom, SFF, SFB, SF storeroom, passages and staircase
Strip ceilings and walls, wash down and prepare all surfaces, line and emulsion all ceilings 2 coats (white). Paper walls with wood chip paper and emulsion 2 coats (cream). Paint all woodwork 2 coats oil colour (white) including new asbestos work.
FFF
Reglaze 2 square clear glass.
General items
Clear all rubbish, sweep out and leave premises clean and tidy on completion.

* Terminology differs from table II. There, two rooms plus back addition per floor were referred to as front, middle, back. Here they are referred to as front, back, back addition. GFF: ground floor front. FFB addition: first floor back addition. SFB: second floor back.

Fireproofing specification
Doors to GFF, GFB, GF back addition, FFF, FFB
Remove hardboard sheeting and fill in the panels solid flush with the frame with plasterboard, or asbestos wallboard not less than $\frac{3}{16}$in thick and thereafter sheet over the whole of these doors with asbestos wallboard not less than $\frac{3}{16}$in thick. Make the doors effectively self-closing by means of spring mechanisms. The added protection to the doors must be fitted on the *side remote* from the staircase.
Doors to SFF, SFB
Remove hardboard sheeting and fill in the panels solid flush with the frame with plasterboard, or asbestos wallboard not less than $\frac{3}{16}$in thick and thereafter sheet over the whole of these doors with asbestos wallboard not less than $\frac{3}{16}$in thick. Make the doors effectively self-closing by means of spring mechanisms. The added protection must be fitted on the *staircase* side of the doors.
Cupboard door on second floor landing
Replace the glazing on the door with glazing of fire resisting quality, no panel of glazing to exceed 4 sq ft in area. Infill the wooden panels with plasterboard or asbestos wallboard not less than $\frac{3}{16}$in thick and thereafter sheet over the whole of the door excluding the glazed section with asbestos wallboard not less than $\frac{3}{16}$in thick. Make the door effectively self-closing by means of spring mechanisms. The added protection to be fitted on the inside of the cupboard.
Second floor landing cupboard
Sheet over both sides of the hardboard sides and chipboard doors with plasterboard or asbestos wallboard not less than $\frac{3}{16}$in thick. Make the doors effectively self-closing by means of a spring mechanism or mechanisms or kept shut when not in use and marked to that effect.
Trapdoor to roofspace on second floor landing
Sheet over the underside of the trapdoor with plasterboard or asbestos wallboard not less than $\frac{3}{16}$in thick.
Spandrel to staircase at ground floor level
Fill in the panels of the spandrel and the doors in the spandrel solid flush with the frame with plasterboard or asbestos wallboard not less than $\frac{3}{16}$in thick, and thereafter sheet over the whole of the doors with asbestos wallboard and the whole of the spandrel with plasterboard or asbestos wallboard. The added protection to the spandrel and doors therein to be fitted on the side *remote* from the staircase enclosure.
Staircase soffit at ground floor level
Line the soffit with plasterboard or asbestos wallboard not less than $\frac{3}{16}$in thick from floor to ceiling line.

As alternatives, the doors referred to above may be constructed to conform to BS459 (half hour type) or be of solid wood at least $1\frac{3}{8}$in thick. The doors are to be made self-closing by means of spring mechanisms of an approved type.
Generally
1 All doors must be a good fit within their frames and all door furniture in good working order.
2 All cracks, holes or gaps in ceiling plaster within the staircase enclosure to be made good.
3 All joins between adjacent sections of protective materials and between this material and other adjacent surfaces are to be properly sealed.
4 All asbestos wallboard is to be fixed by screws.

4 On site

4.01 Two to four weeks after the schedule is prepared the undertakings should have renewed mains as necessary and the direct labour department can start on site. The area foreman programmes the work by trade sequence: usually drains, carpenter, electrician and plumber, bricklayer and plasterer, decorator. Works take from eight to 12 weeks.

4.02 There may occasionally be occupants, for example after a purchase notice (see **2.02**). In these cases occupants are temporarily rehoused, a potential source of delay. They may then decide not to return, **7**.

Variations

4.03 As with all rehabilitation, works cannot be exactly scheduled. There are the usual minor changes such as the amount of plaster to be stripped off, or which falls off, **8**. And there are occasionally more major variations such as the extensive wet rot found in stud partitions in Inderwick Road. Here an extra £2000 of work was needed, requiring a supplementary application to DOE.

Acknowledgements

Thanks to Gerallt W. Hughes MSc, ARICS, AIAS, AIH (assistant borough housing officer—development) and Alfred Brant (principal acquisitions officer) of Haringey Council for their help.

7 *This sort of upheaval (at Inderwick Road) plus the extra the builder would add for working with occupiers in residence makes temporary decanting preferable.*

8 *A common problem; attention to small areas of plaster loosens adjacent plaster and it becomes difficult to find a firm line to stop at.*

Case study 3:
Rehabilitated housing for the disabled

About two people in a thousand use wheelchairs in the home. Probably a quarter of these are effectively chairbound[1]. Since disabled people tend to be poorer than average, they are likely to be found more often than these statistics suggest in housing requiring rehabilitation.

This study concentrates on characteristics of houses for wheelchair users particular to rehabilitation. For a full coverage of wheelchair housing and the special problems of the disabled see the AJ special feature (**25.6.75**)[1] and **Selwyn Goldsmith's** *Designing for the disabled*[2].

1 Scope

Wheelchair housing

1.01 Selwyn Goldsmith gives an approximate working definition of those who need wheelchair housing as 'people who, on account of disability, cannot conveniently be placed in mobility housing'[1]. The three important features of mobility housing are:

- ramped or level access to the dwelling
- all rooms are at entrance level;
- passageways and doors to principal rooms (but not necessarily the bathroom or wc) are wide enough for standard wheelchairs to manoeuvre[3].

So wheelchair housing has stringent requirements. However, the concepts of wheelchair and mobility housing were developed for new building and requirements will inevitably be compromised when starting within existing buildings and tight cost limits.

Case study

1.02 This study is based primarily on the experience of the Notting Hill Housing Trust architects, plus information from an NBA study[4]. It does not aim to be definitive but provides an extensive checklist for wheelchair provision. This applies to conversions within the house. For built-on, special purpose units see *Designing for the disabled*[2] and Cheshire County Council's *Made to measure*[5].

1.03 The main effects of drawing examples from the Housing Trust are that the description of negotiations over finance is biased toward housing associations and there are local characteristics of local authority involvement, catchment and housing stock.

2 Feasibility

2.01 When the architect surveys a house for its rehabilitation potential, he keeps an eye open for units suitable to convert for wheelchair use in terms of their locale (**2.06**) and the houses themselves (**2.07**) **1, 2, 3**. Where conversion is possible, a survey report and sketch scheme are submitted through the housing association to the loan authority; either the local authority or housing corporation.

2.02 Housing associations take on disabled people (owners and tenants) through their house purchase programmes. They may also house people for the local authority. At this stage, the architect is only working in terms of a general need for disabled units. The sketch scheme is not for a particular disabled person. (Though the decision to make a disabled unit is generally taken at this stage, it could be taken later since the stage when the decision is made does not affect the time taken to get cost approvals. In one case the decision was only taken shortly before tender.)

1

2

1, 2, 3 *The three case study houses, all converted to multi-occupation with a unit for a wheelchair user on the ground floor. Interior photographs are of Hammersmith Grove* **1**, *the only one of the three currently occupied.*

3

Extra costs

2.03 No extra costs are allowable under Housing Association Grants (HAGs) for making disabled units. If costs are above HAG ceilings, special application has to be made to DOE. While these will generally be allowed, negotiations add two to four months to the precontract period. The architects strive to get below HAG ceiling to avoid this delay.

2.04 Extra costs are likely to arise from three sources:
- extra space. Roughly, catering for a disabled person takes the equivalent of one extra bedspace. For example, space for a 1p wheelchair unit might otherwise have been used for a 2p unit for able-bodied people. This would reduce the eligible expense (the maximum sum on which grant aid is payable) by £2600
- structural alterations, mainly for easing circulation
- special fixtures and fittings.

2.05 Potential help from local authority social services is not a significant sum; £50 to £100 intended for supplementary facilities to existing dwellings such as grab rails. They may also contribute toward a telephone. (Local authority involvement may vary considerably from authority to authority.)

Locale

2.06 Wheelchair units should preferably be near centres of activity such as shops, doctors, churches and parks. Nearby pedestrian crossings and bus stops may be important. For the self-propelled wheelchair user the area should preferably be fairly flat. Goldsmith[2] suggests a slope of 1:20 for ramps longer than 6 m and this criterion might be applied where possible to the area between the house and local activities. There is no simple way round the problem that acceptable gradients vary considerably for individuals but at this stage there is no individual in mind. The social services department may be able to indicate a range of disabled people they have on their books to check how generally usefully a hilly locale might be.

House

2.07 For wheelchair units, the focus is on the ground floor. Lifts are generally too costly to make use of other floors and are not acceptable as means of escape in case of fire. There needs to be a straight or gentle ramp to the ground floor. This is likely to rule out terraced housing opening directly off the pavement, hilly plots where a ramp from pavement to door would be too steep (see **5.01**), including many houses with basements which often have several steps up to the front door.

2.08 Once inside, there should be generous entrance circulation, corridors (or the potential for making them) 1000 mm, preferably 1200 mm with 775 mm door openings. Internal steps often found between the main house and back addition will entail raising the addition floor and adjustment to doorsets. This will probably be prohibitively expensive if the ceiling has to be raised to provide 2·3 m headroom (except in

kitchens and bathrooms). For bathrooms, the ingenious conversion of a broom cupboard or other minute space is impossible. A bathroom needs to be at least 2·2 m square (see **7.01**).

3 Designing to fit

3.01 Once purchase is completed and detailed design begins, the flavour of the job changes from that of most other rehabilitation. Units are designed with specific clients in mind (other housing associations and local authorities may be different). The architect will be introduced by the social services department, through the housing association, and can get to know the disabled people and any family personally. Beyond finding out details of the disability and some idea of its likely future development, there is the opportunity to fit units to occupants (always remembering that units are part of the housing stock to be differently occupied in future).

3.02 As well as consulting these future occupants during detailed design it is useful to take them on site, perhaps when fittings are on site, but still loose, and again at handover.

3.03 These checks help the architect who is unfamiliar with a disability and its implications. This affects the builder too. Though features such as ramp slopes and surface textures may be carefully specified, the foreman on site is not necessarily very familiar with the specification and what is crucial in it. It is advisable to go over it on site with him and to be on site during special operations like laying ramps.

Cleaning out

3.04 Cleaning out, though specified, may go little further than shovelling up debris and stirring the dust with a broom. Where disabled people will live alone a thorough cleaning out up to 'spring cleaning standards' should be part of the contract.

Examples

3.05 Most illustrations are taken from three schemes for the Notting Hill Housing Trust. Hammersmith Grove, **1**, **4**, is for Mr Matheson, virtually chairbound though he uses a walking frame for the short journey from house to car. Applegarth Road, **2**, **5**, is for a couple, the husband has lost his legs above the knee. He can walk a few steps using artificial legs and walking sticks. Perryn Road, **3**, **6**, is a flat for a chairbound man with no legs. Adjoining is a flat for his sister who looks after him.

3.06 Providing a purpose-built unit may change the dependence of the disabled person on others. The architect could be in a difficult position in that one or more parties may be trying to change this dependence or keep it as it is. Perryn Road, for example, **6**, has been designed as two relatively self-contained units though with easy mutual access. Currently the disabled man and his sister have a first floor flat. It is hoped that the degree of self-containment will lead the disabled man to be more independent. (This self-containment also makes the units suitable for a wider range of future users.)

4 Anthropometrics

Departing from the norm

4.01 Sources referred to earlier[2,3] give fairly detailed information on wheelchair manoeuvring and reach. These are much too extensive to duplicate here but there are several points worth noting. The key point is that published data are usually averages; sometimes there are percentiles. The architect has an individual whose own abilities can be determined. And since the accommodation is likely to be less than perfect, the individual may point out trade-offs which he prefers. For example, positioning a wall where it makes a tight but negotiable turn for a wheelchair may be preferred if it provides space for storage shelving on the other side.

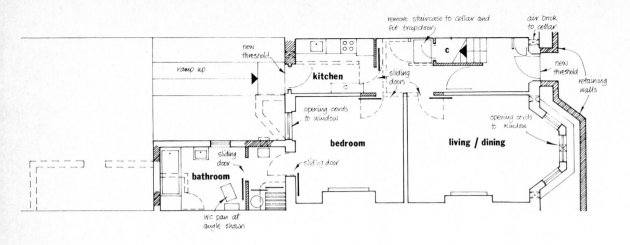

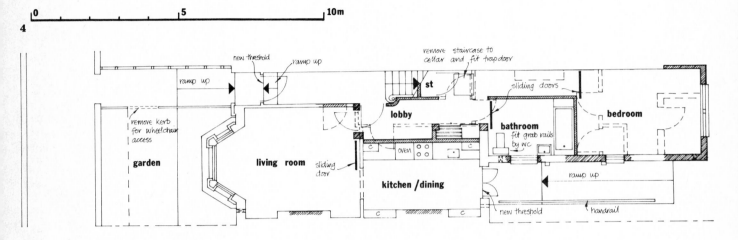

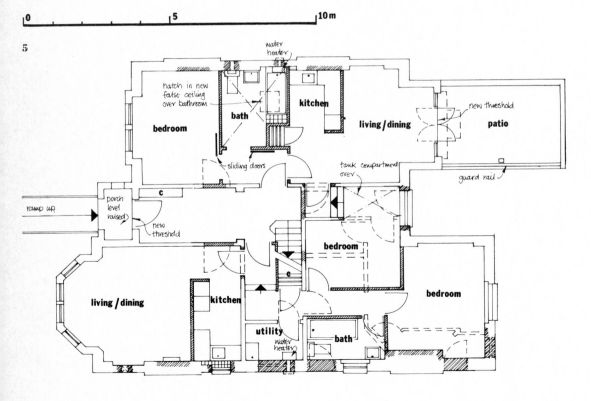

4 *Hammersmith Grove, occupied by Mr Matheson. Ramp, sliding doors and bathroom size are the most conspicuous special features. Broken lines represent demolished work, hatching represents new.*

5 *Applegarth Road, for a disabled man and able wife. The house with a long back addition is more difficult to plan than usual; with a lot of circulation space.*

6 *Perryn Road with disabled unit at top of plan sharing a common entrance with sister's flat and flats on upper floors.*

Disabled and others

4.02 The needs of wheelchair users may conflict with those of family, others using the same house and visitors, some of whom may be disabled too. Within the family, agreement can be worked out on heights, space allocation, etc. But architects must not forget the communal aspects of the house such as switch, lock and handle heights (see **6.01**).

Reach generally

4.03 Where the disabled person lives alone or to reduce enforced dependence on others, make prepayment meters, isolating switches (eg immersion heater), stop cocks and fuses accessible. Curtains should preferably be operated by cords. Sash windows can be operated by cords, **7**, though this may require some attention to weights. When the disabled person lives alone it may be difficult to reach sash window locks. The upper sash can be screwed up and the lower one locked by mortice bolts at the bottom. Windows behind working surfaces, usually in the kitchen, are problematic; in some cases remote opening gear might be fitted.

7 *Bottom sash operated by cords over pulleys at the top of the frame.*

Dexterity generally

4.04 The occupants in the examples are all fairly dexterous, manually. Those who are less so can be helped by devices such as switched sockets with switches on the outside, **9**, rocker light switches, **8**, and lever taps. The references [2,5] provide details of more elaborate measures such as remotely operated taps, pulleys, etc.

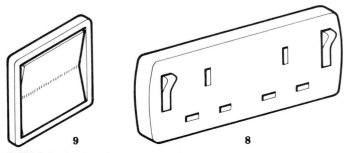

8 *With both plugs in place, switches between sockets are difficult for the less dexterous to reach.* **9** *Similarly a rocker plate, either a special switch or cover for an existing one requires less control.*

Space standards generally

4.05 General wheelchair requirements are 775 mm clear door openings, 1200 mm corridors with 1400 mm needed for a 180° turn. This is of course free space between skirtings and round radiators. As noted earlier, the extra space needed to provide a wheelchair unit is equivalent to about one bedspace. This is used mainly in the bathroom and circulation space, not only corridors but round furniture. For example, a minimal double bedroom for normal use is about big enough as a minimal single bedroom for a wheelchair user.

Simple design

4.06 Though in designing to fit there are many particulars to check, the overall effect as illustrated by the three schemes is of relatively normal appearance. There are evident differences such as the sliding doors, ramps, lack of kitchen base units, perhaps a grab rail in the bathroom and so on. But generally these are 'low profile'; there is no need for conspicuous catering for disability.

5 External

Gradients

5.01 Gradients recommended[2] for unassisted wheelchair users are 1:10 up to 3 m long, 1:16 up to 6 m and 1:20 over 6 m. Knowing the client may make this modifiable. In some cases the disabled person's arms may be too weak for such gradients (or for getting over upstanding weather bars at external doors). At Perryn Road a normal ramp would have been very long to reach back gardens. A small level patio has been built at the rear of the disabled person's flat to provide some, albeit limited, access to the outdoors, **6, 10**.

10 *Raised patio under construction providing some shelter from the wind.*

Resting places

5.02 Resting places, flat areas, may be useful in the length of gradients and are needed at corners and outside doors where the wheelchair user can pause to operate a door lock or handle.

Materials

5.03 Pathways need finishing fairly coarsely, eg in tamped concrete, slabs, rough bricks flush pointed, and tarmacadam with fairly large, say 10 mm, aggregate. Avoid very uneven surfaces, eg setts, unstable surfaces, eg grass or gravel, or smooth ones, eg trowelled concrete or quarry tiles.

Edging

5.04 Ramp kerbs should be at least 75 mm. Wheelchair users may be frightened of falling from chairs and a handrail is useful as a safeguard and reassurance even if it is not used to grip, **11**. Edging kerbs may be put round gulley and to any paths, if desired.

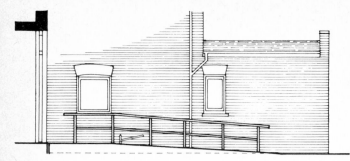

11 *Handrail at Applegarth Road for safety and visual reassurance.*

Refuse

5.05 There will usually need to be space to stop and turn a wheelchair adjacent to bins. A platform for the container used to bring out the refuse may be helpful while manoeuvring. A similar platform may be useful at entrances for milk bottles, deliveries, etc. Locate the bin accessibly for collection, **12**.

5.06 For carports, garages or hardstanding, control gradients and allow at least a metre at the side and rear of the vehicle for unloading. Existing drives may need widening and edging. For a new drive or hardstanding, the local authority will be needed to provide a pavement crossover. Beware taking hardstanding to the building face so that it bridges dpcs and blocks underfloor ventilation, **13**. Slates have been used at Perryn Road to continue the dpc up the face of the wall to above surrounding concrete, **14**.

Gardens

5.07 Usually there is no money to edge paths and provide raised planters. But if there is, remember to reconcile these provisions with the requirements of other flats in the house. There should be some form of provision for clothes drying.

12 *Check if residents are expected to place bins on the pavement for emptying.*

13 *Small parapet to hardstanding with lower surface behind to allow underfloor ventilation.*

14 *Slates sealed to the dpc continuing damp proofing up wall face to avoid bridging dpc by concrete path.*

6 Circulation

Entrance doors

6.01 External doors should be self closing, rising butts are economical and avoid the need for a grab bar. Kick plates can reduce defacement from rubbing of wheelchair footrests. Weather tightness of the threshold is difficult and, though a weatherbar up to 20 mm, **15**, **16**, can be negotiated by a wheelchair, it takes considerable effort. A weather seal fixed to the door is easier, **17**, **18**.

15

16

15, 16 *Threshold keeps out rain but is too high for comfortable movement in and out.*

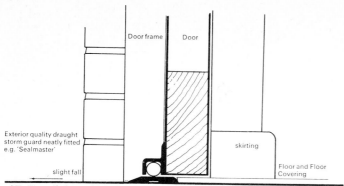

Door frame Door

Exterior quality draught
storm guard neatly fitted
e.g. 'Sealmaster'

skirting

slight fall

Floor and Floor
Covering

17 *Detail from 'Made to Measure'[5]. A smooth run in but it avoids the problem of dpcs.*

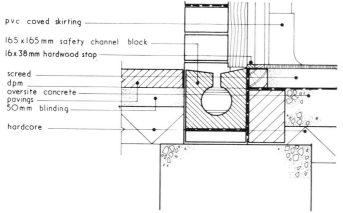

pvc coved skirting
165 x 165mm safety channel block
16 x 38mm hardwood stop

screed
dpm
oversite concrete
pavings
50mm blinding

hardcore

18 *Detail from Spastics Society Field Study Centre (AJ 2.3.77) providing smooth threshold and protection against bridging the dpc.*

Entrance

6.02 Locks and any entry phone should be at a height accessible to all, as should switches in the entrance hall. A time switch is convenient but, if the house door and the flat door are not directly adjacent, the switch will not be near both, and so either leaving or entering must be done mostly in darkness. In such cases a two way switch, one at each door would be preferable. For letters, a wire basket below the letter box saves trying to reach the floor.

Doors

6.03 Side hung doors may be needed at flat entrances and in some restricted places though, generally, sliding doors are more convenient for wheelchair users. There are, however, some disadvantages to bear in mind: extra costs, the strain on the sliding gear often caused by pulling from an angle rather than parallel to the door, difficulty of fitting carpets round the bottom guide, and fireproofing. Sliding doors are difficult to fireproof really well but fire officers are usually fairly tolerant in such special circumstances, **19**.

6.04 Door sets should preferably be 900 mm leaving a 775 mm clear opening. If a few mm extras are needed on the width of side hung doors, a cranked hinge can be used, **20**. A bigger door set, say 1000 mm, is not necessarily an advantage. A 1000 mm door sterilises 26 per cent more floor area than a 900 mm door set; critical in a relatively small room like a bathroom. Side hung doors are better rehung where necessary with the hinges near the corner of the room.

6.05 There may occasionally be opportunities to miss out doors altogether. But usually they are needed for draught control and energy conservation in allowing adjacent spaces to be kept at different temperatures.

Walls

6.06 Radiators and other projections obviously need care in positioning to avoid damage by a chair. Similarly plaster corners need reinforcing, **21**.

Saving circulation

6.07 Rather than easing circulation it can be avoided in part by the use of two way light switches and entry phones linked to a preferred point, perhaps at the bed head, **22**.

Cellar

6.08 Old houses often have cellars which are obviously not accessible to the disabled. At Hammersmith Road there is a trap door and ladder allowing access for an able bodied person for long term storage but saving the floor area previously taken by the staircase, **23**.

19 *Sliding doors are usually convenient, though often less so to other disabled people without chairs. Where the finger grip is found difficult a vertical wooden rod, say 200 mm long, could be substituted to make gripping easier.*

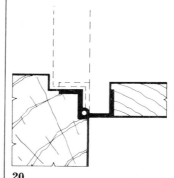

20 *Cranked hinge adds a few mm extra to the clear opening, ie the thickness of the door.*
21 *Unreinforced plaster corner broken by wheelchair handle.*

20

21

22 *Entryphone comprising intercom and automatic openers to front (communal) and flat entrance doors.*

23 *Trap door with iron rung stair into cellar.*

7 Bathrooms

Space

7.01 Space is needed for parking and turning a wheelchair, to transfer to the wc, to position the chair in front of the basin, and to move the full length of the bath for cleaning it and to reach taps and plug. Any clothes line over the bath needs careful positioning to be reachable. Side hung doors should open outwards and any lock be openable from outside in an emergency.

Rails and brackets

7.02 Are grab rails needed? Often yes, though not at Hammersmith Grove, **4, 24**. Any grab rails need fitting to the individual. However, bath edges, basins, shelves and other fittings may be used for support during manoeuvring so need very firm support. Take care specifying fixing on studwork and dry lining.

Baths vs showers

7.03 Ask whether a bath or shower is preferred. It should not be assumed, especially when trying to save space during sketch

24 *Bathroom without elaborate coping for disability. Basin legs get in the way of the chair here and the basin is a little too close to the bath for easy operation of taps.*

design when there is no specific client in mind, that showers are more convenient for severely disabled people. Baths are usually little more difficult to manoeuvre into and, once in, provide much more support than a shower chair. Bathing is more relaxing and helps circulation. Baths are usually put into wheelchair units.

Bath

7.04 Baths should be 1700 mm long with handles at the side and a strong shelf at the head end to sit on for entering the bath, **24**. Where space is tight, the bath could be reduced to say 1500 mm. But some people, such as the future occupant of Perryn Road, prefer to do away with the shelf, finding access direct from a wheelchair equally convenient, **6**.

Basin

7.05 Basins should be 750 mm to the rim, supported on brackets rather than legs. A shelf is needed for razors, make up, etc, and a mirror over the basin large enough for wheelchair users and ambulant people.

7.06 Where, exceptionally, there is a separate wc, a handbasin can be positioned within reach, usually set at right angles to the wc. A recent AJ building study (2.3.77) gave an interesting variation on normal practice, **25a, b**.

25a *Diagonal arrangement of wc and handbasin (see also **25b**).*

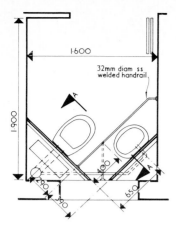

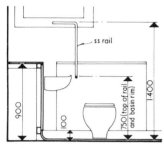

25b *Diagonal arrangement of wc and hand basin (see also* **25a**).

WC

7.07 Find out whether the disabled person wants to get onto the wc from the front or side and position it accordingly. If there is space allow for both approaches to provide for other wheelchair users. Preferred wc height is usually 475 mm whereas most wcs are 405 mm. A few higher ones are available. Disabled people sometimes have collars to put on top to make up the height but this seems unnecessarily *ad hoc* in a newly designed unit. Get a taller wc or build a plinth.

7.08 Fixing grab rails may obstruct fixing a low level cistern. If so, fix a high level one.

8 Kitchens

Surfaces

8.01 Working surfaces are usually 800 mm at Notting Hill, though this can be uncomfortably low for ambulant people, so some compromise may be needed for families. Where there is space the usual process sequence—surface, sink, surface, cooker, surface—is desirable. Carefully levelled surfaces enable heavy pans to be slid from place to place, avoiding lifting. Some base storage units may be possible but some space below the working surface will need to be open kneespace. Use firm brackets and a strong timber as support along the front edge of the surface rather than vertical posts which obstruct manoeuvring.

Eating

8.02 It may be difficult for disabled people to carry food so it is easier to have a kitchen/diner, **26**. It could help if a breakfast bar design was provided allowing heavy casseroles etc, to be slid from working surfaces rather than lifted.

Storage

8.03 The few base units and necessarily low wall cupboards reduce the density of storage on a wall, increasing the desirable kitchen area, **27**. Check what can be reached; long term storage does not need to be very easily accessible, **26**.

8.04 As mentioned, some base storage units may be used. Special purpose mobile storage units are another possibility, **28**, though it may be simpler and more aesthetically compatible with the fitment range being used to cut the plinth from a standard base unit and fit casters. Check that mobile storage is a help; both hands are needed for holding the unit still

while opening door or drawer. A rubbish bin on casters might also be useful.

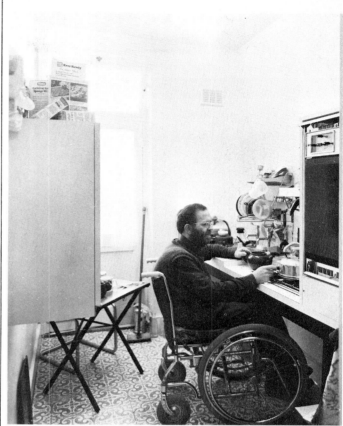

26 *Rather than using the front room,* **4**, *Mr Matheson has a small table for eating in the kitchen and intends eventually to put a bar (shelf) for eating along the wall on the left. Though difficult to reach, the cupboard top provides long term storage.*

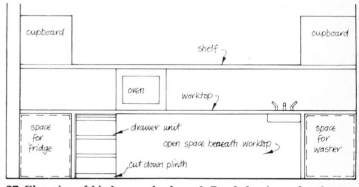

27 *Elevation of kitchen at Applegarth Road showing reduced density of storage that can be made accessible compared with conventional kitchen fitting.*

28 *Special purpose mobile storage unit.*

29 *Fairly cramped kitchen. Small mirror fixed to oven at right of grill for watching food cooking: eye level for ambulent person.*

Cookers

8.05 Split level cookers are usually installed as part of the rehabilitation contract. The hob unit is set level with the 800 mm working surface, the oven lower so that food cooking on the top shelf can be seen. Grills are difficult since they are usually at eye level for the ambulant. Mr Matheson has resorted to a small mirror for watching food grilling, **29**. A lower level grill would of course obstruct the already scarce working surface.

8.06 Where the disabled person does a limited amount of his own cooking, a conventional cooker with a double oven may be acceptable. Though there is no kneespace to conveniently get close to all rings, the top oven incorporating a grill may be more accessible than the equivalent oven and grill in separate fittings.

Sink

8.07 Shallow sinks may be needed to give clear kneespace of 650 mm below. Insulation on the underside to protect legs from burns is seldom necessary. Mixer taps are helpful, positioned off centre and high enough for spouts to be swung over kettles and pans, **30**. Tap holes need to be drilled specially in the factory or on site using a sink unit delivered undrilled.

30 *Swivel tap positioned for easy filling of pans. Swivel arm needs to be high enough to swing over pans resting on draining board.*

Appliances

8.08 Make provision for existing/likely appliances, eg washing machines.

9 Heating

Costs

9.01 Electric heating could possibly be installed as electric radiators may be very small, or substituted altogether by ceiling heating, so reducing obstruction to wheelchair manoeuvre. However, there is no escape from the ensuing large bills in these relatively poorly insulated houses, even if there is continuous heating allowing some use of white meter tariffs. Full central heating is generally necessary with higher than average temperatures, 22°C and perhaps more in bathrooms and bedrooms where undressing can take a long time.

Controls

9.02 Provide the usual controls; time clock and room thermostat or preferably radiator thermostats, if these can be gripped by the disabled person, providing selective room temperature control. Controls need to be within reach and their use explained to occupants.

10 References

10.01 1 Selwyn Goldsmith, 'Wheelchair Housing', AJ 25.6.75 pp1314-1348.
2 Selwyn Goldsmith, *Designing for the disabled*, RIBA, 1976.
3 Selwyn Goldsmith, 'Mobility Housing', AJ 3.7.74 pp43-50.
4 *The elderly and the disabled in rehabilitated housing—guidance for general housing associations*, due out in a few months from the National Building Agency.
5 Cheshire County Council, *Made to measure*, Cheshire CC.
6 *Adapting existing housing for the disabled* DOE Circular 59/78.

11 Acknowledgements

11.01 Thanks for their help to Notting Hill Housing Trust, to chief architect David Page, design team Ian Phillips (Hammersmith Grove), Alison McDonald (Applegarth Road) and Chris Barnet (Perryn Road) and to Kenneth Matheson. We are also grateful for information and comment from the NBA.

Case study 4: The NCB tenant liaison service

Rehabilitation causes upheaval to tenants whether they move out temporarily or remain during construction. A tenant liaison service can keep tenants informed and help them make arrangements to move out or to put up with construction. The service smoothes programming and running the job for both tenants and contractors.

This study deals with the Coal Board's tenant liaison service for local authorities. A similar in-house service could be, and sometimes is, provided by local authorities and housing associations.

1 Coal Board service

1.01 Having rehabilitated some 35 000 coal board (NCB) houses, the NCB also offers its rehabilitation services to local authorities. The tenant liaison service may be provided alone but is more usually combined with design services or with a complete package including construction. The service keeps tenants informed and helps with problems arising from rehabilitation. This also provides information for programming, especially important in providing a flow of units for the contractor. The NCB service is not, of course, unique, but it is more thorough than many. The tenant liaison officer (TLO) is treated by the NCB as being equally important as the clerk of works.

Tenant participation in decisions

1.02 The service is intended to keep rehabilitation running smoothly, not to involve tenants in decision making as ASSIST does (Case Study 1, part 1 AJ 10.11.76, part 2 AJ 8.12.76, part 3 AJ 9.2.76). TLOs are hardly in a position to force tenant involvement on clients though they may be involved in client initiated activities such as local authority meetings with tenants and setting up show houses. However, a similar liaison service set up in-house by a local authority or housing association could provide an organisational starting point for more participatory involvement of tenants.

2 Initial information

2.01 When the liaison service becomes involved in a rehabilitation scheme, tenants will be aware that a scheme is envisaged but will have no particulars of it. Their first detailed information is often a booklet prepared by the liaison service setting out the range of works and how the scheme will be organised from the tenant's point of view.

Booklet

2.02 Works are described in non-technical terms indicating their effects on the tenant and house (unlike a specification). A recent booklet included as its section on bathrooms (which were supplied packaged and craned onto a prepared slab):

A new bathroom will arrive already assembled with a modern white porcelain enamelled bath complete with taps, waste pipes and bath panel.

A new easy clean wash-basin will be installed complete with taps and waste pipes.

Glazed tiles will be fitted round the bath as well as splashback to the basin on exposed edges.

A radiator complete with on/off wheel valve will be installed.

The booklet, typically, covers general works to roofs, walls, floors, heating and redecoration, plus a room by room description of changes.

2.03 The booklet also informs tenants that the liaison service exists and that the TLO will visit them to explain what will happen and when. Should they be out, a note will be left to arrange another meeting. A contact address and phone number is given. (In a phased scheme the contractor's compound may already exist and serve as the TLO's base, **1**.)

2.04 The remaining information usually covers decanting. Tenants are told whether it will be necessary for them to move out and that the local authority, assisted by the TLO, will provide accommodation and help arrange furniture storage. A few notes indicate things to do or remember. For example:

if at work during the day, ensure tradesmen can get in

remove lean-to sheds

remove floor coverings

remove plants from close to the house

lock away items of monetary or sentimental value

if staying, be prepared for services to be disconnected for part of the day

if staying, be prepared for existing heating to be removed (in some cases, arrangements are made for the supply of temporary heating)

if moving out, meters will be read and telephones disconnected.

3 First visit

3.01 The first visit, announced by the booklet, occurs two or three months before work commences. It is important for the TLO to present himself as a helper rather than as a figure of authority. Among other things, the TLO is then more likely to get to know of alterations that tenants have made without telling the local authority.

3.02 The TLO needs to be familiar with current designs and the expected construction programme, and able to give some indication of the starting date and duration of works at each house. The TLO can walk round the house pointing out what

1 *Establishing a presence on site allows people to call at will rather than wait to be visited.*

2 *Houses are vacated for major work like this new back addition. Tenders are generally lower for vacant houses.*

the changes will be like. But tenants' questions will not be confined neatly to the construction process. There may be doubts about tenure, for example, will the rent go up, or, if moved out, will the tenant get back to the same house? And there will be many questions about the arrangements for moving out and the sort of accommodation the local authority is providing. To this end, and to inform programming, the TLO collects as well as imparts information.

3.03 If tenants are moving temporarily, the social services—health visitors, district nurses, doctors, probation officers, etc—need informing about tenants who are ill, disabled, pregnant, receiving meals on wheels, etc. Even when tenants in general are staying, old people and others such as wheelchair users may be offered a chance to move, **2**. Often the old prefer to stay for the company and activity of rehabilitation, though a local community centre (or, perhaps, a vacant house) can be useful as a refuge and a place to cook midday meals. For tenants staying, arrangements may still be made for moving out all but essential furniture.

Questionnaire
3.04 More formally, the TLO completes a questionnaire for each household, covering:

    occupants in house
    present state of health
    best time to call
    whether dwelling is used for any other purposes
    whether all rooms are in use
    shift working (critical if not moving out)
    paving and outbuildings obstructing renewal of mains
    and drains or adding extensions
    condition of garden
    tv aerial
    any pets
    telephone
    main source of heat
    whether help is required to remove floor coverings,
    furniture, lean-tos or outbuildings and to clear loft
    history of damp, uneven floors, smokey chimneys,
    woodworm, etc
    fuel merchant (for solid fuel).

3.05 Where the NCB is not the contractor, a summary of the rate of house availability to the contractor is put into the bill plus other prelims such as a requirement always to leave houses habitable at the end of the day if tenants are staying.

4 Later visits

Checking questionnaire
4.01 The other scheduled pre-construction visit occurs two to four weeks before work starts. The TLO answers queries and checks over the questionnaire to find out whether family circumstances have changed, whether furniture, floor coverings lean-tos or outbuildings will be removed and lofts cleared in time. A proposed starting date is given.

Other visits
4.02 Between this and the first scheduled visit, the TLO will call on an *ad hoc* basis. Tenants can see drawings, kitchen fittings and wallpaper books at the compound, **1**, if this is close, as well as dropping in with other queries. Wallpaper books are taken to other tenants and there are arrangements to be finalised for social services, for moving out and storing furniture. There are many individual problems like access to gardens or care of pigeons belonging to tenants who are moving out. Whatever the problem, the TLO visits rather than sends letters. Apart from better communication generally, some people have a mental block about official letters.

The local authority and tenants
4.03 Using the liaison service could result in local authorities not being directly involved with tenants at all. However, on various schemes, local authority officers have made visits or held meetings with residents' associations in co-operation with TLOs. Though residents' associations are useful, they sometimes fail to articulate individual needs. TLOs often find that those most in need are unable or unwilling to get involved in tenants' associations.

Starting date
4.04 The TLO can only give a planned starting date. The foreman goes to each house about a week before work starts to give a definite date and calls again at the end of the week before the following Monday's start to confirm it.

5 The person for the job
5.01 It is evident that TLOs need to be good listeners, prepared always to get involved even in what may occasionally seem trivial problems. They need to be available outside working hours and, where tenants are staying, to check that houses are habitable at the end of the day or at weekends, for example, no leaks, windows fixed, and services connected. A special type of site staff is needed, too, prepared to be careful with people's homes, to be selective about when they make noise and mess, to clear up after themselves, etc.

6 Construction
6.01 The TLO visits those staying on about every other day during construction to answer queries and sometimes to pick up complaints that tenants are unwilling to make to the builders. For tenants moved out, the TLO will visit the site once or twice and keep tenants informed of progress. Where journeys are difficult, the TLO may on occasion drive anxious tenants to look at current progress and gardens.

7 After construction
7.01 The TLO checks with the foreman on times for tenants to return. Some come back after plastering but before re-decoration. Care is taken in clearing up and reinstating drives, verges and paths.

Visits
7.02 The TLO visits all tenants at the end of construction when the plumber fires the heating system to help explain its working and to provide an explanatory leaflet. There is a preliminary check on snags but the final visit is about a month later allowing tenants to arrange furnishings and acclimatise to the changes. This last visit is part snagging, part feedback on satisfaction with the process and the finished product.

8 Acknowledgements
8.01 Thanks to Mrs J. E. Sanders and Mr P. Garret (tenant liaison officer) of NCB for their help.

Case study 5: Sheltered housing through rehabilitation

Only recently has sheltered housing begun to be built on a significant scale. Though this is almost exclusively new building[1,2], designed by Pollard, Thomas & Edwards for the Notting Hill Housing Trust, we should not ignore the potential of rehabilitation, despite difficulties of assembling enough suitable property for a scheme. Sheltered housing through rehabilitation is new, there is no established tradition. So this case study is intended as an indication of possibilities rather than as a representative solution.

1 Sheltered housing

Categories 1 and 2

1.01 There is some disagreement about what sheltered housing is. It is administratively convenient to define it as Category 1 or 2 housing for the elderly (MPBW Circular 82/69[3]). Category 1 housing comprises self-contained dwellings for the more active elderly, usually with few communal facilities though some access to health care. Category 2 housing is for the less active and must include several communal facilities: warden's self-contained flat, emergency alarm system, common room, laundry, telephone (shared), enclosed and heated circulation. There may be a guest room and warden's office. For both categories the circular specifies standards for space, fixtures, fittings and heating.

A broader view

1.02 Developments are tending to overtake this definition with schemes providing for physically handicapped or mentally ill people who are not all elderly. Reporting on some of these, Melanie Phillips suggested a working definition of sheltered housing as accommodation specifically designed to house and support people with special needs, in which residents lead independent lives backed up by assistance either from a minimal number of staff or from one another. So what sheltered housing becomes, what needs to be designed in future, could be very much more varied than housing the elderly. There is growing interest in providing sheltered care instead of residential homes and living in hospital.

Existing schemes

1.03 There are perhaps 200 000 elderly people living in sheltered housing built by local authorities and housing associations. Housing associations provide a significant proportion; 36 per cent in the first seven months of 1976-7.[4] Schemes to date by housing associations and local authorities are almost all new building, partly because rehabilitation has not been considered, partly because converted property is often less than ideal, partly because it can be difficult to accumulate a large enough block of adjacent properties.

Case study

1.04 This study is of a Category 2 scheme for 50 elderly people at Nevern Road, Earl's Court, London. Designed by Pollard Thomas & Edwards, it has reached sketch design stage. Because there are so few precedents, several features are still under discussion with the DOE as to what is fundable eg double glazing, staggered studs in partitions for sound insulation, garden improvements, etc. So the scheme as built may well be changed from the current design. The lack of precedents also means that the scheme cannot be classified as typical or untypical, though the houses used are certainly not common nationally, **1**.

2 Nevern Road scheme

2.01 Rehabilitation options are few in inner cities. Ground floor space is at a premium, especially for families. And, in any case, to design a scheme convenient for the elderly by housing them only on ground floors would require an enormous number of adjacent properties. So the inner city answer is likely to be, as here, multi-storey probably with lift access to all floors.

House type

2.02 The three houses, **1, 2**, are difficult to make use of. They have 6 m frontages and are about 12 m deep with very high ceilings, **3-9**. Each floor could be converted to one large flat but, because of the limited number of windows per floor, would only make a four person unit, which would be an oversized area compared with cost limits. The alternative is small one-person and two-person units. This is being done in similar houses now under construction across the road.

1 The scheme is for conversion of these three houses. Surprisingly, they were built around 1908 for a Victorian/Edwardian lifestyle that died with the first world war.

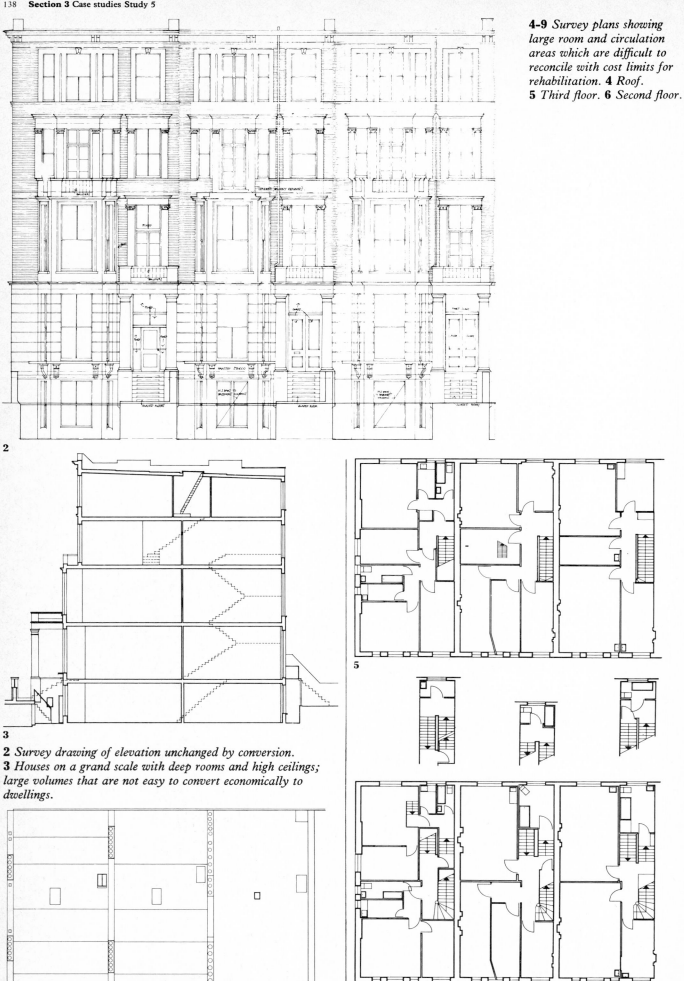

4-9 *Survey plans showing large room and circulation areas which are difficult to reconcile with cost limits for rehabilitation.* **4** *Roof.* **5** *Third floor.* **6** *Second floor.*

2 *Survey drawing of elevation unchanged by conversion.*
3 *Houses on a grand scale with deep rooms and high ceilings; large volumes that are not easy to convert economically to dwellings.*

2

3

4

5

6

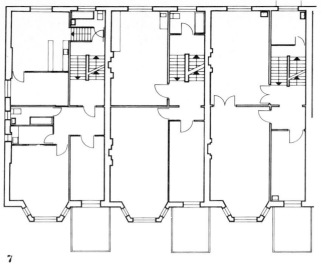

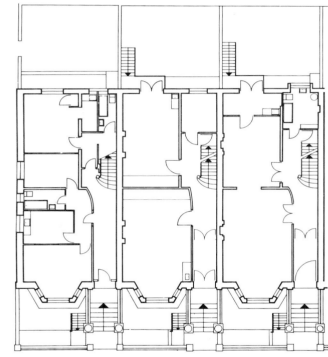

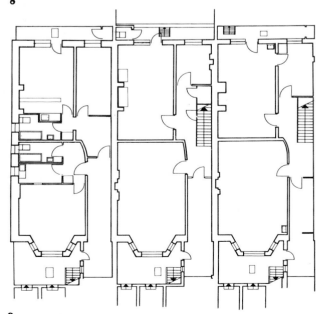

Window and ceiling heights

2.03 The windows are enormous, difficult to control physically, draughty and allow considerable heat loss. The site is also near a dual carriageway which produces sound levels at the houses above 60 dB. There is a limited amount that can be done about these problems though the architects hope to afford double glazing, provide false ceilings in bathrooms and kitchens, and install a centralised boiler for central heating under the pavement vaults to get better heating value for money. Many general rehabilitation schemes now include only partial central heating. But here there are conditions of heating and comfort considered mandatory under Category 2 to be met requiring heating of all spaces.

Radical surgery

2.04 Difficulties in costs converting the houses into flats led the architects to decide on more radical surgery, **10, 11**. A mezzanine is planned on the first floor at the rear to provide lower ceilings and make more use of the available height, **12**. This is only planned for the rear of the first floor as a complete mezzanine would affect the front elevation and require alteration of existing staircases, **13-17**. The other major changes are extensive relocating of partitions, a new top floor and large lift shaft, **18**.

10

7 *First floor.* **8** *Ground floor.* **9** *Basement.*
10 *Houses being converted into small flats, mansard floor being added on top.*

11

11 *Inside the houses shown in* **10**, *many floors staircases and partitions are being renewed or relocated.*

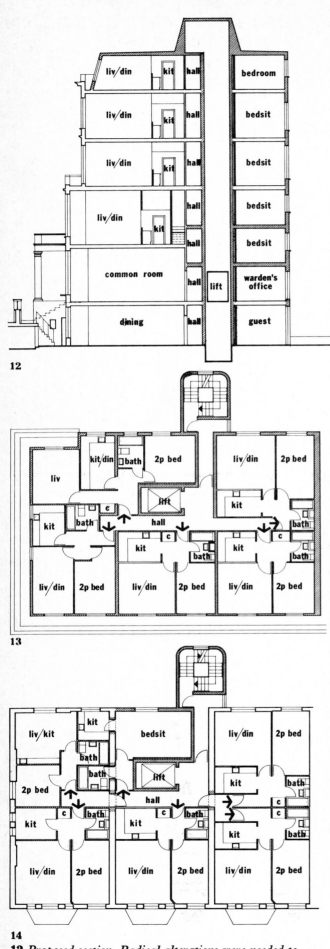

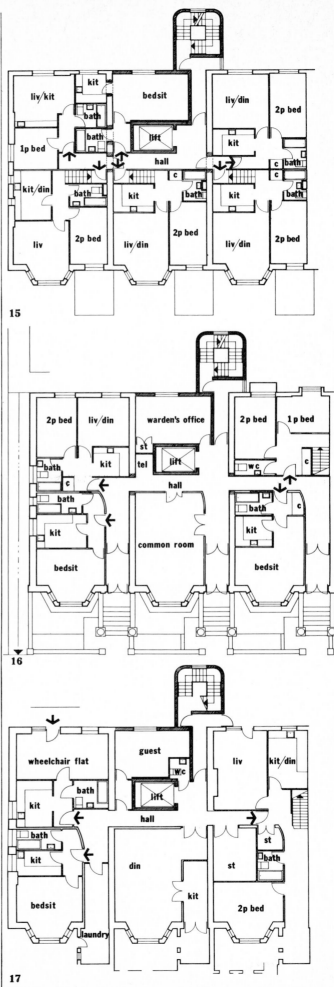

12 *Proposed section. Radical alterations were needed to increase number of flats so as to come within cost limits. Alterations include mezzanines at the rear instead of a first floor, a lift and extra, mansard floor.*
13 *Mansard floor.* **14** *Third floor (second floor identical).*

15 *First floor and upper mezzanine. Lower mezzanine is identical.* **16** *Ground floor.* **17** *Basement.*

18 *Lift shaft being built in houses opposite sheltered scheme. Obscured from view here by the existing ceiling, the shaft goes to the third floor. The height is shown by the brickwork on the left, reaching up to the corrugated iron used to shelter construction of the mansard,* **10.**

19 *From ground floor looking upwards to existing roof boarding in houses opposite sheltered scheme being converted to flats. Though gutting like this is expensive, it is cost effective because some major repair was needed anyway and many more units can be fitted in. Natural conversion would produce few, too expensive units.*

Accommodation

2.05 The three houses provide residential accommodation for 50 old people, a five-person unit for the warden and a single guest room (see table I). There is a common room on the ground floor and communal dining room in the basement. This is for any residents taking meals on wheels and may be for some elderly people from the surrounding area. Cost limits forced the creation of bedsitters adjacent to the lift shaft rather than some more communal space and/or more spacious flats. Cost limits also prevented building out common rooms onto the garden (itself only about 10 m deep).

Table I Schedule of accommodation				
Floor	**1 p bedsit**	**2 p flat**	**1 p flat**	**Other**
Mansard		5		
Third	1	4	1	
Second	1	4	1	
First and upper mezzanine	1	4	1	
Lower mezzanine	1	1	1	
Ground	2	1		
Basement	2			5 p warden unit
				1 p guest room
Sub totals	8 × 1 p	19 × 2 p	4 × 1 p	6 p
Total	56 people			

Access

2.06 There are steps up to the main entrance and down to the basement, **12.** Fortunately, there is space at the end of the terrace to get a ramped access round to the rear entrance and lift shaft. This also provides access to the wheelchair unit in the basement, **17.** The lift should provide access to all floors but if the lift motor proves too obtrusive about the roof line and a hydraulic lift is too expensive, people will have to walk up the last flight of stairs. The lift has to be large enough to accommodate stretchers and coffins.

Costs

2.07 Radical surgery is expensive, **19, 20, 21,** though some major work was needed anyway. Trussed partitions, for example, had been sawn through to make openings so the houses needed

20 *Rear of flats conversion with a feel more like new building than rehabilitation.*

21 *Extensive new partitioning is needed here including false ceiling to bathroom.*

22 *Conversion to flats with houses for sheltered scheme visible opposite.*

bracing with steel, **22**. (Trussed partitions—structural timber framed partitions which carry the weight of floors above and occasionally are used as beams also, needing no support from below.) Fire protection is, of course, more important with the three houses now rated as a hostel. The architects hope that a second lift will not be demanded under Category 2. Fitting out communal kitchens, handrails to stairs (and maybe corridors), grab rails, more lighting, floor finishes, heating standards, etc, are some of the special items that have to be negotiated with the DOE. A summary of Category 2 allow-

ances (extras for building especially for the elderly) and the estimated construction costs of the scheme are given in tables II and III.

3 References

3.01 1 'Sheltered Housing for Old People at Nuneaton and Faversham' AJ 3.10.73 pp787-798.
2 'Queen Elizabeth Close, Norwich' AJ 4.6.75 pp1182-1192.
3 'Housing standards and costs; accommodation specially designed for old people', *MHLG Circular* 82/69.
4 Melanie Phillips, 'Give Them Shelter' *New Society*, 7 April 1977 pp17-18.

4 Credits

4.01 Clients: Notting Hill Housing Trust. Architects: Pollard Thomas & Edwards; job architect: Herbert Reid. Quantity surveyor: Kinsler & Partners. Engineer: Alan Baxter & Associates.

Table II Category 2 allowances

Scheme	10 000
31 units @ £1000	31 000
Guest room	1000
Warden's office	500
Extra for larger lift	6000
	48 500
Wheelchair unit in basement	600
Total	49 100

Table III Estimated construction cost

Yardstick: 12 × 1 p units at £10 900		130 800
19 × 2 p units at £11 900		226 100
1 × 5 p unit at £18 300		18 300
		375 200
Vacancy allowance (extra because houses are part occupied)		28 000
		403 200
Purchase price		138 000
		265 200
Fees at 15 per cent		34 591
		230 609
Less VAT on fees	£2767	
Less VAT on repairs (say)	£2200	
	4967	4967
		225 642
Add Category 2 allowance		49 100
Estimated construction cost		**£274 742**

Case study 6: Rehabilitated housing for single people

Purpose-designed single person housing is relatively uncommon both for rehabilitation and new building, so this case study begins by explaining the current mix of approaches and varying design standards. The second part of the study presents some of the few projects currently being built.

Author **DAVID PEARSON**, an architect/planner, has worked on a number of community-based housing projects in the USA and UK such as the Colville-Tavistock Project (AJ 16.7.75 pp114-116) and is now a HAA project leader with the London Borough of Hammersmith.

1 Introduction

1.01 George Orwell wrote *Keep the aspidistra flying* in 1936, yet it is doubtful if he would need to alter his description of those dingy and depressing bedsitting rooms in lonely lodging houses in Willowbed Road NW to fit much of the housing which is still the only choice for single people today.

1.02 Although central and local government have since implemented policies and improvements in housing, these have mainly concentrated on family accommodation. Single person housing has traditionally been provided by the private landlord. Recently, however, there has been a growing awareness that this is unsatisfactory, that provision must be made for single people as part of overall housing policies. The problem has become particularly acute in inner city areas with the departure of families and the increasing proportion of small households taking their place. The shrinking role of private landlords as providers of housing means that alternatives must be found and planned both in strategic terms and in one-off local experiments or special projects.

2 Demand

Size of the demand
2.01 A joint report by the London Boroughs Association and the Greater London Council (LBA/GLC), entitled *Working party on the provision of accommodation for single people*[1], was published in January 1977 and considered both the immediate problems of finding shelter for the homeless and the broader question of provision in the long term by all London boroughs. The report concludes that 'provision for single people should be considered an essential and integral part of the housing duties of the London boroughs'. It also recommends that 'the local authorities in London should ensure that something in excess of 100 000 small dwellings are provided in all sectors of housing over the next 10 years'. Guidance targets for each individual borough are suggested. For conversions, the aim is 50 000 dwellings; half of these total provisions being suitable for elderly single people.

2.02 The report makes 76 recommendations which stress the need for urgent action and strengthened financial support by the DOE, and give a clear indication of the importance now attached to single person provision by statutory and voluntary bodies. Although no similar appraisal of the need appears to have been made nationally, it is to be expected that there is similar demand across the country in urban areas.

Purpose of this case study
2.03 It is likely that architects, whether employed in private firms, local authorities or housing associations, will become more involved in working on rehabilitation schemes for single people. The aim of this study is to give broad guidance on user research undertaken, current statutory requirements,

1 *Traditional provision for many single people: large old family house subdivided and poorly maintained.*

and roles of housing associations and co-operatives, and finally to review briefly a few examples of the types of provision being made for different groups of single people.

Types of demand

2.04 The term 'single people' covers a wide spectrum of types in terms of age, income and ethnic background. The design of satisfactory housing will therefore vary a great deal according to life styles and aspirations. Although it is difficult to cover the many permutations, the following broad groupings may be helpful in assessing the type of provision most suitable to a particular client group. The surveys described later, carried out by the DOE and York Institute (IAAS), produced typical single person categories on which the groups below are based.

The young mobile person—DOE category (b)

2.05 These will be single people in their late teens or 20s and 30s in all walks of life from students, secretaries, apprentices and itinerant manual workers to young professionals. Many will have a need to find independent housing for the first time away from home. Others will be living in rooms in a shared flat or digs probably close to the centre of town. The accommodation may be sub-standard and in houses in multiple-occupation.

2.06 A growing and important sub-group are young people from immigrant families who may be experiencing special tensions with their parents and who need a supportive environment away from home. If employed, however, young people will generally be prepared to spend a higher proportion of their income on housing. Their need is for both short-term and permanent accommodation, generally furnished and close to the centre. Shared housing may be acceptable so long as each person has his own room for privacy. Many may prefer self-contained bedsitters or small one-bedroom flats.

The older working single person—DOE category (a)

2.07 This group will be in their late 30s up to retirement age and will be in a period of life when a new permanent home will be required. These will include single working people either unmarried or possibly living alone after marital breakdown or the death of a spouse. Many people in this group may have lower incomes but will be fairly stable in their jobs.

2.08 The need for housing is mostly for non-shared accommodation, the ideal being a self-contained one-bedroom flat preferably up to Parker Morris space standards of $32\cdot5$ m^2 including storage.

Elderly retired people

2.09 Elderly people in their retirement have housing needs which depend to a greater degree on health and mobility. Provision can be similar to that for middle aged single people but may range into sheltered accommodation (see also case study 4: sheltered housing AJ 25.5.77 pp991-996). The LBA/GLC report mentioned earlier recommends that half the single person provision should be for the elderly. However, as this type of accommodation has previously received considerable attention, this study concentrates on the other two categories.

3 Types of provision

3.01 Traditionally, the type of provision accessible to single people, young or old, has been in the private sector. For the less well off this has meant living in rooms either as a lodger or in a family house subdivided into single room lettings with shared use of kitchen and bathroom facilities, ie a 'house in multiple-occupation'. Very often the lettings are occupied by a mixture of unrelated households ranging from single people and couples to families with children. This leads, in an uncontrolled situation, to overcrowding, heavy overuse of the

2a *Houses in Liverpool, some of them previously let by private landlords, now developed as part of a scheme of single person student housing (see part 2, AJ 29.6.77).*

2b *Provision common for single people. House subdivided but few fittings or other provisions for a self-contained household.*

3a

few shared amenities, serious fire risk and rapid decline in the standard of general repair and cleanliness, **2a, b**.

Houses in multiple occupation (HMOs)

3.02 In these circumstances it is easy to understand why central and local government have maintained a concerted effort over the years to eradicate the above conditions. The Housing Acts of 1961, 1964 and 1969 contain statutory provisions to enable local authorities to control conditions and the level of occupancy of HMOs and to require registration by landlords. Most local authorities with a high proportion of HMOs have also drawn up a set of local standards suited to their areas. These typically cover:

    natural and artificial lighting
    ventilation
    water supply
    personal washing facilities
    drainage and sanitary conveniences
    facilities for the storage, preparation and cooking of food
    installation and use of space heating appliances
    means of escape in case of fire
    limitation of numbers of persons in occupation.

They may, but rarely do, also specify space standards.

3.03 The sorts of standards adopted are very low when compared with Parker Morris and they are under re-examination by some local authorities which are proposing higher standards.

Space standards in individual dwellings/lettings

3.04 Since section 15 of the Housing Act 1961 does not cover space standards, these are usually not included in local authority standards. Therefore, the only enforceable standard is

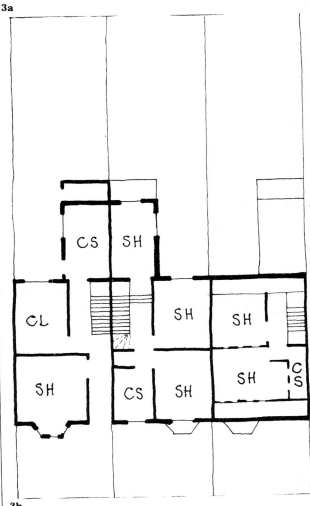

3b

3a, b *Typical analysis by York Institute of the potential of terraced houses to provide for single young people. The plans are possible uses for ground (left), first (centre) and attic (right) floors. (Key: CS—communal services; CL—communal living; SH—single household.)*

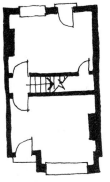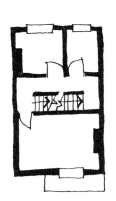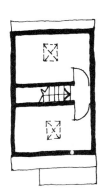

4a

4 *Analysis of terrace use for bedsits to discover how young people live.* **a** *small,* **b** *medium and* **c** *large terraces (see next page).*

4b

4c

contained in section 77 and schedule 6 of the Housing Act 1957.

under 4·6 m²		0 persons
4·6 m²–8·4 m²		½ person (child under 10 years)
8·4 m²–10·2 m²		1½ persons
over 10·2 m²		2 persons

These standards are unsatisfactory for bedsitter accommodation since little usable space is left after bed, sink, cooking facilities, storage and other furniture are installed.

3.05 A higher and more realistic standard has been proposed and adopted by some local authorities which varies according to the number of rooms in the letting, table I.

Table I Minimum standards for single and two-room lettings

Single room used for living—sleeping—cooking
one person	13·9 m²	minimum floor area
two persons	18·6 m²	minimum floor area

Two-room letting with living—sleeping room and separate kitchen
one person	12·5 m²	living/sleeping room floor area
two persons	16·7 m²	living/sleeping room floor area

Two-room letting with kitchen/living room and separate bedroom
one person	6·5 m²	bedroom floor area
	11·2 m²	kitchen/living room floor area
two persons	11·2 m²	bedroom floor area
	14·9 m²	kitchen/living room floor area

Personal washing facilities, food preparation and cooking

3.06 It is generally accepted that one sink in each letting is sufficient for personal washing and food preparation although a few authorities require a wash hand basin as well. Most authorities require the provision of cooking and food storage facilities within each letting.

Bathrooms

3.07 Traditionally, one bath to every 10 persons is the standard used by local authorities but 1:8 or 1:5 are being adopted more often. Also, one wc to every eight persons is traditional, but now 1:6 is more often adopted so long as it is not more than one floor from any letting.

Other facilities and local variations

3.08 As variations occur from area to area, architects should seek advice on accepted standards (and on grants) from the Environmental Health or Housing Departments of the local authority.

4 Work of the York Institute

4.01 Much of this legislation has been aimed at improving conditions for families who are sharing and overcrowded. The research work at the York Institute (Institute of Advanced Architectural Studies) has involved re-evaluating shared accommodation where, as is now becoming more common, this only affects young single people. A continuing programme started in 1973, sponsored by the DOE through BRE, is examining the overall demand for this type of housing with special reference to inner city areas in Leeds, Sheffield and Leicester. The conclusions of the report[2] stressed the need for local and central government to acknowledge responsibility for younger and short-stay tenants in furnished accommodation and to reflect this growing demand by making positive provision in their forward housing programmes and policies and, as an interim measure, to recognise the validity of multi-occupancy property controlled, managed and funded for single young people. The study contains some useful analysis of existing types of local housing stock, ranging from high density small terraces to villa developments, and the potential for different types of occupancy, **3**.

4.02 A second report[3], which surveyed typical dwelling units in 'bedsitland' in Leeds, **3**, concluded with important guidance for future providers and designers.

'The way the accommodation is *managed* is far more crucial to the success of multi-occupancy by single young people than the type of building in which it takes place. Any older housing can, within reason, be used successfully for multiple occupation by single people if sensitively managed.

'Two policy choices and certain key issues will decide the success of any future shared provision, whether purpose-built or a conversion. *Degree of sharing* varying from almost completely separate (eg bathroom and wc as only shared facilities) to completely shared (eg a family house in which each resident has a bedroom but shares kitchen, bathroom and living room). These inter-tenant relationships are fixed by the formal structure of the letting. All the various gradations of sharing may be valid in the right context. *Degree of tenant control* varying from total tenant control to total landlord control. This decision would relate to two areas: first, matters peculiar to individual houses affecting individual housefuls of tenants and, second, matters affecting a whole portfolio of single young person houses under the management of a single housing association or tenants co-operative[4].'

4.03 The initial choices made on these two areas must influence all subsequent decisions regarding the key aspects listed below, so that the whole management and design package is both logical and consistent. The key issues are:

intended occupancy, amount and type of space, facilities, furnishings, selection of individual residents and allocation, tenancy type, household bills, maintenance and cleaning[4].

4.04 So it is important that the architect is involved in the discussion of these overall aspects of the project at initial briefing stage with the client body, as decisions in these areas can have a considerable bearing on proposed design solutions and ultimate user satisfaction.

5 DOE guidance and Leicester scheme

5.01 Apart from the continuing work at York, the DOE study of the needs of single people under retirement age in Leicester is the most comprehensive to date. The DOE has published two Design Bulletins, no 23[5] and no 29[6]. The first is a report of a social survey conducted in Leicester to assess needs; the second gives guidance to designers and others providing new dwellings, and describes the experimental Leicester tower block scheme. A third bulletin is awaited on an appraisal of the occupied tower block scheme in operation.

5.02 It is interesting to note the rather different conclusions arrived at by York and the DOE, based on their surveys. The DOE research showed that there was 'considerable dissatisfaction with existing accommodation—often institutions or substandard rented houses or bedsitters with shared facilities. There was a great desire for purpose built independent accommodation[6].' York, however, found that young mobile singles positively enjoyed sharing and that the type of building was relatively unimportant. Moreover, older buildings such as terraced houses were ideal, being flexible and relatively cheap to adapt to the many permutations of living patterns.

Design Bulletin 29
5.03 DOE Design Bulletin 29 concentrates on provision for the two categories of single people: category (a) older working single people and category (b) young mobile people as described earlier (see paras **2.05-2.08**). For category (a), it recommends a two-room self-contained flat to Parker Morris standards of 32·5 m² including storage. For category (b), it

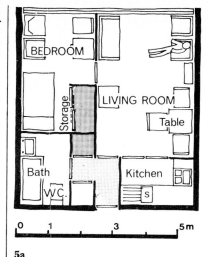

5a

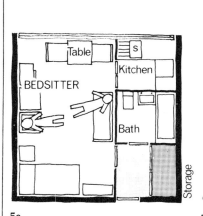

5b

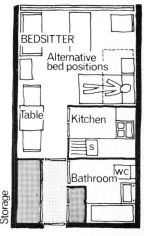

5c   5d

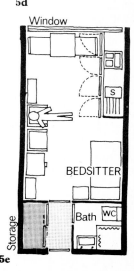

5 *New build proposals for single people from DOE Design Bulletin 29.* **a, b** *32·5 m² PM flats for a middle aged tenant (DOE category a—see* **2.07**). **c, d** *25 m² flats for a young mobile worker.* **e** *Example of undersized flat. Substituting shower for bath saves space but not cost because of plumbing complications. There is little flexibility of furniture arrangement.*

5e

recommends a smaller flat of 25 m² provided with plenty of built-in storage and essential furniture. Shared flats are also proposed so long as each person has his own room. It is suggested that dwellings for up to 10 people sharing amenities are acceptable, table II.

Table II Recommended minimum areas for shared dwellings (including storage) in m². NB (for new dwellings).

	2 *sharing* category (a)	(b)	3 *sharing* (a) & (b)	4 *sharing* (a) & (b)
Houses of one storey	48·5	45	65	85
Houses over one storey	—	—	—	90
Flats	47·5	45	65	85 *pro rata for larger shared flats*
Maisonettes	—	—	—	90 *ditto*

Source: DOE Design Bulletin 29, part IV, p46.

5.04 Note how much higher—almost double—those sharing standards are than even the higher HMO standards given in table I. Flexibility will, therefore, be needed when these are applied to older houses. It is most important that planning authorities recognise this when considering applications and should not be too restrictive or demanding. Early informal discussions between client, architect and the planning authority are essential particularly if shared or hostel accommodation is envisaged. It will also be necessary to discuss the proposals with the local housing or environmental health department to check on any requirements they may have. Needless to say, another vital early consideration will be means of escape in case of fire and fire prevention which may involve smoke lobbies and fire proofing provisions. These provisions may be a large factor adding to costs and may therefore reduce the feasibility of a project for a particular type of property.
5.05 The bulletin gives examples of ideal new dwelling layouts varying from full Parker Morris provision suitable for middle-aged people to bedsitters and shared flats for four or more young people, **5**. It also covers communal facilities, detailed design and provision of equipment, storage, fittings

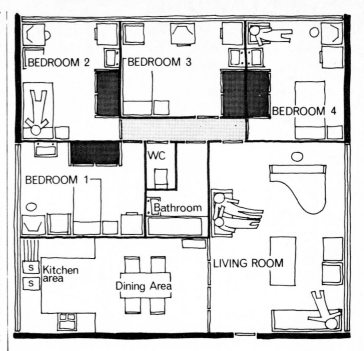

5h

5f, g, i, j *Two-person sharing may be two bedsitters* **f, j,** *one living room and two tiny bedrooms* **i,** *or a flexible arrangement* **g** *which has a bedroom with an optional partition.* **f** *has minimum circulation but wide frontage and so could require a long access corridor in some block plans. Soundproofing should be good between kitchen and bedsits.*
h *More varied layouts are achievable with four people sharing. Little space specifically for circulation though living room is only route to kitchen.*

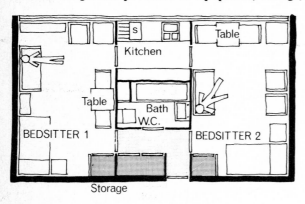

5f

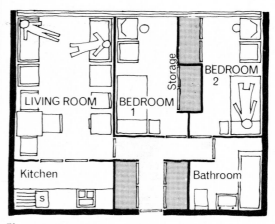

5i

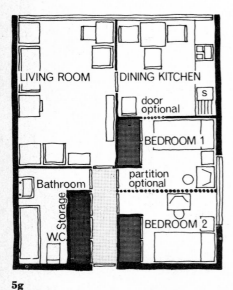

5g

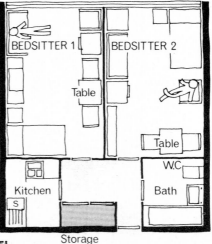

5j

and furniture inside each dwelling, together with all ancillary design considerations such as noise, services, heating, management problems etc. It illustrates the application of these ideas by reference to the 22-storey tower block scheme.

5.06 Much of the guidance in the bulletin is also useful to designers of conversion projects, remembering always that older housing will usually impose special constraints on those ideal standards and that the conversion should be 'natural' for the type of property.

6 Provision by housing associations

6.01 Under the arrangements of the Housing Act 1974, housing associations registered with the Housing Corporation are able and encouraged to provide housing for special categories of need including single people. In DOE Circular 170/74, *Housing corporation and housing associations*[7], priorities are set out for aid via housing association grants (HAG). Projects for single people and those designed to relieve housing stress and homelessness, particularly in inner city stress areas, are specifically listed in para 34 a and b.

6.02 Housing associations may provide for single people either with self-contained units or hostel accommodation in which there are separate bedrooms or living rooms but shared kitchen and toilet facilities.

6.03 Appendix F of the circular gives guidance for new build and conversion projects. So that varying needs can be met, two building standards are given—an 'upper' and 'lower' standard for HAG subsidy purposes.

The standards are:

upper standard	lower standard

1 Communal rooms
Dining and common rooms 2 m² per person | 1·4 m² per person

2 Bedsitting rooms 13 m². All rooms to have wash hand basin and built-in cupboards (2 m²) | *Single rooms* 6·5 m². *Shared rooms* 6·5 m² per person less 10 per cent. Not more than four persons per bedroom. Walls and floors to satisfy Grade II standards for sound insulation.

3 Bathrooms and wc
Approx: 2 baths/showers: 10 residents; 2 wcs: 10 residents. | Approx: 1 bath/shower: 10 residents; 1 wc: 5 residents; 1 basin: 5 residents if not provided in bedroom.

4 Ancillary accommodation
Warden's office, men's and women's wc, cloakroom, kitchen and washing up, stores, bedsitters for staff, etc. | Kitchen and washing up or cooking facilities in each room, laundry, etc.

Note: In the case of old people several modifications apply:
Double rooms of 20 m² may be provided.
All rooms may have an electric fire and a bell near the bed
Dining rooms may provide 1·4 m² per person and common rooms 1·8 m²
One bath to every 10 residents but one bath per floor
A guest room may be provided.

7 Cost limits and HAG

7.01 Details of cost limits and HAGs available for single person accommodation are not included in this case study as

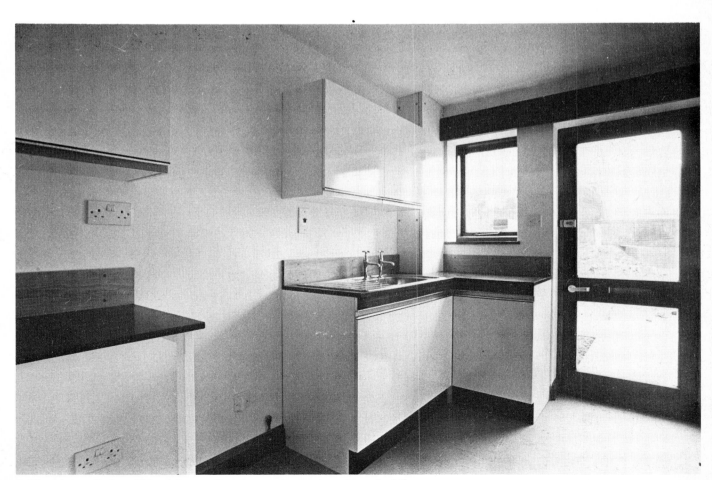

6 *Though cost limits will be tight, quality of provision need not be makeshift.*

revisions are invariably in process. Reference should be made to the latest DOE circulars—the most recent are DOE Circular 24/76 *Cost limits for improvement projects*[8] and DOE Circular 12/76 *Housing for single working people: standards and costs*[9]—the latter deals with new dwellings, **6**.

7.02 If shared accommodation is proposed, it will be necessary to negotiate cost ceilings with the DOE. Ceilings will depend on the standards and amenities provided in the project (eg those bedsitters with shared bathroom facilities perhaps being counted as similar to the cost limits for a normal two-person self-contained flat). Early consultations at sketch scheme stage are essential with the regional office of the DOE. Should the project be in a short-life property (ie less than 10 years' life), the costs allowable will be much less and will depend on the actual life expected. A special grant known as 'mini HAG' is usually payable but this only allows around £1500 for repairs and improvements to each dwelling.

7.03 Provision for ethnic immigrant groups such as young Asians and West Indians is a growing need. A number of community houses have been set up in this way. An example is given in Part 2 (AJ 29.6.77) of a house which caters for young West Indian single people in the Notting Hill area of London.

8 Housing co-operatives

8.01 Recently the alternative of housing co-operatives has been accepted by central government as a means of enabling tenants to exercise real control over their living conditions and to reduce problems such as social isolation and poor housing management. Although not aimed specifically at single people, co-ops would seem to be particularly suited to the needs of both the younger and older categories.

8.02 There are many ways of organising a co-op. One possibility is for an established housing association to purchase privately owned property and then hand over management responsibility to a separately constituted co-operative. Alternatively, when private sector tenants have sufficient expertise and support, they can seek to register as a housing association and purchase and convert one or more properties via Housing Corporation or local authority finance. This type of approach would be very appropriate to the sort of needs identified in the York and DOE research for single people living in houses in multiple-occupation. DOE circular 8/76[10] gives full details and guidance on housing co-operatives.

Society of Co-operative Dwellings (SCD)

8.03 SCD, a secondary housing co-operative (ie a co-op providing advisory and other services to tenants co-operatives), has so far concentrated on producing new build dwellings, though it is now considering rehabilitation projects. In a proposed new build housing co-operative in Slough, emphasis has been placed on communal houses for four to 10 people having their own rooms but sharing bathroom facilities and a large farmhouse kitchen, **4**.

8.04 SCD's experience confirms:
1 the central importance of user control and co-operative forms of organisation in sharing situations
2 the need to give individuals privacy, which requires higher levels of sound insulation to personal rooms
3 the necessity for the DOE to make additional allowances available to cover costs of 2, since the cost per person will still be significantly less than that of providing self-contained flats.

8.05 Three tenants' co-operatives will be featured in the AJ Building study on 29.6.77. Though not for single people, they show how co-operatives can work for new and existing buildings.

9 References

9.01 1 London Boroughs Association/GLC *Working party on the provision of accommodation for single people* Final report Jan 1977.
2 Martin Raper *Housing for single young people* Research Paper 7. Institute of Advanced Architectural Studies. University of York. Sept 1974.
3 Alison Chippindale *A survey of single young people living in multi-occupied houses* Research Paper 11. York. Jan 1976.
4 Alison Chippindale 'Single young people in shared houses' *Housing Review* Oct-Dec 1976.
5 DOE Design Bulletin 23 *Housing single people 1: how they live at present* HMSO. 1971.
6 DOE Design Bulletin 29 *Housing single people 2: a design guide with a description of a scheme at Leicester* HMSO. 1974.
7 DOE Circular 170/74 *Housing corporation and housing associations* HMSO.
8 DOE Circular 24/76 *Cost limits for improvement projects* HMSO.
9 DOE Circular (12/76 *Housing for single working people: standards and costs* HMSO.
See also:
10 DOE Circular 8/76 *Housing co-operatives* HMSO.
11 Inner Area Study: Liverpool *Single and homeless* Report by the consultants, Wilson and Womersley. DOE.
12 Jacky Vincent *The housing needs for young single mothers* Social Policy Research Ltd.
13 W. V. Hole and J. R. B. Taylor *The housing needs of single young people and the use of older properties* BRE Current Paper 43/78.
14 *The new build design manual for single people sharing* The Society for Co-operative Dwellings.

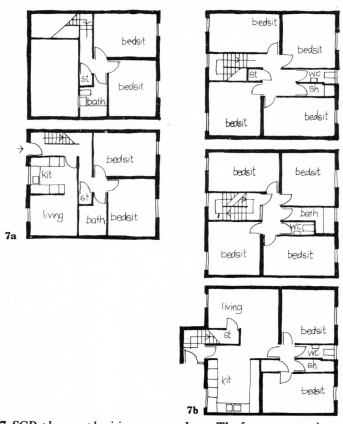

7 *SCD plans emphasising communal use. The four-person unit* **a** *is similar in principle to* **4j**. *The enforced 'community' of* **10** *people sharing* **b** *makes living space in the bedroom important for refuge.*

10 Self-contained bedsitters and two-person standard flats

Single Persons Housing Association (SPHA), Nevern Place, London SW5

10.01 Earls Court has always been the epitome of bedsit land and contains one of the largest concentrations of single people living in houses in multiple-occupation in London. SPHA acquired a terrace of seven large five-storey houses with basements which included a functioning disco and pub, **10a**.

Scheme

10.02 The project was to convert the houses to provide 32 self-contained bed-sitters up to full Parker Morris area of 32·5 m² and 13 units with two bedsitters with shared kitchen and bathroom of 54·0 m². The total 45 units accommodate 58 single people. The disco and pub have been leased back and will continue in operation. A small communal area is provided on the ground floor of one house. The aim is to house essential workers such as teachers, service employees, social workers, etc. Conversion work is to commence shortly. Management pressure by the association on site is not expected to be required as most flats are self-contained, but, in view of the size of the project, this will be reviewed when it is in operation, **10b, c**.

10.03 The estimated capital costs based on the first stage of a two part tender are:

acquisition (including legal fees and allowances)	£318 085
improvement or conversion (including fees, VAT and allowances)	£502 125
Total loan from lending authority (including local authority administration charge)	£828 284

11 Self-contained bedsitters and flats

Liverpool University housing

11.01 Decline of the private rented sector has affected students as it has other single people. In Liverpool the shortage of accommodation is exacerbated by widespread demolition in

10a *Nevern Place terrace with entrance on the left to pub and disco which take up basements and part of the ground floor of the end two houses.*

the city centre which removed potential flats and digs. The university has recently completed a scheme of 383 units, 238 new and 145 conversions in two terraces, **11a, b, c, d**. The scheme is for undergraduate and post-graduate students with a few staff.

Scheme

11.02 The main structural elements and facades were retained, including doors, steps and balustrades. But door furniture was removed and doors sealed with new entrances made at ends or rear of terraces. Catherine Street comprises two terraces of approximately similar houses converted in groups of three. Middle houses have been gutted to provide separate kitchen and bathroom units for the four bedsitters per floor, **11e**. The net accommodation is 47 double bedsitters, six single bedsitters, one one-bed flat, an administrative office and two communal lounges.

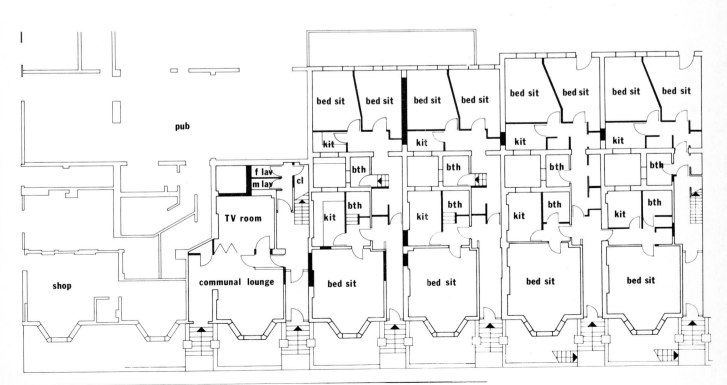

10b *Ground floor. Some bedsits have exclusive use of bathroom and kitchen, others share.*

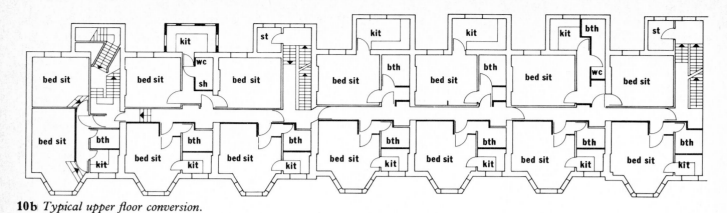

10b *Typical upper floor conversion.*

11a *Site of terraces for conversion in Falkner and Catherine Streets. Other buildings shown are the new student housing.*

11b *Rear of Falkner Street terrace before conversion.*

11c *Major transformation at rear to make these new entrances on some of the houses.*

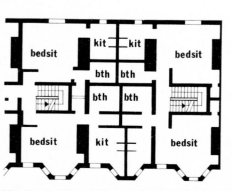

11e *Typical floor plan of three Catherine Street houses planned as four bedsits around service core.*

11d *Interior of site showing new with old.*

11.03 The houses in Falkner Street vary considerably. There is little cross conversion with stairs generally retained and conversion to one flat per floor, **11f**. The Falkner Street terrace now comprises 30 one-bed flats, four two-bed flats and three double bedsitters with their own kitchen and bathroom. Contract costs for Falkner Street and Catherine Street, including a proportion of preliminaries and site works, were £474 165.

12 Self-contained bedsitters with integral kitchen and own bathroom

Godolphin Road, London W12

12.01 When Hammersmith's first HAA was declared around Coningham Road, this large four-storey house had been converted into six 'luxury' bedsitters and one two-bedroom flat by a development company but was vacant and uncompleted, **12a**. The house-to-house survey conducted by the borough showed that over 30 per cent of the households in the HAA comprised single people, a high proportion of these were elderly. As part of the HAA programme, the borough acquired the house and has completed remedial works to most of the flats. The bedsitters are now tenanted by single older working people, some from across the street where they used to live in a similar large house in multi-occupation. The house they lived in previously has also been bought by the borough and is undergoing conversion.

12.02 These bedsitters illustrate how necessary this type of accommodation is, particularly in localised rehabilitation programmes like HAAs. The tenants find the provision adequate for their needs and have been able to move into improved housing and remain in familiar surroundings, **12b, c**.

12.03 Hammersmith borough is also working with housing associations on single person provision both short-term and permanent. In the permanent category, the Shepherds Bush Housing Association is in process of producing two bed-sitter projects. An interesting detail is the proposed integral kitchen/personal washing area, **12d**, which is to be built-in in each bedsitter where bathrooms are shared. The proprietary mini-kitchen unit is combined into the larger storage unit, **12e**. Folding doors close off the whole unit if required.

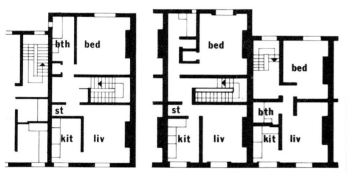

11f *Part of Falkner Street terrace with varying plans converted to one flat per floor.*

12b *View of a bedsit conversion for a single older person.*

12a *Godolphin Road; distinguished house with not very sympathetic addition started by developer before local authority acquisition.*

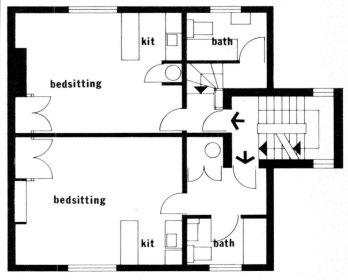

12c *Plan of typical floor.*

13 Bedsitters with shared bathrooms and communal dining/living area

Carlton Terrace, Norwich

13.01 The Broadland Housing Association has carried out a large terrace rehabilitation project where the end house is being converted into a hostel. The remainder of the terrace is being converted into flats some of which will be suitable for single persons to share. The hostel provides nine bedsitters with sharing of bathrooms. A generous communal living room, dining room, kitchen and quiet rooms are also provided, **13a, b, c**.

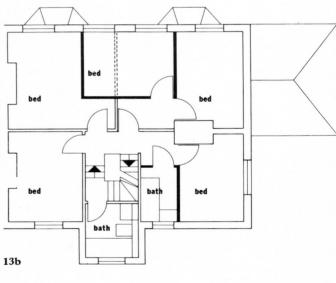

12d *Integration of kitchen and washing facilities. Washing space combined with, but separated from, food preparation area.*

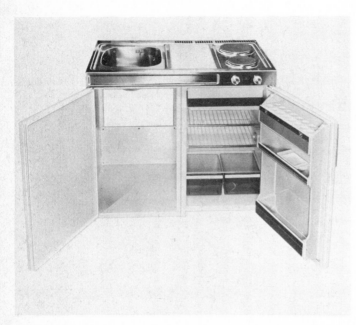

12e *Proprietary combined sink/refrigerator/cooker unit used in* **12d**.

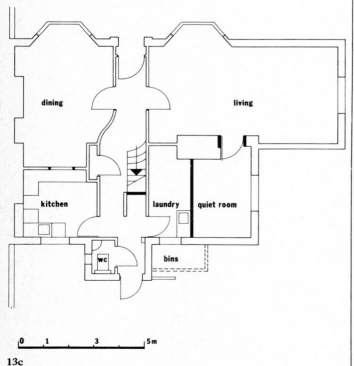

13c

13a *Top,* **b** *first and* **c** *ground floors of hostel. The architect has been able to retain most of the form of the original house, especially on the ground floor. Top floor wc has no bath because sloping ceiling limits usable space.*

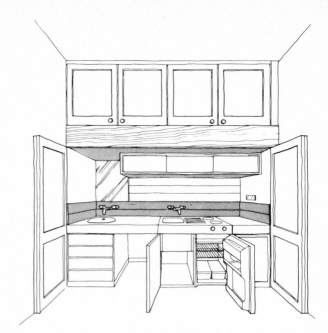

13b

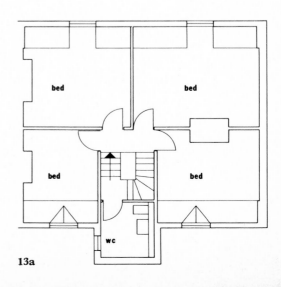

13a

14 Community house: bedsitters (some shared) with shared bathrooms, communal living areas, kitchen and on-site staff

Unity Association, Lancaster Road, North Kensington, London W11

14.01 Homelessness and unemployment are increasing for single young people. These problems are becoming particularly acute in larger conurbations and in areas such as North Kensington with concentrations of immigrant families. Many arise when children of first generation immigrants—West Indian, Asian or African—leave home because of conflicts over life style and identity. Although housing is obviously essential, many of these young people may be in urgent need of a wider range of help including advice, education or training and a period of intensive support before finding more permanent employment and long term housing. To help combat this situation a number of experimental projects have been set up such as the Community House for Unity in the Notting Hill area.

Scheme

14.02 Two large four-storey terraced houses owned by the Notting Hill Housing Trust, a registered housing association, have been leased to the Unity Association to provide communal facilities for young black homeless single people, **14a**. After a rather turbulent beginning, the association obtained a grant under the Home Offices Urban Aid Programme for the project to cover both capital and running costs. The two houses are currently being converted to produce single and double furnished bedsitters for up to 18 people. Communal living, dining and tv rooms are provided on basement and ground floors with administration and warden's offices. Basins are provided in each bedsitter but bathroom amenities are shared. Meals are served by catering staff in the communal dining room. Four full-time staff—co-ordinator, relief warden, cook and secretary—will handle the management and support for the residents. Organisation of employment and training facilities are planned to be close by, possibly in the community space, under the westway motorway, **14c, d, e, f**.

Costs

14.03 The conversion work is being carried out by the Bulldog Building Co-operative, a black organisation using local labour. The estimated cost of the conversion including fees, etc is £32 000 and the annual running cost is estimated at £23 000 to pay for the four full-time staff, catering and administration. The architect who has worked for Unity, John Benson, points out that the capital cost is low largely owing to the use of a community 'self-help' building organisation, **14b**. If Housing Association Grant (HAG) had been used rather than Urban Aid money (HAG was not available when the project was conceived), a higher cost ceiling would have been possible, as evidenced by the Earls Court (Nevern Place) scheme described above, **10.01**.

14a *The single person housing will be in the centre two houses now being converted.*

14b *Members of Bulldog Housing Co-op converting Lancaster Road.*

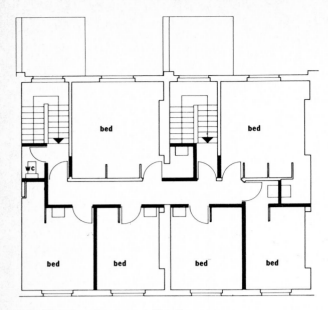

14c *Top floor* (*Lancaster Road*).

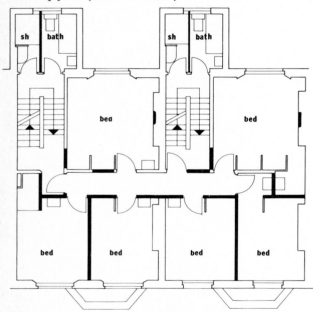

14d *First floor* (*Lancaster Road*).

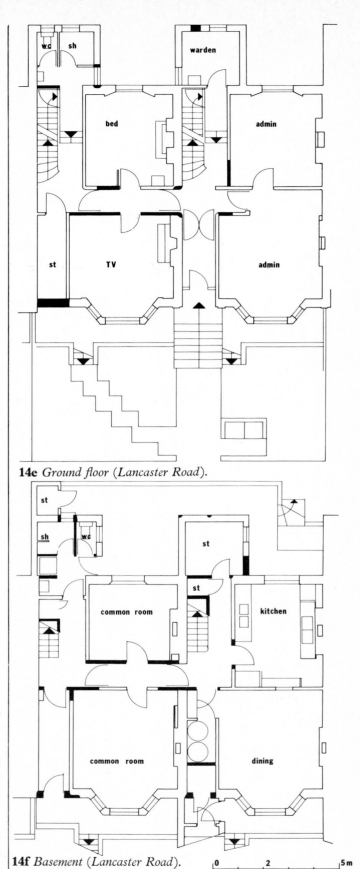

14e *Ground floor* (*Lancaster Road*).

14f *Basement* (*Lancaster Road*).

15 Summary

Size of problem
15.01 Single people are an increasingly large proportion of inner city populations, and there is a lack of planned provision.

Private landlords
15.02 The diminishing role of the private landlord means that central and local government need to co-operate with housing associations and voluntary agencies in providing enough flexible housing.

Importance of briefing
15.03 It is important for the architect to be involved with the client from the earliest stages in any single person project, in the formulation of the whole design/management package. Although the majority of the schemes may simply be self-contained accommodation, there will be many special and experimental projects that require architects to work closely with community and voluntary groups on their own ground.

16 Acknowledgements

16.01 The author wishes to thank the following for their assistance and information:
York Institute of Advanced Architectural Studies, Society for Co-operative Dwelling and Andrews, Downie & Kelly for information on Furnival Avenue, Slough. Stillman & Eastwick-Field and Single Persons Housing Association for help with the Nevern Place scheme. Shepherds Bush Housing Association and Derek Irvine & Assocs. Broadland Housing Association and Edward Skipper & Assocs. for the Carlton Terrace project, Norwich. Unity Association and John Benson for the Lancaster Road scheme. John Saunders of Saunders Boston for Liverpool Student housing. Les Hughes of Notting Hill Housing Trust for general advice. Paul Rydquist of Threshold and the Housing Corporation.

Section four: Improvements and Conversions

Technical study 1
The architect's role

This study of the architect's role introduces the final section of The Housing Rehabilitation Handbook, Improvements and conversions. It takes the form of annotated flow charts for four architects' roles: an architect for a private client, for a housing association and for a local authority both employed in-house and in private practice. The charts deal with the pre-contract phase in which most differences of organisation occur.
There are contributions from JOHN BENSON, GEORGE JONES, PETER COLOMB and DAVID PEARSON.

Improvements and conversions

Early parts of this book on repair and maintenance were mainly technical in emphasis. The case studies expanded on this to include a variety of housing needs, eg disabled and single people, and also put much more emphasis on organisation, eg ASSIST, tenant liaison. This next section of the *Handbook*, Improvements and conversions, maintains the emphasis on organisation but considers space planning and detailing of houses in general.

The section is organised generally in a plan of work sequence, from inception to final account, with occasional asides on subjects that recur at several stages, such as developing standardised documentation.

The sort of extensive works undertaken by local authorities and housing associations but rarely part of the private architect's role.

1 An overview

1.01 The four charts that follow provide an introductory overview of rehabilitation jobs for the newcomer and could be used as starting points for preparing job checklists. (More detailed guidance on checklists is given later in the section in Technical study 3, Standard documents.) The charts were prepared by four architects who have the following roles: architect for private clients, for a housing association and for a local authority, one employed in-house and one in private practice. The charts have not been normalised to produce a set of standard steps because the underlying work stages are evident. Differences in emphasis and style are preserved because they point to significant differences in roles.

1.02 The charts should be read bearing in mind their compilation. Inevitably they reflect to some extent the personalities of those involved and generalisation of clients into four categories produced stereotypes. Nevertheless the overview is broadly indicative of practice. The few paragraphs that follow pick out some of the broad patterns of similarity and difference between the four charts, which begin on the next page.

Institutionalisation

1.03 The charts present a picture of increasingly standardised procedures and communications with clients, least with private clients, through housing associations to the most institutionalised, local authorities. (This stereotype of local authorities is perhaps the most variable with architects able to work informally with officers in some authorities.)

Predictability

1.04 Institutionalisation is in part responsible for predictable communications and hence less comment on them in the charts. Predictability, and lack of comment, also reflects the expertise of the client. The private client is usually inexpert, requiring education and reassurance. The brief will generally be fairly individual. The housing association is concerned with groups of occupants, occasionally individuals, and with the mix of stock it is accumulating. There are likely to be general briefing guidelines and perhaps particular requirements. Local authorities are generally concerned with a durable, relettable mix of stock and may provide standard briefs for most jobs.

Fees

1.05 The architect working for private clients refers to fees often, the others hardly at all. Partly this is because private clients are usually more prompt if accounts are submitted for small amounts often rather than stored till there is a large bill. Partly it is because there is always a worry about whether private clients will pay up at all. With the other clients the doubt is usually only about when.

2 Private architect

2.01 Action

	Comment
Survey stage	
Brief. Agree basis of time fee, date of site visit. Check building ownership and proposed use by client.	*Survey requested.* *Explain what architect does.*
Telephone planning department to check if proposed use matches zoning.	
Get client to check grant possibilities.	*Is building in conservation area, GIA, HAA or listed?*
Check any delays due to backlog for listed building consent/ planning permission.	
Meet client on site for visual survey.	*Warn client if delays or problems envisaged.*
Check client's idea of cost against your own based on rough estimate of £/m² (dependent on use and state of building). Abandon project or continue on agreed approximate budget.	*Architect's costing usually twice client's estimate. Difference to be reconciled in practice by client reducing offer for purchase (if buying), agreeing to spend more or reconciling to lower standard of workmanship.*
Check with planning department any changes from those known previously.	
Write report with time scale based on longest controlling factor expected.	*This factor might be:* *time for planning permission* *time for purchase of property* *time for complex tender documents.*
Agree written proposal.	
Prepare measured survey and detailed structural report. Send these with fee account.	

Sketch design	
Receive fee and instructions to prepare sketch design.	*Client instructs architect.*
Mark up survey drawing with rough proposals with client.	
Prepare elevations. Check costings with own qs if any (on time basis).	
Report to client with fee account.	*Agree with client in principle.*
Make formal town planning by-law and regulations application. Send drawings for comment to means of escape authority.	*Visit planning department to explain drawings to officer concerned. Client makes formal offer to purchase property.*

Detailed design	
Check details with client, especially complicated areas such as bathrooms and kitchens or choice of materials.	
Visit means of escape authority and agree requirements, marking up drawings.	*Inform client of financial influences.*
Complete design drawings and send to client with account.	
Agree design.	*Check there are no known planning or by-law objections and inform client of risk of starting building without official confirmation. Exchange contracts for purchase (better to do this now if changes greatly increase value of building).*
Agree with client type (size) or range of general contractors tendering, explaining cost and time and quality implications.	

Pre-contract documentation
Send probable time programme requirements and drawings to contractors to establish interest.

Prepare services drawings and specification.

Send services out to tender.

Prepare main contractors' drawings and schedules of work.
Receive service tenders.

Agree choice of kitchen fittings, sanitary fittings, lighting, etc.
Check deliveries.

Send drawings for final planning, by-laws, regulations, means of escape checks.

Out to tender.

Check gas and electricity authorities.

Check likely tender amount.
Check progress of planning permission (if not yet confirmed).
Discuss proposals with by-laws, regulations, health and drainage authorities.

Receive tenders.

Agree any changes required for cost reasons with client and contractor.

Agree starting date with contractor to coincide with completion of purchase.

Send client confirmation of agreement with contractor and fee account.

Receive planning, by-law, regulation etc approvals.
Receive fee.

Complete purchase of property.
Contractor starts on site.

Check with client.

Subcontractors may have comments affecting design, eg on boiler size or duct sizes. Services is the largest PC sum so send to tender before main contract to eliminate uncertainty. Main contractor will also tender for services. Compare tenders allowing for contractor's supervision fee if subcontractor used.

Client should order on proforma invoice all critical items on long delivery. (Check restocking charge if project abandoned.)

Undertakings may do internal servicing as well as mains.

3 Architect for housing association (HA)

3.01 Action
Survey stage
Brief. Agree terms.
Find out about access.

Visit site and survey.

Comment

Requirements relate to Housing Corporation standards, to needs HA is trying to satisfy (eg single people, old) and to approval to purchase based on feasibility scheme (usually done by HA).

Send access letter giving choice of date and time. Find out names of tenants—better than addressing letter to 'occupiers'. Enclose prepaid reply for good response.

Sketch design
Prepare survey and sketch scheme.
Indication of programming may be required.
Estimate cost. Check total of the following estimates in relation to the Housing Corporation maximum:
building work cost
legal fees
architect's fees
acquisition costs
VAT

Covering letter. Amount of money available for improvement depends on purchase price.

If sketch makes changes from earlier acquisition feasibility scheme resubmit to Housing Corporation.

Application to planning, regulations, means of escape authorities.

Write to tenant to arrange second visit for checking for repairs, etc.

Detailed design
Working drawings and specification.

Drawings and specification sent to Housing Corporation by HA. Where HA has a large programme the Corporation may agree to a standard job master spec, to avoid delays in approval.

Pre-contract documentation
Phone contractors asking if they wish to tender.

Invite tenders.

Agree tenderers and send client copy of tender documents.

Party wall notice.

Invite tenders from subcontractors such as:
drainage/sewer connection
electricity main
gas main
water main
dpc and timber treatment
roofing.

Receive and analyse tender. Report to client.

If within estimate proceed.
If outside make cuts or go to Housing Corporation to plead special case.

Notify contractor of acceptance and request programme and pre-contract meeting.

Agree vacation of property with HA.
Agree start date.

---

4 Architect consultant to Local Authority (LA)

4.01 Action   **Comment**
Survey stage
Accept/refuse initial inquiry from LA and if accept, request   *Do you want job ? Assess workload and skills.*
further information.

LA sends briefing document.   *Usually well worked out but may be queries.*
Confirm receipt.

Arrange to meet LA officer to confirm brief, check queries and
make individual contacts.

Check whether LA pays for consultants, makes its own officers   *Check consultants with other architects etc if you have no*
available or expects architects to pay.   *regular ones. Check out LA officers if they are to be used as*
                                                                 consultants and fee reduction involved.

Check on tenants and access.
Arrange visit (see HA architect chart).

Survey.

Sketch design
Initial idea.

Check sketch with planning, regulations, means of escape, etc,   *Depending on sketch, other authorities may be affected eg water.*
authorities.

Sketch scheme and report to LA.

Apply for planning permission.
Appoint consultants.

Detailed design
Start detail design and specification.

Send to statutory authorities.

Revisit house for schedule of repairs.

Apply for regulations approval.

Pre-contract documentation

Completed drawings and specification for tendering and to nominated suppliers and subcontractors.

Check contractors on LA approved list and get others added so that a good contractor is likely to produce lowest tender.

Receive and analyse tenders. Check acceptance with LA.

Lowest usually automatically accepted.

5 Local authority architect

5.01 Action

Survey stage

Request to act for LA, briefing documents, timetable and cost limits received.
Send standard acceptance memo.

Comment

Can property (properties) be dealt with as a group contract ? Check recent jobs.

Check if in special area eg HAA, GIA and cost limits delegated by DOE. Also check if within or exempt from section 105 expenditure.

Check date acquired. If over five years ago less delegated costs allowable by DOE.

If property tenanted check rehousing requested by Housing Department.
If no rehousing, inform Department of critical decant dates. Arrange access with tenants (see HA architect).

Are tenants prepared to move ? Hold up in decanting can be major delay if tenants are not rehoused shortly after tenders are received.

If property vacant check temporary securing of property and cutting off services. If not done instruct council works department.
Check keys received.

Security may involve bricking up basement and ground floor doors and windows. What does Housing Department advise ? Extra cost involved.

Survey and report.

Sketch design

Sketch scheme and cost estimate. If total estimated conversion costs are likely to exceed DOE cost limits, report to Housing Department and request instructions on whether to proceed with tenders. If tenders over limits, can deductions be made? If not DOE will have to make decision and extra delays will be involved. Also check if costs can be absorbed in larger contract with other cheaper conversions.

Is brief adequate ? Are unit types, sizes and location in property feasible for property type and cost units.

As for architect consultant to LA.

Check if LA Direct Works Department is to tender with outside contractors.

Technical study 2
Briefing meetings
with clients

**The initial meeting is an opportunity to size up a job
and client. Architect-client relationships are
generally similar to those for new work though the
client tends to be more involved in rehabilitation.
Like the previous study, this one is primarily to
inform the newcomer to rehabilitation. Here, too,
impressions given of clients—private, local authority
and housing association—are stereotyped, indicative
rather than fully representative.
Contributions are from JOHN BENSON, GEORGE
JONES and PETER COLOMB.**

1 Before the meeting

1.01 Briefing will usually be the first significant contact with
clients. It is worth visiting the site beforehand, if only to view
the building(s) from outside. It is usually possible, especially
where institutional clients are involved, to find architects who
have worked for them and so make preliminary checks on their
attitude to architects and architecture. Institutional clients
usually want to meet in their offices but it can be more instruc-
tive if meetings are arranged on site. (As architects come to
work regularly for institutions, such meetings may be replaced
by receiving briefs and conditions of engagement by post.)

2 A profile of the client
Local authorities
2.01 Relationships with local authorities tend to be distant,
with architects taking day to day decisions. Policy decisions
will be discussed but architects generally meet officers rather
than the elected members who, nominally at least, take the
policy decisions.

Housing associations
2.02 Housing associations as clients can vary from a committee
of laymen, concerned with perhaps two or three properties
and discussing them directly with the architect, to a large
organisation with many properties and a full-time liaison
staff. (This variation between committee and organisation is
similar to the difference between a local authority housing
committee and the housing department.)
2.03 In the best cases, liaison is with a group of individuals
whose opinions are channelled through the architect or
quantity surveyor. In other cases, liaison involves sorting out
technicalities while discussion of design and organisation is
dealt with by a committee of the housing association. As with
a housing department, liaison staff are very much involved in
the day to day running of the organisation and are experienced
in all phases from organising finance with the Housing
Corporation through to maintenance.

Private client
2.04 The private client is generally inexpert, but with time
on his hands to think. Rehabilitation is probably a big occasion
in his life, but he has usually little idea of timescale, what his
money will buy, or what an architect does. The architect's
reputation is likely to depend on what the client notices he has
done rather than on the overall quality of design or supervision.
2.05 The key issue is whether the architect feels he can work
with the client and whether the client likes him. Generally,
avoid potential clients who have a great disparity of taste or
sense of humour from one's own unless there is other obvious
affinity. Similarly, look for affinity before risking passing a

potentially difficult client to an assistant. Ask about any
previous architects whom clients have employed and check
on the client with these later. (Potential clients who tell you
how influential they are and how much work then can put
your way have an unfortunate habit of not paying your fee.)
2.06 An architect should take obvious worriers only if he feels
he can cope or needs the work badly. (Coping may recommend
him to the client's less worrisome friends.) If one senses
difficulty ahead, then refuse the job or offer to do it at a high
rate on a time basis (on the RIBA scale, £12 per hour is
equivalent to £8 000 per year). Small jobs should be done on
a time basis.

3 Requirements
Brief
3.01 *Local authorities* generally aim for Parker Morris standards in area, furniture capacity and services, in self-contained
units. Smaller units are usually preferred (compensating for
the predominance of larger family houses in authorities'
stock). This smaller unit size is subject to the house being
converted naturally, ie as little fundamental change to the
house as possible. Designs are not discussed with tenants, so a
flexible but unadventurous design is preferred which mini-
mises external additions and external works. (External works
are more favourably treated in GIAs where there is a separate,
though small, grant for environmental improvements.) The
emphasis is usually on structural soundness and freedom
from all but routine maintenance; client officers are often
surveyors or from other backgrounds with somewhat different
priorities to architects.
3.02 *Housing associations* are also concerned to minimise
structural work and maintenance; for example, full repointing and reroofing are often required. But housing
associations are generally more concerned than local authorities with amenity and, on occasion, there may be specific
tenants to provide for.
3.03 *Local authorities* and *housing associations* give architects
considerable discretion within this fairly tight overall frame-
work. Architects can generally sign Architect's Instructions
for example, and keep work moving rather than having to get
approval from clients first. Apart from contingencies, some
limited overspending may be approved, though, if the client
has to go to DOE to negotiate a new cost ceiling, this could
take up to six months.
3.04 *Private clients* are generally much less interested in
spending to reduce maintenance. Rehabilitation is an opportunity for self-expression, though clients generally have little
idea what is feasible or where the money goes. Whereas local
authorities and housing associations rarely change more
than details after briefing (as a result of change of policy or
personnel), private clients are learning all the time and
perhaps comprising within the family. So the briefing meeting

may provide little more than a declaration of intent and a few first thoughts. If the private client is buying a house, advice should be limited to whether it is suitable for the use envisaged, given the price range. Never advise on whether it will be a profitable speculation.

Service and fees
3.05 *Local authorities* and *housing associations* usually want a full service with specification and drawings, though, occasionally also, a bill of quantities for large jobs (say £100 000). Each house is usually charged separately, though there may be reason, or an attempt made, to pay repetition fees.

3.06 When working regularly for *housing associations*, it can ease cash flow not to charge fees till the G stage. Feasibility studies, stages A and B, are not reimbursed by the Housing Corporation, so housing associations have to pay for their own. Though there is no payment, it may be necessary to do feasibility studies anyway to help the client clarify his ideas.

3.07 *Private clients* will usually have a full service but may only want or be able to afford a design service.

Consultants
3.08 Quantity surveyors are usually used only on large jobs. (A quantity surveyor familiar with rehabilitation can do much of the haggling with contractors.) The architect usually has to employ his own quantity surveyor, structural (and occasionally mechanical and electrical) engineers as required out of fees, though a *private client*, wanting something out of the ordinary, may pay extra for consultants. *Local authorities* may make a deduction in fees for using their technical officers as consultants.

Legal checks
3.09 Ownership will generally be known, though following up absentee landlords can cause delays. Deeds provide a check on ownership and rights of way. Check with the planning department about listing, conservation areas (historic buildings officers are more demanding than housing officers), and statutory areas—GIAs, HAAs, PNs. This may take a couple of weeks. Keep a record of names and telephone extensions and confirm verbal agreements by letter.

3.10 *Local authorities* and some *housing associations* have legal departments which can check on rights of way, rights of light, party walls (inner London), etc. Any litigation is expensive and time consuming. It is important, anyway, to keep on good terms with neighbouring occupiers and owners. Explain pitfalls of rights to light, etc, to private clients and get them to talk to adjoining owners about proposals in principle. Make sure that clients confirm any verbal agreement in writing, pending agreement of detailed drawings.

Programming
3.11 *Private clients* will generally need informing of the realities of programming. Architects can explain likely timing, potential uncertainties and opportunities for regulating programmes, eg, by spending more on a reliable contractor and not changing the brief during the job. *Local authorities* and some *housing associations* will specify the design time. They may also know contractors on the list better than the architect, so it is worth asking them to verify such contractors' programme proposals.

3.12 *Local authorities* and *housing associations* generally know how long finance arrangements and decanting will take. Private clients may well be contemplating house purchase, so it is the architect who is uncertain about work flow. If *private clients* are occupying a house to be rehabilitated, it may be cheaper to move to a hotel temporarily depending on the extent of works and type of contractor. Contract prices are generally higher for occupied houses and contracts run longer.

3.13 For a comparison of decanting possibilities for large clients, local authorities and housing associations, see Technical study 4 'Decanting'.

The initial impression may not be uplifting but few houses are beyond rehabilitation.

Technical study 3
Standard documents

A striking feature of housing rehabilitation is the variety of buildings found. Even in a confined locale it is often necessary to treat each house largely as a one-off project. However, there are repetitions, especially in organisation. This study looks at the scope for standard documents and gives examples of some for early stages of design.
Further examples of standard documents will be given later in the section, which follows a plan of work sequence.

1 Standardising

1.01 Though houses for rehabilitation may appear similar in planning and construction, there are often many detailed differences due, for example, to the preferences of individual workmen or to adapting plans to suit individual clients, **1**. Added to such original differences are various subsequent improvements and conversions plus varied histories of repair and maintenance. So there is little potential for standardising designs except for some details. The main opportunity is in organisation with the development of standard documents.

1.02 Often documentation is a time consuming and tedious process requiring a lot of detailed checking. Using standard documents helps relieve this tedium and, through continual updating, improves completeness and precision, while keeping pace with changing requirements. However, standardising requires investment, both for initial development and updating. So the amount of standardisation appropriate will vary from practice to practice, from a few letters and details to sophisticated specification and billing systems.

Examples

1.03 The sample documents illustrate the potential for standardising at various stages of a job. They indicate the aim of standardising and illustrate ways it can be achieved but cannot generally be copied verbatim. This is partly because it would take several books' length to give complete examples for the various sizes and styles of practice in the public and private sectors, but, also, because going through the process of systematising information for standardising documents can sometimes be as valuable as the documents themselves.

2 Communicating with others

Personal style

2.01 Except when using ready made documents like *The standard form for nomination of sub-contractors*, it is worth considering how far standardisation should go. Institutional clients, some local authorities, for example, may have very standardised communication channels and so it may be appropriate to match their formality of manner. But where architect-client relationships are more informal, and perhaps idiosyncratic, these might be improved by writing more personally. Standardisation could still go as far as keeping a file of points to cover in letters.

2.02 Contact with clients may be predominantly by letter and on that basis an impression is formed of the architect's competence. (*The Honeywood file* by H. B. Cresswell, Faber, is still an illuminating commentary on letter writing.) Letters should be positive, as these two more recent examples illustrate:

'All external openings line up and have level, uncracked sills with the exception only of the main entrance. This has a 20 mm drop to the left hand head indicating some minor differential settlement in the entrance porch.'

Alternatively you could write:

'As far as could be seen all openings were reasonably plumb and level and none of the sills examined had substantial cracks. There was however some indication of differential settlement.'

The first example indicates confidence and ability; the second only that you require a legal let-out if the house falls down due to something you did not notice.

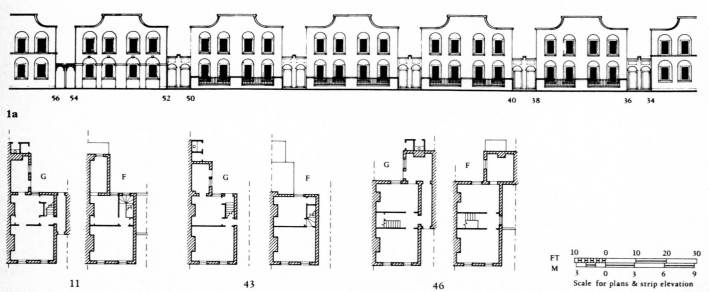

1a

11   43   46

FT
M

10   0   10   20   30
3   0   3   6   9
Scale for plans & strip elevation

1 abc *(overleaf) Even behind a carefully regular facade plans may differ considerably.*

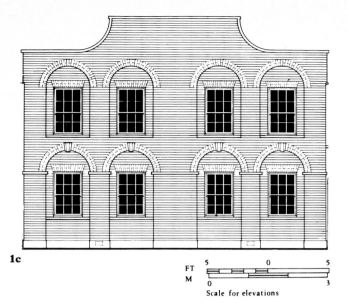

1c

FT
M

Scale for elevations

Uses of letters

2.03 There are several purposes apart from the sending or requesting of information that need considering in preparing standard letters. For example:

● Often more than two parties are involved. A letter ensures and records that all have the same information.

● Many things are forgotten unless written down, including telephone conversations. This applies to large organisations as well as individuals, so it is often worth using confirming letters of decisions agreed in conversation.

● Letters of confirmation can record the state of progress and draw attention to what is critical.

● Letters can be used to trigger action by others.

● A letters file provides a way of checking that one has covered all points adequately from a professional point of view. A file can be looked through regularly like a checklist of communications, reminding one both of urgent matters and those which need dealing with now to avoid future delay.

Letters file

2.04 A sample set of standard communication documents from inception to final account is available in Jack Bowyer's *Small works contract documentation and how to administer it* (Architectural Press). It includes printed notifications, agreement forms, etc, as well as sample letters. The reviewer of the book (AJ 16.2.77) commented that it 'should prove a valuable guide to recently qualified architects . . . Though standard letters should be held in an ever-changing format so that they can be updated with experience, the book forms a good checklist for setting up an efficient documentation system.' There are some omissions as the book deals with matters common to small works generally, not just housing rehabilitation, and it assumes a smooth running job, so there are few of the chasing letters and reminders commonly necessary.

2.05 To help people set up such a system (and decide whether the book itself would be of value) we reprint Bowyer's contents list, §**2.06**. To fit this better to housing rehabilitation the list has been cross checked with the letters file of Levitt Bernstein Associates. The second list is of Levitt Bernstein's letters not covered by Bowyer's book, §**2.07**. This includes letters for architects working for housing associations. The lists include most letters architects would consider standardising, though many practices could manage with only a selection.

Small works contract documents

2.06 1: *Inception of commission to invitation to tender.*
Letter from architect to client: acknowledgement of receipt of commission
Letter from architect to client: confirmation of instructions and Conditions of Engagement

Specimen Memorandum of Agreement
Letter from architect to client: to enclose sketch plans and approximate estimate
Letter from architect to client: acknowledgement of approval of sketch proposals
Letter from architect to client: appointment of consultants
Letter from architect to consultant: confirmation of nomination
Letter from architect to subcontractors: preliminary information
Letter from architect to local planning authority: application for approval
Letter from architect to client: to enclose copies of final production drawings
Letter from architect to local authority building control: application for approval
Letter from architect to quantity surveyor: preparation of bills of quantities
Letter from architect to prospective tenderers: preliminary invitation to tender
Letter from architect to tenderers: invitation to tender
Letter from architect to client: to advise tenders invited

2: *Placing the contract*
Letter from architect to quantity surveyor: to check tenders
Letter from architect to all tenderers: acknowledgement of receipt of tender
Letter from architect to tenderer: return of late tender unopened
Letter from architect to client: report on tenders
Letter from architect to unsuccessful contractor submitting lowest tender: to advise that the tender has not been accepted by client
Letter from architect to client: confirmation of verbal instruction to accept a tender
Letter from architect to successful contractor: acceptance of tender
Letter from architect to successful contractor: to enclose contract documents for signature and return
Letter from architect to client: to seek appointment for signature of contract documents
Letter from architect to contractor: to advise completion of contract documents by employer
Letter from architect to unsuccessful tenderers: to advise that their tender is unsuccessful

3: *The contract I: general*
Letter from architect to contractor: to arrange initial site meeting
Report: site meeting
Letter from architect to employer: insurance of works
Letter from architect to contractor: insurance of works
Specimen Architect's Instruction
Specimen Clerk of Works' Direction
Letter from architect to contractor: subletting
Letter from contractor to architect: datum levels and setting out of works
Letter from architect to contractor: datum levels and discrepancy of dimensions
Letter from architect to contractor: discrepancy between contract drawings and specification
Architect's Instruction, from architect to contractor: discovery of antiquities
Specimen Standard form of Tender for Nominated Subcontractors
Specimen Form of Agreement between Employer and Nominated Subcontractor
Specimen Standard form for Nomination of Subcontractors
Architect's Instruction, from architect to contractor: instruction regarding prime cost or provisional sums
Specimen Form of Tender for use by Nominated Suppliers

Architect's Instruction, from architect to contractor: removal of materials or goods not in accordance with the contract
Specimen Form of Warranty to be given by Nominated Supplier
Architect's Instruction, from architect to contractor: statutory obligations
Specimen Interim Certificate and VAT provision
Specimen Direction of Amounts included for Nominated Sub-contractors in Certificate
Specimen Notification to Nominated Subcontractor concerning amount included in Certificate
Architect's Instruction, from architect to contractor: open up works for inspection or testing
Architect's Instruction, from architect to contractor: restoration and repair after fire
Architect's Instruction, from architect to contractor: postponement of work
Specimen Notification of Extension of Time
Specimen Consent for Nominated Subcontractor's Extension of Time
Notice of Nominated Subcontractor's Non-Completion
Notice of Non-Compliance

4: The contract II: determination
Letter from architect to contractor: notice specifying default
Letter from employer to contractor: determination by employer
Letter from architect to contractor: assignment of agreements
Letter from architect to contractor: removal of materials from site
Letter from architect to contractor: certification of amount of expenses in completion after determination

5: The contract III: the defects liability period
Specimen Certificate of Practical Completion or Partial Completion
Letter from architect to contractor: certification of practical completion, Agreement for Minor Building Works Notice of Delay in Completion
Architect's Instruction, from architect to contractor: to make good a defect within the Defects Liability Period
Letter from architect to contractor: to enclose Schedule of Defects
Schedule of Defects
Letter from architect to contractor: works extra to contract
Specimen Certificate of Making Good Defects

6: The contract IV: the final account
Final account:
    method A
    method B
Letter from architect to contractor: agreement to Final Account
Letter from architect to client: to arrange meeting regarding Final Account
Letter from architect to client: agreement to Final Account
Specimen Final Certificate
Letter from architect to contractor: issue of Final Certificate
Letter from architect to client: to enclose statement of fees and expenses
Letter from architect to contractor: expression of thanks

Additional letters from Levitt Bernstein Associates
2.07 Request for means of escape approval
Application for drainage and ventilation by-laws
Covering letter for priced spec to local authority (as client)
Covering letter for part III to local authority identifying items qualifying for subsidy
Copy of spec to local authority (client) which is being sent to tenderers
Application under Acts for spiral staircase

Application under Acts to unite two adjoining houses
Covering letter with Notice 1, part II TCP Act to occupant (not yet bought out by housing association)
Invitation to tender (pre-priced tender by quantity surveyor)
Covering letter for contract documents
Covering letter for documents supplementing tender set sent
Notice of amendments to tender documents
Gas and electrical meters: notice to contractor of arrangements
Notice on invoices for VAT accounting
Reminder that tender is due
Reminder to contractors on sending notification cards to local authority
Invitation to tender (subcontractors)
Covering letter for notification card set sent to contractors
Invitation to quote for supply
Acceptance of quotation
Refusal of quotation
Invitation to tender for gas installation (and central heating)
To water board to request mains check
Notice (to be returned by contractor) of tender acceptance, price and timing
Notice (to be returned by subcontractor) of acceptance for electrical works
Notice (to be returned by subcontractor) of acceptance for gas works
Notice (to be returned by subcontractor) of acceptance for flooring works
Notice (to be returned by subcontractor) of acceptance for central heating
Covering letter compliments slip to housing association with copies of Architect's Instructions

3 Internal documents

3.01 A communications file is just one of the documents that can be used in standardising office procedures. At this early stage in a job, initial contact with clients, it may be worth setting up a system for monitoring progress. This is done, in the examples given here, using a general job checklist and individual job diaries. The examples are from Levitt Bernstein Associates, a medium sized practice doing a lot of rehabilitation for housing associations in inner London.

Checklist
3.02 Checklists are often prepared but not used as a day to day working tool because people have in effect learnt them. But they can be useful on a longer term basis for checking back that items are complete and for looking ahead for potential delays. Checklists can provide a formalisation of procedures within the office so that several people may work separately on different aspects of the same job. And they provide a brief introduction to office procedures for new staff. Like communications files, checklists need periodic updating.
3.03 The sample checklist, §**3.05**, is for a particular practice working for a particular housing association in a particular area at a particular time. It must be read as a working, rather than model, document. It does illustrate, however, the range of items and degree of detail that can be worth covering, both external communications and co-ordination within the practice.

Diary
3.04 The checklist provides a standard procedural document. The job diary is kept for each job, cross referenced to the checklist. The diary provides a check on completeness (and, if necessary, liability) by recording both actions and their explanations. This makes decisions more open to scrutiny and reduces the gloss likely to be put on after the job by post-rationalisation. Again the example, §**3.06**, is a working document for particular circumstances, **2**. It illustrates the sort of information worth recording.

Checklist example

3.05 (Abbreviations include: Trust—the housing association; HAG—housing association grant; LBA—Levitt Bernstein Associates; SL—standard letter. Dates on section headings refer to checklist revision dates up to the end of the Cornwallis Road job.)

1.00   *Loan application*   (9. 1975)
1.01   Receive go ahead from Trust.
       Do survey (see survey form in negs drawer).
       Do drawings (1:100).
       Do HAG financial statement (form in negs drawer).
       Do estimate (form in negs drawer).
1.02   Tell appropriate partner in group when loan application is ready to be checked.
       All this should be within two weeks of instruction from the Trust.
1.03   One copy of all completed loan application documents to be given to Jack Crozier (estimator).
1.04   Hand completed documents to Nancy (office co-ordinator) for forwarding to Trust (LBA only).

2.00   *Planning application*   (4. 1976)
2.01   Planning application should be made concurrently with loan application and submitted not less than four days after submission of loan approval to Trust.
       Fill in form TP1 (form in local authority forms drawer). Standard letters: Haringey SL 53, Islington SL 43.
       Check orally with planning department that house is suitable.
2.02   If Trust is not yet owner of property send form TP11 (in local authority forms' drawer)

2 *21 Cornwallis Road, London N19, whose rehabilitation is described in the job diary.*

informing present owner of proposed conversion.

3.00   *Follow up*   (9. 1975)
3.01   All revisions and changes will be dealt with through the Trust.
3.02   Inform Trust when number of units or people per unit are changed for any reason as it may require a revised loan application.
3.03
3.04   When both loan approval and completion of contracts on purchase of house are in, claim 35 per cent fees on estimated conversion cost, less contingencies.

4.00   *Working drawings and spec*   (4. 1976)
4.01   Receive go ahead from 'office co-ordinator' to prepare working drawings and spec.
4.02   Prepare drawings and specification.
       Have spec checked (LBA: David L, David B, MB, ARP: Tony).
       Send tender documents to Trust who now have to obtain Housing Corporation approval of tender documents before the job goes out to tender.
4.03   Send three copies of plans to Trust for approval and to enable it to assess rent and rates.
4.04   Send off for approvals:
       means of escape (SL 41)
       district surveyor (SL 42)
       drainage (SL 44)
       uniting of premises (SL 62)
       adjoining owner for consents (SL 72).

5.00   *Subcontractors' quotes:*   (9. 1975)
5.01   Get quotations for: (as applicable)
       timber treatment (to be confirmed after opening up) (SL 21)
       dpc and damp proof treatment (SL 21)
       ironmongery (SL 23)
       sanitary fittings (SL 23)
       kitchen fittings
       electrical installation
       gas installation and fittings
       central heating
       flooring.
5.02   Get quotes for specialist work:
       mouldings
       joinery
       staircases (SL 26)
       metal work
       roofing.
       Include estimated prices in spec part III.
       If not available before tender stage, base on prices and rates in subcontract standard quotations file.
5.03   Ask Thames Water Authority to inspect and state whether or not new supply is required (SL 27).
       Include provisional sum in summary sheet.

6.00   *Tendering*   (9. 1975)
6.01   Go out to tender and inform 'office co-ordinator' (SL 31).
6.02   Trust receives tenders in architect's presence.
6.03   Check tender and priced schedule and inform Trust of lowest correct tender received.
6.04   Get OK from Trust.
6.05   Send copies of tenders and tender list to borough valuer.

6.06   Fill in form BC4 (in negs drawer).
Send copy of priced spec and tender list to borough architect.
6.07   Write to all other contractors and list results in numerical order only (do not include names) (SL 03).
6.08   Chase approval of BC4 through Trust.
6.09   When BC4 approval received apply for 75 per cent fees.
6.10   Check with Trust before agreeing starting date with contractor.
6.11   Prepare contract documents.
6.12   Send two copies of contract documents to contractor for signing and then pass on to Trust (or arrange meeting).
6.13   Inform Trust of planning permission and give it original, keeping a copy on file.
6.14
6.15   All contract documents should be kept in central file.
6.16   Check all necessary approvals.
6.17   Check contractor's insurance.
6.18   Ask Trust what preconversion costs were and send letter to council certifying amount for payment (SL 49).
6.19   See manual for negotiated prices.
6.20   Send copy of spec to Trust.

7.00   *Start on site:*   (9. 1975)
7.01   Inform Trust if works do not start on contract date, giving reasons. Let Trust know when works do actually start.
7.02   Ask Trust to supply signboard or window sticker as soon as work has started.
7.03   Provide contractor with two sets, unpriced contract documents and drawings.
7.04   Arrange first site visit and issue first AI (standard AI no. 1).
7.05   Arrange for Metropolitan Damp to inspect as soon as builder has completed demolition.
7.06   Form BC2 to be sent to the Trust every fortnight to indicate actual, in relation to programme, performance.
7.07   Let Trust know of any retrievable items on site, such as fireplaces, galvanised sheets, etc.

8.00   *During contract*   (4. 1976)
8.01   Issue certificates monthly, whether requested by the contractor or not, together with direction and subcontractors' notification, where relevant.
8.02   Certificates for amounts over contract sum must be sent to Trust with copies of priced variations and explanation for increase in costs (Trust will forward to council).
8.03   Inform Trust immediately if any extra works are required or delays expected.
8.04   Inform Trust when consultation with tenant is required for selection of decorations.
8.05   Check in manual on liquidated and ascertained damages should they occur.
8.06   Check in manual in the event of squatters.
8.07   Notify Trust as soon as all roofing work has been completed so that Trust Maintenance can inspect and send back its report.
8.08   Send off application forms for connection of gas and electricity at least four weeks before completing. Sign forms on behalf of Trust.
8.09   Check copies of VAT invoices and send separate certifying letter to council with copy to Trust (Islington SL 47).

8.10   Builders should contact Islington Drainage two weeks before handover so that they can have access to site to inspect.
8.11   Consult manual in the case of determination of contractor's employment.

9.00   *Practical completion*   (9. 1975)
9.01   Check spec and schedule items against work done and against practical completion check list.
9.02   Inform Trust that job is ready for inspection. Make inspection with Trust.
9.03   Inform borough valuer that job is ready for inspection.
Make inspection with him.
9.04   Inform housing assistant of handover date and ensure keys are ready.
9.05   Issue practical completion certificate and issue further interim certificate (not penultimate).
9.06   One month after practical completion issue penultimate certificate including draft final account.
9.07   Apply for 100 per cent fees due as soon as final account is approved.
9.08   Place six months maintenance date in your diary.
9.09   Send guarantees to Trust and also copy of report where relevant.
9.10   Send 'as built' drawings showing final positions of all stop valves and drain cocks to Trust maintenance department.

10.00   *Six months defects*   (4. 1976)
10.01   Arrange to inspect with contractor.
Draw up schedule of defects.
10.02   Send copy of schedule of defects to Trust and inform it when defects are remedied and approved by the architect.
10.03   When every item is checked and complete issue final certificate (releasing retention) together with final account summary.
10.04   Inform Trust when it takes over responsibility for repairs.

Diary for 21 Cornwallis Road, London N19
3.06 (Abbreviations include: C33—the housing association; LBA—Levitt Bernstein Associates; HTC—Holloway Tenants Co-operative; BSR—bed-sitting room; DS—district surveyor; LA—local authority.)

Date	Action	Comments/check list
24.1.73	C33 instruction to LBA to prepare loan application. House located in HTC area and tenanted.	1.01
5.2.73	Dimensional survey of property; house in very bad condition.	
6.2.73	Provision conversion proposal based on Unit Mix of: 1 five-person maisonette 1 one-person BSR flat shared garden access. Preliminary financial statements indicates low funding levels.	1.01 Dwg no 21 CWR 01 Pre-HAG funding see FS
13.3.73	Proposals reconsidered for reasons of: ● bad structural/finishing conditions ● low funding levels, ie high subsidy (above norm) ● vendor unwilling to sell rear of yard making it too small for shared use. At this time, LA finance availability subject to number of persons housed (ie bedspaces). Property re-evaluated. Decision to put forward as single family house with eight bedspaces. Financial implications: ● lower conversion cost ● lower LA subsidy levels. Forwarded to client for Funding Application to LA.	Dwg no 21 CWR 01a

Date	Action	Comments/check list
162		
24.5.73	Funding approved by LA on condition that works commence within four months of date of approval and are completed within 12 months.	
	During the intervening period it is evident that the sitting tenants are unwilling to move unless a guarantee to their being rehoused in the same location is forthcoming. Furthermore, a HTC survey of their members' housing needs shows a preference for small units.	
10.73	LA increases standards to be expected in conversion work.	
7.11.73	LBA approached LA architect's department with a view to amend the proposed upgrading of this house in order to provide two units as originally proposed. LA indications are favourable.	3.01 (changed)
10.11.73	Scheme revised and re-submitted for further approval. The unit mix now is: 1 one-bed, one-person flat / 1 three-bed, four-person maisonette / with terrace for maisonette. Plans are drawn 1:50 as basis for working drawings. Units replanned and are now more or less in final form.	
10.1.74	LA approval of revised scheme. House still tenanted.	
	Lull	
18.4.74	Application for approval under Town and Country Acts.	2.01
	Application for Approval under the London Building Acts (Amendment) Act 1939—Section 35 (Means of Escape).	4.04
1.5.74	Instruction to prepare tender documents by client	4.01
21.8.74	Planning officer voices concern regarding terrace arrangement for maisonette. Overlooking/loss of privacy problems, although existing roofs are in use for hanging out washing, etc.	
28.8.74	Invite planning officer to meet on site to discuss overlooking problem.	
1.9.74	Instruction by C33 to invite tenders.	
4.9.74	Meeting with planning officer on site. Resolved problem by raising parapets to sides of terrace above eye level at rear dropping to shoulder height at front.	
17.10.74	Completion of working drawings and tender documents.	4.02
18.10.74	Confirm points agreed with planning officer by letter enclosing elevations.	
	Send tender documents to LA architect's department for comments.	
	Application to GLC DS office for approval under relevant London Building Acts (Amendment) Acts. Includes structural calculations.	
	Application for Approval of Drainage Works to LA.	4.04
	Out to tender on builder's work to seven contractors.	6.01
	Out to tender on subcontractor works.	5.01
	Quotations for supply items invited.	5.02
30.10.74	LA architects query bedroom layout to four-person unit.	
31.10.74	Approval for means of escape received.	
31.10.74	DS office requests further information.	
4.11.74	Reply to LA architect's department showing furniture layout to bedrooms of four-person unit in accordance with Circular 36/67 and Design Bulletin No. 6.	
7.11.74	Tenants vacate property; client secures to deter squatting.	
11.11.74	LA architect's department still disagrees.	
15.11.74	Send additional information to GLC DS office.	
	Attempt to justify bedroom layout to LA architect's department.	
	Return of tenders for builder's work; only three out of seven received.	6.02
	Tenders for subcontract work received.	
	All supply item quotations in.	
16.11.74 to 1.12.74	Negotiations with lowest tenderer. Reduced tender sum from £17 288·43 to £14 961·17 by remeasuring and adjusting measured allowances. Adjust PC sums in the light of tenders for subcontract works received. Proposed contract period 26 weeks.	
2.12.74	Make recommendations to client	6.05
25.11.74	GLC office replies with minor queries. Chimney Breast Certificate issued in pursuance of the London Building Acts (Amendment) Act 1939 Section 17 (2).	
9.1.75	Reply to GLC DS office confirming queries raised in letter of 25/11/74. Under the London Building Acts (Amendment) Act 1939 write to adjoining owners specifying works affecting party walls. Meet with LA architect's department to discuss conversial layout to bedroom floor. Agree in principle to accept the comments made since the family situation of the incoming tenants has changed. Only two bedrooms now required.	
17.1.75	LA architect's department agrees.	
10.1.75	Client accepts tender. Contractor informed.	
3.2.75	Drainage works approved.	
6.2.75	Planning approval received.	
11.2.75	LA approves tender.	
15.2.75	Fixed tender period runs out.	
21.2.75	Invite contractor to meeting in order to discuss programming, etc.	
28.2.75	Not having heard from the proposed contractor send express letter voicing our concern.	
4.3.75	Send telegram to contractor.	
7.3.75	Meet contractor. He wants an increase in the tender price since the tender period has run out on 15.2.75. Builder confirms start on site 31.3.75.	
12.3.75	Request client's brief regarding negotiations for a percentage increase.	
14.3.75	Client agrees for a negotiated percentage increase subject to approval.	
27.3.75	Increased costs accepted by client. Increase works out at 2·8 per cent per month for 1½ months = 4·2 per cent.	
	Tender total amended by addendum. Contracts signed by employer and contractor.	6.11
	Start on site. Projected completion 26.9.75. Issue of first Architect's Instruction giving details of contractor's obligations, nominated subcontractors and suppliers.	
	Impress contractor of the need to place official orders for subcontract and supply items as early as possible. He is to enter into Forms of Contract.	
	Agree regular site visits on Thursdays but point out since site was on way to the office, the architect could visit whenever necessary.	7.04
4.4.75	Receive copies of Builder's Official Orders, etc.	
2.5.75	First valuation: stripping out complete demolitions complete.	8.01
	Back extensions, rear wall built, main wall propped. RF foundations complete. DS notes bit. felt dpc built into structural wall. Contractor inserts lead cored dpc as specified. Agree areas of plaster repairs. Roof stripped. Instruct contractor to extent of timber replacement. Substitute s/h Welsh slates for h/d asbestos slates.	
5.6.75	Second valuation: dpc injected below all floor joists. Recall dpc subcontractor because run of injection to front wall below ground level externally. Timber treatment complete. Main roof completed. All rsj below structural brickwork in place. External brickwork at rear complete, repointed and measured. Decide to replace whole of ground floor flooring in timber.	
3.7.75	Third valuation: drainage except rear manhole complete. All new/modified external openings complete. Window repairs complete. Decide to draught proof all sashes as an extra. Four box frames/sashes replaced to match existing. First fixing electrics complete. No need to replace LEB head and incoming main. Roof terrace complete. Railings fixed.	
7.8.75	Fourth valuation: plaster repairs nearly complete. Issue internal decorations schedule chosen by incoming tenants. CH first fix complete. Bathroom fittings in. Kitchen fittings in. Plumbing complete. Plaster repairs measured.	
28.8.75	LA inspection. Officer passes both units as satisfactory Fifth valuation.	9.03
2.9.75	Practical Completion Certificate issued, four weeks early. Release of retention. Original tenant moves back into newly converted maisonette.	
17.10.75	Final account agreed with builder. Certificate issued.	9.06
30.1.76	Tenants complain of hot water coming from cold-water taps. Call on house with heating subcontractor. Expansion pipe had come off clip and fallen into CW tank in attic. Rectified.	
5.3.76	Final inspection with client's representative. Builder on site also. Defects list containing minor items issued.	10.01
13.4.76	Certificate Making Good Defects, revised Final Account and Final Certificate issued.	

Technical study 4 Decanting

Architects may advise on decanting—whether and how occupants move out during rehabilitation—either making proposals or indicating the extent of disruption rehabilitation will cause.
Though the decision to decant at all is determined largely by the extent of works and occupants' preferences, there are also cost considerations in deciding whether to move and how this should be arranged. This study looks at some of the alternatives.

1 Deciding to stay

1.01 When there is a choice of whether to move, the costs of a move can easily be calculated. But the savings are more difficult to measure. There are unquantifiable factors such as the effects of living on what is effectively a building site, the effects of having occupants resident on quality of workmanship, or the disruptions of moving from home. There is likely too to be an addition to contract price if dwellings are occupied. Though this price will not appear as a separate item, some contractors will admit how much vacant units are worth to them, while for others this will have to be surmised from a knowledge of current rates. Contractors will of course vary. They will not all have experience of working with occupants resident and as mentioned in Case study 4, 'Tenant liaison service', working carefully round occupants requires a particular sort of site staff. In one recent case, contractors were asked to price having occupants in residence. Two contractors charged £50 per house, one £75, one £100, one £3000 (an ultimatum) and one nothing. This last contractor thought there were also advantages to having houses occupied: materials and equipment are more secure and staff work more tidily, **1a, b.**

Owner-occupiers
1.02 Owner-occupiers are likely to be most reluctant to move since they are most personally involved in results of rehabilitation and have to make their own arrangements.

Tenants
1.03 Tenants of private landlords, housing associations and local authorities will generally be offered alternative accommodation where works are extensive. However, as the case study on 'Tenant liaison service' illustrates, tenants may prefer not to move because of the disruption of moving to a new place and back again, or in the case of older people because they like the company and activity during rehabilitation. Occasionally, tenants will be concerned that if they move out, especially to a rehabilitated vacant dwelling, they will have to stay there and not be allowed back home.

Rehabilitation with occupants in residence
1.04 Disruption can be eased by providing a place such as a vacant house or community centre which occupants can use to escape dirt and noise during the day and prepare midday meals. If works are not very extensive as is often the case with inter-war dwellings, disruption may be made bearable by working very fast. Interior works to inter-war dwellings may be confined to refitting bathrooms and kitchens, rewiring and altering heating systems. The GLC, for example, has experimented on inter-war flats, trying to crush all this into a weekend. It is now trying a few contracts that do it in four days, **2.**

1a   1b

2

*1 In some cases the radical change necessitates decanting, **a**. In others change is fairly minor but contractors usually still prefer to be able to treat the house as a building site, **b**.*
2 Flats like these or inter-war semis often require rehabilitation straightforward enough to programme very tightly.

1.05 For older properties, work could be speeded using prefabricated units, **3**, though experience suggests that they are generally too expensive and often unsympathetic to existing buildings in form and materials.

Greenwich inter-war flats
1.06 The NBA have reported* on an inter-war scheme in Greenwich, London involving the range of works noted above. These took about six weeks, carried out by Greenwich Direct Labour Department. The authority said that working

* Decanting costs: three case studies National Building Agency. 50p.

3 *Prefabricated kitchen and bathroom units in a HAA.*

with tenants in residence added nothing to the cost of rehabilitation itself. There was however some additional expenditure. To provide access to the kitchen for refitting, rewiring and fitting a boiler a temporary kitchen unit and cooker point were provided in the living room. The costs incurred per dwelling (at 1974 prices) were:

	£
kitchen unit (used five times)	13·00
two cooker point reconnections	10·50
making good	9·00
redecoration of living room	45·00
clearing up each day	20·00
total cost per dwelling	97·50

The cost per dwelling to the local authority was £97·50 plus £2 per week rent reduction during rehabilitation. The annual loan charge (1974) was about £11 per year.

2 Possibilities for decanting

Owner occupiers
2.01 Savings on contract price (and perhaps time) plus avoiding day to day disturbance may make moving worthwhile

either to friends and relations or hotels (and taking holidays) during rehabilitation.

Tenants
2.02 Tenants may be provided with temporary houses or mobile homes, or find accommodation for themselves with friends or relations, or move permanently. The next few paragraphs outline parts of two NBA case studies in Sheffield and Reading. In Sheffield, tenants were offered several choices of move and the local authority was able to build up a sufficient stock of vacant dwellings for temporary accommodation. In Reading, the local authority has not been able to build up a stock so has bought mobile homes.

Sheffield
2.03 Sheffield's Wybourn estate comprises 1700 houses built in the 1920s being rehabilitated over two and a half years and taking seven to eight weeks per house. Tenants had four options:
permanent rehousing away from the estate (these transfers provided 130 houses before the contract began)
temporary rehousing within the estate (in unimproved, and later improved dwellings)
permanent rehousing within the estate (moving to vacant improved houses)
temporary rehousing by tenants (self-help; staying with friends and relatives)
With other normal vacancies, these options produced a stock of 300 dwellings either for temporary rehousing or in the course of rehabilitation. Costs (at 1974 prices) are given in table I.

Table I Decanting costs (1974 prices) from NBA case studies

	Temporary rehousing £	Sheffield Permanent rehousing £	Tenant self-help £	Reading Mobile homes £
Removal expenses (averaged)	32	16	32	80
Furniture storage	—	—	12	
Redirection of post	2	2	2	
Other costs including loss and damage	10	5	10	—
Rent reductions	18	—	—	
Reconnection of services	22	11	22	17
'Fit for letting' costs	10	—	—	15
Total	94	34	78	112
Annual loan charge 20 years at 10 per cent	11	4	9	13
Purchase of 18 mobile homes				50 580
Cost of ancillary items (excluding television sets)				4 302
Site costs, fees, etc				15 000
Transport and assembly, etc				2 340
Total (excluding re-instatement work)				72 222
Annual loan charge 20 years at 10 per cent				8 480
Annual apportioned loan charge for 1080 dwellings				8
Management cost (apportioned)	7·50	7·50	7·50	20
Annual loan charge	1	1	1	2·50
Loss of rent excluding rent reduction	60	60	60	—
Annual loan charge	7	7	7	—
Annual estimated loan charge/u :t improved	19	12	17	25·50

Reading
2.04 Reading, with a programme in 1974 of around 150 house improvements per year, bought 18 three-bedroom, twin-unit, mobile homes. They were located ten minutes walk from the rehabilitation site. They are expected to last about eight years occupied regularly for periods of about seven weeks. Costs (at 1974 prices) are given in table I.

Housing associations
2.05 The NBA study from which these figures are taken also presents costs (at 1971 prices) to housing associations of delays in decanting and of purchasing mobile homes.

Technical study 5
Surveys

Initial surveys provide information needed for sketch schemes. Later, detailed surveys are needed for drawing up a repairs schedule and detailed specification of alterations.
This study deals with individual or small groups of houses. For organising house condition surveys prior to declaring GIAs, HAAs or PNs (a job usually done by local authority surveyors) readers are referred to DOE Area Improvement Notes 1 *Sample house condition survey* **and 2** *House condition survey within a potential GIA.* **The study is based on information from PETER COLOMB.**

1 Initial surveys

Aims
1.01 An initial survey should gather information on which sketch designs can be based, comprising:
● survey drawings to scale showing the complete house;
● notes on the *general* condition of the house;
● notes/drawings of any special features;
● notes/drawings of the environs of the house.

Things to take
1.02 Large tape (at least 15 m); small tape (5 m, stiff metal type); rod (2 m, usually a folding rule for taking heights); pencil; rubber; paper in stiff backed pad or on clipboard (thin paper is useful as plans can be overlaid); pocket knife (for probing timber, holding the end of a tape and sharpening pencils); old, warm clothes (unoccupied houses, and cellars and roofspaces generally, are cold and dirty); proof of identity (to tenants); camera; any necessary keys; torch; binoculars (for inspecting roofs from ground level); mirror (a dentist's or wide angled car mirror for looking in tight spaces, eg inside eaves).
1.03 Two people on a survey make holding tapes easier. One can talk to occupants while the other does initial drawings. It may help to know your own dimensions, eg a 300 mm foot or a 1 m stride.

Assessment of condition
1.04 At this early stage of a job, only an overall idea of condition is necessary. A more rigorous inspection for repairs will occur later. Look for defects that will require major work, eg badly sagging roofs, disintegrating load bearing walls, extensive timber decay. You may be able to take advantage of these in conversion by rebuilding in a different form. Services (electricity, gas, water) are usually only worth saving either if in very good condition or on a very limited budget.

Method in observation
1.05 At first, surveys are difficult and time consuming but with practice the informed eye picks out only the essentials. It may be worth developing a survey checklist though more for the later detailed survey than for this initial one.

Procedure
1.06 If a house is tenanted spend some time explaining what you envisage doing to the tenants' home. Ask occupants about leaks, damp, blocked drains, previous repairs and maintenance, etc. Occupants know the recent history of the house and can be helpful in identifying defects though their explanations may be misleading. Alleged penetrating damp may be due to condensation for example.
1.07 Most tenants are worried about being moved out at short

notice and need informing and reassuring about timetables. This is especially so for squatters who are more concerned about eviction orders than what will happen to the house. It is most important to generate a good relationship with occupants to ensure their co-operation. If houses have been squatted or used as doss houses they may need cleaning.
1.08 If the building is unoccupied, be careful where you put your feet. Timber decay may be fairly rapid at critical places such as immediately inside the front door. Look round carefully for concealed cellars and lofts. If there are no hatches to roofspaces these will have to be made to allow detailed inspection later. For M-roofs and others with several slopes there is usually only a hatch to one of the roof spaces. Lack of access hatches indicates lack of maintenance. The dictum 'out of sight, out of mind' applies to maintenance, especially of roofs, **1**. Look at the general state of repair, noting major defects and botched repairs.
1.09 Try to identify structural walls including stud partitions, eg from joist directions (at right angles to the run of floorboards). And try to establish if walls reduce in thickness as they rise. This should be shown by different measurements on different floors, by steps in walls beside staircases, **2**, and differences in window reveals. Structural walls generally run

1 *Out of sight repairs can be the most primitive of patching. Slates and other debris in this box gutter probably help rainwater to flow into both roof spaces.*

through from floor to floor though structural studwork is occasionally offset. The structure is usually fairly clear, especially if you think back to how the house could have been constructed.

1.10 Take photographs of interiors and exteriors as reminders. All initial drawing and measuring should be done by whoever draws up the survey. Other people's notes tend to be incomprehensible.

Initial drawings

1.11 Walk round the house again making drawings of each floor plan. These are easier to deal with later if drawn to the same scale. Pacing out rooms as a rough guide can help here. Start on the floor where the structure is clearest. This can serve as a master plan on which other plans are overlaid. Draw sections of complicated parts like stairs and sketch any special features (with dimensions), eg mouldings, window seats, shutter boxes. Photographs help too.

1.12 Note on plans: joist directions, door swings, fireplaces, incoming service mains and meter positions, sanitary fittings and kitchen sinks, manholes (position, invert level and direction of flow), gulleys, rwps, direction of floor joists, number of risers on stairs (note winders), services not to be renewed. Take special care at places that are likely to be problems in rehabilitation, eg restricted heights or widths. Note any beams below ceilings. On some houses it is worth drawing a roof plan too.

1.13 Occasionally a more three-dimensional drawing is needed to record cracking (or occasionally the paths of services). This can be done with a composite elevation—like a cardboard cutout of walls and ceiling that might be bent into a three dimensional model, **3**.

1.14 Draw a site plan and note fences, walls, steps, trees, outbuildings, etc. In GIAs, where there will be environmental improvements, take note of public spaces, eg back alleys, pavements, street furniture.

Measuring

1.15 Establish a convention about the point you measure to, especially on door and window openings. It is easiest to measure the door itself and the brick window opening, but it does not matter much how it is done as long as you are consistent. It is a useful check if dimensions are duplicated, for example measuring the full room dimensions and comparing this with the sum of alcoves and chimney breast dimensions. When measuring along the floor, remember to allow for the thickness of skirtings. Surfaces are often uneven, waving in and out by 5 mm, so fine accuracy cannot be expected.

1.16 Check diagonals to see if the house is square and if not, take diagonals in every room. Take as many overall dimensions as possible, both of the house (party wall to party wall and front to back) and of each room. Measure room heights, window sill and head heights, door heights, heights of landings above floor levels, floor thicknesses, wall thicknesses (noting wall construction).

1.17 If surveying repetitive houses (a terrace for example) measure a typical house, draw it up, get prints, then go back and mark on any differences in other houses.

Drawing up the survey

1.18 It saves time and effort if the survey drawing via copynegative can be used for sketch design and thereafter working drawings. This needs remembering during measurement and in the choice of scale, position of sections, etc.

1.19 Draw the survey as soon as possible after measuring while it is still fresh in the mind and cryptic notes are decipherable. First it is useful to rough out each floor on a separate sheet then overlay them to check vertical alignments.

2 Detailed surveys

2.01 After agreement on sketch design (which should include a schedule of major repairs) a detailed, measured schedule of repairs is needed of those parts to remain after rehabilitation. The more comprehensive the schedule, the more complete the ensuing specification. Repairs may be needed for a variety of reasons:

standards have changed, eg improved roof and floor ventilation, introduction of dpcs;

maintenance has been neglected, eg roofs, **1**, external joinery;

even with adequate maintenance materials wear out, eg slates and their nailing. And those features designed to the lowest factors of safety fail first, eg parapets, flat roofs, tall chimneys;

houses, or parts of them, were originally badly built or badly converted, eg back additions;

alterations have affected the serviceability of what remains, eg blocking underfloor ventilation or bridging dpcs.

2.02 Method may help, say room by room starting at the top of the house and element by element outside, eg chimney, aerial, parapets and projecting party walls, ridges, hips and valleys, eaves, box gutters, gables, etc. However, for rainwater goods and internal services it may be easier to follow them round the building rather than noting their occurrence as elements or per room.

2.03 Section 2 'Repair and maintenance', covered most conceivable defects and their repair. This can be used as a check for completeness of repairs covered or as a basis for drawing up a repair checklist for your practice. The current section 'improvements and conversions', will give details of alterations to houses.

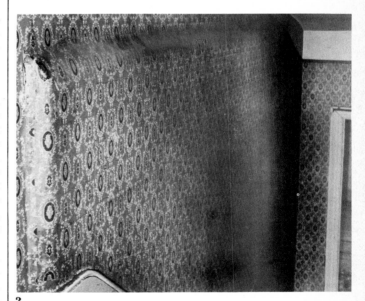

2

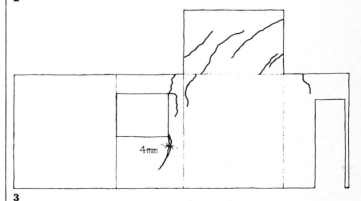

3

2 *Reduced thickness in a wall at the side of a staircase.*
3 *Composite drawing of walls and ceiling recording cracks rather than using separate plans and elevations.*

Technical study 6
Areas for improvement

Improvement proposals for individual older houses may be affected by their being in areas of special control or action initiated by the local authority, ie HAAs, GIAs and PNs. DAVID PEARSON, HAA project leder in Hammersmith, London, outlines the nature of these areas and their potential effects on design.

Section 5, Information sheet 1 deals with grants in detail, both inside these areas and elsewhere.

1 Area-based approaches

1.01 Repeated analyses of census data and house condition surveys show that most of the worst housing problems tend to be geographically concentrated in certain local areas. These slums or twilight areas have been singled out by successive governments for priority action employing measures ranging from persuasion and voluntary action to compulsion. All these measures have aimed at concentrating resources and special powers in small areas supposedly containing the core of the problems.

1.02 There is some disquiet with these area-based approaches because not all problems are as localised as the designated areas are intended to deal with. Also, often not enough areas are declared to cover all an authority's problems but there is no half-way stage, no mechanism for doing less, but in more areas. There is, as yet, no official suggestion for making a change.

2 General improvement areas (GIAs)

Nature of areas

2.01 These areas introduced under the Housing Act 1969 for England and Wales but recently revised under the Housing Act 1974 usually contain around 200 to 300 houses. Although a GIA may have housing problems, they will be less extreme than in HAAs which were set up to deal with areas of multiple stress. The area should contain more owner-occupiers and less tenants renting from the private sector.

Improvements

2.02 The basis of GIA action is to give higher house renovation grants to owner-occupiers for carrying out improvement to individual dwellings while the local authority undertakes to complete a scheme of environmental improvements to streets and open spaces; £200 per house is allowed for this. Sixty per cent improvement grants are available to owners for improve-

1 Flowers Streets' GIA in Liverpool (the subject of an AJ Buildings illustrated article on 6.4.77).

2 Cleaning out and reinstatement of canal and banks plus some planting in the Rochdale industrial GIA.

ments and repairs to form self-contained accommodation. However, the owner must specify, when applying for a grant, whether the accommodation is to be for owner-occupation or available for letting for five years. If let, the rent must be a registered rent fixed by the rent officer. If necessary, the local authority has compulsory powers and may also be willing to purchase some property in the area.

2.03 There are now many GIAs complete or nearing completion, **1**. Industrial GIAs have been developed occasionally by individual initiative, **2**, but will be backed by legislation soon. They are only concerned, however, with promoting environmental and infrastructive improvements by industry.

Treatment areas

2.04 Treatment Areas were introduced in the Housing (Scotland) Act 1969 as the Scottish counterpart to GIAs. They have been replaced by HAAs in the 1974 Act.

3 Housing action areas (HAAs)

Basis of areas

3.01 As experience was gained from implementing GIAs and Treatment Areas following the 1969 Acts, it became clear that there are areas of stress, generally in inner cities, with high proportions of tenants in dwellings owned by absentee landlords. The increased financial incentives only served to aggravate the already unsatisfactory conditions.

3.02 All too often, development companies and speculators cashed in on the help offered by local authorities to obtain grants for improving multi-occupied properties to produce 'luxury' conversions. With the original tenants winkled out, the new flats were let or sold to higher income households from elsewhere. This displacement of residents, or 'gentrification', convinced many local authorities and voluntary agencies that a new form of controlled area initiative was essential.

3.03 The Housing Act 1974 introduced housing action areas (and priority neighbourhoods—para **4.01**) to supplement revised GIAs. The Housing (Scotland) Act 1974 introduced

HAAs to replace Treatment Areas. These could be HAAs for improvement or for demolition, though only the former is covered here.

Nature of areas

3.04 HAAs usually comprise around 300 to 500 houses, though Birmingham has some as large as 800. Extreme housing problems usually exist and intensive action is required to arrest the causes of dereliction, physical and social. The areas chosen as HAAs will typically contain high proportions of tenanted properties owned by private landlords where there is sharing or lack of Standard Amenities (and in Scotland often not meeting the Tolerable Standard).* The properties will be in a poor state of repair but, in the main, capable of rehabilitation to form good accommodation with a 15 to 30 year life, **3**. Socially, account should be taken of the degree of overcrowding, multi-occupation, harassment, evictions and homelessness.

Timing

3.05 Having decided to declare an HAA, the local authority in England or Wales has five years, with a possible two-year extension, to secure a significant improvement in the living conditions in the area. HAAs can subsequently be converted to GIAs with emphasis switching from individual houses to environmental works (in England and Wales).

Grants

3.06 Greater incentives are given to private owners and landlords to improve their houses and tenanted dwellings via 75 per cent grants which in cases of hardship can be increased to 90 per cent of the eligible/approved costs. As with GIAs, owners must declare the intended occupation of new flats at the time of application for a grant.

3.07 Environmental grants are a new type of grant available in HAAs in England and Wales to help improve conditions outside the house. They are restricted to privately owned

Standard Amenities:
fixed bath or shower, wash basin and sink;
hot and cold water supply to above;
wc.
A house is of *Tolerable Standard* if it:
is structurally stable;
is substantially free from rising or penetrating damp;
has satisfactory provision for natural and artificial lighting, for ventilation and heating;
has an adequate supply of piped, wholesome water available within the house;
has a sink provided with a satisfactory supply of both hot and cold water within the house;
has a water closet available for the exclusive use of the occupants of the house and suitably located within the house;
has an effective system for the drainage and disposal of foul and surface water;
has satisfactory facilities for the cooking of food within the house;
has satisfactory access to all external doors and outbuildings.

3 *Scottish tenements frequently figure in HAAs. The areas are often run down industrially and houses, rented from absentee landlords are below the tolerable standard.*

4a

4b

4a, b *The effects of environmental improvements inevitably vary with the type of housing. Backcourts of tenements,* **a,** *can be transformed to some extent but the fronts,* **3,** *can show little sign of change. Improvements in Black Road GIA, Macclesfield,* **b,** *give a sense of rejuvenation.*

properties and can be used for such things as repair of boundary walls, gates, steps, external redecoration of the house, tree planting, etc, **4a, b**. The grant is only £50 per dwelling but can be increased by local authority contributions. The grant is so small that it is often not used. The environmental grant in Scottish HAAs is £200 per house, used by the local authority (as in English/Welsh GIAs).

Compulsion

3.08 Increased compulsory powers are also available to local authorities whereby compulsory improvement notices can be served under section 88 of the 1974 Housing Act on each dwelling in a house. (These powers do not exist in Scotland. The only power is compulsory purchase if work is not done in 9 months.) These notices require the owner carrying out improvements to install standard amenities for the exclusive use of each dwelling and to bring the property into a good state of repair generally. The works must be completed in 12 months from service of the notice. If after 6 months there is unsatisfactory progress, the local authority may further consider compulsory action which could include arranging for the works to be carried out in default or the making of a compulsory purchase order under section 43 of the Housing Act 1974.

3.09 An alternative is the early use of Compulsory Purchase Orders on a large scale for the worst tenanted properties, allowing landlords time to come forward with satisfactory proposals. Block CPOs are no doubt a most direct and effective way of achieving definite results but the Government is changeable in its attitude to this approach and will need convincing that the authority can cope with the improvement

5 *Compulsory purchase was suggested for substandard and overcrowded houses with absentee landlords such as these in Colville/Tavistock in London, the first HAA, (AJ 16.7.75 p114).*

programme and not leave properties, once purchased, empty and unimproved, **5**. There is also a provision called 'Notification Procedure' for HAAs in England and Wales whereby owners intending to sell a tenanted house or give Notice to Quit to a tenant must inform the local authority first.

Tenure

3.10 The local authority must be satisfied about the housing arrangements of the tenants both during and after the works are carried out and may in England and Wales assist with either temporary rehousing or with permanent rehousing usually with an agreement from the owner that nominee(s) from the council list will be accepted into the improved accommodation. Obviously, these provisions are complicated and time consuming and because of this many authorities are unwilling to use these new provisions.

4 Priority neighbourhoods (PNs)

4.01 The idea behind these areas in England and Wales was originally that, with the intensive action in HAAs or GIAs, the immediately surrounding areas could appear neglected, with resulting blight and perhaps accelerated decay. These areas once termed 'safeguard areas' were to be declared as a holding operation pending the probable declaration of an HAA. These areas—of which very few have been declared—will have similar prevailing conditions to HAAs. Only 50 per cent grants are available as they are outside designated areas, and no compulsory powers are provided. The only real provision is that of the notification procedure as described for HAAs. The provisions as they stand are generally weak and many authorities have decided to wait and declare either HAAs or GIAs.

5 Implications for the architect

5.01 Therefore, for an architect working within one of the above areas, the main effects on rehabilitation activity are likely to be in finance, control and timing.

Level of financial aid

5.02 The levels of grants available will have primary bearing on the economic feasibility of rehabilitation proposals at sketch scheme stage. If the client is a private owner or landlord, the main question he will want advice on is—can the house be economically improved or would it be to his advantage to sell it, perhaps to the local authority or housing association? This will involve the architect in not only providing an economic feasibility study but also investigating tenant

housing and rehousing arrangements. If the property is in an HAA or GIA, the local authority will be as concerned about the social factors as the physical proposals. For instance, if the house is multi-occupied, the improvement package must consider what is to happen to the tenants if the client's instructions are to provide a smaller number of self-contained flats.

Level of control and time limits

5.03 Area-based approaches in HAAs (para **3.05**) have a statutory period for completion and local authorities will most likely expect a faster service in production of material for improvement grant applications. The architect should also check if there are any statutory notices requiring completion of works within a certain period. There may be other policy requirements or aims for the area such as achieving rehousing of families with children in self-contained accommodation with access to gardens.

Environmental treatment

5.04 Apart from proposals for the house and tenants, there may be environmental schemes in process and this could affect the plans for external items and redecoration, **6**.

Advice

5.05 In many HAAs and GIAs, local project teams have been set up working from local offices in the area. It is best to consult these teams at the earliest opportunity and discuss all of the above factors before making any proposals to the client.
5.06 Full details and guidance for HAAs, GIAs and PNs in England and Wales are given in DOE Circular 14/75, *Housing action areas, priority neighbourhoods and general improvement areas*. For HAAs in Scotland, the corresponding document is SDD Circular 67/75, *Housing below the Tolerable Standard: housing action areas* and its accompanying Memorandum 68/75.

6 *Environmental scheme in Deeplish Road, Rochdale, involving road closure, pavement widening, echelon parking, planting and street furniture.*

Technical study 7 Sketch schemes for housing conversion

Every house is different in its combination of original design, subsequent alteration and state of repair. Yet there are many ideas common to houses that apply at sketch scheme stage. The study begins with a brief listing of them followed by a commentary on a series of sketch schemes for converting three houses. The schemes are by JOHN BENSON, PETER COLOMB and GEORGE JONES.

1 Approach

Natural conversions

1.01 Natural conversion—respecting the existing qualities of a house and making as little change as possible—has gradually become the norm for rehabilitation. Though quality varies enormously, even the most run-down house may have distinctive proportions, mix of materials, shapes of rooms and circulation spaces, and features such as mouldings, architraves, skirtings, etc. Very infrequently is there now dogmatic insistence on Parker Morris standards involving major costs for little discernible change of amenity, eg moving partitions a few centimetres.

Differences between clients

1.02 Though a similar approach of sensitivity and parsimony can apply for all clients, some will want more radical change to produce more personalised schemes, eg some owner-occupiers, landlords and tenants' co-operatives. This will involve the balance of standards and costs, which may be higher or lower than the Parker Morris norm for average occupants. There may however be pressure on individual clients from local authorities giving grants and from mortgage companies to achieve this norm as a minimum.
1.03 While local authorities and housing associations are likely to be concerned with low maintenance and 30-year life, individual clients often put less emphasis on repair. Major items like roof replacement might be left for a few years and individual clients may prefer less fail-safe repair once aware of the risk and costs. For example, only minimum rather than total replastering might be done on the understanding that there is a risk of more becoming detached in future, requiring replacement. Such a policy may reflect not only current priorities but cash flow, since individual clients may not be able to afford enough work at one time to last 30 years. (Significantly the eligible/allowable expense of £5000, the maximum cost for rehabilitation on which grants are paid, is often considerably below that spent per house by local authorities.)
1.04 Individual clients have of course the opportunity to suit themselves such as in the quality of spaces (eg making an open plan or removing a ceiling to give a double-storey height), in the distribution of spaces (eg making bathrooms relatively small or large and having more of them), in the quality and number of fixtures and fittings (eg in bathrooms and kitchens) and in catering for particular activities (eg hobbies) and possessions (eg sports and gardening equipment, freezers).

Priorities for repair

1.05 Improvements should focus on critical elements of the building such as roofs, dpcs, wall structure, existing timber, etc, for the real expected life of the property, which could be subject to rehabilitation continuously over several generations.

Where there is a major item of repair such as replacing a roof, it can be a good opportunity to effect a conversion at relatively little extra cost, eg making part of the roofspace habitable or a store.
1.06 This study considers the mass of housing requirements in the price range which relies on grant aid to effect improvements. Requirements for special needs can be found in some of the case studies: Case study 3 *Three wheelchair units*, Case study 5 *Sheltered housing*, Case study 6 *Single person housing*.

New standards for old buildings

1.07 Hopefully, rehabilitation will provide houses as good as new, but the mix of qualities may well be different. There may be more sense of place for example but perhaps less thermal comfort. Trying to achieve new housing standards item by item in old buildings often mars existing qualities and can be impractically expensive. The next few paragraphs point out some of the potential conflicts.

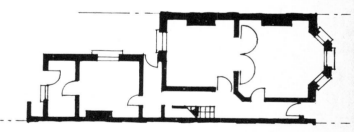

1 *Typical plan for a house around* 1890 *with elongated plan due to back addition.*

Relationships between rooms
1.08 Modern house plans tend to be nearer square than those of older houses which often have long back additions and so may be three or more times as long as they are wide, **1**. This can make movement between rooms tortuous. In large houses of this shape, making units self-contained may be difficult since landings provide circulation between rooms and access to upper floors.
1.09 Many small terraced houses, 4 m or less frontage, open directly off the street letting in dust and draughts and providing little convenient space for storing bulky items like prams and bikes. Fuel delivery and storage (solid/oil) may also be awkward.
1.10 Depending on the position of services, stacking bathrooms and kitchens for convenient servicing may conflict with convenient planning. The run of joists can complicate resiting stairs (expensive) and artificially ventilating interior bathrooms and kitchens. Ventilation ducts may have to run vertically to the roofspace rather than immediately horizontally to the exterior.

Physical environment

1.11 Principal rear rooms may be shaded from the sun by back additions. Orientation and fenestration may originally have been selected expressly to avoid sunlight, at least around midday. The sound insulating properties of old houses are often as good as in new houses but it can be difficult to avoid placing noisy rooms such as living rooms and kitchens over quiet ones such as bedrooms.

1.12 225 mm solid brick walls have higher U-values than cavity walls, especially when damp. Dry lining to improve insulation is fairly expensive, generally not grant aidable and may produce cumbersome and unattractive details at windows, doors, fireplaces, skirtings, cornices, dados, etc. Stud partitioning has less thermal capacity than masonry. Services will generally be replaced to new standards but solid walls, high ceilings and large, draughty sashes can make old rooms expensive to heat.

Space standards

1.13 Providing accommodation similar in area to new building may involve fewer, larger rooms, especially in big houses for multi-occupation. Multi-occupied houses and small terraced houses may be overcrowded by modern standards. The client is usually responsible for housing people displaced.

Regulations

1.14 New work or re-erection has to comply with building regulations. These regulations may also be insisted on by mortgage companies or local authorities giving grants where new work is not involved, for example, digging out floors to provide statutory floor to ceiling heights. Regulations commonly affecting sketch schemes cover enclosure of escape routes in case of fire, location of drainage stacks inside houses where the original is replaced, and allowable heights of spaces. Allowable heights vary with the use of spaces and, where there is mixed use, the stricter standards apply. So in kitchen/dining rooms for example, height standards for dining rooms usually apply rather than the generally more lenient standards for kitchens. Standards vary between the Building Regulations 1976, the Building Standards (Scotland) (Consolidation) Regulations 1971 with Amendment Regulations for 1973 and 1975, and the inner London Constructional By-laws 1972 (with a 1974 amendment on high alumina cement). In inner London, architects can choose whether building regulations or by-laws apply. For room heights the building regulations are generally more lenient.

Contraction

1.15 Back additions are often poorly constructed, with inadequate foundations, poor bonding to the body of the house, built-in drain pipes etc. Demolishing back additions and sealing a basement/cellar could be more economical than repair and make the house more compact and easier to run.

Expansion

1.16 Excavation of ground against basement rooms could bring them back into habitable condition, opening out onto gardens near ground level, though care should be taken that shallow foundations are not undermined. Additions could be built or extended though these would often not produce convenient plans. Prefabricated additions are only usually economic where there is a significant, accountable cost saving from speed of erection. Making a roof terrace can provide some outdoor space (more an advantage in multi-occupied houses with limited access to gardens), **2**, **3**. However, flat roofs are prone to leak and there may be noise annoyance to people living below. Mansard additions are fairly expensive (for example for the private client a case can usually be made in economic terms for moving house rather than expanding into the roof). Mezzanines are generally too expensive and conflict with fenestration, though there are exceptions.

2

3

*2 Extra floor added to terrace. The house with an M-roof at the left hand end of the terrace is the original form of the whole terrace. Roof terraces are provided at the front, pictured here from the inside, **3**.*

Self-containment

1.17 As mentioned (para **1.08**) self-containment may be difficult to achieve in multi-occupied houses. Also with more, smaller units on upper floors the vertical circulation area is larger. These units are unsuitable for older or infirm people. (Units with better views can be some compensation for lack of mobility.) If a large unit is made on upper floors it may be difficult to provide access to a separate garden, **4**, so a roof terrace, **2**, may be more convenient. There may be difficulties of providing space and access to separate meters, tanks, boilers and storage (especially for upper units) for bulky items such as fuel (solid/oil), bikes, prams etc.

Communal areas

1.18 In multi-occupied houses there are often difficulties in defining responsibility for care of communal spaces, both internal and external. Though fencing parts of gardens simplifies allotting responsibility for upkeep, the result is often unattractive. Tenancy agreements will define responsibility for cleaning communal spaces inside but general care may increase if these are attractive. Spending extra on finishes and some furnishings could be a good investment for the client.

2 Sample schemes

2.01 To illustrate how the points made so far combine in sketch designs we present conversion schemes for three terrace houses. These are a small 1850 house, a larger 1890 house with a long back addition, and a five-floor house (including basement and attic) of 1870. These are common house types to illustrate common problems and opportunities. It is not claimed that they are a representative sample of all houses rehabilitated.

4 *Separate access to separate areas of garden; a straightforward solution organisationally but not very elegant.*

Parker Morris standards

2.02 Though Parker Morris standards were devised for new local authority dwellings, they do indicate the sort of density of occupation likely to be sought in local authority, housing association and other low cost rehabilitation. So the Parker Morris accommodation is given for each of the sample houses.

The space standards themselves are given in tables I, II and III. For some of the reasons noted previously, eg tortuous circulation routes and existing room sizes, conversions are likely to require more space per person than the standards suggest.

Table I Parker Morris standard for dwelling space (m²)

	6 people	5 people	4 people	3 people	2 people	1 person
3-storey house	98	94				
2-storey centre terrace	92·5	85	74·5			
2-storey semi or end terrace	92·5	82	72			
Maisonette	92·5	82	72			
Flat	86·5	79	70	57	44·5	30
Single-storey house	84	75·5	67	57	44·5	30

Table II Parker Morris standard for general storage space (m²)

	6 people	5 people	4 people	3 people	2 people	1 person
Houses*	4·5	4·5	4·5	4	4	3
Flats and maisonettes:						
Inside the dwelling	2	2	2	1·5	1·5	1
Outside the dwelling	1·5	1·5	1·5	1·5	1·5	1·5

* At least 2·5 m² should be at ground level.

Table III Parker Morris standard for wc provision

1, 2 and 3-person dwellings	1 wc; may be in bathroom
4-person two- or three-storey houses and two-level maisonettes, 5-person flats, Single-storey houses	1 wc; in separate compartment
Two- or three-storey houses and two-level maisonettes at or above the minimum area for 5 people, flats and single-storey houses at or above the minimum area for 6 people,	2 wcs; one may be in bathroom

Where a separate wc does not adjoin a bathroom it must contain a washbasin.

3 House built in 1850

3.01 This house throws up several problems centred on its small size and restricted circulation. Two variants are given:
● 4 m frontage two-storey terraced house with single-storey back addition, **5**;
● 5·2 m frontage two-storey terraced house with two-storey back addition, **6**.

Parker Morris

3.02 4 m frontage house. Ground floor 32 m². First floor 28 m². PM accommodation (equivalent to a flat or single-storey house) is 61 m² for three people.
5·2 m² frontage house. Ground floor 40 m². First floor 40 m². PM accommodation (two-storey centre terrace, separate wc) is 79 m² for four people.

Commentary

3.03 *Circulation on the ground floor is through all **5**, or some, **6**, of the rooms. In the smaller house, **5**, there is a problem of dirt and draughts getting in through the front door. Separate circulation routes can be created in both the 4 m frontage, **7** and 5·2 m frontage, **8**, variants though this reduces the size of already quite small rooms. Even with a fanlight over the front door and light from upstairs these corridors are dark.*
3.04 *The ground floor addition is the obvious place for a bathroom in both variants, **7**, **8**, since the first floor addition is only accessible through another room. Where a separate wc is needed this can be located in the existing rear entrance and a new entrance made in the rear room, **8**. A combined wc and bathroom may provide a better quality space and not be significantly less convenient since there is unlikely to be space for a washbasin in a separate wc.*
3.05 *If the ground floor is used as a living space there is little*

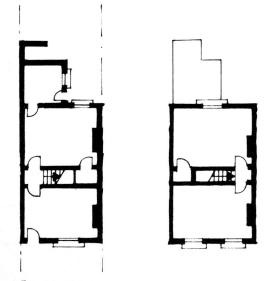

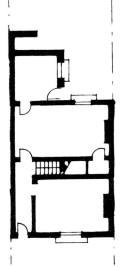

5

6

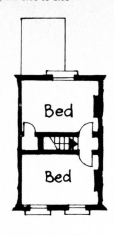

7

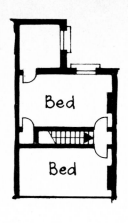
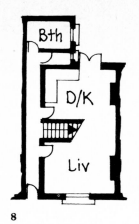

8

*alternative to a combined dining/kitchen area, **7, 8**. However these plans do not provide for a semi-formal dining space screened from pans, washing up, etc. This can be achieved by setting the working surface across the room with a higher cupboard/shelving/ breakfast bar screening it from the dining area, **10**. However, the new rear entrance in plan 8 would require a break in the working surface for circulation to the outside. The kitchen could be more*

*convenient without the circulation route but this would involve instead using the original rear entrance, **6**, and a smaller combined wc and bathroom. A bar, **9**, would be more effective for a larger plan, **10**.*

3.06 *Another possibility is to extend the rear room alongside the addition, **11**, but this is expensive for the space provided and greatly limits daylight penetration.*

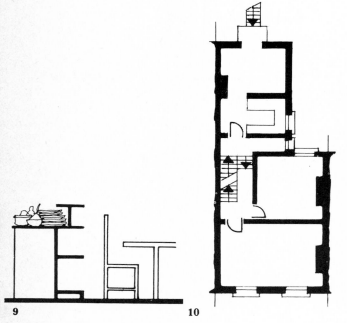

9   **10**

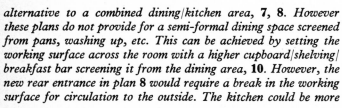

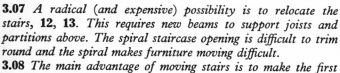

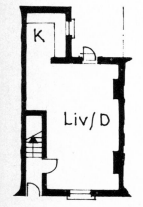

11

3.07 *A radical (and expensive) possibility is to relocate the stairs, **12, 13**. This requires new beams to support joists and partitions above. The spiral staircase opening is difficult to trim round and the spiral makes furniture moving difficult.*

3.08 *The main advantage of moving stairs is to make the first*

*floor addition accessible independently and so more suitable as a bathroom, **12, 13**. This frees space on the ground floor, so providing more opportunities for arranging food preparation, dining and living space.*

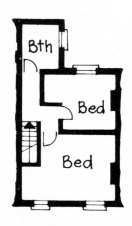

12

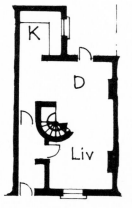

13

3.09 *If the stairs are not moved, the first floor addition is much less usable (when the upstairs is used for bedrooms). It might provide a workroom, playroom, store (much needed in these small houses) or dressing room-cum-wardrobe,* **8, 9**.

3.10 *The first floor addition is more easily used if the first floor is living space,* **14, 15**. *(If living upstairs is contemplated, it might be worth building up the rear addition of the smaller 4 m frontage house, if its foundations are adequate.) Advantages of living upstairs can include better views, no impact noise from bedrooms used as playrooms and more fire safety. Fire tends to spread upwards and the main fire sources are the kitchen and boiler. Disadvantages include insecurity about sleeping downstairs, any potential adverse reaction to this 'strange' layout from unknown future occupants and impact noise on bedrooms.*

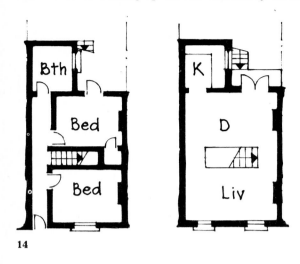

14

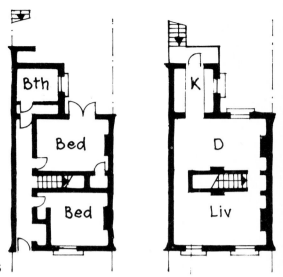

15

3.11 *Storage space is needed in these small houses and is especially difficult for bulky items like prams and bikes near the front door. This can be provided by using part of the original front room immediately inside the front door,* **15**. *Losing space from a bedroom may be preferable to losing it from a living room.*

3.12 *To increase the house's volume, giving more sense of space the staircase walls and ceiling can be partially removed. Piers are needed to support a valley gutter and insulation for the roof,* **15, 16, 17**. *RSJs across the house could replace the piers.*

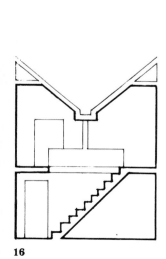

16

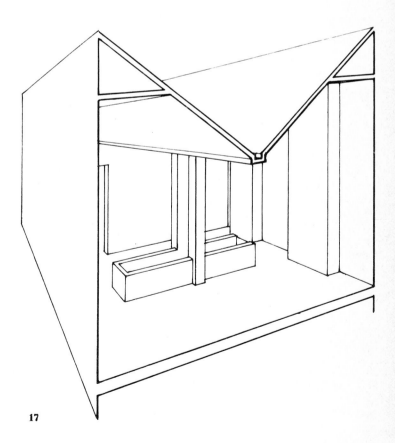

17

4 House built in 1890

4.01 A two- or three-storey house with a two-storey back addition, **18**. Where there is an attic floor, it is sometimes too low for conversion to habitable use though if this use is already established it can continue. Other rooms often have good proportions and mouldings, especially the principal rooms on the ground floor. The back addition is often substantial and sound though reliant on its chimney for structural support. Drains usually run along the back of the terrace.

Parker Morris

4.02 Ground floor 59 m² or 50 m² plus 9 m² circulation space where the house is subdivided. First floor 59 m². Attic (if present) 33 m².
For a single-family house PM accommodation is:
seven people at two storeys;

too large for family use at three storeys.
For subdivision, PM accommodation for two storeys is:
ground floor two-person flat at 46 m²;
first floor three-person flat at 58·5 m².
For subdivision, PM accommodation for three storeys is:
ground floor two-person flat at 46 m²;
first floor two-person flat at 46 m² (not three-person because of circulation space to attic floor);
attic floor one-person flat at 31 m²;
or combined first floor and attic to give a five-person maisonette at 84 m².

4.03 These are the mathematical possibilities but a glance at the plans, **18**, shows that there are generally too few, and too large rooms to provide these numbers of bedspaces on the upper floor(s) and no convenient way of providing a self-contained flat on the first floor with an attic flat above.

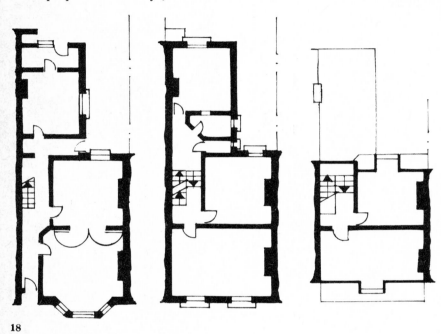

18

Commentary (house)

4.04 *Conversions as a single family house, **19**, **20**, assume that any attic could be left virtually unchanged since there is adequate space elsewhere for most sizes of family. The attic floor might be used as work, play, living or sleeping space either as two rooms or opened up.*

4.05 *The kitchen and back kitchen are knocked together with the outside wc put in working order, **19**, or a new wc installed accessible both from the house and the garden, **20**.*

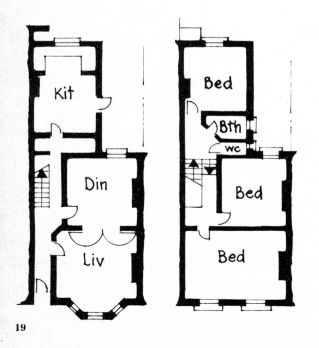

19

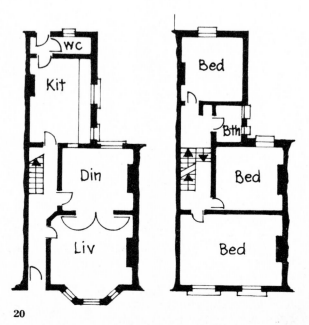

20

4.06 *The original rear entrance lobby can be used for a boiler or as a store, 19. A wc here probably is not practicable since it is unlikely to be large enough to include a washbasin and space is also needed for a lobby. One small type of basin, that fits upright into the thickness of a partition might be used. If the boiler is in the kitchen, these original walls can be removed and a vista provided through the whole ground floor, 21. A further sense of openness is provided by a glazed conservatory alongside the addition.*

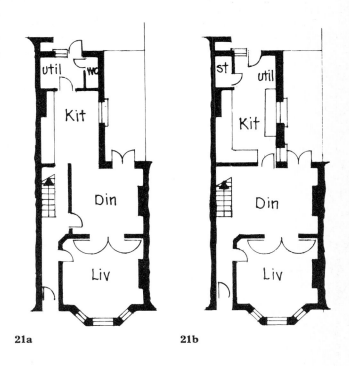

21a 21b

Commentary (subdivided house)
(Hatching on doors indicates entrances to units.)
4.07 *The most convenient subdivision for self-contained units is two flats in the two-storey house or a maisonette over a flat in the three-storey houses, 22, 23. These conversions assume any attic floor is as existing, 18. An external stair can provide self-contained access to the garden for the upper unit, 23. Further external space for the maisonette is provided by a roof terrace on top of the addition. However, flat roofs become more prone to leakage if walked on and railings may be unsightly from garden.*

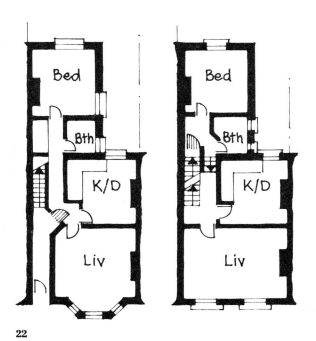

22

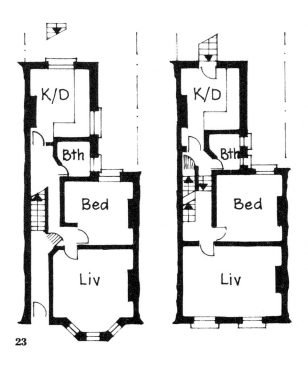

23

4.08 *A more spacious feeling maisonette can result from making different use of the attic. A bathroom in the attic releases the first floor bathroom and lobby space for kitchen space, 24. However, it is then a long way from garden to bathroom and so important to have the outside wc working or the first floor wc retained with a small basin.*
4.09 *It is often difficult to arrange the common entrance space with the entrance doors and framing in an attractive way. And while putting the upper unit door at the top of the stairs helps to keep hall and stairs light, putting the lower unit entrance near the foot of the stairs tends to create a dark corridor inside, 22, 23, 24. One less obtrusive alternative is to place the lower unit entrance door beneath the turn in the stairs, 25. This does however create a longer route into the flat, especially its living room and more communal space to care for. Understair space might be used for communal bulky storage, eg prams and bikes (combined with any deduction from the ground floor front room—see 15).*

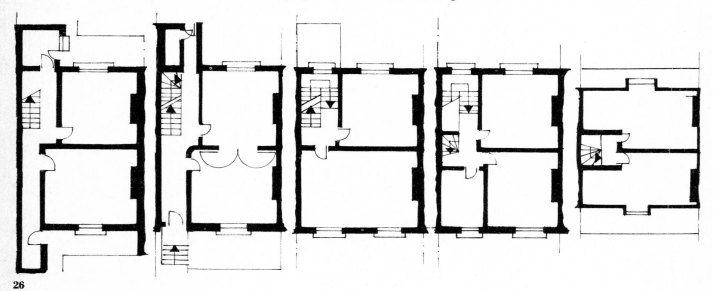

24   25

5 House built in 1870

5.01 This house is on five floors, including basement and attic, **26**. Most of the problems of circulation, locating bathrooms, storage etc, apply as for the other houses. So the commentary for this house focuses primarily on the options for subdivision. Back additions are often poorly built and may need demolishing.

Parker Morris
5.02 Basement 53·6 m². Ground floor 53·6 m². First floor 50 m². Second floor 50 m². Attic floor 37 m². There are numerous permutations. The following example indicates the number of bedspaces suggested by Parker Morris. Basement plus ground floor maisonette of 94·5 m² for six people; first

floor slightly undersize for 46 m² two person flat; second floor plus attic maisonette of 73·5 m² for four people.
5.03 These figures suggest an occupancy averaging more than two bedspaces per floor. As in the 1850 house, rooms are too few and too large to provide for these numbers of bedspaces. The lower maisonette can hardly provide bedspace for six, for example. Though circulation is eased if few large units are provided and by the fact that there are not long landings as in the 1890 house, **18**, the clients of such large houses (probably local authorities and housing associations or perhaps landlords) may well want to make use of them to provide more smaller units. Small units are increasingly in demand and often most conveniently provided as flats and bedsitters in large houses.

26

Commentary
5.04 *One flat per floor seems the largest possible number of separate units (except for planning bedsitters). However, three flats with a maisonette above makes better use of the reduced space in the attic, for probably no fewer occupants, **27**. Removing the stair in the basement provides a little more space.*
5.05 *In **27** and the next two conversions **28**, **29**, it is assumed that the back addition needs demolishing. In each case the bathrooms and kitchens are stacked vertically for ease of servicing.*

The winding attic stair is replaced providing more comfortable, better lit use and ease of furniture moving.
5.06 *Conversions **28** and **29** provide a two-storey maisonette with a three-storey maisonette above, though the lower one in **29** is much more spacious (for two persons instead of four). More planning flexibility and a little more space is provided by re-locating stairs in the upper maisonette, **28**. In both cases, the lower maisonette entrance is at basement level so that the upper maisonette can use the original front door.*

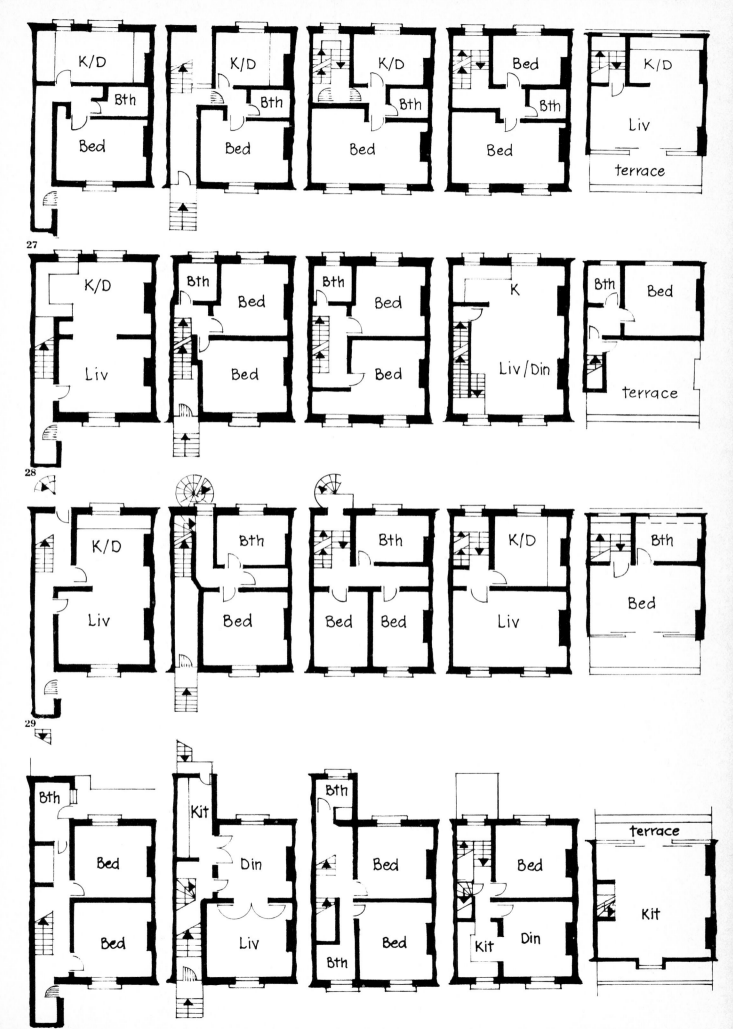

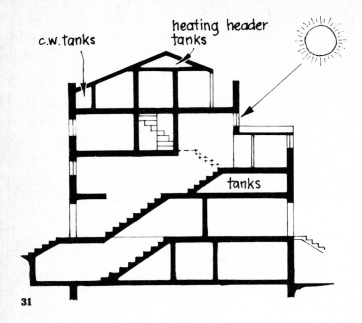

31

5.07 *A spiral staircase provides self-contained access to the garden, 29. A straight run of steps would take up a lot of space since it needs to descend one and a half or even two storeys. There is also a roof terrace for the upper maisonette, made larger for 28, by having a small bathroom, just a wc, washbasin and perhaps a shower.*

5.08 *Another two-maisonette conversion uses the attic floor as living space with the original stair opening into it, 30. A fire door will be needed at the foot of this stair. It also provides a separating ventilated space between the attic and the first floor bathroom. The rear addition is retained, perhaps extended in the basement to provide a terrace outside the ground floor kitchen. By building a half-storey void on the extension (used for tanks) a bathroom can be added to the first floor to meet the half landing,*

30, 31. This can be a full bathroom or as here, where there is already one close by, comprise a wc, washbasin and cloakroom.

5.09 *Another variation, again retaining the addition and using the attic as living space is two maisonettes with a flat between, 32. As in the four unit conversion, 27, there is little opportunity to provide self-contained access to the garden for the upper unit, so an outdoor terrace becomes even more important than in the two-maisonette conversions, 28, 29, 30.*

5.10 *In conversion 32 and in 30, retaining the back addition provides bathroom space, so allowing less disruption of the usually large and attractive principal rooms on the ground floor, also in conversion 32, and where the addition is removed, 27, 28, 29, there are internal bathrooms requiring artificial lighting and ventilation but not in 30.*

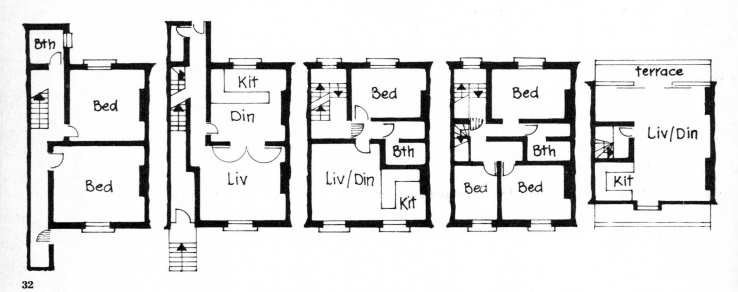

32

Technical study 8
Sound insulation

This study of sound and the following study of fire deal largely with the same elements: walls, floors and doors. However, the problems are different in character. Sound insulation measures are frequently difficult to construct, improvements may be less than hoped for, and sound insulation is not mandatory, so is often under-financed. In contrast, fire requirements are mandatory so money has to be found for improvements which in practice are usually simple to construct. When dealing with sound and fire, it is usually easiest to sort out sound insulation and then check fire resistance.

1 Noise annoyance

1.01 The definition of noise as unwanted sound (BS 661) highlights its subjective character. The perceived noisiness of sounds depends on our expectations and ability to adapt, not just on the sound's physical properties. Our perceptions differ with the activity we are engaged in, eg sleeping, mending a bicycle, watching television. Inevitably the appropriate sound insulation varies from person to person, context to context. In practice this has been condensed to a set of grade standards.

2 Grade standards

2.01 Though building regulations do not come into force, there is likely to be considerable noise annoyance if protective measures are not taken. The standard grades are often difficult to meet constructionally but, as the following definitions (from CP3, chapter III) indicate, they are expected to provide only partial protection.
Party wall grade Noise from neighbours is acceptable to the majority. (This is based on a one brick party wall.)
Grade I Noise from neighbours causes only minor disturbance; it is no more of a nuisance than other disadvantages which occupants may associate with living in flats. (This can be for either walls or floors. It is based on the highest insulation practicable vertically between flats: a concrete floor with floating floor above.)
Grade II With this degree of insulation, the neighbours' noise is considered by many occupants to be the worst thing about living in flats. Even so, at least half of occupants are not seriously disturbed.
Worse than grade II If insulation between flats is as low as 8 dB worse than grade II (8 dB represents about a doubling of loudness), noise from neighbours is often intolerable and likely to lead to very serious complaints.

Grade curves

2.02 The curves, **1**, **2**, express sound insulation in terms of components: airborne and impact sound insulation. The airborne sound grade curves, **1**, are of insulation; the aim is to get up to or above the curves. The impact sound grade curves, **2**, are measures of the sound penetrating floors from a standard source; the lower curve indicates less sound penetrating the floor, ie better insulation. So the aim here is to get down to or below the curves.
2.03 Tables II and III, given later, contain a column headed *slope*. This refers to the notional slope of the airborne sound insulation curve. Thus the tables give a single figure average for insulation and a slope to indicate how this varies over the frequency range. Slope A is low—less than 4 dB per octave, B is medium—4 to 6 dB per octave, and C is high—more than 6 dB per octave. Slope B, around 5 dB per octave, is usually

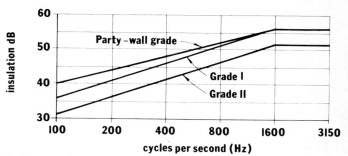

1 *Grade curves for airborne sound insulation.*

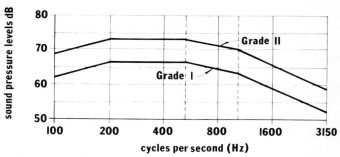

2 *Grade curves for impact sound insulation.*

preferred. Slope C is a steep slope and therefore relatively poor insulation at low frequencies. This is the range where insulation is always poorest. And although hearing degrades with age this is relatively little at low frequencies. So the old find poor low frequency insulation no more acceptable than others do.

3 Planning

External

3.01 Where possible, avoid making space for other people's children's play, starting engines and other noisy activities near windows or in 'canyons', ie between closely spaced buildings where sound is easily reflected up to higher level windows. Screen/garden walls and hard paving may help reflect sound through windows. However, brick boundary walls can be useful in screening windows near the ground from traffic noise. Double glazing protection is rarely affordable. If used, it would probably be casements fitted inside existing windows.

Internal

3.02 Divide noise sources, such as living rooms and circulation routes in multi-occupied houses, fromquiet spaces such as bedrooms, both horizontally and vertically. Stacking living room above living room, bedroom above bedroom is a convenient way of doing this.

3.03 If rewiring several units per floor, avoid putting switches and sockets back to back in party partitions.

3.04 Run ventilation ducts from internal bathrooms and kitchens away from bedrooms.

3.05 If old, high level cast iron wc cisterns are retained, these can be a source of considerable structure-borne sound. Put resilient strips on top of brackets supporting the cistern. And fit an extension tube to the inlet to take the water inlet below the level of water in the emptied cistern, **3**. (But note that some water authorities do not allow these tubes, due to the risk of back siphonage.)

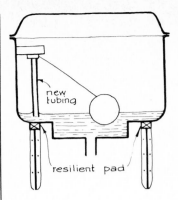

3 *Measures to reduce structure borne sound from cast iron wc cisterns.*

4 Doors

Upgrading

4.01 Doors with an eggbox core or panels of framed doors are lightweight, about 5 kg/m², providing insulation around 21 dB. This may be reduced to only 17 or 18 dB where there are substantial air gaps at the perimeter (maybe as much as 20 000 mm²). These gaps must be largely removed before increasing door weight itself can significantly improve insulation. A total weight of around 25 kg/m² should then provide 25 or 26 dB of insulation.

4.02 Though any dense timber materials could be used, doors usually in need of upgrading are entrance doors in multi-occupied houses. Since these are generally fire doors, ie doors onto an escape route, upgrading needs to cater for fire performance, (see technical study 9 'Fire' **3.05**).

4.03 Similarly, sealing gaps round doors for acoustic performance must often be reconciled with integrity in case of fire. Reducing gaps round doors to 3 mm as is recommended for fire resistance (see technical study 9 'Fire' **3.02**) often requires planing and lipping doors, since both door and frame are likely with time to have become out of square. Less elaborate is fixing metal draught strip to the frame and threshold. (Unfortunately, this makes the door stiff to close and so likely to be slammed, causing more noise.) A synthetic rubber seal, **4**, plus threshold seal closes gaps and muffles the impact of closing. It also controls cool smoke and is probably adequately resistant to flame (integrity) so would not need intumescent strip(s) to provide half-hour fire protection. However, fire officer's opinions may vary (see study 9, 'Fire' **3.03** and figures **1**, **2** and **3**).

Doors in partitions

4.04 The insulation provided by doors and partitions are interdependent, the insulation of the whole usually being limited by that of the door. Table I illustrates this interdependence, assuming a door area around seven per cent of total partition area. CP3 chapter III provides data for other percentages.

Reducing incident sound

4.05 Other occupants passing entrance doors in multi-occupied dwellings may cause noise annoyance. This may be helped by reducing the reverberance of the circulation route with acoustically absorbent materials. Since the circulation route is also usually a fire escape route, however, choice of materials must be carefully checked against surface spread of flame (see technical study 9 'Fire' **8.01**).

5 Walls

5.01 Existing walls are very difficult to upgrade with confidence that there will be a significant improvement. Because walls and floors are constructionally integrated, flanking transmission of sound is likely to largely bypass the effects of any surface treatment to walls. So for example, battening out with absorbent quilt infill and plasterboard finish will probably make only a few dB improvement at the most, and that mostly at middle and high frequencies.

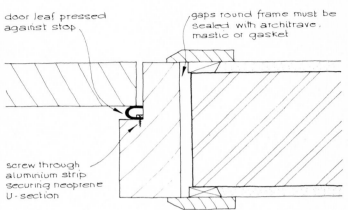

4 *Door seal made with proprietary neoprene U-section held in place by screwing through an aluminium strip. The U-section can be bent back for screwing.*

Table I Insulation values of partitions with doors						
Construction	**Insulation value of partition**					
	25 dB	**30 dB**	**35 dB**	**40 dB**	**45 dB**	**50 dB**
Any door with large gaps round edges (15 dB)	23	25	27	27	27	27
Light door with edge-sealing treatment (20 dB)	24	28	30	32	32	32
Heavy door with edge-sealing treatment (25 dB)	25	29	33	35	37	37
Double doors with sound-lock (air-space or lobby) (40 dB)	25	30	35	40	44	48

5.02 To make a significant improvement, embracing lower frequencies, usually requires a separate leaf spaced to give a 100 to 150 mm air gap; for example, studwork with a 50 m quilt of glass fibre or mineral wool stapled between and finished in 19 mm plasterboard. Any joists into the wall would require instead stopping off on the studwork. Another method, where there is a masonry partition, is to add an extra skin of masonry, supporting any joists on a ledger or hangers. Both this and the studwork would, however, require new foundations. Effective treatments such as these are, unfortunately, generally too expensive.

5.03 Table II gives some wall constructions and their acoustic properties (from CP3 chapter III). Where existing partitions vary acoustically around the building, it may be possible to plan to make use of the acoustically best partitions in the most sound-sensitive places.

5.04 When constructing stud partitions note that putting a quilt between studs gives 2 to 3 dB improvement. If studs are staggered and quilt used, airborne insulation can be improved by up to 10 dB.

6 Floors

Constructional problems

6.01 The most effective acoustic treatments for existing floors are generally those that cause most inconvenience constructionally: increasing floor heights and/or lowering ceilings.

Table II Sound reductions of partitions

Construction	Approx mass (kg/m²)	Average sound reduction (100 to 3150 Hz)	Slope	Comment
Single sheets or slabs				
6 mm plywood	4	21	B	
18 mm chipboard	12	26	B	
25 mm chipboard	14	27	B	
22 mm t & g boarding	12	24	A	
6 mm asbestos cement sheet	12	26	B	
9·5 mm plasterboard	10	25	B	
12·7 mm plasterboard	12	26	B	
3 mm glass	7	23	A	
4 mm glass	10	25	A	
6 mm plate glass	17	28	A	
9 mm plate glass	26	30	A	
Stud frame partitions (finish to both sides)				
12 mm fibre insulation board	7	20-22	A	Porous
3 mm hardboard	6	23	C	
6 mm plywood	7	24	C	
18 mm blockboard	22	30	C	
9·5 mm plasterboard	20	30	C	
9·5 mm plasterboard and plaster skim coat	30	32	B	
9·5 mm plasterboard and 13 mm plaster	65	35	B	
3-coat plaster on wood or metal lath	75	35-37	B	
13 mm plaster on 25 mm woodwool slab	75	37	B	
50 mm compressed straw slab	34	33	B	
50 mm compressed straw slab and skim coat	45-50	35	B	
Single leaf walls (finish to both sides)				
50 mm compressed straw slab skimmed	27	30	B	
50 mm woodwool slab plastered 13 mm	70	35	A	
100 mm hollow clay block plastered 13 mm	120	37	B	
100 mm clinker block plastered 13 mm	185	43	B	
200 mm hollow clinker block plastered 13 mm	170	42	B	
200 mm hollow dense concrete block plastered 13 mm	240	45	B	Grade II
112 mm brick plastered 13 mm	270	45	B	Grade II
225 mm brick plastered 13 mm	480	50	B	House party wall grade Grade I
175 mm dense concrete plastered 13 mm	460	50	B	Do

Floors

6.02 Where a floor is raised by acoustic treatment only, say 10 mm, an angled fillet at the threshold can save the floors of adjacent spaces being raised, **5**, (the door bottom will need trimming). Where the increase is greater, 50 mm or more, floors of adjacent spaces will need raising. This will be expensive, especially if (as is likely) this involves a landing approached by stairs, because all risers of staircases are required to be of equal height. Adding 50 mm to a landing involves adjusting each tread height to equalise rises on staircases above and below.

Ceilings

6.03 Below ceilings there is often adequate height from floor to ceiling and above window heads to install a thickened or extra ceiling. However, there are often cornices, roses and other mouldings that would be obliterated by such treatments.

Approach

6.04 Because of these problems at ceilings and floors, treatments are given in two groups. The first involves no (significant) thickening, ie no addition to ceiling surface and only 10 mm or so addition to floor level. The second involves significant thickening, ie 50 mm or more to floors and/or additions to ceilings.

6.05 As table III indicates, the common measures for improving floors are pugging and floating floors; usually both are needed. The overall performance given in the last column is the lower of the two, impact and airborne performance.

No thickening

6.06 *Carpets* Carpets with underlay are found to make a significant improvement to impact sound insulation (BRE

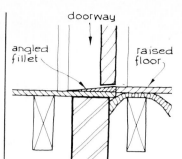

5 *Where acoustic treatment such as floating a floor raises the floor level only a few mm, an angled fillet at the threshold avoids raising floors to the same height in all other spaces at that level.*

5

CP 27/77). Compare the scale of improvement in **6** with the space between grade curves in **2**. For example, it seems likely that carpet could bring construction 4 in table III to grade I, though low frequency performance is not very good. So installing a carpet with underlay may be cost effective even for owners of unfurnished accommodation who would not normally pay for carpeting. Where there is no underfelt, pinning sheets of hardboard to floors helps seal plain edged boarded and poorly fitting t & g floors.

6.07 *Pugging (deafening)* The usual materials for pugging are slag wool (100 to 200 kg/m³) to provide 15 kg/m² and dry sand (1600 kg/m³) to provide 80 kg/m². While the lighter pugging is generally easily supported on the ceiling, the heavier may cause problems both for ceilings and joists. Lath and plaster ceilings cannot generally be relied on to support the load and plaster may become detached from laths and/or laths detach from joists. Also joists in old houses tend to be shallower (not always) than used today and may not be strong enough—check from table IV. (Pelleted slag wool is increasingly difficult to obtain. Mineral wool is an available but inferior substitute.)

6.08 If floors need strengthening, extra joists could be added or extra timber bolted to existing joists. This bolting on may be necessary anyway where joists are sagging and new timber provides a level top surface for laying either a level floor or as a base for a floating floor, **7**, (see **6.10**).

6.09 When joists are strong enough, either originally or strengthened, the ceiling itself may still fail. Sand can be supported on pugging boards, **8**, though there is some loss of acoustic performance. Available results suggest an average loss of about 2 dB over the frequency range, though this is probably greater at lower frequencies, less at higher.

6.10 *Floating a floor* To float a floor the top surfaces of joists must be flat, **7**, otherwise the floor will rock and occupants will nail it down, losing the acoustic benefits. The floating

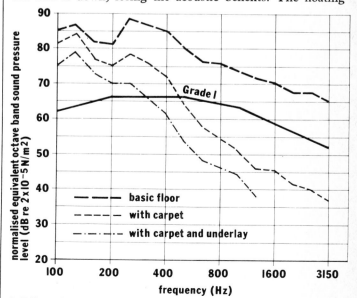

6 *Effect of carpet on impact sound transmission. The basic floor is 25 mm plain edged boards, 175 × 50 mm joists at 375 mm centres spanning 3660 mm with 12·7 plus 9·5 mm plasterboard. (From BRE CP 27/77.)*

Table III Wood joist floors

Number	Construction	Average sound reduction (100-3150 Hz) dB	Slope	Sound insulation grading in dwellings Airborne	Impact	Overall
1	Plain joist floor with plasterboard and single-coat plaster ceiling (no pugging)					
	Thin walls	34	C	8 dB worse than Grade II	8 dB worse than Grade II	—
	Thick walls*	36	C	4 dB worse than Grade II	5 dB worse than Grade II	
2	Plain joist floor with plasterboard and single-coat plaster ceiling and 15 kg/m² pugging on ceiling					
	Thin walls	39	C	4 dB worse than Grade II	5 dB worse than Grade II	—
	Thick walls*	44	C	Possibly Grade II†	Possibly Grade II†	Possibly Grade II†
3	Plain joist floor with 19 mm lath-and-plaster ceiling (no pugging)					
	Thin walls	40	C	Probably 4 dB worse than Grade II†	Probably 6 dB worse than Grade II†	—
	Thick walls*	45	C	Grade II	Grade II	Grade II
4	Plain joist floor with 19 mm lath-and-plaster ceiling and 80 kg/m² pugging on ceiling					
	Thin walls	45	B	Grade II	Grade II	Grade II
	Thick walls*	48	B	Grade II or possibly Grade I†	Grade II	Grade II
5	Floating floor with plasterboard and single-coat plaster ceiling (no pugging)					
	Thin walls	39	C	4 dB worse than Grade II	3 dB worse than Grade II	—
	Thick walls*	44	C	Possibly Grade II†	Possibly Grade II†	Possibly Grade II†
6	Floating floor with plasterboard and single-coat plaster ceiling and 15 kg/m² pugging on ceiling					
	Thin walls	43	C	2 dB worse than Grade II	2 dB worse than Grade II	—
	Thick walls*	48	C	Grade II or possibly Grade I†	Grade II or possibly Grade I†	Grade II or I†
7	Floating floor with 19 mm lath-and-plaster ceiling (no pugging)					
	Thin walls	43	C	2 dB worse than Grade II	Grade II	—
	Thick walls*	48	C	Grade II or I‡	Grade I	Grade II or I‡
8	Floating floor with 19 mm lath-and-plaster ceiling and 15 kg/m² pugging on ceiling					
	Thin walls	45	C	Possibly Grade II†	Grade II†	Possibly Grade II†
	Thick walls*	48	C	Grade II or I‡	Grade I	Grade II or I‡
9	Floating floor with 19 mm lath-and-plaster ceiling and 80 kg/m² pugging on ceiling					
	Thin walls	49	B	Probably Grade I	Probably Grade I	Probably Grade I
	Thick walls*	50	B	Grade I	Grade I	Grade I

* At least three walls below the floor not less than 415 kg/m², eg 225 mm brick walls. Generally, though, studwork is lighter than say 112 mm masonry, it is not far below 225 mm masonry in performance with respect to flanking transmission. So stud partitions are to be thought of as near equivalents of thick walls.
† Assumed from other measurements
‡ May give Grade I with very thick walls

Table IV Span of joists (metres) to support dead load of 50 to 125 kg/m²

Joist size (mm)	Spacing of joists (mm) 400	450	600
38 × 75	0·87	0·79	0·62
38 × 100	1·36	1·24	1·00
38 × 125	1·88	1·73	1·40
38 × 150	2·41	2·23	1·83
38 × 175	2·82	2·66	2·27
38 × 200	3·21	3·03	2·64
38 × 225	3·61	3·41	2·96
44 × 75	0·98	0·89	0·70
44 × 100	1·51	1·39	1·12
44 × 125	2·08	1·92	1·56
44 × 150	2·60	2·45	2·03
44 × 175	3·02	2·86	2·48
44 × 200	3·45	3·26	2·83
44 × 225	3·87	3·66	3·18
50 × 75	1·08	0·99	0·78
50 × 100	1·66	1·53	1·23
50 × 125	2·27	2·09	1·71
50 × 150	2·76	2·61	2·21
50 × 175	3·22	3·04	2·64
50 × 200	3·67	3·46	3·01
50 × 225	4·11	3·89	3·39
63 × 150	3·09	2·92	2·54
63 × 175	3·59	3·40	2·96
63 × 200	4·09	3·87	3·37
63 × 225	4·59	4·34	3·78
75 × 200	4·43	4·20	3·67
75 × 225	4·97	4·71	4·11

Data from England and Wales Building Regulations Schedule 6, Table 1

floor should rest on a 25 mm resilient quilt draped over the joists and continuous over the floor's area. Glass wool and mineral wool are the usual materials. Beware substitutes. The acoustic absorbance of the quilt is needed between joists, so resilient strips only on joist tops are less effective. Also, some other materials can lose their resilience. The quilt should be taken up round the edge of the floorboards, **9**.

6.11 To construct a floating floor like this, **9**, the floor is made up in 500 to 1000 mm wide sections with battens projecting 100 mm beyond them to allow sections to be screwed together when laid. The height increase is solely due to the quilt; a 25 mm quilt crushes down to about 10 mm over joists.

6.12 Battens should ideally be 50 mm × 50 mm but this depth may conflict with piped services notched into the tops of joists. Battens could be reduced to 25 mm deep or simply notched themselves.

Thickening

6.13 *Floor surface* If there is no height restriction, a conventional floating floor can be used, **10**. With battens on joists, the floor is easier to construct. This raises the floor by the batten thickness, say 50 mm, plus 10 mm for the quilt. Pugging is of course generally still needed. However, a recent

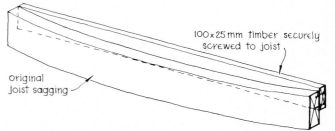

7 *Extra timber bolted to existing joists to provide a level surface. The size of the added member illustrated does not greatly increase strength. Reference to table IV suggests size of timbers required.*

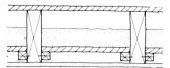

8 *Pugging supported on boards rather than the ceiling. Though there is some loss of airborne sound insulation, using pugging boards is better for fire resistance. Pugging directly on ceilings increases stress on them and makes them likely to collapse more readily in a fire.*

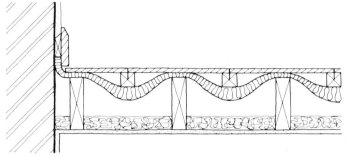

9 *Floating floor with slag wool pugging between joists. Floor level is raised about 10 mm, the thickness of the compressed 25 mm quilt.*

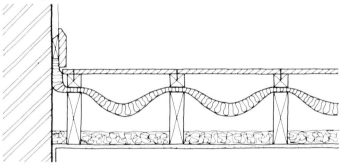

10 *This floating floor is easier to construct though vulnerable to workmen nailing battens to joists.*

trial indicates that grade I overall can be achieved by treatment solely to the top surface with a floating incorporating pugging, **11**. This increases floor height by about 75 mm.

6.14 *Ceiling surface* As an alternative to pugging boards, extra layers can be added to the ceiling. (Occasionally, where there are cornices, it may be possible to add an extra layer to the ceiling which butts up against the cornice and bond these two with plaster and skim.) A sure but elaborate method uses metal lath and three layers of plaster. Slightly less elaborate is two 12·5 mm layers of plasterboard with chicken wire sandwiched between. (The chicken wire is to limit collapse during fire. It contributes to providing one-hour fire resistance where there is 80 kg/m² pugging and a floating floor.) Generally it is preferable to keep the original lath and plaster ceiling since its weight is acoustically useful.

6.15 Even where several layers are added, the ceiling may be stained if the sand is at all wet. A polythene sheet is a worth-while protection.

6.16 *Extra ceilings* Where there is adequate headroom, a new independent ceiling can be very effective. Recent trials in houses with thick walls, plain edged boarded floors and lath plaster ceilings showed that new ceilings could achieve grade I. New ceilings were built 150 mm below the existing, supported on new joists notched onto ledgers (or could be on joist hangers). A 50 mm quilt was draped over the new joists, **12**. Note that there is no pugging or floating floor, so constructionally this measure may be easiest to take.

6.17 If headroom is a little more restricted, the old ceiling could be removed and new joists set between existing ones, **13**. If the quilt is at least 50 mm, the new ceiling is heavy (say 19 + 12·5 mm plasterboard) and flanking transmission low (heavy walls below), then grade I will probably still be achieved (BRE CP 27/77). In both cases (**6.15** and **6.16**) stud

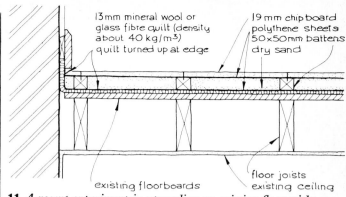

11 *A recent experiment in upgrading an existing floor without pugging in the ceiling, improving both airborne and impact insulation. (From BRE CP 27/77.)*

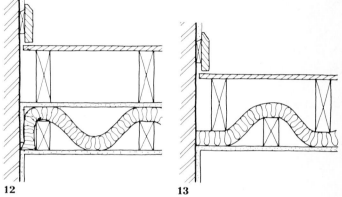

12 *Improving an existing floor, both impact and airborne sound insulation, by installing a new ceiling. The existing floor has plain edged boards and a lath and plaster ceiling. It is preferable to hack back existing wall plaster to below ceiling level, run new plasterboard to the exposed wall masonry and make good the wall plaster to achieve an effective seal.*
13 *A variation on 12, less good acoustically but saving on headroom. (From BRE CP 27/77.)*

partitions instead of thick walls on the floor below should not seriously degrade insulation.

7 Pipes

7.01 Where pipes and ducts pass through walls and floors, they need sealing into them to the same acoustic standard as the surrounding material.
7.02 For sound plus fire protection treatment is difficult. Silicone rubber sealants work but are very expensive. One possible treatment is to slot a sleeve of tubular thermal insulation onto the pipe; it is a tight fit but do not slit it. In masonry make an oversized hole to take the pipe with its insulation and mortar it in. In timber, etc, drill a slightly undersized hole so that the insulation is gripped. In either case cut off the insulation below the surface. The ends should then be sealed in a way agreeable to the fire offices. Plaster may be acceptable. Asbestos rope wound round the pipe was used but tends to fall out and can be a danger to work with.

8 Lead

8.01 The affordable acoustic uses of lead are very limited. A recent trial laying 60 kg/m² lead sheet on plain edged floor-boards increased airborne insulation by 4 to 5 dB between 125 and 1600 Hz. Impact transmission was reduced by 10 dB at lowest frequencies but only 2 to 4 dB at other frequencies. Hanging lead sheet in wall cavities seems to have had some effect in muffling conspiratorial conversions in prisons in experiments about 300 years ago, but is not practicable as an effective partition protection.

Technical study 9
Fire

This study of fire is related to the previous one on sound. Generally, the acoustic treatments given there meet or can easily be made to meet fire requirements.

1 Standards

1.01 Building regulations and fire officers' current practice are the main sources of standards. The Fire Precautions Act, which is retrospective in its certification, is currently only applied to hotels and hostels, offices, shops and railway premises with no immediate prospect of its extension to dwellings generally. ISO (International Standards Organisation) may produce some agreement on terms and standards in the next two or three years. Currently, for example, there are fire doors and smoke doors but no agreed definition of the latter.

Stability/integrity/insulation
1.02 Codes generally refer to fire resistance in terms of:
stability—resistance to collapse or excessive deformation
integrity—resistance to passage of flames and hot gases
insulation—resistance to excessive temperature rise on the unexposed face.
Fire resistance of walls and floors is generally given as a single figure, say half-hour. This means that stability, integrity and insulation are all to be of half-hour duration. The English/Welsh building regulations have a *modified half-hour* standard, involving half-hour stability, 15 minutes integrity and 15 minutes insulation.

Fire resisting and fire check doors
1.03 Doors are classified in terms only of stability and integrity. Thus for example a 30/20 door is one with 30 minutes stability and 20 minutes integrity. The conventional terms for doors are expressed as follows:

30/20 door	half-hour fire check door
30/30 door	half-hour fire resisting door
60/45 door	one-hour fire check door
60/60 door	one-hour fire resisting door

Smoke control
1.04 *Integrity* refers to the passage of flames and hot gases. Where cool smoke reaches a door any heat activated protection, commonly intumescent strips, will not be triggered. The standards required for smoke control vary locally.

Requirements
1.05 Most fire doors will be required to be half-hour firecheck, some half-hour fire resisting. Partitions and floors are usually half-hour, except over basements and other high risk areas where one hour is required. Requirements vary between Inner London, England and Wales, and Scotland. Requirements also vary with local conditions and practices. In Inner London, for example, a lobby is required between habitable rooms and escape routes. Talk to fire officers at sketch scheme stage. (Single family houses are exempt from most regulations.)

2 Planning

2.01 Planning can help contain fire sources, mainly kitchens and boilers, and keep them away from escape routes, especially in multi-occupied houses. Escape routes may involve jumping out of windows or climbing over roofs (by prior written agreement) into adjacent houses. Consider the likely mobility of potential occupants.

3 Doors
Repair or replacement?
3.01 If doors are weak or warped they may fail through lack of stability (say excessive deformation) or lack of integrity (say through cracks, split panels). It may be cheaper to replace rather than upgrade a door. However, a door may have attractive mouldings and panelling worth preserving. And door openings may be far out of square, so that a new door would require cutting to shape.

Fit
3.02 Doors need to fit tightly in their frames and hard against door stops which should project 25 mm from the frame. Where one-hour check/resistance is needed, stops should be rebated into the door frame. A tight fit of door to frame means a gap of only about 3 *mm all round*, though the bottom is less critical; most of the pressure is at the top of the door. Planing round the edges and adding a lipping may be needed to get this tightness. Synthetic rubber or metal draught strips provide sealing against smoke. Rubber should carbonise in a fire forming an outer layer which contributes to integrity.
3.03 Where fit is good, integrity can be improved by adding intumescent strips to the door and/or frame depending on the resistance required, **1**. As mentioned, these strips are heat activated so do not stop cool smoke. Alternatively to metal or rubber draught stripping, intumescent strips could be combined with a smoke control brush, **2**. Strips should last up to 20 years, though they are vulnerable to wear and tear and to vandalism. Larger timber sections might be more effective in the long term if authorities could agree on these.

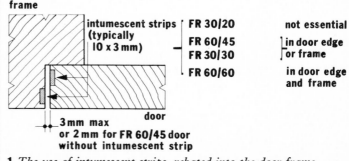

1 *The use of intumescent strips, rebated into the door frame and/or door, to achieve different standards of fire resistance.*

Hinges

3.04 Doors on escape routes must be self-closing and in some cases in England and Wales (and by local discretion in Scotland) rising butt hinges may be used. However, they require trimming the door top near to hinged edge and thickening of door stops to preserve lap (where the trimming has taken place). Given current labour costs it is often easier and cheaper to fit a closer mounted in the frame.

Upgrading

3.05 *Panelled doors* Where it is acceptable to fill in panels, fitting is often time-consuming and the new surface layers difficult to detail. A new door is probably more convenient. Where panelling is worth preserving, asbestos insulating board or other similarly thin material can usually be fitted to one, or where necessary both sides, within the depth of the frame and new mouldings planted on to mask the joint, **3, 4**.

3.06 *Intumescent coatings* These will increase fire resistance but are vulnerable to being painted over or rubbed down during later decoration. Before applying on intumescent coating, the door usually needs rubbing down to bare wood. Glass fibre should preferably be added in the first coat; follow manufacturer's instructions closely. Some fire officers will not approve this treatment.

3.07 *Sandwich panelling* Though relatively expensive, this least obtrusive method involves sawing the door in two vertically and interleaving a panel of asbestos insulating board or equivalent substitute.

Asbestos

3.08 Beware specifying asbestos products unless it is likely that prospective contractors will take adequate precautions. Several companies, including asbestos product manufacturers, now produce asbestos substitutes of similar specification.

4 Walls

4.01 Walls are usually of adequate fire resistance. For example, timber studwork with 12·7 mm plasterboard both sides skimmed gives half-hour fire resistance. Schedule 8 of the English/Welsh Building Regulations gives a long list of constructions and their fire resistances. (Schedule 8 covers most constructional elements, not just walls.)

5 Floors

5.01 Half-hour fire resistance is generally required, though one hour is needed for floors over basements which separate units and other high risk areas. Table I gives example for upgrading existing constructions. Note that for the first construction, a plain edge boarded floor with lath and plaster ceiling, upgrading with a 25 mm quilt could be part of a floating floor construction. Also 5 mm hardboard is effective while producing only a marginal floor thickening. (Schedule 8 of the English/Welsh Building Regulations gives several other examples. Once the resistance of an existing floor is known, examples of the sort of additions needed are indicated in table II.)

Fixing

5.02 Because of the risk of charring, both by direct exposure to fire and heat conducted along fixing nails and screws, fixing of boards to ceilings should be deeper than that necessary merely to secure the board in place. (Deep fixing is also useful in supporting the weight of sand pugging for sound insulation.) For example 30, 40 and 60 mm nails at 150 mm centres are recommended for 9·5, 12·7 and 19 mm plasterboard respectively. Asbestos insulating board or substitutes should be screwed, say 50 mm screws at 300 mm centres, depending on their weight.

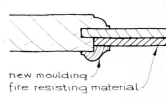

new moulding
fire resisting material

2   **3**

2 *Use of intumescent strips and a brush to achieve fire resistance and smoke control. The strip should have been positioned to avoid a break at the hinge.*
3 *Section of door showing fire resisting layer added to one side of a door panel and a new moulding planted on.*

Table I Improving the fire resistance of timber floors

Existing construction	Upgrading	Fire resistance
Plain edged board or badly fitting t & g. Joists not less than 38 mm wide. Lath and plaster ceiling not less than 16 mm		30/15/15 (modified half-hour)
	5 mm medium or high density hardboard or 5 mm plywood screwed or nailed to floorboards. Joints in existing boards and new material not to coincide.	half-hour
	9·5 mm plasterboard or 6 mm asbestos insulating board (or substitute)	half-hour
	25 mm mineral wool or glass fibre quilt laid above existing ceiling and fixed to sides of joists. Or draped over all floor in floating floor.	half-hour
	9·5 mm plasterboard fixed below ceiling with 9 mm gypsum plaster finish	one-hour
	9 mm vermiculite/gypsum plaster on plasterboard or metal lath fixed below existing ceiling	one-hour
	12 mm asbestos insulating board (or substitute)	one-hour
Plain edged boards or badly fitting t & g. Joists not less than 38 mm wide. 9·5 mm plasterboard with skim coat		
	9·5 mm plasterboard with 9 mm lightweight gypsum plaster finish	one-hour
Plain edged boards or badly fitting t & g. Joists not less than 38 mm wide. 12·7 mm plasterboard with skim coat		
	9·5 mm plasterboard with 9 mm lightweight gypsum plaster finish	one-hour
	9 mm lightweight gypsum plaster on metal lath	one-hour
21 mm t & g boarding. Joists not less than 38 mm wide. 13 mm fibre insulating board with 5 mm gypsum plaster finish		
	9·5 mm plasterboard	half-hour
	6 mm asbestos insulating board (or substitute)	half-hour
21 mm t & g boarding. Joists not less than 38 mm wide. Lath and plaster not less than 16 mm		
	9·5 mm plasterboard with 9 mm lightweight gypsum plaster finish	one-hour
21 mm t & g boarding. Joists not less than 38 mm wide. 9·5 mm plasterboard with skim coat		
	9·5 mm plasterboard with 9 mm lightweight gypsum plaster finish	one-hour
	13 mm lightweight gypsum plaster on metal lath	one-hour
	2 layers of 9 mm asbestos insulating board (or substitute). Joints not to coincide with joints in boards	one-hour

Table I continued

Existing construction	Upgrading	Fire resistance
21 mm t & g boarding. Joists not less than 38 mm wide. 12·7 mm plasterboard with skim coat		
	9·5 mm plasterboard with 9 mm lightweight gypsum plaster finish	one-hour
	9 mm lightweight gypsum plaster on metal lath	one-hour
	12 mm asbestos insulating board (or substitute)	one-hour

Data from Gordon Cooke (AJ 25.8.76) and BRE digest 208 *Increasing the fire resistance of existing timber floors*, forthcoming December 1977, Crown copyright, reproduced by permission of the Director, BRE.

Table II Contribution of ceilings to fire resistance of floor

Thickness	Construction	Contribution in minutes
13 mm	fibre insulating board to BS 1142 : Part 3	10
16 mm	gypsum plaster on timber lath	20
16 mm	gypsum plaster on metal lath	30 to 35
13 mm	vermiculite or perlite/gypsum plaster to BS 1191 on metal lath	50
9 mm	gypsum plasterboard	9
13 mm	gypsum plasterboard	18 to 20
19 mm	gypsum plasterboard	25
—	2 layers of 9 mm gypsum plasterboard	16 to 18
6 mm	asbestos insulating board	20 to 25
9 mm	asbestos insulating board	30 to 33
13 mm	asbestos insulating board	40

Table III Surface finishes of walls and ceilings

A Inorganic group	Brickwork, blockwork, concrete, plasterboard, ceramic tiles, plaster finishes (including rendering on wood or metal laths asbestos boards). Acceptable in all locations.
B Cellulosic group (not flame retardant treated)	Timber, hardboard, particleboard (chipboard), blockboard. Not acceptable on escape routes, ie staircases, corridors, entrance halls.
C Cellulosic group (flame retardant treated)	Acceptable in all rooms, provided evidence of suitable treatment is available. Not acceptable on escape routes, ie staircases, corridors, entrance halls.
D Woodwool slab	Acceptable in all locations.
E Thermosetting plastics (decorative laminates)	Acceptable as for Group B, unless shown to be of flame retardant grade (evidence to be provided) in which case acceptability will be as for Group C.
F Thermoplastic plastics (expanded polystyrene wall and ceiling linings)	Acceptable on inorganic surfaces in thicknesses not exceeding 5 mm on walls, 12 mm on ceilings, provided not finished with gloss paint, in same situations as Group B*.
G Thin vinyl and paper coverings (other than heavy flock wallpapers)	Acceptable in all locations, provided they are on an inorganic surface.
H Heavy flock wallpaper	Acceptable as for Group B, unless shown to be of flame retardant grade (evidence to be provided) in which case acceptability will be as for Group C.

* Expanded polystyrene tiles or surfaces which have been painted with gloss paint should be removed.

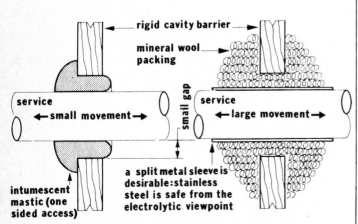

4 *Where there is small gap around services passing through a cavity barrier, fire resistance may be maintained with intumescent mastic or mineral wool packing. The mastic will provide sound insulation if it does not soften and move, or is not made to intumesce (expand) by hot service pipes. Check with manufacturers. The mineral wool is not an effective acoustic insulant.*

6 Meter cupboards

6.01 Gas meters should not be placed on an escape route and not under stairs in single family dwellings over two storeys. The local gas regulations should be consulted. They vary from area to area and seem to change about every 18 months.

6.02 Electricity meters should usually be in a half-hour cupboard if on escape routes.

6.03 For plastics meter cupboards see DOE Circular 97/77.

7 Fire escapes

7.01 Spiral staircases may be unacceptable to fire officers (and users). Regulations vary about siting escapes away from windows. Protect from the weather where necessary.

8 Spread of flame

8.01 Pressure impregnation is best for timbers. It can give Class 0 for plywood (depending on adhesives) and Class 1 for solid timber. Impregnation forms an adequate layer but this may be removed by working the material on site. So impregnation should be done on cut sections. Impregnated timber is not usually available ex stock.

8.02 Surface coatings (applied like paints) do not usually give Class 0. Intumescent coatings swell in heat to about 10 mm, giving Grade 1 to timbers. Generally, coatings are liable to be abraded, decorated over and so on. They may be incompatible with extant finishes. To check whether existing materials are adequate, see table III which classifies surfaces according to their spread of flame characteristics.

9 Glazing

9.01 Glazing to doors and fanlights on escape routes should be 6 mm georgian wired glass. Regulations vary on permissible areas.

10 Ducts and pipes

10.01 Ducts and pipes need fire stopping with material of the same resistance as any fire resisting wall or floor through which they pass. A seal can be made, for example, with mineral wool or plaster; 4 shows method of fire stopping cavity barriers.

11 Hostels

11.01 The articles on the Fire Precautions Act noted in the introduction to this study cover hostels. Designers should consult them for information on escape routes, emergency lighting, heat and smoke detectors, fire fighting equipment, and so on.

12 Sheltered housing

12.01 Sheltered housing seems problematic; it is difficult to ascertain which regulations will be enforced and it is worth checking at an early stage. In one recent case, the fire officer classed a new scheme as flats whereas the building regulations inspectorate classed it as an old people's home. It is not, it seems, a hostel.

13 Further Information

13.01 *Fire protection: increasing the fire resistance of existing timber doors.* Building Research Advisory Service Technical Information TIL45, BRE.

Technical study 10
Services

This study is mainly focused on heating, with additional information on services supply: water, gas, electricity, telephones, tv aerials and alarms. These will generally be replaced with new services to current standards. This study covers aspects specific to rehabilitation.

For services that are repaired rather than renewed see Section 2, Repair and maintenance, Technical study 6, Interiors.

1 Energy conservation

Who pays?

1.01 These first paragraphs indicate possibilities for energy conservation as a prelude to installing a heating system. Some should be part of any good design. Others, such as insulation, require specific expenditure and the client will need persuading to make such long term investments. Owner occupiers are usually on tight budgets and pre-occupied with first costs, but with rising fuel bills they are increasingly aware of energy saving as a long term relief. Landlords in both public and private sectors are not generally responsible for fuel bills. They tend to have little interest in long term savings, though there are exceptions.

Temperature and comfort

1.02 Keeping temperatures to a minimum obviously conserves energy. Lower temperatures are generally more acceptable where conditions are more controlled, rather than where temperatures and air movements fluctuate.

1.03 While a well balanced system will achieve designed temperatures in constant conditions, this is lacking in flexibility. Temperatures in various spaces cannot be adjusted for preference, economy or change of use. Heating systems with a single space heating thermostat do not provide this flexibility, nor respond effectively to localised heat gains from appliances such as lights, cookers, or tvs, from people or from the sun. To provide flexible local control, localised thermostats are needed wall mounted in each space linked to emitters or, in a wet system, use thermostatic radiator valves *plus* a room thermostat to prevent cycling, ie the boiler heating itself and circulation water when all valves are closed.

1.04 In selecting design temperatures remember to keep bathrooms, wcs and perhaps bedrooms warm for the aged and infirm.

Ventilation

1.05 There is likely to be a lot of air movement due to leaks, especially around sashes, and simply to there being a large volume of air in high ceilinged rooms. Ventilation heat losses can be high. Ventilation rates may be as much as 3ach/hour.

1.06 Draught stripping is important but difficult to make effective on sashes. Repositioning beads to give a tighter fit of sashes should help. It is unlikely that air movement will be brought below one air change per hour, so condensation risk is not great, given some heating, except in bathrooms and kitchens.

1.07 Most treatments to windows are not very practicable. Double glazing (a casement type inside the sash) might be cost effective if there was also a significant noise problem. Fitting insulating shutters externally is a possibility; easier, in fact, with sashes than with casements, where casement windows on upper floors would have to open inwards. There is not generally room to install new internal shutters, but it is worth getting old shutters that have been screwed or painted shut working again, **1**. (See Repair and maintenance section, Technical study 6 Interiors, para **2.05**.) Heavy curtains are effective but not usually specified by the architect.

Roof

1.08 For pitched roofs lay 50 mm, or better 75 mm of insulation between joists, eg mineral wool. If in quilt form do not tuck its ends into the eaves so that eaves ventilation is prevented. This is more critical if there is roofing felt, which limits ventilation. Insulation lowers the winter roof space temperature, so lag all tanks and pipes including overflows.

1.09 Insulating flat roofs to extensions is rarely economic unless roofs are being replaced. Insulation to the ceiling increases the risk of interstitial condensation, so a vapour barrier is desirable above the ceiling and where possible good roof ventilation, eg 25 mm holes at 150 mm centres, in any eaves soffit or a continuous 10 mm gap.

1 *Shutters can significantly increase thermal comfort, but settlement of the structure may leave the window opening out of square so that shutters are difficult to close.*

Ground floor

1.10 If a screed is to be added to a solid floor, lay 50 mm of expanded polystyrene below it.

1.11 For suspended timber floors above earth, where much of the floorboarding is being removed for timber treatment and services installation, the whole floorboarding could be lifted for little extra cost and a 50 mm insulating quilt draped over joists. (This is not a floating floor: nail through the quilt.) Check underfloor ventilation.

External walls

1.12 Many external walls are 225 mm brickwork, not very effective as insulators—especially when wet. While insulation improves them, its positioning significantly affects thermal performance.

1.13 *Insulation in theory* A lightweight, ie low thermal capacity, structure reaches comfort conditions relatively quickly in response to heating, therefore making more economical use of an intermittent heat input. Intermittance is usual whether people are out at work or continuously resident but only use the heating system for restricted periods. Unfortunately, in summer the structure will warm quickly in response to solar gain and tends to overheat. Shading devices, perhaps doubling as window insulators, would help (see **1.07**).

1.14 In contrast, a heavyweight, ie high thermal capacity structure reaches comfort conditions relatively slowly, and so is more suited to continuous heating, perhaps for example sheltered housing. However, summertime performance is more stable than for lightweight structures.

1.15 While it is not possible to completely transform the structure of a building, some of the characteristics of different structure weights can be produced by choice of position for insulation. A good insulator (better than masonry) positioned on the inside gives a response to heating more like a lightweight structure. Table I indicates how brickwork and some better insulators compare in their response to heating. (Improving insulation is not of course directly related to improving thermal capacity.) An insulator on the outside will have very little effect on the rate of reaching comfort conditions or responding to solar radiation but will produce a slower rate of heat loss, as for a heavier structure.

1.16 The effects of thermal capacity are not of course restricted to walls but effective action can only rarely be taken on roofs and floors.

1.17 *Insulation in practice* The choice of any insulation's position is not usually free. Insulation on the outside is unlikely to be affordable or aesthetically acceptable unless it is part of a weatherproofing treatment such as boarding or tiling. (See section 2, Repair and maintenance, Information sheet 5, Separate layers.)

1.18 In general, internal insulation is more appropriate both theoretically and practically. (For drylining see section 2, Repair and maintenance, Technical study 6, Interiors, para **3.17**.) Construction such as plasterboard on battens cools the wall behind, increasing the risk of condensation. So battens should be treated and a vapour barrier put between them and the lining, **2**. To reduce condensation risk the air space could be ventilated. Only vertical battens can then be used; horizontal ones stop vertical air movement, **3**. Moving air is, of course, a poorer insulator than still air. The void behind linings can be a useful space for running services, **4**.

1.19 Though plasterboard is not the best of insulants, plaster is generally the most practicable finish. Insulation can be

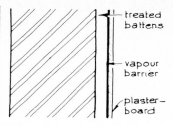
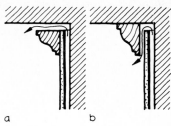
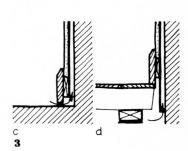

2 *Dry lining an interior.*
3 *Ventilating behind dry linings. At the top, coves can be used, **a**, **b**. For solid or upper floors, **c**, ventilation may be blocked by floor coverings. Skirtings should be fixed high enough to allow for this and occupants informed of its purpose. Ventilation from below the floor, **d**, is more fail-safe.*

4 *Battening for dry lining fixed to counterbattens provides space for cables.*

improved by using a composite of polystyrene sheet bonded to the back of plasterboard. For example, a sheet of 9·5 mm plaster plus 13 mm polystyrene has a U-value of 2·5 W/m² °C, that of 12·7 mm plaster plus 25 mm polystyrene is 1·3 W/m² °C. Where a polystyrene-plasterboard composite is used it provides good insulation on its own so battening could be dispensed with. The thickness of any battens (hence air space) and lining has of course to be reconciled with fitting round openings and masking any ceiling mouldings.

Cavity fill

1.20 Cavity walls can be found back to the mid-19th century. The most effective step is to close the top of the cavity where this is open, since a ventilated cavity leaves a 275 mm cavity wall with a U-value little lower than that of a 110 mm wall.

1.21 Cavity fill can be used in some cases, though not all cavities are suitable for filling due to being too narrow, bridged, discontinuous, etc. The builder could open cavities for inspection but any prospective installer will anyway open up cavities, if in doubt, since he has to write the guarantee. (For cavity fill, check that the installer has an Agrément Certificate. This covers not only the product but the installation team.) Cavity fill is relatively expensive for the benefit produced but cheaper than dry lining.

2 Central heating

2.01 New heating is generally central except in small units, such as bedsitters. In the current financial situation, however, a system may not cover all spaces in the dwelling. If it does not, try to persuade the client to install a large enough boiler and accept a pipe layout that provide for extending the

Table I Speed of response of different wall materials		
Material	Thickness required for U-value of 1 W/m² °C (mm)	Temperature rise (°C) resulting from the application of 1 kW for 1 hour
Brickwork	700	0·06
Timber	120	0·68
Wood wool	83	1·40
Fibreboard	42	4·80
Expanded polystyrene	25	96·00

heating system to the whole dwelling in future.

2.02 'Central' usually refers to a plant feeding all emitters in one dwelling. Where a landlord controls heat supply, eg in a hostel or bedsitters, a system central to the whole building may be appropriate. Monitoring shows fuel costs up to 25 per cent higher than for individual dwelling plants: lag pipes.

3 Fuels

Solid fuel
3.01 Solid fuel is usually burned in a radiant fire, providing heat to radiators and water via a back boiler. It is often liked for its warm glow. Such systems are slow to respond to control, though response can be improved with fans in emitters. In summer, either the radiant fire is lit or a separate heat source must be used for heating water.
3.02 Fuel storage, delivery (especially for terraces) and ash disposal can be awkward, more so in multi-occupied dwellings. There is a prospect of *relatively* stable prices in the long term.

Oil
3.03 Oil fired systems can respond well to control. Oil delivery and storage space can be difficult for terraces and multi-occupied dwellings. The simplest systems are gravity fed, requiring the storage tank outlet higher than the boiler. There is evident concern about price stability since it is largely outside UK control, despite the North Sea reserves.

Gas
3.04 Gas fired systems can respond well to control. Gas prices are more in UK control than oil but there is longer term concern about exhaustion of reserves (a heating system may last 20 to 30 years). There is some concern about explosions. For supply, see **10.01**.

Electricity
3.05 Systems respond well to control. In some cases it may be impracticable to bring in a supply of other fuel. Despite white meter tariffs (between 23·00 and 07·00), electric heating is to be avoided where possible. For supply see **11.01**.

Liquid petroleum gas (LPG)
3.06 LPG needs cylinder storage space and access for delivery. It costs about as much as electricity.

4 Wet systems

Boilers and flues
4.01 Where there is space available, position boilers and other system components for ease of maintenance.
4.02 Radiant solid fuel or gas (for small dwellings) fires with back boilers are compact, fitting into almost any existing fireplace. And original back boiler pipework can often be re-used. Gas responds more quickly than solid fuel to controls and can usually heat the back boiler without the radiant fire being in use. So it is practicable to use the gas system for summer water heating.

5 *Heating flue outlet cowl, ill matched to existing pots.*

4.03 Freestanding boilers can be compact; wall mounted gas boilers more so. Boilers with balanced flues may be up to 25 per cent more expensive than conventionally flued ones, but this is likely to be matched by the extra cost of installing the conventional flue itself. This usually involves opening up a chimney stack, threading a liner down it to connect with the boiler outlet and capping the flue with a Gas Board approved cowl (which does not blend with existing pots, **5**).
4.04 Where a balanced flue is used as air inlet/fume outlet, it must:
● not be onto a right of way (eg around the end of a terrace)
● not be less than 300 mm below an opening or close to the side of one
● be fitted with a guard if less than 1800 mm above ground level
● not be at ground level
● not be near an entrance
● not be beneath eaves or balconies.

Air for combustion
4.05 Adequate ventilation to conventionally flued boilers is a matter of agreement between manufacturers, the Gas Board (if involved), and building inspectors. The English/Welsh Building Regulations suggest a deemed-to-satisfy figure of 550 mm^2 air inlet per kW output. This inlet is to be directly from the outside through a wall or from a ventilated underfloor space.
4.06 If a gas boiler is in a separate compartment this must be ventilated, whether the boiler has a conventional or balanced flue. There must be two permanent air vents to the compartment, one at high and one at low level (see table II which is of Gas Board stipulations). For oil fired boilers, check with the building inspectorate.

Table II Gas boiler compartment ventilation area (mm^2/kW output)

Position of opening	Conventional flue		Balanced flue	
	Air from adjacent space	Air direct from outside	Air from adjacent space	Air direct from outside
High	1100	550	1100	550
Low	2200	1100	1100	550

Emitters
4.07 Put panel radiators near (preferably under) windows, at least 50 mm from the wall and 100 mm from the floor. A thin layer (say 4 mm) of foil faced polystyrene behind radiators will reduce direct heat loss to the outside. Double panel radiators are less efficient emitters than single ones per unit surface area.
4.08 Convectors can sometimes be useful because they are more compact, though generally more expensive than panel radiators. The price differential decreases with increasing output. Fan assisted convectors respond quicker to controls, though they are more expensive and can become noisy in operation. Fan assisted convectors should be positioned opposite windows to allow good mixing of air. Convectors have a lower casing temperature than panel radiators, so they may be safer for children and the old.
4.09 Finned skirting radiators are sometimes preferred for appearance. They are relatively expensive, difficult to clean and almost impossible to paint unless sprayed off site.
4.10 Do not forget emitters in circulation spaces.

Pumps
4.11 Check that stop taps are fitted either side of pumps to allow removal for maintenance/replacement. They are likely to wear out in a few years and can become noisy toward the end of their lives. It may be possible to put them somewhere that is not noise-sensitive. (Some boilers may have pumps attached, located within the boiler casing.)

Water heating
4.12 For water heating combined with space heating, an

indirect cylinder is preferable, ie one in which water is heated in the cylinder by a coil or sleeve, rather than water to the hot taps passing directly through the boiler. Thus the same water—from boiler to coil or sleeve and back—circulates continually, limiting corrosion and furring. In many localities contractors add corrosion inhibitor for extra protection.

4.13 An existing hot water cylinder can be converted by replacing the immersion heater with an indirect coil. There is then no separate means of summer water heating. So for fuel economy in summer, good system control is essential—see **6.03** and **6.04**.

4.14 If a hot water cylinder supplies more than one bathroom, the supply to taps is more constant if there is a separate draw off from the cylinder for each bathroom, rather than their being supplied in turn.

Pipework

4.15 There are two layout types, one pipe and two pipe systems. In a one-pipe system heated water runs from one emitter to the next in series and so cools considerably as it circulates. It is difficult to design a one-pipe layout that meets design temperatures, **6**. In a two-pipe system, feed and return to emitters are separate so emitters are fed in parallel, **7**. Plan pipe layouts to reduce building work and where possible, pipe runs.

4.16 *Microbore systems* These use loops of pipe (usually 6 mm diameter) to and from each emitter from centrally located manifolds, **8**. This centralising of feeds and returns is likely to increase overall pipe length, but the pipe is cheaper than rigid pipe and easier to install.

4.17 In some cases a two-pipe system may be cheaper than the usual microbore system. If pipes are sized down to the minimum for the heating load carried, microbore piping can often be used where two-pipe systems divide to feed each emitter. This avoids the greater overall length of piping usual for microbore systems. For pipe sizing, see **8.04**.

4.18 *Pipework installation* For solid floors try to avoid putting pipes under screeds, except perhaps at thresholds, since maintenance and later adaptation are virtually impossible. Non-microbore piping run at right angles to joists should be near loadbearing walls, where the loss of strength from notching joists is not very critical. Many old joists are broader but shallower than would be used today, so notching is more critical structurally. Though running pipes parallel to joists avoids the labour of notching them, most or all floorboards must be lifted to get the pipe in, so this may be more labour intensive.

4.19 Where hot and cold water pipes follow the same route, they could be put in separate notches or the hot pipe insulated. This keeps cold pipes cool and reduces heat loss in hot pipes.

4.20 Where there is no insulation, hot pipes may creak on joists as they expand and contract. A thick felt pad or piece of insulation quilt firmly fixed in the notch can ease their movement.

4.21 A metal plate over the notch can help maintain joist strength if necessary and prevent nailing into pipes, **9**. Problems of notching do not occur with microbore pipework. It can be threaded through holes drilled at the neutral axes of joists.

4.22 Support any surface mounted pipes at about 1·5 m centres, more frequently at vulnerable points such as skirtings. (Microbore pipework is too soft and vulnerable to damage for surface mounting.) Insulate pipes in roofs, under floors and other cool places. Insulation on pipes chased into walls reduces the risk of new plaster cracking. (However, chasing is risky because nails may be put through pipes accidentally. Pipes are not like cables, whose positions ought to be predictable—vertically above switches and below power points.)

Feed and expansion tanks

4.23 These tanks need to be higher than any radiator, so they

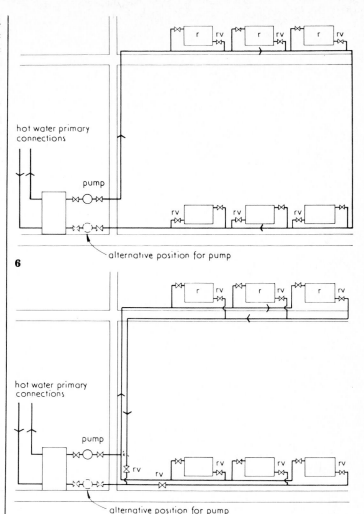

6

⋈   rv regulating valve
⋈   isolating valve
7

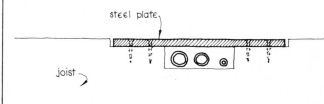

8

9

6 *One pipe system; radiators fed sequentially.*
7 *Two pipe system; feed and return on separate circuits.*
8 *Manifold with six and eight mm pipe outlets.*
9 *Steel plate to strengthen joists and protect services from nailing.*

may be awkward to fit where there are rooms in the roof to be heated. In one case a tank was put in an unused chimney.

5 Warm air heating

5.01 Warm air heating can be installed but may involve removing ceilings. Metal ducting (square or round) wrapped in insulating quilt may be 150 to 200 mm deep. Ducting of foil faced expanded polystyrene may be a little shallower. Since grilles should discharge below windows, it is unlikely that the direction of joists will be appropriate to allow all main and distribution ducts to reach the extremities of the building within the depth of the floor. So often a new, lower ceiling will be needed, **10, 11**. This new floor could also be a sound insulation measure—see this section, Technical study 8, Sound, paras **6.15** and **6.16**.

Supply

5.02 Outlet grilles, **12**, should be at least 300 mm from walls and 1 m from corners. If near a corner, angle the vanes to direct air away from it. Outlet grilles should be at least 2 m apart.

5.03 Systems do not usually need return ducts from each room. Instead, a short duct can be put through a wall from rooms to a central collecting space, usually a hall. The return duct then draws air from the collecting space. (But see **5.05** for fire precautions in flats and maisonettes.)

Boilers

5.04 Boilers are relatively bulky compared with those for wet systems, **13**. Their ventilation requirements are similar—see **4.05** and **4.06**. There are sometimes problems of sound propagation from boilers; bends in ducts near boilers and acoustically absorbent duct linings can help reduce this. Some boilers have a separate chamber for water heating which can be used independently in summer.

Fire in flats and maisonettes

5.05 CP 3, Chapter IV states that ducted heating systems should not cause the spread of smoke or fire from rooms to circulation spaces or from living rooms to bedrooms in flats and maisonettes. Precisely what this entails is unclear but for gas fired systems the following measures will probably be acceptable:

- no grilles to be more than 450 mm from the floor
- the return air path should be ducted and connected to the heater (compare **5.03**)
- the room thermostat maximum should not exceed 27°C and should be mounted between 1370 and 1830 mm high
- there should be no grilles through any wall of an escape route (compare **5.03**).

6 Controls

6.01 Controls should be easy to understand. Provide an instruction book if the installer does not and ensure that systems are explained to occupants.

Solid fuel fired systems

6.02 Control possibilities are limited due to the system's slow response. A hot water cylinder thermostat and a room thermostat are usual and fans can be added to emitters to speed response. When the room thermostat indicates no further heat requirement, the fire will continue to produce heat for some time. As the circulating pump switches off, surplus heat must be allowed to circulate by gravity, either to the hot water cylinder or to one or two radiators. The installer will generally do this as a matter of course.

Warm air heating

6.03 Warm air heating can be fitted with a single room thermostat and a hot water cylinder thermostat. A timer giving, say, two heating periods a day is useful for near continuous

10 *Corridor ceiling accommodating warm air trunking and other services.*

11 *Even in small rooms a new, lower ceiling is likely to be needed to accommodate trunking.*

12 *Warm air outlet grille set near window.*

13 *Bulky boiler, trunking and flue for one flat.*

heating and essential for intermittent. Set to two short periods a day with the room thermostat turned down, systems may provide summer water heating.

Other wet systems

6.04 Wet systems can have two more types of control beyond those for warm air systems. Each emitter can have a thermostat, so allowing flexibility of temperature control (see **1.03**). A motorised valve allows choice of priority between water and space heating. If the thermostat is turned down in summer, a priority control is not necessary for providing water heating only (though a larger boiler may be needed for winter use—see **8.05**, boiler sizing). Position thermostats out of direct sunlight.

7 Commissioning

Wet systems

7.01 Wet systems should be flushed out when they are complete and any corrosion inhibitor added as they are filled. Run the system for an hour and allow it to cool to check for obvious leaks before covering up piping. Run the system to check that all control permutations are working, including the clock if fitted. Then keep the system running for two or three weeks, so that the building has time to heat through, before finally checking design temperatures. Only after this length of time may expansion and contraction of the system reveal leaky joints and even nailing through pipes. A nail may initially pierce a pipe and seal the hole.

7.02 Running systems for a few weeks helps dry out the construction and provides better conditions for subsequent trades, such as decorators, and thereby perhaps more care is taken.

Warm air systems

7.03 Check for leaks and noise before covering up the ducting. Again prolonged running is preferred so as to warm the structure before being sure of design temperatures.

8 Calculation

Aim

8.01 Generally calculation will only be used as a rough guide to size plant and check installers. They will do their own estimating anyway since they are responsible for achieving design temperatures. It is useful to get an idea of emitter sizes at a fairly early stage to find out how much space they will require.

8.02 With this in mind, the calculation procedure is approximate. It considers only heat losses to the outside, not to adjacent terraced houses or other dwellings in multi-occupied houses. If for some reason it is necessary to consider heat losses to these and there is no specific information on the heating system used, assume they are at the lowest likely design temperature, 13°C.

Space heating

8.03 1 Calculate areas of roof, external walls, windows and lowest floor in m².

2 Using the U-values from Table III, multiply the areas for each space by their U-values, then by the temperature difference (between −1°C and the design temperature).

3 Calculate the volume of each space in m³.

4 Multiply this volume by 0·72 W/m³ for adequately sealed spaces (say 1·00 W/m³ for poorer seals). This assumes about 1·5 air changes per hour. Internal bathrooms and lavatories will have no fabric heat loss, but ventilation losses will depend on fan rating and pattern of use. If this averages, say, three air changes per hour then take ventilation loss as volume × 0·72 × 2.

5 Sum the losses from 2 and 4 for each space. This is the emitter output. Manufacturers' data give sizes.

6 Sum all losses. This gives total output. See **8.05** for boiler sizing.

Table III U-values

Construction	U-value (W/m² °C)
Solid walls	
110 mm brickwork + plaster	3·0
do + 25 mm cavity + 10 mm foil backed plasterboard	1·5
do + 25 mm expanded polystyrene + 10 mm plasterboard	0·9
225 mm brickwork + plaster	2·1
do + 25 mm cavity + 10 mm plasterboard	1·5
do + do + 10 mm foil backed plasterboard	1·3
do + 25 mm expanded polystyrene + 10 mm plasterboard	0·8
335 mm brickwork + plaster	1·7
do + 25 mm cavity + 10 mm plasterboard	1·3
do + do + 10 mm foil backed plasterboard	1·1
do + 25 mm expanded polystyrene + 10 mm plasterboard	0·7
Cavity walls (top of cavity sealed)	
275 mm brickwork + plaster	1·6
do + 25 mm cavity + 10 mm plasterboard	1·2
do + do + 10 mm foil backed plasterboard	1·0
do + 25 mm expanded polystyrene + 10 mm plasterboard	0·7
Solid floors (U-value varies with area because of edge exposure)	
15 m × 15 m	0·26
15 m × 7·5 m	0·36
7·5 m × 7·5 m	0·45
3 m × 3 m	1·07
Suspended timber floors	
15 m × 15 m	0·45
15 m × 7·5 m	0·61
7·5 m × 7·5 m	0·68
3 m × 3 m	1·05
15 m × 15 m + 25 mm quilt over joists	0·33
15 m × 7·5 m + 25 mm quilt over joists	0·40
7·5 m × 7·5 m + 25 mm quilt over joists	0·43
3 m × 3 m + 25 mm quilt over joists	0·56
Roofs	
Pitched roof, slates/tiles, roofing felt, plaster ceiling	1·9
do + 50 mm glass fibre insulation	0·54
Flat 150 mm concrete roof with 20 mm asphalt	3·3
do + ventilated cavity + 50 mm glass fibre + 10 mm plasterboard	0·53
Flat three-layer felt + 25 mm boards + joists (cavity unventilated) + lath and plaster	1·02
Flat three-layer felt + 25 mm boards + joists (cavity ventilated) + 25 mm quilt + 9·5 mm foil backed plasterboard	0·77
Windows	
Wood frame + single glazed	4·3
do + double glazed	2·5
Metal frame + single glazed	5·6
do + double glazed	3·2
Roof glazing	6·6
Horizontal light with skylight (ventilated space between)	3·8
Insulating quilt (0·034 W/m °C)	
25 mm quilt	1·36
50 mm do	0·68
75 mm do	0·45

Pipe sizing

8.04 Pipe size depends on heat load, so as piping for a two-pipe system branches toward the emitters it could be reduced in size. The heat requirements from 5 and 6 can be used for sizing pipes using Table IV. This table of 'ideal' heat carrying capacity is for low velocity systems. Installers, especially of microbore systems, commonly risk noise and dirt accumulation by using three or more times the velocities assumed here; each pipe then has about three times the heat carrying capacity given in Table IV. (In practice, microbore pipe sizing is further simplified by using 6 mm or occasionally 8 mm pipe from manifolds to all emitters.)

Boiler sizing

8.05 There are various schools of thought on boiler sizing, most of which lead to oversizing. But boilers running well

Table IV Approximate pipe sizing

Pipe size (mm)	Maximum heat carrying capacity (kW)
6	0·4
8	0·8
10	1·4
12	2·6
15	5·0
22	13·3
28	24·7
35	50·8

below capacity are relatively inefficient.

8.06 If there is a diverter value giving priority either to water or space heating then boilers can be sized on the space heating. Otherwise the two loads need summing. Add 2 to 3 kW to the space heating load (this also speeds warm up).

8.07 Boilers still rarely run near peak capacity and calculations ignore solar gain (admittedly irregular) of around 100 W/m² for south facing windows, gain from people, say 100 W each, and from appliances. So boiler size could be the demand given in step 6 of the calculation plus say 25 per cent for warming up to this steady state. Most installers will be dogmatic about the convention they use because they are usually responsible for guaranteeing temperatures. There is limited advantage in oversizing boilers to get quick response since oil and gas boilers respond quickly anyway. Also, there is no point in the heating system responding much more quickly to control than can the building structure. However, for solid fuel back boilers response is slow and oversizing by, say, 25 per cent to improve this is worthwhile. (This is 25 per cent on top of any margin already added.)

9 Water

Supply
9.01 *A* Check the size of the existing main and work out proposed requirements.

9.02 *B* Ring the Water Board and find out who is the area representative. Speak to him and:

state points in *A*

check on date of existing installation to establish likely life

inform him of likely contract starting date and arrange a site meeting if it is thought necessary

establish acceptance of any special equipment that you may be using, eg instant electric water heaters, no cold water storage tanks, mains pressure heating systems, etc, and also any special requirements.

9.03 *C* Confirm all points agreed in *B* in writing with copies to all interested parties, eg services consultant (if any) and general contractor. (Where no contractor has been chosen, include the letter as an appendix to contract documents). The letter could usefully include a sentence to the effect, 'please inform me if I have misunderstood any of the points discussed and correct me in your letter of acknowledgement'.

9.04 *D* If necessary, obtain a quotation for replacement of a new main. This will require a drawing or marked up ground plan/site layout on which *all* mains should be marked. Remember that one trench on site can be sufficient for all new mains runs, if properly organised. That is, a 100 mm land drain or PVC pipe and draw line laid for a new electricity mains cable and a closed ended insulated barrel of correct size (see **10.01**, *A*) for gas.

Water main
9.05 If the main is of lead, it is better replaced. Where the main goes to a basement it may descend from pavement level on external walls. Lag it, providing a weatherproof finish.

9.06 Separate mains are needed to each unit in multi-occupied houses if separate water rates are to be paid.

Cold water tanks
9.07 If cold water tanks are on back addition roofs, put new ones indoors. Put them high to produce a good head but remember that each unit in multi-occupied houses must have access to its own tank. All tanks could be in the roofspace if access was via, say, a trap in a communal space, eg landing. If a new tank is put in a roofspace, ensure that the trap door is (or is made) big enough to get the tank through. Plastic tanks are easier as they can be bent to some extent. The tank should have a fitted (and in cold spaces an insulated) cover. Hardboard or expanded polystyrene slabs are not usually permitted on their own as cover materials.

14 *Compact plumbing unit with hot and cold water storage. Illustration shows connections to vent stack, basin and wc.*

14

15 *Plumbing unit incorporating a boiler.*

9.08 It may seem easier, where permissible, to avoid using a cold tank. However, they usually pay off. For example, there is some stock if mains supply is cut off; they are needed for cold supply to showers; and they provide a place for introducing solvent for de-furring hot water pipes.

Combined units
9.09 Where space is limited there are several compact units available combining hot and cold water storage, **14**, and in a few cases containing boilers too, **15**. They are designed to fit in alcoves at the side of chimney breasts so may be less than 300 mm deep. Hot water storage should be about 70 litres per person per day. For cold storage, see Building Regulations.

Instantaneous water heaters
9.10 Instantaneous water heaters may be useful in small dwellings such as bedsitters where space heating is supplied by one or two radiant sources. Multipoint gas heaters are no

longer permitted in bathrooms (only heaters with balanced flues are acceptable).

10 Gas

Supply
10.01 *A* as for water (**9.01**)
B as for water (**9.02**)
C as for water (**9.03**)
Plus:
10.02 Send two copies of proposed alterations and indicate position of all meters, equipment and proposed supply runs. Request that one set is returned with any special regulation requirements marked on. (This is important. Of the undertakings, the Gas Board's regulations are prone to change.)
10.03 *D* Arrange a site meeting to establish new service routes and meter positions.
10.04 *E* Confirm all points agreed at the site meeting in writing as before (**9.03**).
10.05 Remember that quotations are only kept for six months and unless a letter is sent to the Board to keep the file active, it will be archived after that time.

Gas mains and meters
10.06 Meters cannot be in circulation areas in multi-occupied dwellings, so they must be inside each unit or outside the house, commonly combined with a bin store. The external location is useful because any main through floors should be in a duct, eg a larger sized pipe, vented at each end, eg with air bricks. The main itself may be 50 mm diameter copper pipe, though flexible pipe around 15 mm is coming into use.
10.07 Gas supply may not be demanded in the private sector, though it is worth providing if fairly economical to give flexibility of future fuel choice. In the public sector it is generally necessary for providing choice of cooking fuel.

11 Electricity

Supply
11.01 Procedure as for gas but drawings are not normally required other than to indicate the line of a new main (or existing duct and draw line) and proposed meter positions. The total number of power points, lighting and cooker or heating circuits will be required to complete an application for a metered supply.
11.02 It is almost impossible to get a supply unless the form is filled in at a showroom and signed by the building owner.

Electricity main and meters
11.03 Check there is space to bring in a main; local boards have restrictions on radii to which mains can be bent. For multi-occupied dwellings, there may be restrictions on the number of supplies taken straight from a main. If this number is exceeded the service head fuseboxes, distribution boards etc, can take a lot of space—up to the size of a small single wardrobe. Check with the board how much ancillary equipment will be involved in providing a supply to several units.

Circuits
11.04 Plan ring main layouts to minimise building work (cable is cheap) remembering to supply communal spaces with lights and power (requiring a landlord's meter in multi-occupied houses) and power to controls, fans and boilers of heating systems. Extract fans and their timers, for bathrooms and kitchens, can usually be run off the lighting circuit. It is useful to have two lighting circuits, crossing over between floors so that each circuit supplies some fittings on each floor. Thus if there is a circuit failure there are always some lights available. For failures, contact breakers are preferable to fuses and quite cheap. Put the fuse or contact breaker box where it can easily be reached.

11.05 On circuit diagrams mark all door swings and radiator positions to ensure that outlets and switches are not covered up.
11.06 The contractor will test the system and supply a certificate to the Electricity Board. The board may accept this or carry out a full test of its own.

Installation
11.07 Clip cables in floors to the sides of joists and if crossing joists drill holes at neutral axes and thread the cables through. Keep cables out of contact with hot pipes.
11.08 Cables chased into walls should run vertically only. PVC cover strips beneath plaster are little protection against nails but may allow cables to slide in the wall, making wiring of outlets and switches easier. Galvanised metal strips are more protective, **16**. Conduit is generally used only in specially vulnerable positions but even that is not completely safe, **17**.

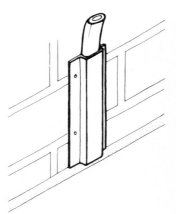

16 *Galvanised cover giving some protection from nailing.*

17 *End view of conduit; conduit and cable were pierced by a masonry nail.*

12 Telephones
12.01 Check with the Post Office on cable routeing at an early stage, or get the electrician to run telephone cables within the house. In large schemes every dwelling may be wired, as is common for new housing.

13 TV aerials
13.01 Get the electrician to run tv aerials at the same time, though not adjacent to, existing cables. In schemes with around eight or more units, a communal aerial may be cheaper than individual ones.

14 Alarms
14.01 Alarm systems tend to be fitted after completion, disrupting decorations and leaving trails of surface wiring. Where possible, get the system installed as part of the contract and require wiring to be chased or otherwise concealed.

15 Postscript

A sanguine note
15.01 Undertakings tend to be slow moving and uncompromising in their requirements, so contact them early while there is some room to manoeuvre on the design. Keep a record of people contacted and their telephone extension numbers. Confirm all conversations in writing and seek an acknowledgement of receipt.
15.02 Regulations, or at least their interpretations, vary from area to area. They are also liable to change, (notably gas regulations). So keep up to date on current regulations and check outline and detailed intentions with undertakings. Delays over controversies may last for weeks.

Technical study 11 Structures

Natural conversion—working in sympathy with the existing built form—will limit the structural changes needed during rehabilitation, though radical change may occasionally be required. This study covers common structural changes required in natural conversions.

1 Structural change

Natural conversions
1.01 Natural conversion—rehabilitating in sympathy with what exists—is an approach as applicable to structural change as to changes affecting proportions and features of existing buildings. The benefits are not only aesthetic. Understanding the structure and working with it should provide good value for money.
1.02 It is of course possible to make almost any change given enough money. On occasion gutting a building may be necessary if the structure is unsound or if radical change is required to provide a cost-effective new use for the building, eg Case study 5, Sheltered housing, AJ 25.5.77 p991 (CI/SfB 81 (W6)). But commonly the low budgets available for rehabilitation urge natural conversion on the designer.

The conversion process
1.03 To achieve natural and cost effective rehabilitation it is important to consider the new pattern of loading *during* conversion as well as afterwards and the ease with which conversion work can be done. The following are key points to consider when envisaging the process:
● will propping be required and will the structure on which the props bear be affected?
● since needling and propping can be expensive, with props passing down through several floors to earth, can structural changes be made 'self-scaffolding'? That is, can new structural members be installed before existing ones are removed?
● will sagging or other movement during conversion disrupt surfaces, especially plaster?
● can joinery, plaster mouldings and other vulnerable items be protected from damage during rehabilitation?
● is there space for people to work, eg on foundations or in roofs?
● is there space to bring in materials, eg long members or large sheets?

2 Understanding the structure

2.01 Understanding the structure is a prerequisite of designing a natural conversion that is relatively easy to construct. The following points generally apply.

Settled loading pattern
2.02 Old buildings will usually have reached a settled pattern of loading, the points of high stress being evident in settlement and distortion of the fabric. Floors, roof structures, stud walls and masonry jointed with lime mortar can have undergone considerable plastic movement over their life. Generally do not disturb the settled loading pattern by attempting to push them back into square. Try to follow existing lines of structure when building additions.

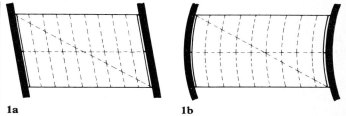

1a   1b

1 *Schematic illustrations of stud walls made loadbearing by movement of the structure:* **a** *shows leaning walls imposing a racking load on the stud partition;* **b** *shows bowing walls, in this case at both ends of the partition. The studwork provides some restraint to the outward bowing wall through noggins being built into it, and some buttressing to the inward leaning wall. This restraint or buttressing may have little effect on the bowing walls, but does load the previously unloaded studwork.*

Basements
2.03 The quality of structure in basements is often difficult to determine. Cross walls may be acting as essential buttressing to perimeter walls against external earth pressure. Walls may be bowed from floor to ceiling and/or from end to end. Basement walls may derive their stability from the dead load of the structure above. Generally avoid making significant alterations to basements below ground level.

Loadbearing studwork
2.04 Many original stud walls were designed to be loadbearing, while others may have become so. For example, intersecting walls may be leaning, imposing a racking load, **1a**, or may bow and the stud wall provides restraint or buttressing, **1b**; or roof beams and floors formerly passing over stud walls may have sagged and so bear on them.
2.05 There are several pointers *generally* associated with studwork designed as loadbearing:
● stud walls continue vertically from floor to floor
● if there is a beam beneath a wall it is probably loadbearing
● walls at right angles to joists are more likely to be loadbearing than those parallel to joists
● with plaster removed a gap can sometimes be seen above stud walls not loaded from above
● loaded studs 'sing' when struck
● a last resort—a loaded stud grips a saw blade.

Previous changes
2.06 Many old houses have been altered several times in their life: timbers may have been notched or cut through, walls moved, roofs recovered in different materials, additions built or demolished, foundations affected by changing water tables, etc. The result will be a factor of safety somewhere between 10 and 1.1. It is often difficult to uncover changes and hence

be confident about factors of safety. This is an argument both for being circumspect—expecting the unexpected—and for converting as naturally as possible.

2.07 RSJs may be found which can only be identified from old structural steel handbooks. In the case of filler joist floors (ie RSJs with fillers such as hollow pots spanning between) they may date from 1900 though for houses built since 1910 their RSJs can mostly be found in 1930s tables. Previously to this, steel sections will be found built up from plates and rivets rather than rolled.

2.08 *Follies* Some previous changes will have been badly built; check where possible. For example:
- holes in roofs and floors may have no trimmers
- openings in walls may have no lintels
- lofts may be used without strengthening ceiling joist
- chimneys may be cut back on lower floors but left intact on upper floors with no support.

Future settlements

2.09 Structural changes inevitably re-distribute loads to some extent. This can be ameliorated in several ways.
- Try to avoid local load concentrations. For example, load a blank wall rather than one with a large window area where masonry between windows is effectively acting as a column and so is already relatively heavily loaded. For new beams use large bearing areas and padstones where necessary to spread loads.
- Use relatively weak, plastic mortar mixes to accommodate movements in masonry, eg a 1:2:9 cement/lime/sand mix. Some builders are reluctant to bother with lime but may be goaded by specifying bagged ready-mixed lime mortar.
- Despite your specification, sawn timber and joinery may have fairly high moisture contents on delivery. However, they may dry out considerably over a few years if fully exposed to central heating. Similarly, existing joinery is likely to be dried out and hence shrink considerably from the effect of new heating. Allow for this or at least warn the client.
- Limit settlement of new foundations and hence settlement of new relative to existing parts of the building by using deep, lightly loaded footings (eg up to 5 tonne/m²) or rafts.
- With a redistribution of loads following structural changes, foundations on shrinkable clays may recover. However, this is likely to be at a rate similar to original shrinkage. So, for example, a building which settled 10 mm in its first 20 years would take a long time to recover three or four mm.

Buttressing and bracing

2.10 When contemplating structural changes note the buttressing effects of one wall intersecting another and of chimney stacks buttressing adjacent walls. Also note the bracing effects against racking of boarding nailed to floors, and of braces, lath and plaster and any brick infill in stud partitions.

3 Examples

3.01 The following plans are annotated to illustrate the structural implications of a variety of possible conversions. These three plans, **2**, **3**, **4**, are the same ones used for the sample sketch schemes comprising Technical study 7 published in AJ 21.9.77 p551.

4 Openings

General guidelines

4.01 Where possible:
- line up openings vertically from floor to floor
- keep openings away from corners
- keep openings tall and narrow rather than short and wide
- keep openings as small as possible
- locate openings where there is adequate bearing for lintels: providing bearing is often difficult in perimeter walls, especially party walls, without building piers
- put a sill beneath an opening where this is near the footing, **5a**, **b**. Generally **5a** would not need a sill to re-distribute load beneath an opening but **5b** would. The sill needs to be near rigid to avoid bowing
- sills may also be needed further up the building where it is desirable to redistribute loads beneath openings
- where conversions require rooms which straddle major internal partitions and so require new openings, a partial opening can be acceptable rather than one that spans the full width of the new room, **6**.

Openings in masonry—door sills

4.02 *For sills in external walls* a concrete sill is appropriate, **7**. As the sill is exposed to the weather ensure that there is adequate concrete cover on reinforcing bars to avoid spalling.

4.03 *For sills in internal walls with timber floors* take the brickwork down two courses below finished floor level and cast in its place a new sill, **8**.

4.04 *For sills in internal walls with new concrete floors* reinforce the top of the slab around the opening. If the existing floor was free of the wall, ie not structurally connected, then make the new floor free too, **9a**. If the existing floor loaded the wall then place reinforcement to link wall and floor, **9b**.

Openings in masonry—lintels

4.05 Where possible use traditional detailing for heads and reveals of external openings, eg brick arches. For timber sizing see Schedule 6 of the English/Welsh Building Regulations 1976. For sizing internal or external steel lintels see Information sheet 1, Steel beam sizing.

4.06 *Partial self scaffolding* It is sometimes possible to make the insertion of a steel lintel in masonry partially self scaffolding. The opening itself does not need needling and propping

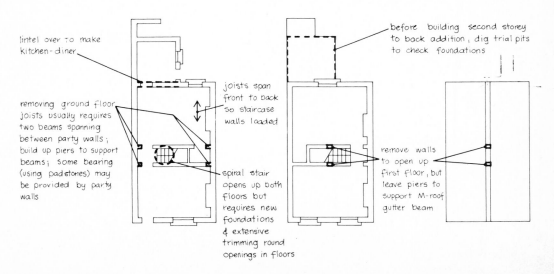

lintel over to make kitchen-diner

removing ground floor joists usually requires two beams spanning between party walls; build up piers to support beams; some bearing (using padstones) may be provided by party walls

joists span front to back so staircase walls loaded

spiral stair opens up both floors but requires new foundations & extensive trimming round openings in floors

before building second storey to back addition, dig trial pits to check foundations

remove walls to open up first floor, but leave piers to support M-roof gutter beam

2 *Likely structural changes for conversions to small 1850 house*

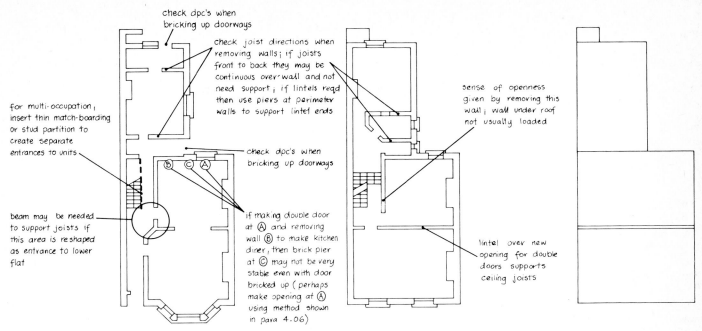

check dpc's when
bricking up doorways

check joist directions when
removing walls; if joists
front to back they may be
continuous over wall and not
need support; if lintels reqd
then use piers at perimeter
walls to support lintel ends

sense of openness
given by removing this
wall; wall under roof
not usually loaded

for multi-occupation,
insert thin match-boarding
or stud partition to
create separate
entrances to units

check dpc's when
bricking up doorways

beam may be needed
to support joists if
this area is reshaped
as entrance to lower
flat

if making double door
at Ⓐ and removing
wall Ⓑ to make kitchen
diner, then brick pier
at Ⓒ may not be very
stable even with door
bricked up (perhaps
make opening at Ⓐ
using method shown
in para 4.06)

lintel over new
opening for double
doors supports
ceiling joists

3 *Likely structural changes for conversions to medium sized 1890 house.*

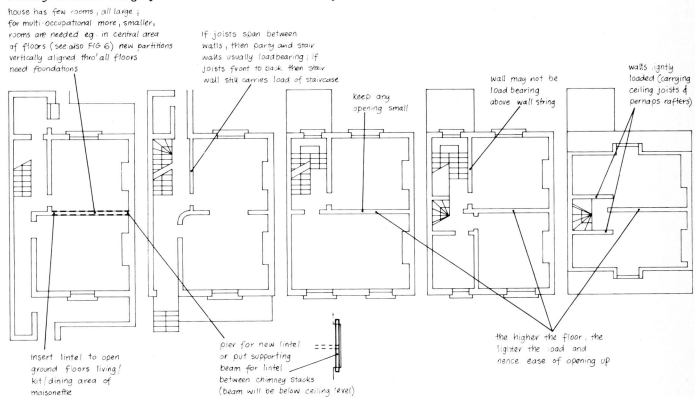

house has few rooms, all large;
for multi-occupational more, smaller,
rooms are needed eg. in central area
of floors (see also FIG 6) new partitions
vertically aligned thro' all floors
need foundations

if joists span between
walls, then party and stair
walls usually loadbearing; if
joists front to back then stair
wall still carries load of staircase

keep any
opening small

wall may not be
load bearing
above wall string

walls lightly
loaded (carrying
ceiling joists &
perhaps rafters)

insert lintel to open
ground floors living/
kit/dining area of
maisonette

pier for new lintel
or put supporting
beam for lintel
between chimney stacks
(beam will be below ceiling level)

the higher the floor, the
lighter the load and
hence ease of opening up

4 *Likely structural changes for conversions to large 1870 house.*

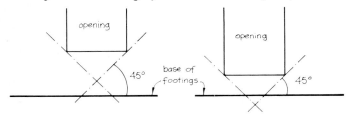

opening

opening

base of
footings

45°

45°

5 a, b *Rule of thumb for use of sills beneath openings.*
*Where 45° lines intersect below footings **b**, a sill is*
needed

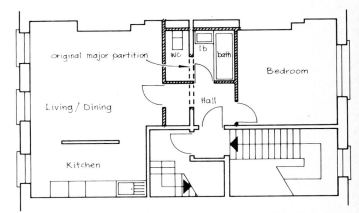

original major partition

wc

lb

bath

Bedroom

Living / Dining

Hall

Kitchen

6 *Opening in spine partition kept as small as possible.*
The remainder of the spine partition is incorporated in the
new plan.

but it is advisable to relieve the wall of loads by propping floors and roofs bearing on it. The procedure involves removing half the wall thickness where the lintel will be fixed, installing a steel channel, removing the second half of the wall thickness, installing a second channel and bolting them together, then removing masonry below to form the opening, **10a-f**.

4.07 There are several preconditions for making an opening in this way:
● roofs and floors bearing on the wall should be propped down to the ground
● the masonry should be of good quality and lightly loaded enough to bear all the load on half the thickness
● the wall must be divisible in half, ie one or two bricks thick
● making the opening should not endanger the stability of the surrounding structure. This is unlikely to be a problem since the wall with a strip half its thickness missing, **10b**, is generally providing more support to the adjacent structure than it will be when the opening is made, **10f**. So if the opening is safe, making it should be.

4.08 Where a sill is required to redistribute a load below an opening, as for example in **5b**, the partial self scaffolding method may still be used. Sill and lintel would be installed by the same method. Then vertical strips of masonry are removed between the ends of sill and lintel and steel columns bolted in place, **11**. Finally the masonry is removed to form the opening. Note that no bearing area is required in the masonry for the lintel. As for concrete, the sill must be near rigid to avoid arching.

Openings in studwork
4.09 Many stud partitions are structural, supporting floors, roofs or walls above. They may also tie in or buttress external walls. Lath and plaster help the studs form a stiff membrane so if plaster is 'live' replaster with bonding and finish. For timbers see Schedule 6, English/Welsh Building Regulations 1976. For steel beam sizes see Information sheet 1, Steel beam sizing.
4.10 *Single door opening* Small openings are easily made self-scaffolding. Where a brace in the studs is cut, some substitute is needed to replace its effect. In **12** the opening is framed by doubling up studs both sides of the opening with a trimmer halved in for the opening head. A 150 × 25 mm board is screwed to studs (ie within the depth of the plaster) as bracing. The opening can be made to size or to the next largest whole number of studs and the new door frame secured by new noggins.
4.11 This, **12**, and the opening details that follow involve cutting the sole plate which rests on the joists. Its continuity usually needs restoring; see **4.15** for details.
4.12 *Larger openings* For larger openings needling is easy once some lath and plaster is removed though propping can still be expensive. With needling and propping the head of a new opening could be made as in **13**.
4.13 *Larger openings—self scaffolding*. For self scaffolding the beam must be formed before the studs are cut. The beam could be formed using two 200 × 50 mm boards bolted to the studs masked by a deep architrave, **14**. Using the deep architrave is obtrusive. Less so is to form a beam in the depth of the plaster using plywood sheet, **15**. Because ply is unlikely to be the same thickness as the plaster, or to butt against it without a crack forming, the joint could be masked with a picture rail. If plaster is also in poor condition the whole wall could be finished in plasterboard and skim coat.
4.14 If there is not sufficient height from the top of the opening to the cornice or ceiling for installing ply to form a beam it could be formed in the stud wall on the floor above. Any floor joists above the opening would need hanging from the newly formed beam. Remember that the ply itself will not act as a simple beam since its thickness to depth ratio will be greater than 1:6.

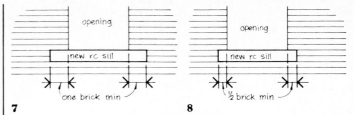

7 *Rule of thumb for installing sill in external masonry wall.*
8 *Rule of thumb for sill in more lightly loaded, internal masonry wall.*

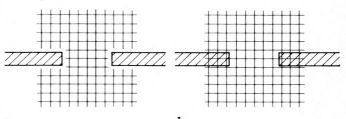

9 a, b *Top reinforcement for new concrete floor at openings. Use reinforcement layout **a** where original floor did not load wall, **b** where it did, with concrete through wall.*

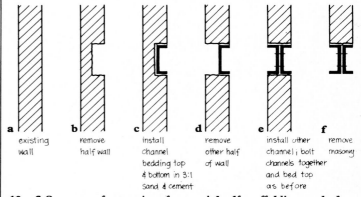

10a-f *Sequence of operations for partial self scaffolding method of installing steel beam.*

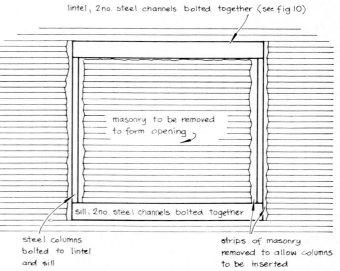

11 *Structural framing of an opening, using the method of* **10 a-f** *to fix lintel and sill, then joining their ends with steel columns.*

4.15 *Restoring continuity of sole plates* Check first that the sole plate is carrying a load. Restoring continuity is anyway a precaution against a non-loadbearing stud partition becoming loadbearing due to structural movement—see **2.04**.
4.16 Where joists run parallel to the opening which is not over a joist, a new sole plate can be supported on solid noggins between joists, **16**.

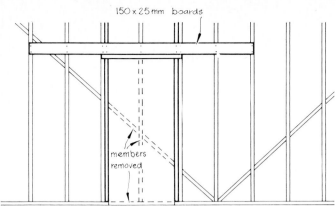

150 x 25mm boards

members removed

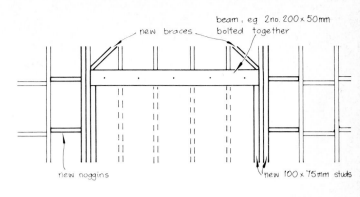

new braces

beam, eg 2no. 200 x 50mm bolted together

new noggins

new 100 x 75mm studs

12 *Restoring bracing effect when making an opening in a stud partition. Lath and plaster is removed, brace cut and new studs installed before fixing boards either side of studwork and halving in the new head.*

13 *Detail for a larger opening than **12**. Noggins removed, extra studs added to edges of opening. Studs cut and beam supported in new inner studs (100 × 75). The cut studs are skew nailed to the new beam.*

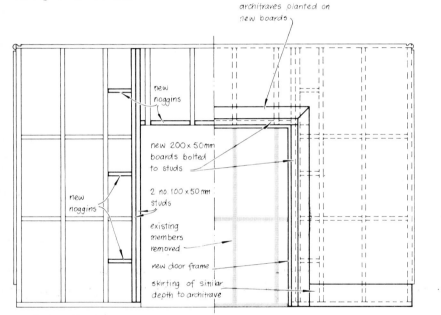

architraves planted on new boards

new noggins

new 200 x 50mm boards bolted to studs

2 no. 100 x 50mm studs

existing members removed

new door frame

skirting of similar depth to architrave

new noggins

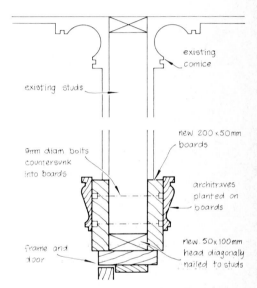

existing cornice

existing studs

9mm diam bolts countersunk into boards

new 200 x 50mm boards

architraves planted on boards

frame and door

new 50 x 100mm head diagonally nailed to studs

14 *Self scaffolding of a large opening. Lath and plaster removed and new studs added at opening edges. 200 × 50 boards bolted to either side of all studs to make a new opening head. Existing studs are then cut to form the opening. Boards continue down both sides of opening for continuity of thickness. Deep architraves (perhaps built up from several pieces) are planted onto the boards.*

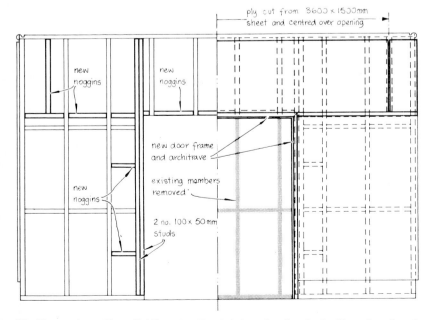

ply cut from 3600 x 1500mm sheet and centred over opening

new noggins

new noggins

new door frame and architrave

existing members removed

2 no. 100 x 50mm studs

new noggins

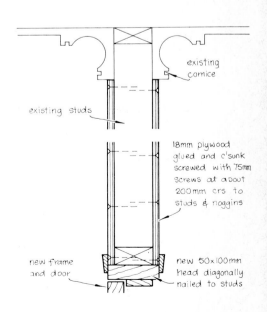

existing cornice

existing studs

18mm plywood glued and c'sunk screwed with 75mm screws at about 200mm crs to studs & noggins

new frame and door

new 50 x 100mm head diagonally nailed to studs

15 *Alternative self scaffolding detail. Ply sheet fixed to both sides of studwork to form beam, installed in the same sequence as **14**. Ensure that one 3600 mm long sheet, not two 2400 or 1800 mm long sheets are used. The ply to plaster joint is masked by picture rail or continuation of the architrave. Skim any vertical joints between ply sheets.*

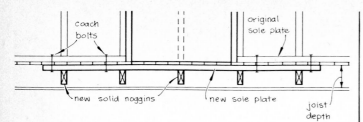

16 *Stud partition parallel to joists but not resting on one. Nail planks across opening through lath and plaster to existing studs either side of the partition at say 500 mm from the floor to temporarily tie the opening before cutting the sole plate. Withdraw floorboards to install solid noggins and new sole plate. Bolt new sole to old and replace floorboards.*

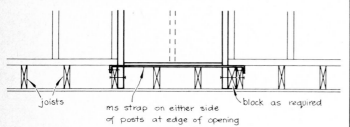

17 *Stud partition at right angles to joists. As for **16**, use planks to temporarily tie opening. Sole plate must be cut to get in new studs before steel straps are fixed at both sides of partition. Notch straps into joists so that floorboards lie flat.*

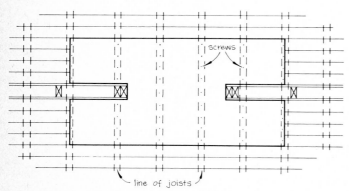

18 *Tie opening with planks so that the sole plate can be cut and new studs installed before fixing ply.*

4.17 Where joists run at right angles to an opening the sole plate ends can be connected with the aid of mild steel straps both sides of the opening, **17**. Alternatively, if the existing sole plate is well spiked to joists, an 'H' shaped sheet of ply the same thickness as the floorboards can be used as a tie, **18**.

5 New stud partitions

5.01 New stud partitions on existing timber floors need fixing at the head and sole. It is most convenient for a new partition parallel to joists to be positioned above a floor joist and below a ceiling joist (though these will not always be vertically aligned). Where the sole and head come between joists use supporting noggins, **19**, or an extra joist, **20**. If the partition is long the joist, **20**, is cheaper; if short the noggins, **19**, are cheaper. Joists, **20**, may need to be wide or doubled up.

6 Additions

6.01 Where a new addition is built it may settle and/or rotate significantly relative to the existing building. Use deep footings or a raft to limit settlement and make a movement joint between old and new, **21**. Do not bond the addition to the existing structure unless limited settlement is assured. Such a movement joint could be masked by vertical tiling.

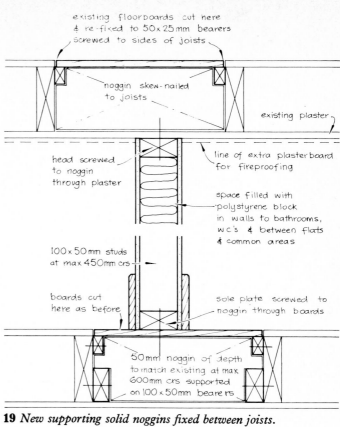

19 *New supporting solid noggins fixed between joists.*

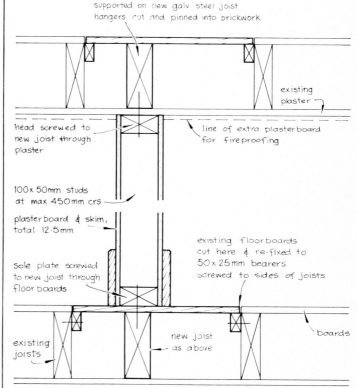

20 *Alternative to **19**, new joists support head and sole.*

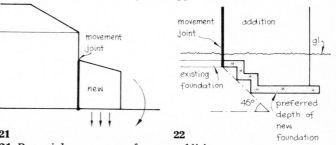

21   **22**
21 *Potential movements of a new addition.*
22 *Stepping down avoids undermining existing foundations.*

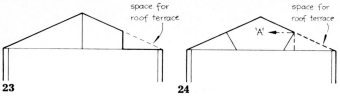

23 *The roof should not in theory spread, if supported at the ridge, when part of the rafters are removed to make a roof terrace.*
24 *With no ridge support, cutting rafters leads to spread and some restraint in the direction arrowed will be required. For example use large purlins tied together at gable/party walls and a large timber (or steel) ridge.*

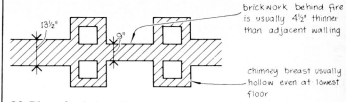

26 *Plan of existing chimney.*

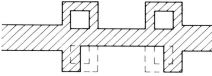

27 *Brickwork modified to provide wider opening and piers for lintel or brick arch (tied with steel strap).*

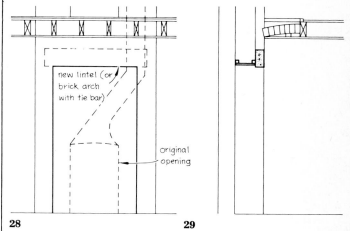

28 *Likely path of flue in existing fireplace.*
29 *Try not to disturb the hearth above when installing the lintel. Close flue with, say, 12 mm ply having a ventilation opening covered with fly mesh to catch any falling debris.*

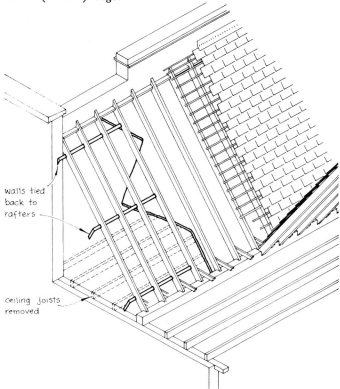

25 *Before removing ceiling joists tie wall to rafters with steel straps (say 30 × 5 mm) notched into and screwed to rafters and turned down say 100 mm in the masonry. Then screw ply to underside of rafters to make stiff membrane. Joists can now be removed.*

6.02 As well as a movement joint allow plenty of overlap on flashings and do not fix cast iron rainwater goods externally, or other rigid piping internally, firmly across the joint.
6.03 When designing foundations for additions check existing adjacent foundations by trial pit and make trial holes to check bearing capacity of soil. For light additions a raft can be used. Generally use large, deep foundations to limit stress (say up to 5 tonne/m²) and hence settlement. Existing foundations are often shallow so new ones will need to step down, **22**.

7 Roofs
Terraces
7.01 Where the ridge is supported there should be no spread of the roof from cutting rafters, **23**. But with purlins strutted at mid-span some restraint in direction 'A' is needed, **24**, such as tying purlins together at the party walls.

Open roofs
7.02 Where ceilings are removed under M-roofs to create more dramatic space, any tying effect of joists on front and back walls or parapets is lost, **25**. These walls will tend to fall out so tie them back to the first few rafters with steel straps

and cover the rafters with sheets to create a stiff membrane before the ceiling joists are removed.

8 Staircases
8.01 Generally leave existing staircases alone. Any new ones should be parallel to joists since this reduces the amount of trimming round the opening. Pick up the newel post on a trimmer rather than joist to provide more stiffness.

9 Chimneys
9.01 Chimneys are stiff, stable and often on deep foundations, so important structurally; beware of moving them. In major work a chimney can be cleaned then filled with reinforcement and concrete for added strength. New major beams can be tied into it.
9.02 Retaining the fireplace reduces the likelihood of condensation and leaves open the possibility of fuel burning. Sweep flues then burn wood to help reseal old parging.
9.03 Only brick up fireplaces when absolutely necessary and put in an airbrick at high level in the room. Make sure the air brick enters the flue for that room; two openings in one flue constitute a fire hazard.
9.04 Cap pots with drop in cowls or wire mesh.

Cooking alcoves
9.05 Where space is tight it can be worth opening chimney breasts to form cooking alcoves, **26, 27, 28, 29**. In London Chimney Certificates and Party Wall Notices are required for removing a chimney breast.

Technical study 12 Interior finishing

Finishing of rehabilitation jobs is much like new work once repairs have been carried out. These notes on interiors provide points of difference to check. The choice of interiors will of course depend not only on budget but whether the client is an owner occupier, housing association (in which case the future tenants may be known) or local authority (which usually requires a flexible, low key design).

1 Joinery

Timber mouldings

1.01 Skirtings, architraves, picture rails and dados are still available in some ornate shapes. The mouldings available such as Ogee, Ovolo and Torus may not match exactly but are usually compatible. Deep skirtings can be made up from several pieces, **1**.

1.02 Extra moulded timber may be needed for repairs or when openings are made or closed. To get an exact match, mouldings in one room could be renewed completely and the salvaged pieces used in other rooms for repair. Remember to make architraves thicker than skirtings to avoid exposing the skirting's end grain where the two meet, **1**. Changing mouldings may involve patching plaster and making good decorations.

Doors

1.03 Existing mouldings may be damaged; removing and planting on new ones may be quicker than piecemeal repair. Doors in poor repair could be moved to less conspicuous positions though doors often differ from floor to floor in large houses. They tend to be less elaborate in basements and towards the top of the house.

1.04 Repairing doors with split panels and loose joints may seem expensive for preserving appearance. But even this, plus any trimming for new floor finishes may be as cheap as fitting a new door to an old, out of square, perhaps non-standard opening. Trimming or specials may be needed to fit new metric doors to imperial openings.

1.05 For fireproofing of doors see this section, Technical study 9, 'Fire' (AJ 23.11.77 p1051).

Floor to skirting joints

1.06 Wall and floor settlements can leave a variable gap between skirting and floor. Where this gap is large but localised the floorboards can be lifted and joists firred up. For larger areas possibilities include:
● leaving the gap—it is characteristic of old buildings and can be useful for carpet laying
● laying a thick carpet to cover it
● masking it with cove planted over the joint **2a,b**
● scribing a cover piece and cutting to follow the floor contour. This is added to the skirting, **3**.

2 Plaster mouldings

2.01 Plaster mouldings are still available though expensive by rehab standards (see Yellow Pages of telephone directories or AJ adverts and Architectural Salvage for availability). Cornice can cost around £1 per foot, central ceiling roses (say) £40.

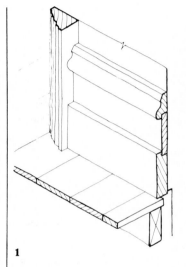

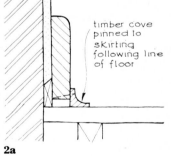

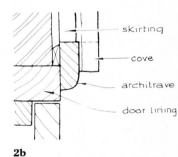

1 *Skirtings built of several pieces may be thick. Architraves should be thicker to mask end grain at openings. New deep skirtings could be devised from available profiles.*
2a *Section of skirting with skirting-to-floor joint masked by cove.*
2b *Plan of cove finishing at opening. To save shaping, the cove could be stopped at the architrave face (dotted line).*

timber cove pinned to skirting following line of floor

skirting
cove
architrave
door lining

2a   **2b**

3 Finishes

Ceramic wall tiles

3.01 Even with thick application of adhesive to fill hollows, the shiny finish of ceramic tiles will tend to show up unevenness in the wall plaster. For a true surface, skim first.

3.02 Specify plastering, fixing and grouting according to use, eg a dense sand/cement render in expanded metal as a base for tiles in showers. Join tiling to fixtures with non-setting mastic. For plastering specification see BS 5492: 1977.

3.03 Since the electrician finishes some time before the tiler starts it is very difficult to co-ordinate switch and socket positions with tile spacing so that they are central in one or a group of tiles. If there is some datum for tiling such as a spashback or corner, the likely tile positions are more predictable and the architect could mark outlet and switch positions on the wall to suit. For general co-ordination a clause can be put in the electrician's and tiler's specifications that electrical boxes in kitchens and other tiled areas should be fixed with the bottom at, say, 1 m from the floor and that the tiler must set out from a horizontal line at this height.

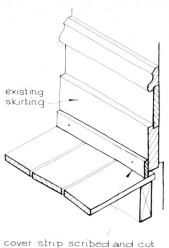

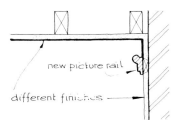

3 *Cover strips can appear to be part of skirting mouldings while being scribed to follow uneven floors.*

existing
skirting

cover strip scribed and cut
to fit uneven floorboards

3

new picture rail

different finishes

4a

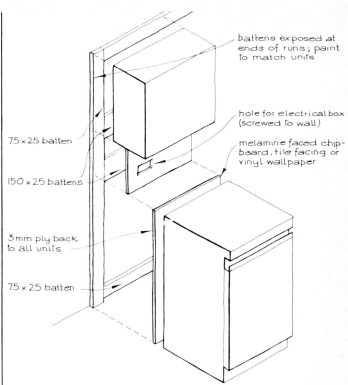

battens exposed at
ends of runs; paint
to match units

75 × 25 batten

150 × 25 battens

3mm ply back
to all units

75 × 25 batten

hole for electrical box
(screwed to wall)

melamine faced chip-
board, tile facing or
vinyl wallpaper

5 *Battening out of uneven wall to support kitchen cupboards.*

4b

4 *For an uneven wall to ceiling junction bring the ceiling finish down to a new picture rail. Putting blocks at intervals for nailing the rail could be necessary on poor walls, **4a**, or at door head height where a rail is more likely to be used for hanging things—with the obvious extra cost.*
4b *view of a rail installed.*

Floor lino

3.04 Lino sheet or tiles need a flat, stable substrate. Pack and nail springy boards as necessary. Uneven floorboards can be covered with preshrunk hardboard; say 4 mm (or shrink the hardboard on site by wetting). Fix sheets with ring shank nails at 100 mm centres or use a nailing machine, but not staples. Nail more heavily around the edges. Using 18 mm nails prevents nailing through floorboards into services.

Painting

3.05 There is rarely money for extensive burning off of paint. Burning window frames frequently results in cracked glass: paint strippers are safer. Alternatively a caustic bath can be used if locally available. Dipping a door will cost around £5. This involves transporting the door to and from the bath, scraping off the now loosened paint and leaving it for at least two weeks to dry out before repainting. It is not very good for the timber. Never dip veneers.

3.06 Gloss paint shows up unevenness; eggshell less so but can look as though it has not been done. It is also more liable to chip. Vinyl emulsion provides a fairly easily-maintained finish to walls and can be continued over woodwork, eg book shelves.

3.07 Where there is no cornice the junction between wall and ceiling is often irregular. So there is no clear line for making a change of decoration, eg of colour or a change from ceiling emulsion to wallpaper. A neat junction can be made by bringing the ceiling finish down to any picture rail, or installing one either at door head height or 25 mm from the ceiling, **4a**, **b**.

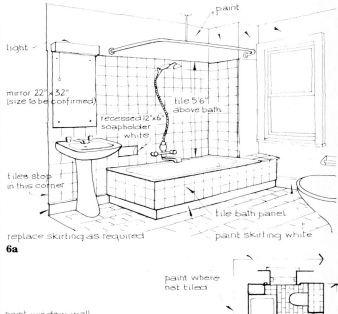

paint

light

mirror 22"×32"
(size to be confirmed)

recessed 12"×6"
soapholder
white

tiles stop
in this corner

replace skirting as required

tile 5'6"
above bath

tile bath panel

paint skirting white

6a

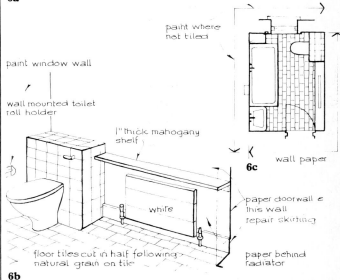

paint where
not tiled

paint window wall

wall mounted toilet
roll holder

1" thick mahogany
shelf

white

floor tiles cut in half following
natural grain on tile

6b

wall paper

6c

paper door wall &
this wall
repair skirting

paper behind
radiator

6a,b,c *Specification of finishes, in this case for a guest bathroom. Check that views, eg a and b, show all angles/corners. A plan, c, is a useful check for completeness and for relating the 3D drawings.*

3.08 Colour is, of course, a matter of personal taste. Where occupants are not known, a light colour can give character for little or no extra cost. However, plain white is a good base on which new occupants can put their own colours and show up defects, so may encourage contractor to produce a better finish.

Wallpaper
3.09 Where there is a client to choose patterns, papering can be as cheap as painting and less revealing of slight unevenness in walls. Even so walls need to be well prepared: emulsioned anaglypta or wood chip paper to mask poor surfaces is the hallmark of poor work.

4 Fixtures

4.01 Fixtures need planning and installing bearing in mind that rooms are frequently not square and walls and floors uneven. Floor mounted units can be packed underneath to get top surfaces level. But remember where there is a large top surface, eg a range of kitchen units, to level up starting at the highest point in the room and use this as the datum level for the remainder. Where the gap between plinth and floor is appreciable, a fascia for the plinth can be cut from ply, melamine, etc, scribed to follow the floor.
4.02 For wall mounting of fixtures on uneven internal walls, battening provides a true surface, **5**.
4.03 When planning fixture layouts note that sills of sash windows may be too low for working surfaces to run beneath them. For privacy, eg in bathrooms, mirrors can be put inside existing glazing.

5 Specification

5.01 Drawing is an alternative to some written specification **6a,b,c,d,e**. It can be easier for people to see at a glance if it is complete. It may also be more comprehensible than a written specification and more likely to be followed by site staff who either skim over the written specification or do not read it at all. The main disadvantage is that being particular to a job it is difficult to formalise feedback in a way equivalent to developing standard clauses in a written specification. Such a sketch may also be of dubious validity in a dispute. It is generally more appropriate for small builders.

6d,e *The photographs show the finished scheme:* **d** *shows view* **6b**, **e** *below shows view* **6a**.

6e

Information sheet 1
Steel beam sizing

This section gives a step by step calculation procedure for steel beams in simple loading and restraint conditions, namely simply supported (not fixed ended) members with uniformly distributed loads, centre and off-centre point loads. Data are provided on weights of building materials and available steel sections.

1 Units

1.01 It is impossible to use one set of units consistently that does not involve extremely large numbers or minute fractions. To partially alleviate this and to make data tables compatible with other available information, the calculation of loads is in kilonewtons and metres, the subsequent calculation of stresses and deflections in newtons and millimetres.

1.02 For reluctant Europeans the following conversion factors may be useful. (Strictly, pounds and kilos should be measures of force, ie lbf and kgf.)

1 lb = 0·45 kg = 4·45N

1 kg = 9·81N

1 lb/ft run = 1·49 kg/m run = 14·59 N/m run

1 kg/m run = 9·81 N/m run

1 lb ft² = 4·88 kg/m² = 47·88 N/m²

1 kg/m² = 9·81 N/m²

2 Approximate calculation

2.01 Steel beam sizing is a matter of trial and error. To limit detailed trial calculation this approximate calculation can be done first to get beam sizing about right. It is usually adequate in this approximate calculation to check bending only, since shear and deflection are rarely critical.

2.02 The selfweight of a beam becomes prominent when the beam is lightly loaded. The costs of beams are such that, especially when small, oversizing costs little and in some cases may be advantageous if a larger beam is more easily available or more easily built in.

2.03 Because achieving enough end restraint to permit no rotation is very difficult to guarantee, all beams are assumed to be freely supported rather than having fixed ends.

Procedure

2.04 *Loading.* Assess spread and point load. Double point load and divide by the span to give an equivalent load/m run; see **3.01**.

Sizing. Choose a beam one-twentieth of the span and look up its self weight in table II.

Total load. Add loading to self weight to give a total load/m run (w).

Units. Convert to N and mm: see **3.04**.

Elastic modulus. Calculate $\frac{wl^2}{8}$, divide by 165 N/mm² and check the elastic modulus for the chosen section in table II.

Detail. If the beam is about right do detailed calculation.

3 Detailed calculation

Step 1: loading

3.01 Domestic construction is generally fairly light: the weight of finishes such as render or vertical tiling for example is usually negligible. From table I assess the dead and imposed

Table I Loads of building elements

Imposed loads	Load (kN/m²)
Housing	
floors	1·5
flat roofs	0·75
pitched roofs (on plan)	0·75
stairs—dwellings not exceeding three storeys	1·5
—all others not less than	3·0
not more than	5·0
(and at least the same loading as the floor to which they give access)	
Residential buildings (eg hostels)	
bedroom/dormitory	1·5
dining	2·0
toilet room	2·0
communal kitchen (but check equipment)	3·0
lounge	3·0
laundry	3·0
corridor	4·0

Reduction of imposed loads with height Number of floors including roof	Percentage reduction in total imposed load on all floors carried by member under consideration
1	0
2	10
3	20
4	30
5-10	40

Dead loads	Load (kN/m²)
Floor	
Boards + joists + lath and plaster ceiling	0·8
Roof	
Flat roof:	
asphalt + boards + joists + lath and plaster ceiling	1·2
felt + boards + joists + lath and plaster ceiling	0·85
Pitched roof:	
lath and plaster ceiling + timber joists and	
roof structure + plain clay tiles	1·6
roof structure + single lap clay tiles	1·3
roof structure + plain concrete tiles (gauge 75-112 mm)	1·6 to 1·9
roof structure + single lap concrete	1·4
roof structure + slate (Welsh/Cornish) thin	1·1
thick	1·4
roof structure + slate (Westmorland) thin	1·4
thick	1·7
Masonry walls	
114 mm brick + plaster	2·0
229 mm brick + plaster	4·5
343 mm brick + plaster	7·0
458 mm brick + plaster	9·0
Stud partitions	
Stud + plasterboard both sides	0·4
Stud + lath and plaster both sides	0·8
+ brick on edge (75 mm) infill	2·5
+ half brick (114 mm) infill	3·0
Water	
(eg water in tanks—1000 kg/m³)	

For further information on weights of elements see BS 648, *Schedule of weights of building materials;* for loading limits see CP 3: Chapter V: Part 1, *Loading.*

loads on the beam, either per unit length (w) or point load (p).

Step 2: select a steel section

3.02 Based on experience a steel section is selected from table II, then tested by trial and error. For a uniformly distributed load add the self weight of the beam selected to the load calculated in step 1. For a point load add twice the self weight to the point load. For self weight in both cases, use the load given per metre in kilonewtons. The weight in kilogrammes given in brackets in the table is for use when ordering from stockists.

3.03 Table II shows steel sections that should be readily available from stockists. Most steel tables show a wider range

Table II Properties of steel sections

Nominal size (mm × mm)	Imperial equivalent (inches)	Mass per metre run (kg)	Self load per metre run (kN)	D/T ratio	Radius of gyration (r_y)	Web area (A_w) (mm²)	Elastic modulas about x-x axis (mm³)	Moment of inertia about x-x axis (mm⁴)
Joists								
203 × 102	8 × 4	(25·3)	0·25	19·5	22·5	1177	226 × 10³	2294 × 10⁴
176 × 102	7 × 4	(21·5)	0·21	19·8	22·5	943	171 × 10³	1519 × 10⁴
152 × 89	6 × 3½	(17·1)	0·17	18·4	19·9	745	116 × 10³	881 × 10⁴
127 × 76	5 × 3	(13·4)	0·13	16·7	17·2	572	75 × 10³	476 × 10⁴
102 × 64	4 × 2½	(9·7)	0·09	15·5	14·3	418	43 × 10³	218 × 10⁴
76 × 76	3 × 3	(12·7)	0·12	9·1	17·8	388	42 × 10³	159 × 10⁴
Channels								
305 × 102	12 × 4	(46·2)	0·45	20·6	29·1	3109	539 × 10³	8214 × 10⁴
254 × 76	10 × 3	(28·3)	0·28	23·3	21·2	2057	265 × 10³	3367 × 10⁴
229 × 76	9 × 3	(26·1)	0·26	20·4	21·9	1737	228 × 10³	2610 × 10⁴
203 × 76	8 × 3	(23·8)	0·23	18·1	22·3	1442	192 × 10³	1950 × 10⁴
178 × 76	7 × 3	(20·8)	0·20	17·3	22·5	1173	150 × 10³	1337 × 10⁴
152 × 76	6 × 3	(17·9)	0·18	16·9	22·4	975	112 × 10³	852 × 10⁴
127 × 64	5 × 2½	(14·9)	0·15	13·8	18·8	813	76 × 10³	483 × 10⁴
102 × 51	4 × 2	(10·4)	0·10	13·4	14·8	620	41 × 10³	208 × 10⁴
76 × 38	3 × 1½	(6·7)	0·07	11·2	11·2	387	19·5 × 10³	74 × 10⁴
Universal columns (can be useful where depth of section is critical)								
203 × 203	8 × 8	(46)	0·45	18·5	51·1	1483	449 × 10³	4564 × 10⁴
152 × 152	6 × 6	(23)	0·23	22·4	36·8	930	166 × 10³	1263 × 10⁴
Universal beams								
305 × 165	12 × 6½	(40)	0·39	29·8	36·7	1853	560 × 10³	8500 × 10⁴
305 × 127	12 × 5	(37)	0·36	28·4	25·8	2187	470 × 10³	7143 × 10⁴
305 × 102	12 × 4	(25)	0·25	44·8	19·2	1768	288 × 10³	4381 × 10⁴
254 × 146	10 × 5¾	(31)	0·30	29·2	31·9	1534	352 × 10³	4427 × 10⁴
254 × 102	10 × 4	(22)	0·22	37·4	20·2	1473	225 × 10³	2863 × 10⁴
203 × 133	8 × 5¼	(25)	0·25	26·1	29·4	1179	231 × 10³	2348 × 10⁴

but of varying availability. Generally, where there are several weights for a serial size of steel section, the lightest is likely to be most readily available and is given in this table.

Step 3: convert to newtons and millimetres
3.04 Multiply point loads in kN by 1000 to convert to newtons. Multiplying uniformly distributed loads (in kN/m) by 1000 converts kN to N, dividing by 1000 converts m to mm. The net result is the number unchanged. For example:

50 kN/m run = 50 N/mm run

From now on all values are in N and mm. Thus, for example, a span of 2·5 is now 2500.

Step 4: allowable bending stress
3.05 Because of web restraint conditions found in practice, allowable bending stress varies with the steel section used. To establish this stress, look up the $\frac{D}{T}$ ratio and the radius of gyration (r_y) for the selected section in table II. Divide the length (1) in mm by the radius of gyration to give an $\frac{1}{r_y}$ ratio.

Using this and the $\frac{D}{T}$ ratio look up the allowable bending stress in table III. Note that a value of $\frac{1}{r_y}$ below 90 is treated as 90, a value of $\frac{D}{T}$ below 10 is treated as 10. Intermediate values can be found by linear interpolation.

Step 5: select formulae
3.06 Table IV gives formulae for common, simple loading conditions. Select the appropriate set for bending, shear and deflection.

Step 6: bending stress
3.07 Calculate the maximum bending moment using the formula selected in step 5. Then calculate the elastic modulus required by using the following formula:

$$\text{Elastic modulus} = \frac{\text{maximum bending moment (calculated)}}{\text{allowable bending stress (from table III)}}$$

(Units as appropriate: w in N/mm; p in N; 1, a and b in mm; elastic modulus in mm³; bending moment in N mm; allowable stress in N/mm².)

3.08 Look in table II for the elastic modulus of the section. This must be greater than the value of elastic modulus just calculated. If it is not greater, choose a larger steel section, adjust self weight and recalculate allowable and maximum bending stresses. (Factors associated with greater strength are increased r_y and elastic modulus, and a smaller $\frac{D}{T}$ ratio.)

3.09 If the calculated value of elastic modulus is appreciably less than the value in table II, use a smaller section and again recalculate.

Step 7: shear stress
3.10 Allowable shear stress for the steel sections in table II is 100 N/mm². Look up the web area (A_w) for the selected section in table II and calculate the maximum shear stress using the formula selected in step 5.

(Units as appropriate: w in N/mm; p in N; 1, a and b in mm; A_w in mm²; shear stress in N/mm².)

3.11 The calculated value of shear stress must not exceed 100 N/mm². If it does, pick a section with a larger web area (A_w). Recalculate bending as well as shear stress. Shear stress will rarely be critical if bending strength is adequate. Exceptionally it may be critical for very heavily loaded beams or very short spans.

Step 8: deflection
3.12 The degree of deflection is usually expressed as a fraction of the length, eg one in 300. The allowable deflection is the

Table III Allowable bending stress (N/mm²)

l/r_y	D/T ratio							
	10	15	20	25	30	35	40	50
90	165	165	165	165	165	165	165	165
95	165	165	165	163	163	163	163	163
100	165	165	165	157	157	157	157	157
105	165	165	160	152	152	152	152	152
110	165	165	156	147	147	147	147	147
115	165	165	152	141	141	141	141	141
120	165	162	148	136	136	136	136	136
130	165	155	139	126	126	126	126	126
140	165	149	130	115	115	115	115	115
150	165	143	122	104	104	104	104	104
160	163	136	113	95	94	94	94	94
170	159	130	104	91	85	82	82	82
180	155	124	96	87	80	76	72	71
190	151	118	93	83	77	72	68	62
200	147	111	89	80	73	68	64	59
210	143	105	87	77	70	65	61	55
220	139	99	84	74	67	62	58	52
230	134	95	81	71	64	59	55	49
240	130	92	78	69	61	56	52	47
250	126	90	76	66	59	54	50	44
260	122	88	74	64	57	52	48	42
270	118	86	72	62	55	50	46	40
280	114	84	70	60	53	48	44	39
290	110	82	68	58	51	46	42	37
300	106	80	66	56	49	44	41	36

From BS 449 : Part 2, *The use of structural steel in buildings.*

Table IV Formulae for bending, shear and deflection

Simply supported beam—uniform distributed load

Maximum bending moment	=	$\frac{wl^2}{8}$
Maximum shear stress	=	$\frac{wl}{2A_w}$
Maximum deflection	=	$\frac{wl^4}{161 \times 10^5\,I}$

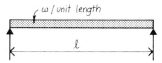

Simply supported beam—centre point load

Maximum bending moment	=	$\frac{pl}{4}$
Maximum shear stress	=	$\frac{p}{2A_w}$
Maximum deflection	=	$\frac{pl^3}{101 \times 10^5\,I}$

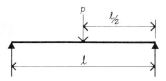

Simply supported beam—off-centre point load
(Dimension 'b' refers to the larger dimension, 'a' to the smaller).

Maximum bending moment	=	$\frac{pab}{l}$
Maximum shear stress	=	$\frac{pb}{A_w l}$
Maximum deflection	=	$\frac{pl^3}{101 \times 10^5\,I}\left(\frac{3a}{l} - 4\left(\frac{a}{l}\right)^3\right)$

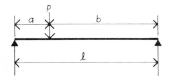

length (l) divided by this fraction, eg $\frac{1}{300}$.

3.13 Look up the moment of inertia (I) of the steel section in table II and calculate the deflection using the formula selected in step 5. This calculated value should not exceed the maximum allowable deflection, eg one in 300. If it does, pick a new section with a larger moment of inertia (I). Recalculate bending and shear stresses and deflection.
(Units as appropriate: w in N/mm; p in N; 1, a and b in mm; I in mm⁴; deflection in mm.)

3.14 To restrict the chance of masonry cracking it is safer to use a deflection of $\frac{1}{450}$. When the beam is used in underpinning even greater stiffness is desirable, achieved using a limiting deflection of $\frac{1}{900}$

3.15 *Assumptions made include:*
● sections are rolled 43 grade steel
● deflections for simply supported beams with an off-centre point load are accurate to 2·5 per cent
● for point loads, adding twice the weight of the beam to allow for self weight is correct for bending but excessive for shear. However, it is bending not shear that is usually critical
● Young's modulus, 'E' for steel is 210 000 N/mm²
● beams will effectively be simply supported not fixed ended.

'Triangle of masonry' method
3.16 In some cases the load on a beam can be taken as a triangle of masonry, as illustrated in table V. This simplifies calculation of loading and requires different formulae. However it is only safe to use this calculation based on lighter loads when you are confident that the spread of loads above the beam will not be changed at some time in the future, eg by forming a new opening above the beam.

3.17 The formulae appropriate are given in table V. The load W is based on a triangle of masonry of base angle 60°. This has a surface area of $0\cdot43 \times 1^2$ (where the beam length 'l' is in metres). W can be calculated by multiplying this surface area by the appropriate load from table I. Having done this proceed to step 2, para **3.02**.

Table V Formulae for 'triangle of masonry' method

Maximum bending moment	=	$\frac{Wl}{6}$
Maximum shear stress	=	$\frac{W}{2A_w}$
Maximum deflection	=	$\frac{Wl^3}{126 \times 10^6\,I}$

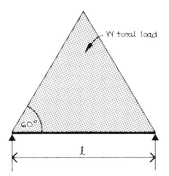

4 Example of detailed calculation
4.01 The terraced house, **1**, is two up, two down with a central stair. Joists run front to back bearing on the staircase walls. All walls are solid, one brick thick and plastered. Ceilings are lath and plaster below joists. Floors are boarded. The timber pitched roof is finished in fairly thin Welsh slates.
4.02 A single-storey extension is to be added requiring a 1·6 m wide opening in the rear wall, **1a**. A beam will be required over this opening to carry the weight of the wall above it (say 3 m to the eaves), dead and imposed loads from half the 3·5 m span of the first floor room and from half the 8 m span of the roof, **1b**. It will not carry any load from the new extension roof. The beam's length is measured to the centre of the padstones, in this case 1·9 m. (Units used are: (p) is point load, (A $_w$) is web area, (r$_y$) is radius of gyration, (w) is load per unit length, (W) is load of triangle of masonry, (l) is length of beam between centres of padstones, (I) is moment of inertia, (a) and (b) are distances between an off-centre point load and the beam ends—see table IV.)

Step 1: loading
4.03 *Wall*—one brick thick, plastered, 3 m high. From table I the load of the masonry is 5·5 kN/m² of wall area.

Wall load on beam	= 4·5 × 3
	= 13·5 kN/m run

4.04 *First floor*—boards, joists, lath and plaster ceiling. From table I dead load is 0·8 kN/m², imposed load is 1·5 kN/m². The beam supports load from half the span of the room, ie 1·75 m.

Floor load on beam	= (0·8 + 1·5) × 1·75
	= 4·0 kN/m run

4.05 *Roof*—lath and plaster ceiling below joists, timber roof structure and fairly thin slates. From table I dead load is 1·1 kN/m², imposed load is 0·75 kN/m². The beam supports load from half the span of the roof, ie 4 m.

Roof load on beam	= (1·1 + 0·75) × 4
	= 7·4 kN/m run

4.06 Total dead and live loads on beam

$$= 13\cdot5 + 4\cdot0 + 7\cdot4$$
$$= 24\cdot9 \text{ kN/m run}$$

Step 2: select a section
4.07 Experience or approximate calculation suggests a RSJ 127 × 76 mm. Its self weight is 0·13 kN/m run from table II.

Total load on beam

$$= 24 \cdot 9 + 0 \cdot 13$$
$$= 25 \cdot 03 \text{ kN/m run}$$

Step 3: convert to newtons and millimetres
4.08 Total dead and live load on beam
$$= 25 \cdot 03 \text{ N/mm run}$$

Step 4: allowable bending stress
4.09 From table II for a 127×76 mm section, $\frac{D}{T}$ ratio is $16 \cdot 7$, r_y is $17 \cdot 2$.

Thus $\frac{l}{r_y}$
$$= \frac{1900}{17 \cdot 2}$$
$$= 110 \cdot 5$$

From table IV, with $\frac{D}{T}$ of $16 \cdot 7$ and $\frac{l}{r_y}$ of $110 \cdot 5$, the allowable bending stress is 165 N/mm^2.

Step 5: select formulae
4.10 The load is uniformly distributed.
The formulae applicable from table V are:

Maximum bending moment $= \dfrac{wl^2}{8}$

Maximum shear stress $= \dfrac{wl}{2A_w}$

Maximum deflection $= \dfrac{wl^4}{161 \times 10^5 \, I}$

Step 6: bending stress
4.11 Bending moment
$$= \frac{wl^2}{8}$$
$$= \frac{25 \cdot 03 \times 1900 \times 1900}{8}$$
$$= 112 \cdot 8 \times 10^5 \text{ Nmm}$$

Elastic modulus required $= \dfrac{\text{maximum bending moment}}{\text{allowable bending stress}}$
$$= \frac{112 \cdot 8 \times 10^5}{165}$$
$$= 68 \cdot 4 \times 10^3 \text{ mm}^3$$

The selected 127×76 mm section has a modulus of $75 \times 10^3 \text{ mm}^3$ from table II, so is adequate in bending.

Step 7: shear stress
4.12 Web area (A_w) from table II is 572 mm^2.

Maximum shear stress $= \dfrac{wl}{2A_w}$
$$= \frac{25 \cdot 03 \times 1900}{2 \times 572}$$
$$= 41 \cdot 5 \text{ N/mm}^2$$

Since the allowable shear stress is 100 N/mm^2, the joist is acceptable in shear.

Step 8: deflection
4.13 Moment of inertia (I) from table II is $476 \times 10^4 \text{ mm}^4$.

Maximum deflection $= \dfrac{wl^4}{161 \times 10^5 \, I}$
$$= \frac{25 \cdot 03 \times 1900^4}{161 \times 10^5 \times 476 \times 10^4}$$
$$= 4 \cdot 25 \text{ mm}$$

Say the limiting degree of deflection is one in 300 then:

allowable maximum $= \dfrac{1}{300}$
$$= \frac{1900}{300}$$
$$= 6 \cdot 3 \text{ mm}$$

So the actual deflection, $4 \cdot 25$ mm, is less than the allowable maximum of $6 \cdot 3$ mm. The joist's deflection is acceptable. But if the more stringent criterion suggested earlier, in paragraph **3.14**, of a deflection of one in 450 is used, the allowable

deflection is $\dfrac{1900}{450} = 4 \cdot 2$ mm.
The joist is then on the borderline of acceptability.

5 Choice of beam
5.01 The chosen joist, 127×76 mm is adequate in bending, shear and deflection. However, the width of 76 mm is not effective for supporting a 225 mm wide wall. This simple example in fact involves such a small opening that a concrete lintel could easily be used instead. In general though, where the joist selected is much narrower than the masonry supported, a plate can be welded or bolted on top of the joist to collect the load from the masonry. Universal beams and columns have usefully wide flanges. Alternatively a pair of joists could be used, for this example say two 76×76 mm joists. Calculation involves halving the loading assessed in step 1, and then proceeding as before with the other steps.

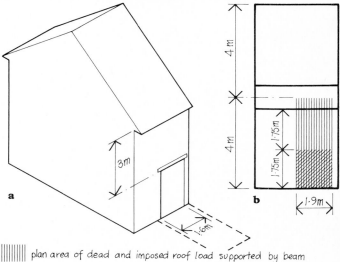

|||||| plan area of dead and imposed roof load supported by beam

//// plan area of dead and imposed first floor load supported by beam

1a *Part of a terrace showing the 1·6 m opening required for a new rear extension.* **1b** *Plan of terrace showing the plan areas of floor and roof to be supported by the new beam.*

2 *House requiring beam in its rear wall to make an opening into the new rear extension. Avoid, where possible, making the opening so close to the corner.*

Section five: Administration

Technical study 1
Notes on running the job

Rehabilitation generally involves a higher proportion of site supervision and other organisational work than new building. With unforeseen work being discovered during rehabilitation and the unpredictability common among small builders, jobs are also likely to run less smoothly. These notes cover problems frequently encountered that are particular to rehabilitation jobs.

1 Contracts

1.01 While this study is not concerned specifically with contracts it is assumed that some legally binding agreement exists, eg in Minor Works form or some kind of schedule of works agreement. It may be tempting to be casual about contracts for small private jobs, at best because the small builder seems trustworthy and personally involved, at worst because he may go bankrupt one week and appear under another name the next leaving little chance of redress. Use of the courts to enforce contracts may also seem unlikely due to the time and expense involved. Yet though we are not about to become as litigious as, say, the USA, there may well be more recourse to the courts in future to establish liability and seek redress. *Anns v London Borough of Merton*, though concerned with a larger scale of works, could be taken as a pointer in this direction.

2 Selecting contractors

Private clients

2.01 Private clients can be offered a range of sizes of contractor. Check with local architects and visit jobs both in progress and complete if you do not know the local contracting scene. Generally the smallest contractors are slow, enthusiastic and cheap; the largest are sometimes fast and always expensive.

Local authorities

2.02 Local authorities have lists of approved contractors for tendering (or perhaps a direct labour department). Local contractors who are known to be good could be recommended for addition to the list. To find out who is good on the list

(since only a selected number may be asked to tender) or to find other local contractors worth recommending, consult a friendly local authority officer, local architects and visit jobs. Time spent on this is an investment.

2.03 Local authorities must take the lowest tender which usually results in using a small contractor.

Housing associations

2.04 Though working to tight cost limits, housing associations should be in the strongest position of the three; they may have a broad experience of builders, as have local authorities, without having to accept the lowest tender.

This can be useful, for example if housing associations want to spend more on better quality work so limiting future maintenance, or because the lowest tender seems underpriced so the contractor is likely to get into financial difficulties during the job.

3 Cost control

Estimates

3.01 Estimates of costs are generally less accurate than for new work, mainly because of defects unforeseen during the survey which can increase repairs costs and perhaps the feasibility of some proposed improvements. So get as much information to any qs as early as possible to help make cost estimates definite and get as large a contingency sum as possible.

Contingency sum

3.02 Agree with clients how a contingency sum should be spent. For local authorities it may be fixed, eg one per cent or

. . . bankrupt one week and appear under another name the next . . .

. . . defects unforeseen during the survey. . .

. . . a fire of architraves, skirtings, fire surrounds. . . that you wanted kept. . .

£1000, whichever is less. Clients may agree to a maximum sum the architect can spend without consulting them.

Variations
3.03 Small variations, eg repair of rotten lintels found during the job, can usually be accumulated until there is a pageful. Send Architect's Instruction, priced, to the client, contractor and site.

Timing payments
3.04 Do not overpay at the start of a contract since this leaves little profit in later work which is then liable to be skimped (contractors often price early items relatively highly anyway to produce a quick cash flow).

3.05 Local authorities prefer few, large bills for ease of processing. Private clients usually pay better if bills are small and frequent. Send in a fee account with each certificate.

3.06 Private clients' pockets are always too small to accommodate their ambitions. Do not cut corners unless these are carefully explained to the client and it is made clear that if cutting the corner does not work, it might be more expensive for the client than by doing the work in the best way, eg the risks of using cheap materials or re-using materials in unnatural situations. If the risk is not explained to the client or if the architect deludes himself into thinking a job can be done for a figure which he knows is unrealistic, he may be tempted to blame the contractor for construction failure rather than himself.

4 Organising building

Checks before starting on site
4.01 Some at least of the following items are not strictly the architect's responsibility (as specified by contract). But it may well help the smooth running of the job to make an unobtrusive check where appropriate.
Is the contractor insured?
Has the client raised his insurance to cover new work?
Have materials with long delivery times, eg sanitary ware, been ordered?
Has the programme been agreed with the contractor?
Have dates been agreed with statutory undertakings to start work?
Are telephones, water and electricity available on site?

Providing information on site
4.02 Get a lot of information to the contractor's office and to site early on. Rehabilitation contracts are usually short for a particular house—a few weeks—so late information is liable

to disrupt programming and perhaps cause delays due to new ordering.

4.03 Be on site on the first morning and go round the house(s) explaining key points of specification and drawings (which the site staff may not have read or even received). Arriving any later than this you may be warmed by a fire of architraves, skirtings, fire surrounds and the like that you wanted kept.

4.04 Send any subsequent drawings and written instructions to the contractor *and to the site* unless confident the contractor will pass them on promptly.

Standards
4.05 Though standards are specified in the contract documentation, there are several ways in which standards can be established and maintained in a less formal manner.
Establish and enforce standards early on. Praise the good, blame the bad: this is best done though the foreman.
Arrive at the beginning of critical operations like setting out, checks on equipment, work that will be covered by floor screeds, plaster, decorations etc rather than after the event.
Make spot-check visits.
If you want poor work ripped out and done better, check first if there will be unacceptably long delays due to ordering replacement materials.
Be on site for specialist subcontractors, eg gas board, electricians. They sometimes please themselves about standards and it can be extremely difficult to get them back on site once they have left.
Finishes tend to be neglected, though they are important in occupants' minds. Ensure that the contract covers clearing out, painting and decorating, then thorough cleaning eg windows, working surfaces, taps, etc, not just a builder's finish.

Site meetings
4.06 Hold regular meetings to check progress and the future programme.
Check that ordering of materials allows for unexpected delays.
Discuss variations and send Architect's Instructions to the client, contractor and site.
Write minutes of key items and send them to the client, contractor and site.
If there are complex questions, go away to think. If significant extra costs are likely the client will need consulting anyway.

Snagging
4.07 Try to do this as you go, including subcontractors' work, to avoid a lot of small unprofitable jobs left at the end of the contract which are difficult to programme and time-consuming.

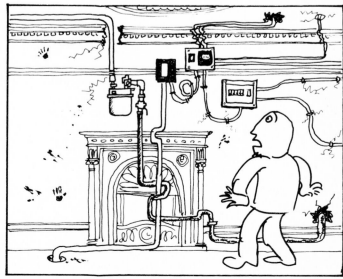

. . . they sometimes please themselves about standards. . .

. . . treating the client's home like any other building site. . .

Defects liability period

4.08 Notify the client and contractor two to four weeks before the six-month liability period is ended. Make sure the contractor also takes notes of work he agrees to do and send a confirming letter.

5 Ending a contract

5.01 Determining the contract is drastic, unpleasant and probably expensive in the long run, so not to be contemplated lightly. These notes are intended to give the architect a sense of the worsening relationships and standards of work that can occur so that an impending crisis can be recognised and, where possible, avoiding action taken. The legal side of determination is better left to a solicitor.

5.02 Whether a contract is determined or a contractor chooses to leave prematurely, the dispute is usually ostensibly about the quality and rate of work. However this is often the end of a chain of (sometimes predictable) events in which the initial blame may lie as much with the client as the contractor (at least in the private sector). This is illustrated by the following all-too-common examples.

Causes of deterioration

5.03 *Negotiating reductions to the tender.* This may be because some items seem overpriced or because the tender price is more than the client can afford, so he cuts down in expensive items. Either way, the contractor's overall profit is reduced.
This leads to
slow progress and discontented labour
which leads to
a reduction in the standard of workmanship.
This leads to either
refusal by the client to pay within 15 days of certificates. This indirectly determines the contract. The contractor could sue for loss of profit.
Or it leads to
anger by architect and client, and hence reduced valuations due to omission of condemned work
which leads to
the contractor being unwilling to work at all.

5.04 *Accepting the lowest tender from a contractor you have not worked with before.* After demolition and initial works the builder realises he had underpriced and goes away or instigates the deterioration described in **5.03**. If the contractor is evidently making a loss discuss this with the client.

5.05 *Clients living on site.* Where clients do not move out they can become frustrated by the inefficiency of the contractor, pub lunches, decorators smoking and leaving cigarettes in the wc, etc. These may be symptomatic of general inefficiency or just the builders treating the client's home like any other building site (though the contractor should be prepared for this). Acrimonious exchanges may result in slowing progress and deterioration as in **5.03**.

5.06 *Clients move in and decide on additions.* Despite there being good reason for the contract period being extended, the client moves in on the date originally programmed (in some cases he may be paying for a hotel or boarding with friends or relatives). Once in, the client adds more and more small items, eg joinery. This slows work and the client makes slower payment. The contractor then refuses to complete snagging and further additional items.

5.07 *Fees and favours.* The client is determined to extract the last ounce of goodwill by offering more work with friends (which may not materialise) and does not pay all contractor's certificates or architect's fees. The architect advises the contractor of this, who leaves the site while he has not lost too much. The architect resigns.

Manner of determination

5.08 The legal details of determining a contract are covered in the *AJ Legal handbook*—CI/SfB (Ajk).

5.09 Whether one of the reasons noted above pertains or the contractor is simply not very good, the client may need to cut his losses by determining the contract. If the contractor is given notice to quit but asked to do all he can before he leaves, both standards and work rate drop further. So determine the contract in a clearcut way.

5.10 Be absolutely certain that the fault has occurred and that the contractor knows it has occurred.
Give the contractor every chance to put it right.
Make certain that the client both knows and understands what is happening.
Read the contract again.

5.11 There can be no completely normal procedure for such irregular events, but the following example gives a sense of the care involved.

5.12 *Example of determination.* The architect notes a fault, eg that there is only one man on site and he is playing patience. The architect phones the contractor to complain and phones the client to tell him about it. If the fault persists (things may well improve temporarily) write to the client to notify him and write to the contractor telling him that if the fault is not rectified so that work resumes satisfactorily, then the client will be forced to start proceedings to determine the contract (send a copy to the client).

5.13 If the fault still persists be sure that determination is the right course. Is the client definitely prepared to take legal action? If so then list all faults fully and send these to the

. . . only one man on site and he is playing patience. . .

client with a report stating the likely consequences of determination, such as delays and extra costs.

5.14 If the client agrees to go ahead call in a solicitor. Have a notice sent by registered post or recorded delivery to the contractor saying that he has 14 days to rectify the fault, and that if this is not done then within 10 days afterwards he will receive notice determining the contract.

5.15 Rather than being unwilling, the client may leap to litigation. But determination is unpleasant and should be avoided where possible. In any case resist pressure from the client to terminate the contract for 'unreasonable or vexatious' reasons.

5.16 Where the initial (14 day) notice brings only temporary rectification and the architect notes the fault on future site visits, the architect should complain to the contractor by letter and check with the client that he is still willing to determine. If the fault persists a letter can be sent within 10 days determining the contract.

After determination

5.17 *Rights.* The client is entitled to employ other people to finish the job and to use the previous contractor's plant (owned, not hired), materials and subcontractors. At the end of the job all monies are added up, and if this comes to more than the original contract sum then the contractor owes the client money. It may come to less because the client withheld certificate payments to the original contractor who was dis-

charged. These should be paid up to the value of the contract sum.

5.18 *Action.* On the day of determination the following (check with the solicitor) will probably be necessary.

Make a valuation of works done, materials in the contractor's yard, etc (or get the qs to do this).

Change the locks on doors to make the site secure.

Contact all subcontractors and suppliers informing them of what has happened. Check whether they are willing to continue and what monies are outstanding.

Sort out who owes who what at the end of the contract.

5.19 Following this the client may want advice on finding a new contractor. The price for completing the works will be higher than their valuation in the existing tender (including allowance for inflation).

6 Supervising works

6.01 A book on supervision of housing rehabilitation is to be published by the Architectural Press, written by Levitt Bernstein Associates, entitled *A supervisor's guide to rehabilitation and conversion* (£5·95 hardback, £3·95 paperback).

7 Planning applications

7.01 Three articles on 'Making a planning application' have been published in the AJ: see 20 and 27.9.78 and 4.10.78.

Information sheet 1
Grants

This section covers conditions for receipt of renovation grants by house owners. The main variations are between England & Wales and Scotland, any historical significance a house may have, and whether it falls within a GIA or HAA.

1 General conditions for obtaining renovation grants

Ownership

1.01 An applicant must be a freeholder or have at least five years of a lease to run before receiving a house *renovation grant* (renovation grant is a generic term used to cover improvement, intermediate, special and repairs grants in England & Wales and improvement and repairs grants in Scotland). The owner-occupier must certify that the dwelling will be his main residence for five years after the date when the works have been approved by the local authority as complete—the *certified date*. Similarly a landlord must certify that the dwelling(s) will be available as permanent residence(s) for five years from the certified date. Under section 83 of the Housing Act 1974 charities (eg Historic Building Trusts) need not provide certificates of future occupation.

1.02 If these conditions are subsequently broken the local authority may claim back all the grant plus interest. Owners or landlords can choose to pay back grants with interest, so releasing themselves from the grant conditions. The DOE has stated that owner-*occupiers* need not repay the grant where they need to sell the house, but where making a profit on improvement was not the reason for the sale. In practice this release from grant conditions is at the local authority's discretion.

Second homes

1.03 No grants are available for second homes. Local authorities can make grants for second homes where these are to become main residences, but do not usually do so.

Rates

1.04 Rates are likely to be raised at the next revaluation where major improvements or conversions have been made. The local authority will probably suggest the amount of likely change, if asked.

Rents

1.05 Where a landlord improves a house he can apply to the local authority for a Qualification Certificate changing a controlled tenancy (ie fixed rent) to a regulated tenancy (ie 'fair' rent). Inevitably, rents go up.

1.06 Tenants can get some indication of likely rents and rent rebates from the local authority at an early stage. There may be friction during rehabilitation between landlords and tenants who do not want all the improvements and attendant rent increases.

Standards

1.07 Grants can be a mixed blessing since standards may be set as a condition of grant payment that owners do not want to achieve. Information on statutory minimum standards is given in paragraph **4.01**. Many local authorities have become more sympathetic to old buildings from their own experiences

of rehabilitation, carrying out more natural conversions rather than insisting dogmatically on Parker Morris standards. Hopefully this attitude rubs off on their attitude to grants for owners.

1.08 Although in many cases the building regulations do not apply (see Building Regulations, Section 3, A5ff, or Building Standards (Scotland) (Consolidation) Regulations, A9) many local authorities insist on some if not all regulations being met as a condition of grant, eg lowering floors to achieve $2 \cdot 3$ m floor to ceiling heights. An early visit to the dwelling by the local authority improvements officer will indicate what the extra local requirements are. If there are many of these that the client does not want, receiving a grant can be uneconomic.

1.09 If the house to be rehabilitated is being bought, any mortgage company involved usually imposes another, overlapping set of required works.

2 Limits of renovation grants

Percentage local authority contribution

2.01 When grants are given they cover a percentage of the agreed costs of rehabilitation. A local authority may consider a builder's estimate overpriced. Also some works are grant aidable as a right, others at the local authority's discretion. So grant is only payable for agreed items of work at the full or revised (downwards) price. Local authorities' contributions are:

- 50 per cent of rehabilitation costs generally
- 60 per cent of rehabilitation costs in GIAs
- 75 per cent of rehabilitation costs in HAAs (this may be raised to 90 per cent in cases of hardship (in Scotland only 50 per cent is payable on works not specified by the local authority)
- less than 50 per cent of rehabilitation costs may be given for non-residential buildings converted to dwellings.

Eligible/approved expense

2.02 Grant aid is not payable without limit. There is a cost ceiling above which the owner pays all the rehabilitation costs. In England and Wales this is called the *eligible expense*, in Scotland the *approved expense*. For example, if the eligible/approved expense for a particular grant is £5000, the local authority can pay 50 per cent of rehabilitation costs, ie up to £2500. If costs go above the eligible/approved expense of £5000 the local authority still pays only £2500 and the owner must pay all costs over £5000.

Rateable value limits

2.03 Grants are generally only payable where the house has a low enough rateable value. In *England and Wales* the ceilings are:

- £600 for conversions in Greater London
- £400 for improvements in Greater London

Table I Rateable value limits for rehabilitation by district in Scotland

Islands		Column A £	Column B £
	Orkney	70	175
	Shetland	70	175
	Western Isles	70	175
Region	*District*		
Borders	Berwick	85	215
	Ettrick and Lauderdale	80	200
	Roxburgh	80	200
	Tweeddale	100	250
Central	Clackmannan	95	240
	Falkirk	100	250
	Stirling	100	250
Dumfries and	Annandale and Eskdale	85	215
Galloway	Nithsdale	80	200
	Stewartry	80	200
	Wigtown	85	215
Fife	Dunfermline	95	240
	Kirkcaldy	90	225
	North East Fife	90	225
Grampian	City of Aberdeen	90	225
	Banff and Buchan	80	200
	Gordon	80	200
	Kincardine and Deeside	80	200
	Moray	75	190
Highland	Badenoch and Strathspey	75	190
	Caithness	70	175
	Inverness	80	200
	Lochaber	75	190
	Nairn	75	190
	Ross and Cromarty	70	175
	Skye and Lochalsh	70	175
	Sutherland	70	175
Lothian	East Lothian	110	275
	City of Edinburgh	110	275
	Midlothian	110	275
	West Lothian	95	240
Strathclyde	Argyll and Bute	75	190
	Bearsden and Milngavie	115	290
	Clydebank	105	265
	Cumbernauld and Kilsyth	100	250
	Cumnock and Doon Valley	80	200
	Cunninghame	90	225
	Dumbarton	110	275
	Eastwood	100	250
	East Kilbride	115	290
	City of Glasgow in respect of houses in HAAs for improvement or for demolition and improvement declared in accordance with Part II of the Housing (Scotland) Act 1974	120	275
	City of Glasgow in respect of houses not in such HAAs	110	275
	Hamilton	115	290
	Inverclyde	100	250
	Kilmarnock and Loudoun	90	225
	Kyle and Carrick	90	225
	Lanark	110	275
	Monklands	115	290
	Motherwell	110	275
	Renfrew	100	250
	Strathkelvin	105	265
Tayside	Angus	85	215
	City of Dundee	100	250
	Perth and Kinross	95	240

- £350 for conversions elsewhere
- £225 for improvements elsewhere.

Here 'conversions' refers to producing more units of accommodation as a result of rehabilitation or, at the discretion of the local authority, providing the same number of units but of a significantly better standard, eg in layout.

2.04 The rateable value limits for *Scotland* are set out in table I. *Column A* is the limit for a single house that is improved or where a number of houses are converted into a lesser number. *Column B* is the limit for a single house converted into two or more houses.

Unforeseen costs

2.05 When additional work is discovered during rehabilitation which could not reasonably have been foreseen, such as timber decay, local authorities can increase the amount of grant aid (at the same percentage) even where this exceeds the eligible/approved expense.

Owner's contribution

2.06 The owner's contribution to costs may still be difficult for him to raise. Many authorities have loan schemes to assist poorer owners (Scottish local authorities must make loans for specified works in HAAs—see paragraph **4.01**).

VAT

2.07 Repair and maintenance are taxable, alterations are zero rated. Grant aid can be paid on VAT if it is included in the builder's estimate.

2.08 Clarification of VAT may be obtained from your local VATman: see 'Customs and Excise' in the telephone directory. There is also a free leaflet which gives some guidance on distinguishing repair and maintenance from alterations plus a description of VAT rules, called *Value Added Tax: construction industry alterations and repairs and maintenance*, HM Customs and Excise Notice No 715.

Second grants

2.09 Local authorities can pay a second grant to an owner who has received one already for the same dwelling. However, there needs to be a good reason why all works were not included in the first grant application.

Do-it-yourself

2.10 Only the costs of materials and other people's labour are eligible for grant aid in DIY rehabilitation.

3 Grant application procedure

Timing applications

3.01 Some standards are phrased in such terms as 'adequate' and 'satisfactory', so it is important to find what these mean to your particular local authority and hence what may have grant aid. If much work is turned down for grant aid it may become uneconomic and require a change of design.

Discuss drawings with the local improvement officer and be present when he does a survey of the dwelling to determine required repairs. This is important to timing because meetings to approve grants are usually held infrequently—every four or more weeks. A query will result in the application being resubmitted to the next meeting several weeks hence.

Submission

3.02 Most local authorities now have a set procedure for processing grant applications and standard forms for some items. Get forms and submission instructions and follow them to the letter to avoid queries and hence resubmissions.

3.03 After an informal discussion of drawings and final agreement with clients, submission of grant applications usually involves the following documents.

Certificate of ownership There may be a local authority form for this. Or a letter is needed from a mortgage company, or submission of deeds or a letter from the client's solicitor.

Certificate of future occupation There may be a local authority form for this, a written undertaking to fulfil for residence/ letting requirements set out in paragraph **1.01**.

Local authority forms Variable in content but mostly for basic data, eg addresses.

Specification of works

Plans Generally submission of plans (several copies) is separate from submission for building regulations approval and any planning permission. These approval/permissions cannot be taken as approval of the grant itself.

Builder's estimate This may need to be broken down to separate repairs and replacements from (any) improvements and conversions. For some grants repairs and replacements may have to be split into basic amenities and associated repairs. And a further item may be needed embracing any other works, even though grant aid is not being sought for them.

Fee estimate An estimate of professional fees.

Provisions for tenants Landlords may be required to say what provisions are being made for tenants during rehabilitation or what will happen to existing tenants if conversion reduces the number of units in a house.

Timing of works

3.04 Do not start work before grant approval is received in writing. If you do, the grant may be invalidated.

3.05 Local authorities may provide postcards or otherwise get you to inform them when works reach various stages, eg structural work, wiring, drain laying, completion, etc. Failure to do so can invalidate the grant.

3.06 A time limit is generally set for the works, usually a year from grant approval.

Grant payment

3.07 Once the local authority approves the completed works it will pay the grant within one month (local authorities can pay instalments during the work). Grants are being raised every year to 18 months so always check on the current level.

Grant refusal

3.08 You must be given an explanation for refusal. If there is hope, try again. You could appeal within six months of refusal to the DOE, Welsh Office or Scottish Office as appropriate but this is likely to be long-winded (several months). Also, the local authority may be following agreed priorities and not be able to afford aid for works which would receive aid from another authority with fewer demands on its funds.

Environmental grants

3.09 All grants to owners are available for work within the boundary of the site. Environmental grants are available to *local authorities only*, for external works in public parts of the site of an HAA or GIA. (Grants can also be given to housing associations, eg for improving backcourts of tenements to provide drying areas, bin stores, fences, paths and trees.)

4 England & Wales and Scotland

4.01 Detailed renovation grant conditions and up-to-date details of allowable/eligible expenses are given in one of two free leaflets available from local authorities. In England and Wales it is called *Your guide to house renovation grants*. In Scotland it is called *Improve your home: grants available*.

There is also a leaflet available for Northern Ireland, called *Housing renovation grants: a brief guide*. It is available from local authorities or the Northern Ireland Housing Executive, 1 College Square East, Belfast 1.

5 Disabled people

5.01 Brief notes on rehabilitation grants for disabled people are given in the two leaflets mentioned in paragraph **4.01**. For more detailed guidance see *Housing grants and allowances for disabled people*, 25p, from the Royal Association for Disability and Rehabilitation, 25 Mortimer Street, London, W1M 8AB. This leaflet covers England and Wales only.

6 Historic buildings

6.01 While this handbook does not generally deal with houses or areas of outstanding architectural or historic interest it may be that some of the grants available can be used. However most are from limited funds, discretionary and provided too slowly for rehabilitation.

Eligible/approved expense for listed buildings

6.02 In England and Wales the eligible expense for listed buildings is higher than for other houses, as outlined in table II. In Scotland increasing the approved expense is discretionary.

Grants available

6.03 For England and Wales the Civic Trust provide a free leaflet, *A Civic Trust guide to grants and loans available for conservation*. For Scotland a similar leaflet is due to be published around the end of 1978. See paragraph **6.08** for addresses of the Trusts.

6.04 There are two main types of grant, for *repairs* and for *conservation*. These are discretionary and payable after other sources of finance, such as improvement grants, have been exhausted.

Repairs grant

6.05 Repairs grants are for repair and maintenance of buildings or groups that are of *outstanding* architectural or historic interest. For information on these contact the appropriate Historic Buildings Council—see paragraph **6.08**. There are also Town Schemes for rehabilitation of whole groups or areas of outstanding historic buildings—contact the local authority.

Conservation grants

6.06 In *Outstanding Conservation Areas*, currently about 10 per cent of all Conservation Areas, conservation grants are available for environmental improvements. They are available for the buildings not outstanding themselves but which contribute to the quality of an outstanding area. They also cover landscaping, restoring traditional paving and other external works. Apply to the Historic Buildings Council.

6.07 For England and Wales there is a small sum administered as a conservation grant by the Civic Trust for fabric and environmental upgrading in non-outstanding conservation areas. Contact the Civic Trust.

Addresses

6.08 Civic Trust, 17 Carlton House Terrace, London, SW1Y 5AW.
● Historic Buildings Council for England, 25 Saville Row, London, W1X 2BT.
● Historic Buildings Council for Wales, Pearl Assurance House, Greyfriars Road, Cardiff.
● Civic Trust for Scotland, 24 George Square, Glasgow G2.
● Historic Buildings Council for Scotland, 25 Drumsheugh Gardens, Edinburgh, EH3 7RN.

Charitable Aid Foundation

6.09 The Charitable Aid Foundation's *Directory of grant-making trusts* lists some charitable trusts who may aid conservation work. The directory is available at main reference libraries. A new edition is in preparation, from the Trust at 48 Pembury Road, Tonbridge, Kent, TN9 2JD price £25·00.

7 Insulation grants

7.01 Though the recently instituted insulation grant is not specifically part of rehabilitation work it can be applied for simultaneously (an improvement grant may not cover insulation). The insulation grant is for 66 per cent up to a maximum of £50 for lagging tanks and pipes in roof spaces and for loft insulation (where there is *no* existing insulation. This does not apply to flat roofs). Contact the local authority.

8 Current grants

8.01 Check that the rates of grant aid, ceilings, eligible/approved expense, etc are still current. The values given here were current for the end of 1978.

Table II Eligible expense limits for listed buildings

Grade	For improving a dwelling	For converting a dwelling of three or more storeys
Grade I	6000	6800
Grade II*	5600	6400
Grade II	5300	6100